T0129256

THE VERDICT OF HISTORY

THE VERDICT OF HISTORY

The Great Trials. From Ancient Times To Our Days.

VIRGINIA LALLI

authorHOUSE®

AuthorHouse™
1663 Liberty Drive
Bloomington, IN 47403
www.authorhouse.com
Phone: 1 (800) 839-8640

© 2016 Virginia Lalli. All rights reserved.
Translation of Sara Pasetto

No part of this book may be reproduced, stored in a retrieval system, or
transmitted by any means without the written permission of the author.

Published by AuthorHouse 05/09/2016

ISBN: 978-1-5049-8678-6 (sc)
ISBN: 978-1-5049-8679-3 (hc)
ISBN: 978-1-5049-8677-9 (e)

Library of Congress Control Number: 2016904754

Print information available on the last page.

Any people depicted in stock imagery provided by Thinkstock are models,
and such images are being used for illustrative purposes only.
Certain stock imagery © Thinkstock.

This book is printed on acid-free paper.

Because of the dynamic nature of the Internet, any web addresses or links contained in
this book may have changed since publication and may no longer be valid. The views
expressed in this work are solely those of the author and do not necessarily reflect the
views of the publisher, and the publisher hereby disclaims any responsibility for them.

CONTENTS

"To find justice, one must be faithful to it; like all divinities, it only appears to those who believe."
Piero Calamandrei
"Elogio dei giudici scritto da un avvocato".
"An ode to judges written by a lawyer"

"Ius est ars boni et aequi."
Ulpian, recalling Celsus's definition.

To my parents

PREFACE

A juxtaposition of the terms "trial" and "history" is an ordinary matter for anyone who engages with the law; it is also normal for anyone who is interested in "legal facts", whether from reading the news, from personal experience or from perusing the pages written by famous authors throughout the centuries.

In etymological terms, the judicial "process" itself derives from the past tense and from the past participle of the Latin verb "procedere": it indicates the re-presentation of a path that has already been completed and that is inevitably already "history", since it is addressed again before a court. Indeed, when a trial takes place, a set of human actions are recalled and submitted for evaluation to a figure who will have to hold them – or their outcome – to a standard of legality, to clear or punish those who performed those actions. This standard of legality, albeit placing a claim to eternity, is highly mutable in time and place, such that it is often nothing more than a pretext for something "other" than legality.

Before the judge, therefore, the parties offer different interpretations of a set of previously occurred facts, to which a behavioural rule that is "currently in force" must be applied, a rule that will act as a filter of the "history" recounted in court, to enable the judgment to be handed down. This judgment will sanction an "absolute" and unchallengeable truth (as per the concept of res judicata, i.e. the impossibility to modify what was finally declared in a judgment) in terms of innocence or guilt.

Thus, each trial – no matter how minor and obscure – is inevitably a phenomenon through which the past, a story, are evaluated: therefore, "intentions" to act or mere ideas should never be put on trial; this is a rule of Civilization that should always be kept in mind by those who are involved in a "trial". Actually, history is replete with trials conducted in relation to previous facts not to identify the wrongdoing therein, but to prevent someone from acting, feeling or thinking "for the future" in some way, even if fully aware that "historical" facts are not "juridically" reprehensible, and that the harm perhaps consisted precisely in the action of the institution of power, which "held" the trial.

Indeed, readers should always bear in mind that a trial is "held" between "parties" such that a judgment is "handed down" by a "judge", upon consultation with "attorneys", within a system of rules that constitutes the "standard procedural code". To hold; to hand down judgment; to advocate for or summon; to judge, or make justice by issuing a judgment; to follow a procedure: it is difficult to fail to see how trials, how every trial, in recalling History (whether with a capital or a lowercase "H"), invoke a ritual with a sacred character. Indeed, it could not be otherwise. Suffice it to consider that the main function of law – applied precisely in the context of the trial – is to achieve that ne cives ad arma ruant, as written in the Roman Law of the XII Tables. This law was both juridical and "sacred", and regulated and enabled peace among the cives. In other words, the main function of the trial is to make tangible a law that prevents citizens from resorting to arms. But why should citizens even resort to arms? This would happen if, without observing a Law that regulates private and public human relations, citizens sought to make the "particular" (as Machiavelli would call it) prevail over other private parties or over the Republic itself.

Thus arises the eternal dilemma: the trial leads to a truth, which once "ritually" ascertained and "ruled upon", becomes absolute and intangible. However, can procedural rules constrain the reality of the facts? Could not the procedural limitation of "admissible" evidence, the very interaction between the "parties" in court denature the historical and natural Truth, in favour of a "political" truth, a truth "of power", which is "instructive" and "exemplary" and has nothing to do with the truth of Justice that all citizens in all place and time seek, in the pursuit of which rivers of ink have been spilt, and, since ancient times, innumerable clay tablets and sacred steles have been engraved?

Precisely herein lies the risk inherent in every trial: the risk that its "holding" denature the straightforward recalling of historical facts and deeds, leading to a "judgment" that fully traces the Latin maxim summum jus, summa injuria: *extreme justice is extreme injustice.*

This book presents a number of exemplary trials that have taken place in history. These trials show that often the Law has served as a façade for the need to protect the "collectivity", "decorum", "order", "Peace", "humanity" itself; a need which was often no more than a modest cloak for the injustice or the revenge sought by a successful party, once "part" of a historical, political, ethical event, and "judge" of those same facts of which he had been – previously or simultaneously – the direct or indirect "counterpart"! This is true of Socrates, as well as of Catiline; Sacco and Vanzetti, and the German Nazi leaders; Wilde and Galileo.

Despite the immobility of res judicata, *"History" emerges. History, decided upon by Judges in all ages and places, has its revenge, judging trials herself and enabling – as a genuine* magistra vitae – *the handing down, through the centuries, of new judgments through which the absolved individual becomes the guilty party, the accuser becomes the accused, and the party declared guilty is absolved. This quasi-cathartic process is perhaps what enables "those most ferocious of beasts" – human beings – to moderate its adjudicatory action, and to avoid extreme injustice from always being the foundation of the law established in judgments.*

Reading Virginia Lalli's beautifully written pages on the trials of history, presented as dusty volumes from the archives of the Courtroom of Time exhumed for an evaluation that might, sometimes, become a "revision", will enable readers to reflect on the contemporary acuity and fallacy of judicial proceedings of the past, identifying many analogies with contemporary Historical facts and legal current events. Also, it enables practitioners to examine, with ever greater rigour, the real essence and purposes of the sacred rite that is the "trial", in which the factual account must always be followed by multiple and continuous "revisions" to reach judgments

that respect Jus and Jura, Law and Justice. All this takes place before History takes on the task of revision, a History that cannot be stopped by means of laws and trials but can be more unpredictable and implacable than any trial, even though it may no longer apply to the living, to whom alone trials are addressed!
Rome, 2 May 2015

***Avvocato* Juan Carlos Gentile**

DEMOSTHENES AND THE DISTRACTED JUDGES

from the *Noctes Atticae*, Aulus Gellius (Rome AD 130 - Rome AD 180).

One day, the famous orator Demosthenes was discussing a case that could involve the death penalty. When he noticed that the judges were not paying attention, he said "Listen to me just for a while. I am about to tell you a new and cheerful story".

The judges thus prepared to listen to him. Demosthenes began: "One day, a young man hired a donkey to travel comfortably from Athens to Megara. In the middle of his journey, the midday heat became unbearable and neither trees nor shelters offered shade. The young man stopped the donkey, unmounted, and sat on his saddle so that he could take shade under the animal.

The donkey owner became irate, claiming that the rental of the donkey did not include the rental of its shadow. The young man retorted that the shadow could not be separated from the donkey and thus, the shadow had to be included.

The two men began to fight and punch each other. At the end, they agreed on a decision that conformed to law.

As soon as Demosthenes saw that he had the judges' full attention, he suddenly came down from the platform. The judges called to him and beseeched him to finish the story. He said: "What? You can listen to a story on a donkey's shadow, and you cannot listen to the case of a man whose life is at stake?"

1

THE TRIAL OF SOCRATES

I say again that the greatest good of man is daily to converse about virtue, and all that concerning which you hear me examining myself and others, and [...] the life which is unexamined is not worth living.

Apology by Plato[1]

Plato's Apology was written as a direct testimony of Socrates' trial for impiety.
This trial took place on a morning in May 399 BCE, at the Heliaia, the court of Athens.
Three accusations were made against Socrates (Athens 469 BCE - Athens 399 BCE) before the Heliaia: impiety, corruption of youth, and introduction of new deities and non-recognition of the traditional ones. For these, Meletus and Anytus asked for the death penalty to be inflicted upon the old philosopher. At the time, criminal cases could only last one day: therefore, the trial began early at sunrise and ended at sunset.
Socrates began by saying: "I cannot in a moment refute great slanders". At the time of the trial, Socrates was seventy years old,

---

[1]   Taken from http://classics.mit.edu/Plato/apology.html. In this chapter, the quotations of Plato's *Apology* of Socrates are taken from http://classics.mit.edu/Plato/apology.html.

1

was married and had three children. It was the first time for him to appear in court.

"Thus," continued Socrates, "I must defend myself against two categories of accusers: those who are in court and those who have slandered me for a very long time now." He noted that there was also a third category of accusers: a number of "Athenian citizens, much more fearsome than Anytus and Meletus".

This category counted several members and had engaged in criticism of Socrates for a very long time, to the extent that those who attended the trial had already heard him speak when they were adolescents, and thus accused without allowing him the chance to defend himself.

"These citizens cannot be named," said Socrates, "except for certain dramatists." These in particular had managed to persuade others, who in turn then convinced yet others. This brought Socrates to say that to defend himself, he "must simply fight with shadows".

"Yet Socrates, a victim among many of that satire, felt in court that the origin of his troubles lay precisely in the fame and in the face that the dramatists had thrust upon him; and Anytus shrewdly took advantage of this to win over popular opinion and lend credibility to his accusations".[2]

The most important dramatist named by Socrates was Aristophanes. The latter had poked fun at Socrates in his comedy *The Clouds* (verses 264-266), written in 423 BCE. As told by Socrates himself, in that play he is portrayed to walk among the clouds and "talking a deal of nonsense".

The Clouds describes Socrates as a sophist and a naturalistic philosopher who lived in a house called a *phronisterion* (thinking place) and who taught "unjust dialogue" to prevail over "just dialogue". It was no coincidence that in the play's debate between Just Dialogue and Unjust Dialogue, the latter casts doubt upon traditional morality. Even a value such as respect for one's parents becomes relative, seeing as Zeus himself rebelled against his father Chronos.

---

[2]   Franco Massara (ed.), *I processi dell'età classica*. Edizioni di Cremville. Geneva. 1970. p. 70. Author's translation.

"In addition, in the comedy, Socrates presents the supreme divinities specific to intellectuals: the Clouds 'alone are divinities, all the rest is nonsense' (v. 365) and, out of carelessness and superficiality, Strepsiades will be led to swear on 'fog' and to get rid of the gods of the Olympus."[3]

However, according to Plato's *Symposium*, Socrates was actually on friendly terms with the comic poet.

In comedies, Socrates was usually assimilated to the Sophists, a current that in reality he opposed. In his view, for a mere fee, the Sophists (who included figures such as Gorgias from Leontini, Prodicus of Ceos and Hippias of Elis in their midst) would teach one to say everything and its opposite through the art of eloquence. According to the Sophists, there was no single truth that applied to all, because of the relativity and mutability that they believed were at the basis of laws, customs, religions and of all possible "truth" in scientific realms. Therefore, Man was the "centre of the universe" and words were extremely powerful "extrinsic means of persuasion". Socrates, on the other hand, felt the need to "replace these devastating teachings with a renewal that was at once both scientific and moral".[4]

Socrates' greatest supporter was Chaerephon, who once consulted the Oracle at Delphi to ask whether there was anyone more knowledgeable than Socrates. The priestess of Delphi, the Pythia, answered that there was nobody wiser. Unfortunately, buBy the time of Socrates' trial, Chaerephon had died, but the trial was attended by Chaerepon's brother, who referred the episode. Thus, Socrates said: "[f]or wherever a man's place is, whether the place which he has chosen or that in which he has been placed by a commander, there he ought to remain in the hour of danger; he should not think of death or of anything but of disgrace. [...] [I]f, I say, now, when, as I conceive and imagine, God orders me to fulfil the philosopher's mission of searching into myself and

---

[3]   Aristophanes. *Le Nuvole*. Milan. Bur Rizzoli. 2001. P. 25. Author's translation.

[4]   F. Ballotto. *Platone, Apologia di Socrate*. Milan. Principato. 1957. P. 10. Author's translation.

other men, I were to desert my post through fear of death, or any other fear; that would indeed be strange, and I might justly be arraigned in court for denying the existence of the gods, if I disobeyed the Oracle because I was afraid of death: then I should be fancying that I was wise when I was not wise. For this fear of death is indeed the pretence of wisdom, and not real wisdom, being the appearance of knowing the unknown; since no one knows whether death, which they in their fear apprehend to be the greatest evil, may not be the greatest good."

Likewise, Socrates could not live quietly, maybe exiled, because it would equate with disobeying God: this would be impossible to him, for he perceived the greatest good of man to be "daily to converse about virtue, and all that concerning which you her me examining myself and others, and that the life which is unexamined is not worth living. [...] And yet what I say is true, although a thing of which it is hard for me to persuade you."

Meletus argued that Socrates was guilty because he corrupted youths. Socrates answered that, if he corrupted youths, he could not possibly be doing so intentionally: to corrupt people means to make them evil, which exposes oneself to the risk of being harmed by them. At the very worst, this could only be done involuntarily, and thus could not attract a criminal sanction. Indeed, these sanctions made sense only if imposed for intentional deeds, and could not lead those who may have made unintentional mistakes to understand the reasons for their wrongdoing.

In the ensuing dialogue with Meletus, Socrates "maieutically" asked questions that eventually led the accuser to doubt himself. Socrates asked: "Would you say that this holds true in the case of horses? Does one man do them harm and all the world good? Is not the exact opposite of this true? One man is able to do them good, or at least not many; the trainer of horses, that is to say, does them good, and others who have to do with them rather injure them? [...] Happy indeed would be the condition of youth if they had one corrupter only, and all the rest of the world were their improvers."

In other words, Socrates demonstrated that Meletus was no expert on the education of youth and indeed had never been interested in such matters.

According to another accusation leveled by Meletus, Socrates did not believe in the existence of the gods, but rather believed that the sun was made of stone and the moon of earth, and that neither were deities.

Socrates replied that this accusation was better made against Anaxagoras; in any case, youths could hear these ideas at the theatre, for an admission ticket costing no more than one drachma. Socrates brought Meletus' contradictions to the fore in the space of only a few remarks. He got Meletus to admit that people only agree to spend time with those who bring them good, fleeing from those who bring them evil. Therefore, Socrates could not possibly be teaching evil; otherwise, nobody would spend time with him. Alternatively, if Socrates did teach evil, he did so unawares and as such, in accordance with Athenian law, those who err unintentionally were not to be put to trial but rather to be educated.

Socrates' merciless destruction of Meletus continued as he refuted the accusation of eschewing the traditional gods in favour of new ones (namely, the Socratic *daimon*): Socrates showed that it was impossible to not believe in the traditional gods yet profess faith in certain other gods, such that Meletus ended up contradicting his own accusation. Then, Socrates only had to prove that he believed in one of the city gods and that his *daimon* was the offspring thereof. This he did by means of an analogy. He first stated that there could not be the existence of human things and not of human beings, of horsemanship and not of horses, or flute-playing without flute players. Likewise, there could not be new gods if these did not originate (even as impure offspring) from the existing gods.

However, even if the Athenians decided to disregard Anytus' call and to free Socrates on the condition that he no longer engage in philosophy, Socrates stated that he could not obey the Athenians and ignore the gods; he could not refrain from engaging in philosophy and exhorting and advising.

But what was the nature of Socrates' speeches? What was their content? Socrates himself provided us with a description that Plato reports in his Apology: "O my friend, why do you who are a citizen of the great and might and wise city of Athens, care so much about laying up the greatest amount of money and honor and reputation, and so little about wisdom and truth and the greatest improvement of the soul, which you never regard or heed at all? [...] "And if the person with whom I am arguing says: Yes, but I do care; I do not depart or let him go at once; I interrogate and examine and cross-examine him, and if I think that he has no virtue, but only says that he has, I reproach him with undervaluing the greater, and overvaluing the less. And this I should say to everyone whom I meet, young and old, citizen and alien, but especially to the citizens, inasmuch as they are my brethren. For this is the command of God, as I would have you know; and I believe that to this day no greater good has ever happened in the state than my service to the God. For I do nothing but go about persuading you all, old and young alike, not to take thought for your persons and your properties, but first and chiefly to care about the greatest improvement of the soul. I tell you that virtue is not given by money, but that from virtue come money and every other good of man, public as well as private."

Are these things so evil as to deserve the death penalty?

Or, said Socrates, would the Athenians have "injured [them]selves more than [they] would injure [him], by wrongfully imposing the death penalty against the gift of the god who placed [him] alongside the city, to arouse, persuade and reproach [them] one by one, always and in all places fastening upon [them]." Chosen by the heavens, Socrates argued that he had strived to fulfill his tasks to the best of his abilities, neglecting his own concerns and living in utter poverty. He came to the Athenians as a father, as an elder brother, to exhort them to be virtuous.

Socrates noted that some may have wondered why, with all his wisdom, he did not enter politics and advise the state. He explained that he was willing to advise citizens but not the state because his *daimon* prevented him from doing so. It would be impossible for someone to save himself if he legitimately opposed the state and yet sought to avoid injustice or illegal deeds from being committed in the city.

Socrates stated that "as part of the Council"[5], "[their] tribe of Antiochis had the presidency at the trial of the generals who had not taken up the bodies of the slain after the battle of Arginusae; and [the Athenians] proposed to try them all together, which was illegal, as [the Athenians] all thought afterwards."

Socrates was the only Prytaneis to disagree and appeal to refrain from committing illegalities. For this, the Prytaneis were willing to put him to trial and imprison him, but Socrates nevertheless preferred to risk and remain on the side of justice and the law.

The Oligarchy of the Thirty then gained power. These "sent for [him] and four others into the rotunda, and bade [them] bring Leon the Salaminian from Salamina", as they wanted to execute him (his only fault being that he supported democracy).

On that occasion too, Socrates showed that he did not fear death, but was instead concerned with refraining from injustice or impiety. While his four companions went to Salamina, Socrates returned home. The government was overthrown and Socrates could not be put to death.

The *daimon* thus appears to be an interior calling inspired by divinity, that ceaselessly spurs one to a quest for justice without ever being sated, and to remain vigilant because nothing can ever be taken for granted.

As for the death penalty called for by Anytus, Socrates wondered aloud whether perhaps he should not rather receive a reward. He had "never had the with to be idle during his whole life; but has been careless of what the many care about – wealth, and family interests, and military offices," and other public honours; he sought rather to "persuade every man among [the Athenians]

---

5   The Bulè consisted of 500 members. Each of the ten tribes of Athens appointed 50 individuals, divided into ten classes. The representatives of each tribe held the direction of the Council (Prytaneum) for one-tenth of the year.

that he must look to himself, and seek virtue and wisdom before he looks to his private interests", to become better and wiser.

"What do I deserve to suffer?" asks Socrates. "A reward for a benefactor who educates you, or to enjoy the support of the Prytaneum".[6]

There were five hundred persons eligible to vote. Ultimately, Socrates was found guilty by a margin of only thirty votes: 220 were cast in his favour and 280 against him. If only thirty more people could have been persuaded, perfect parity would have been reached and no penalty could have been imposed, as established by the law of the time. Yet, when Socrates' friends offered to help him flee the city and escape all the accusations, he answered:

"I do not want to escape; one must never commit an injustice, even when one has suffered from one." After the judges had read out the penalty, the accused was to propose a "counterpenalty". Indeed, according to the laws of the Athenian tribunal, both the accused and the accuser had to propose a penalty and submit it to a vote. But how could Socrates propose a penalty for himself, that is, for one who is well aware that he has not committed any crime? The possibilities open to him were prison, exile or a sum of money – the latter of which, however, Socrates did not possess. He did not consider incarceration and enslavement to be just; therefore, it was all the less likely that he would have considered exile to be honourable: if he was sentenced by the people whom he loved, who else could ever accept him and his philosophy? Especially since he was incapable of refraining from engaging in philosophy, out of obedience to God and personal conviction.

However, Socrates predicted, those who voted for his death would receive an even worse revenge from Zeus.

"What, then, is death? Death is one of these two things: either it is as if one becomes nothing, a loss of consciousness, or, as commonly said, death is a change, a migration of the soul from this place to another. If death means to have no consciousness,

---

[6] The Prytaneum's building hosted the first magistrate, the holy hearth of the *polis*. Foreign ambassadors, decorated citizens and the winners of Olympic Games were hosted there with public monies.

then it is akin to sleeping. If death is a migration from this place to another, and it is true that in the new place, one can meet all those who are already dead and the greatest heroes of ancient times, what greater good can there be than death, o Judges? If in the Hades one finds the true judges and those who were just in life, how is this transmigration to be despised?"

Finally, in Socrates' view, a just man could not possibly receive harm; nor could his life be neglected by the gods. As a consequence, his circumstances were no coincidence. This was why the mark of God did not attempt to force Socrates to backtrack, as well as the reason why Socrates did not hate those who voted against him or accused him of wrongdoing.

His friend Crito visited him in prison and tried unsuccessfully to convince him to escape; he could have done so easily, also because his friends had the financial means to bribe the prison guards.

As Socrates' execution approached, his followers watched him sleeping peacefully.

When he awoke, he told them about his dream: "I thought a beautiful and majestic woman was approaching me, dressed in white and calling me by name, telling me:

"O Socrates, on the third day you will reach the florid land of Phthia".

"Listen to me and save yourself, I would lose such a friend as is impossible to find" said Crito.

But Socrates was serene, leaving those who survived him without a trace of doubt: without knowledge, life itself has no value and can be abandoned without much regret. The philosopher needs the city, because his research is not self-sufficient but takes place in a community; however, he cannot live in a city that does not accept this research.

In any case, neither Meletus nor Anytus could cause Socrates' downfall. He continued on his path all the same without concern for his life, just like the heroes who fought at Troy. Each citizen, regardless of the modesty of his means, should only be concerned with acting justly, for the good of the city: this is why Socrates refused to leave the place that God assigned to him. The death penalty would damage not Socrates, but the Athenians, who would lose someone who constantly pushed them towards virtue. To explain why he could not escape, Socrates told a tale in which he personified the Laws.

In his tale, the Laws warned Socrates that "one must account for one's behaviour, because by escaping, you will destroy the Laws and the City, at least in part. What value and effectiveness do you believe that can have? What would happen if judgments handed down had no force between private parties, but were, on the contrary, jeopardized by them?

Socrates said that it could be replied that the judgment was unjust.

The Laws, in turn, argued back that "it is by means of Laws that your mother and your father could marry and you could be born." Socrates had nothing to answer to this nor to the Laws on education, in accordance with which Socrates too was raised. "The Laws have justly imposed upon your father to educate you in music and in gymnastics."

"It is always necessary to fulfil that which is ordered by the City and by the Nation or to convince these of what is right. However, if it is not holy to exert violence against one's mother or father, is it not perhaps much less so to exert violence against the Nation?

"However, us Laws have also made it possible for any Athenian citizen who so wishes, after passing the *docimasia* exam and proving to know the city's legal system, and thus the condition in which the citizen would find himself if he did not like it, to go wherever he wishes. And none of the Laws prevents or prohibits you from emigrating to form a colony, or to a foreign country, if the Laws or the City are not to your liking.

"We propose, and do not severely impose, this action.

"You have granted to us such strength and accepted to lead your life as a citizen under our protection. Here, you have performed every activity and had your children, because you loved the city beyond any doubt. Moreover, during the trial, you had the chance to sentence yourself to exile, if you wished; that which you seek to do now against the city's will, you could have done then, with its agreement.

"In fact and not in name only, you agreed to live your life as a citizen, in accordance with our content; but now you wish to escape, going against the customs and commitments according to which you agreed to conduct your life as a citizen. You are about to violate the pacts and commitments that you have made with us without coercion nor deceit, over the course of seventy years.

"If you flee to Thebes or Megara, you will live in an oligarchy and as an enemy to their Constitution. In Thessalia, there is much confusion and immorality. You will have to praise men of all natures, serving them. And what else could you do in Thessalia if not hold banquets, as if you had emigrated there only to feast? What would be of all your teachings on justice and other virtues? Perhaps you wish to live because you would like to raise and educate your children. Do you think you could educate them, among such customs?

"Thus, obey your nurturers the Laws, and do not value children, life, or any other thing more than justice. Like this, once you reach the Hades, you can defend yourself in all these things before those who reign there. Escaping would not be the right thing to do, neither here nor in the afterlife.

"Do not let Crito persuade you."

Thus Socrates chose to drink the poison, and his belly soon began to freeze. Shortly after, his voice would be heard for the last time: "O Crito", he reminded, "we still owe one rooster to Asclepius. Do not forget to give it to him.

"I must beg of you one thing: when my sons have grown, if you believe that they care for riches and other things before virtue, and if they wish to appear great although they are nobodies, scold them, harassing them like I harassed you. Make sure that they become ashamed of themselves, as I did with you, because they do not care for the things that they should be concerned with, and because they believe they are worthy when they are worthless. If you do this, you will have treated me with justice, myself and my sons."[7]

"Very well," answered Crito, "do you have anything else to say?"
Socrates did not answer. After a brief moment, he shuddered. Crito closed his mouth and his eyes.

"Echecrates, this was the end of our friend, the best man, we can confidently say, of all those whom we have known – incomparably the wisest and the most just".

*   *   *

Socrates felt neither indignation nor surprised when he heard the death sentence issued against him, because it was not wholly unexpected to him. What was surprising, rather, was the minuscule difference between those who believed him guilty and those who did not. Meletus narrowly escaped having to pay a fine, if Socrates had not been condemned to death.

In terms of the law, Socrates opposed the death penalty with a counterproposal of an adequate reward, such as remaining a Prytaneis with the support of public monies. He deemed this appropriate because he was a benefactor of the city, a man who educated and improved his fellow citizens.

Ultimately, those who won the Olympics with four- or two-horsed chariots or with a single horse received the same reward; however, as Socrates said, "these only make you seem happy, while [he] makes sure that you are happy".

It was not pride that led Socrates to advance this request, but a sense of justice.

He argued that he deserved neither prison, a fine or exile, because he had never harmed anyone.

Socrates declared to his judges that the Athenians would have to suffer the shame of having sentenced a wise man to death.

Those who sentenced him would not, by their judgment, free themselves from his teachings: others like him would certainly emerge and would be just as difficult to bear. It was pointless to

---

[7]   *Apologia. Op. cit.*, p. 109 (author's translation).

repress those who criticize: the only way to avoid their statements is to improve oneself.

Socrates represented the often inconvenient and unpopular figure of the philosopher and of the wise man who reminds people that it is not possible to live, work or govern without striving to know and pursue virtue. This is not a waste of time, but rather an opportunity to improve oneself and become more complete individuals. Thus, philosophy was once a transdisciplinary field that cut across several realms of knowledge. Humanity instead often twists and allows itself to be twisted by the worst forms of exploitation and instrumentalization, to achieve its ends.

Against this backdrop, philosophers easily become inconvenient; they might be met with removal from the scene, or on the contrary become an opportunity for growth. The choice often lies with history and with each individual. We may choose to ignore philosophical arguments, but we do so at our own risk and peril, and may also inflict consequences upon society and civil coexistence.

This is Socrates' legacy.

2

THE CONSPIRACY OF CATILINE

For the renown which riches or beauty confer is fleeting and frail; mental excellence is a splendid and lasting possession.

Sallust, *De coniuratione Catilinae*

I have taken upon myself, as is my habit, the general cause of the downtrodden.

Lucius Sergius Catiline

In *De coniuratione Catilinae* (Conspiracy of Catiline), Sallust (Amiternum, 86 BCE – Rome, 34 CE) wrote that "[Rome] had grown great through toil and the practice of justice, [...] great kings had been vanquished in war", but then, slowly, "[t]hose who had found it easy to bear hardship and dangers, anxiety and adversity, found leisure and wealth [...] Hence the lust for money first, then for power, grew" – the roots of all evils.
Virtue started to decline and vices to grow; and the latter were sometimes punished. However, the infection quickly spread. What was divine could no longer be distinguished from what

was secular; the city changed deeply and its government, which was once the best, the most just, became cruel and intolerable[8]. In such a vast and corrupt city, Catiline (Rome, 108 BCE – Pistoia, 62 BCE) easily attracted a multitude of followers.

Sallust paints a rather dark portrait of Catiline. Apparently, Catiline was of lively intellect and robust in constitution, but had a perverse and depraved character. He was drawn to tumult, violence, burglaries and discord since young. He had incredible physical strength and could easily withstand deprivation of food, warmth and sleep. His spirit was intrepid, cunning and fickle, and he was singularly talented in deceit and dissimulation. Catiline was greedy and skilled; ardent in his passions, not ineloquent, but had little judgment; he was uninhibited and always ready to engage in extreme behaviour[9].

"Since a young age", wrote Sallust, "Catiline had nefarious relations with a young girl from a noble family, with a vestal, and so forth, against law and morality. He fell in love with Aurelia Orestilla, in whom no good man ever found anything to praise except her beauty. Since she was reluctant to marry him because he already had a son, it is generally believed that Catiline had this son murdered so as to free his home for the criminal marriage. His villainous soul, at odds with the gods and with men, could not find rest neither asleep nor awake, such the remorse tormented him. His pale complexion, his bloodshot eyes, his gait now fast, now slow: everything in his appearance and behaviour revealed the perversity of his heart".[10]

Catiline hatched a plot to take over the Republic.

---

[8] Sallust. *De coniuratione Catilinae*, X. In this chapter, quotations from this work are taken from http://penelope.uchicago.edu/Thayer/E/ Roman/Texts/Sallust/Bellum_Catilinae*.html.

[9] Id., V.

[10] Sallust, *De coniuratione Catilinae* XV.

"In his *Parallel Lives*, Plutarch recounts the conspiracy of Catiline[11] as the most serious attack ever made on the Roman state and its socio-institutional system since the City's very foundation. And yet, no Latin author dealt with the rebellions led by Sertorius, Lepidus and Spartacus, which preceded Catiline's endeavor by only a few years.

Why is it that even two centuries later, not a single aristocratic historian did not condemn Catiline's effort and no good man who, upon hearing Catiline's name, was not seized by disdain and horror – while those of Sertorius, Lepidus and Spartacus himself had been forgotten or processed?

There is indeed a reason. And a good one: Catiline's so-called conspiracy was the first – albeit failed – revolution in History"[12].

Lucius Sergius Catiline was born in Rome in 108 CE to the senator Lucius Sergius Silus and Belliena, who had two more children, one son and one daughter. Catiline belonged to the *gens* Sergia, one of the hundred *familiae* who, as the legend goes, were the founders of Rome. At the time, most Roman *familiae* of highest descent enjoyed embellishing their genealogical heritage and the Sergi were no exception: they claimed to descend from Sergestus, the companion of Aeneas.

In 73 CE, Publius Clodius accused Catiline of raping a vestal, an extremely serious act of sacrilege and crime that attracted penalties of live burial for the woman and death by bludgeoning for the man. The vestal's name was Fabia. She was the sister of Terentia, Cicero's wife who later married Sallust as her third husband. Catiline was found near Fabia's cell, engaging in suspicious behaviour. He was put to trial and cleared of any guilt. However, some doubt lingered; and Cicero and Sallust understandably harboured ill feelings towards him, beyond any merely political reasons[13].

---

[11] Plutarch. Parallel Lives. Life of Brutus, 5; Life of Cato, 22; Life of Caesar, 7, Life of Crassus, 13.

[12] M. Fini. *Catilina*. Oscar Mondadori. 1996. Milan. P. 11. Author's translation.

[13] Id., p. 13.

Actually, with his second marriage to Aurelia Orestilla (his first wife Gratidia, who gave him his only child, had died), Catiline had settled down in sentimental terms. Cicero and Sallust accused him of killing his only son so that he could marry Orestilla. However, for the moment, the crime went unprosecuted; Cicero may have exploited the family tragedy to discredit the rebel[14].

Once Catiline was done with war and civil unrest, at the age of twenty-six, he devoted himself to politics. His career ascended swiftly and brilliantly. In 78 BCE he became a quaestor and thus joined the Senate; by 74 BCE he was a legate in Macedonia; in 70 he had been made an aedil, and in 68 a praetor (governor) in Africa. In other words, he had obtained every honour by the time that Silla, his mentor, died; at this point though, since he had passed from the aristocratic party to the democratic one, he became isolated. "The year was 66 BCE and Catiline was forty-two years old. The time had come for him to aim to become consul. In springtime, he returned from Africa to take part in the rallies for the elections of the consuls that would be held in 65 BCE, the year when he would reach the requisite age. However, on the way, he encountered the ferocious hostility of the aristocratic oligarchy. The interpreter of this hostility was a man who, in terms of temperament, habits, skills, character and life view, was extremely different from him, in fact the complete opposite: Marcus Tullius Cicero"[15].

When Cicero was about twenty years old, he completed his studies in law, rhetoric and philosophy. He moved to Rome and lived in a small house that his father had bought in the *Carene*, a neighbourhood on the outskirts of the city. He planned to become a lawyer.

Cicero also began to engage in political activities, and his career was as swift and brilliant as that of Catiline. He became a quaestor at the age of thirty (76 BCE), aedil at thirty-seven (70 BCE), praetor at forty (66 BCE) and consul at forty-three in 63 BCE, the year of his dramatic confrontation with Catiline.

---

[14]   Id., p. 14.

[15]   Id., p. 20.

At the beginning of his political career, Cicero supported the democrats, albeit without much fervor. He soon left them and for some time pondered the possibility of founding a centrist party based upon his class of provenance (the horsemen) and forming an alliance with the *optimates* against the plebes to defend the interests of the merchant bourgeoisie, which was beginning to establish itself as a class in those very years against the aristocracy. However, when the aristocrats proposed him as a candidate consul, he shifted to their side[1].

He delivered four speeches in a row against the agrarian law proposed by the tribune Servius Rullus, which sought to establish a more equal distribution of land. He fought against the proposal to re-confer civil rights upon the children of outlaws, who had been deprived of all such rights; this move however had the effect of boosting the support for Catiline. Cicero opposed all proposals for reform.

Cicero defended existing privileges and as a consul, delivered a speech (entitled *Pro Othone*) asking that horsemen be reserved fourteen rows of seats at the theatre.

"For him, the *concordia omnium* consisted simply in the immutability of the social hierarchy and the preservation of the power of the aristocratic oligarchy among the ranks of whom Cicero, as all good bourgeois, aspired to settle, so as to share their status and privileges, while always proclaiming noble words: *humanitas, dignitas, virtus*, love for the Nation, for traditions, for the penates, for the Gods"[2].

His boastfulness became legendary. Even Plutarch, who overall depicted him favourably, wrote that "he felt immoderate satisfaction when he was praised"[3].

Cicero constantly talked about how he had discovered and foiled Catiline's conspiracy, to the extent that he had bored everyone. Plutarch writes that "[o]ne could not go to the Senate, attend

---

[1]   Plutarch. *Life of Cicero*, 11. Author's translation.

[2]   M. Fini. *Op. cit.* p. 26. Author's translation.

[3]   Plutarch. *Life of Cicero*. P. 6. Author's translation.

an assembly meeting or to go court without having to listen to Cicero talk about Catiline and Lentulus. He ended up filling even the books and treatises that he wrote with praise, and his words, so sweet and graceful, became annoying and heavy for those who listened; it seemed that, by some sort of fatality, he had been stuck with the prerogative of annoying others"[4].

Cicero was utterly incapable of understanding his opponent: they were complete opposites of one another. And his dismay was documented in writings dated after Catiline's death, which sought to evaluate him with greater equanimity. Thus, in the *Pro Celio* speech, seven years after the conspiracy, Catiline was portrayed as a true aristocrat: "Who, at one point, was better thought of by eminent personalities, and who more intimate with wrongdoers? Who, more than he, supported the honest and at the same time was more nefarious for this city? Who was immersed in the most obscene pleasures and most resistant to fatigue? Who more than he was more rapacious and at the same time more generous? These were truly exceptional qualities, his capacity to befriend many people, to keep that friendship with deference, and let all partake in everything that he owned, to help all by means of money, support, with the most tiring services and, if necessary, even with crime... I myself, I will say, was almost fooled by him once"[5].

From the fourth century BCE, far-reaching transformations had started to take place in the aristocracy. Since the patricians (the original nobility, the families that had founded Rome) continued to decrease in number (in 366, only twenty-one clans remained), after some decades of strife, rich plebeians were admitted into the nobility. "However, these had a very different mentality from that of the old patricians, whose primacy was based on blood, tradition, *auctoritas*, honour, honesty, truth to one's word, loyalty, courage, valour in battle – that is, on that set of traits that the Romans summarized with the term *dignitas*. *Dignitas* originally

---

4   Plutarch. Parallel Lives. Life of Cicero, 24.

5   Cicero. *Pro Caelio*, 6, 13, 14. Author's translation.

had nothing to do with wealth. However, with the advent of the new aristocracy and of the horsemen, wealth became the only standard against which to measure the worth of a man.

The dominant oligarchy continued to refer to the ancient virtues and love for the nation, but it was actually driven only by a thirst for personal power, and practiced corruption on a systematic scale"[6]. The discontent and frustration that had been festering for decades among the poorer classes of the Roman population (that is, its majority) found a first outlet with the Gracchi. In 133 BCE, the tribune of the plebeians Tiberius Graccus proposed an agrarian law that sought to redistribute to the landless those public lands that had been arbitrarily taken over by landowners.

From that moment onwards, for almost one century, until the extinction of the Republic and the advent of the principality, Roman politics was dominated by two parties: the *optimates* and the *populares*. The former defended the interests of the aristocracy, and the latter those of the plebeians. "In words only. Indeed, also the leaders of the *populares* were senators and aristocrats, and it soon became clear that they used the name of the Gracchi and of the plebeian support that this guaranteed only to contrast their opponents. Rarely, if ever, in seventy years did the leaders of the *populares* do anything to seriously address social problems, limiting themselves only to some marginal and instrumental concessions or to those free distributions of wheat that were seen favourably by the *optimates* too, because they kept the population content without having to give up anything." The plebeians could not find a leader to truly champion their interests, because they were too poor and too uneducated to provide one from their own ranks. On the other hand, the aristocrats, even those to claimed to be *populares*, only cared for their own personal aims. Then again, the brutal and exemplary end of the Gracchi was an eloquent warning to all, one that paralyzed even those who were sincere.

---

6   M. Fini. *Catilina Op. cit.* p. 41. Author's translation.

In the words of the English historian P.A. Brunt, "among the members of the upper classes, few were willing to be accused of irresponsibility and violence, to be called seditious agitators by their peers, and to entrust their career to the ephemeral favour of the masses."[7] "In seventy years, there was only one of these: Catiline"[8].

In his home, Catiline displayed as a symbol the eagle of Marius, Silla's great antagonist, who was considered the champion of popular aspirations, also because of his humble origins.

However, Catiline's most remarkable features were a bravado, a boldness, a bravery that neared temerity, which he proved throughout his life, in war and in peacetime[9].

Before resorting to violence, Catiline attempted legally to become a consul three times, and he was rejected by means of tricks and fraud.

In 66 BCE, Catiline ran for the elections. The aristocrats immediately sought a remedy. They convinced the consul Lucius Volcatius Tullius, who presided over electoral rallies, to reject his candidacy on the grounds that it had been submitted late[10]. Then, to exclude him definitively, the aristocrats prompted Publius Clodius to prosecute Catiline for bribery supposedly committed during his time as governor in Africa, exploiting the complaints (which were a wholly ordinary occurrence) made by some delegates from his province. The law absolutely prohibited those who were under trial from running for an official position.

Despite the hostilities, Catiline, defended by the great Horace, was acquitted of all wrongdoing. He then submitted his candidacy again, in 63 BCE.

The struggle was among three candidates: Cicero, supported by a great part of the Senate and by the horsemen, Catiline and Hybrida, who enjoyed the support of Caesar and Crassus, the leaders of the democratic party and of the plebeians. Hybrida

---

7   P.A. Brunt. *Op. cit.* pp. 142-143.

8   M. Fini. *Op. cit.* p. 4. Author's translation.

9   Id, p. 13.

10   Sallust. *Op. cit.* XVIII.

was a weak, ambiguous man who was easily manipulated and blackmailed. Cicero made a secret pact with Hybrida for their voters to elect the two of them; this was possible because the votes were cast in secrecy and each voter could express two choices (there were two positions of consul to be filled).

Cicero came first, Hybrida second by a very narrow margin and Catiline was third.

Catiline ran for the position of consul for the third and final time in 63, to enter into function in 62 CE. He ran alone. Crassus, Caesar and the democrats did not support him because his ideas were too radical. He was supported only by the plebeians; these, however, could scarcely be enough.

Catiline thus began his electoral campaign, which was extremely aggressive, also because he no longer had to consider Crassus' and Caesar's views. In a speech that deeply affected the aristocrats and the bourgeoisie, he said that "a faithful defender of the poor could not be anyone other than he who was poor himself, the needy should not believe the promises of the rich and fortunate[11]". He added that the leader of those who sought redemption should have been a man who was courageous but also as poor. He, who owned almost nothing, was suitable because of the fruitless electoral campaigns and legal fees he had to pay. He concluded his speech with a highly inflammatory accusal: "In the Roman Republic there are two bodies, one is frail and infirm and has a head without a brain; the other is vigorous and healthy but has no head. If I will be able to earn it, I will be that head as long as I live". During the hearing, Cicero called Catiline to explain his statements. "Defiant as ever" wrote Cicero[12], "Catiline did not provide any justification", but repeated, in the *Curia*, before the élite of the Roman State, every point made in the private meetings. He then suddenly left the Senate, unspeaking[13].

---

[11] Cicerone. *Pro murena*, 51. Author's translation.

[12] Ibid.

[13] Ibid.

In those days, a reform introduced during the 3rd century had profoundly changed the situation at the Senate: the aristocracy and the bourgeoisie no longer were guaranteed the majority.

The consequence was that the candidates, who were always in fact aristocrats, began to engage in a ferocious war to gain the support of the plebeians. Electoral campaigns became incredibly expensive and entailed artistic displays, banquets and presents, if not actual bribery.

In the elections held in 63 BCE, Cicero, who presided them insofar as he was a consul, threw a first curveball to Catiline. With a weak excuse, he postponed the rallies the very day before the elections from the second half of July to the first half of August[14]. This protracted the duration of the campaign, which favoured the rich candidates. In addition, a great proportion of Catiline's supporters were farmers living in the Italic countryside and could not afford to stay long in Rome. Decimus Junius Silano, supported by Caesar, and Lucius Murena, by Crassus, were the winners. Once more, Catiline was not elected.

A few days later, one of the losing candidates, Servius Sulpicius, and the austere Marcus Porcius Cato accused Murena of having rigged the elections: his employees (*divisors*) had been caught bribing voters[15].

At the trial, which took place towards the end of November of 63 BCE, Murena was defended by three great lawyers: Cicero, Hortensius and Crassus. Cato, who led the prosecution, noted the anomaly (or rather serious injustice) of a consul who defended as a private person, as a lawyer, someone who was charged with rigging the very rallies that he had presided and the legality of which he was required to ensure. Cato also noted the paradox in which Cicero was caught: after he, as a consul, had pushed for the approval of the strictest law that had ever been issued on the subject of electoral wrongdoing, the *lex Tullia*, now, as a lawyer, he fought against it.

---

[14]   Ibid.

[15]   Id., p. 54.

Still, there was nothing to be done. Murena was acquitted. It was a political judgment. Catiline left Rome to ponder a plan. In theory, if Murena had been sentenced, precisely Catiline should have taken his place as first runner-up.

Why did the aristocracy fear Catiline to the point of blocking him from the very beginning, with all sorts of legal and illegal means? Cicero and Sallust portrayed him as a common criminal, a delinquent, someone who had killed his own son and wife. But if these were the issues, he could never have had such a prestigious career.

In 70 BCE, a few years before these facts, the position of censor was reintroduced ten years after Silla had abolished it. This was a judicial position among whose tasks was that to watch other the morality of the senators. There was a general "clean-up" operation and 64 senators out of 300 (over one-fifth of the assembly) were expelled from the *Curia* for "unworthiness"[16]. Catiline was not one of these[17]. When, in November of 64 BCE he was trialled for official misconduct, several very important individuals testified in his favour. These also included his political opponents, such as Lucius Torquatus, a hyper-conservative consul[18].

Just before the trial, Cicero himself offered to defend Catiline in court. He wanted to gain his favour in view of the elections to be held in 64 BCE, in which both of them would have run. Catiline refused the offer, because he deeply scorned the orator[19].

The aristocratic oligarchy feared Catiline's political, economic and social plan. This plan, which in 66 BCE was a mere draft, became increasingly precise in the four years during which Catiline tried to become a consul with legal means.

---

[16]   Livy. *Periochae*, XLVIII. Author's translation.

[17]   M. Fini. *Op. cit.* p. 55.

[18]   Cicero. *In toga candida*, 8.

[19]   Id., 19.

We are familiar with the details of the *lex Servilia* presented by the tribune Servius Rullus, upon direct proposal from Catiline, because Cicero himself wrote four speeches against it[20].

The *lex Servilia* consisted of 40 articles and had three goals: 1) ensure a more equal distribution of wealth 2) restart the agricultural sector, which had been dramatically impoverished by the development of large agricultural estates and 3) drastically reduce the ranks of the Capital's plebeians, which, as time had gone by, due to the crisis of small businesses and to the use of slave labour, had expanded greatly in number and become ever more lazy, because they lived off the free distributions of wheat; they had also become increasingly riotous, to the point that they posed a real threat to public order[21].

Cicero would later issue an indictment against the agrarian law (in a speech entitled *De lege agrarian*).

However, Catiline's economic plan included other proposals too. The most important of these was the cancellation of debts and the annulment of the law which punished insolvency with arrest and imprisonment.

The agrarian law would adversely affect the large landowners (thus, the aristocrats in particular); the cancellation of debts, the bankers and financiers (that is, the horsemen especially).

"The political and constitutional aspects of Catiline's plan proposed a return to the origins, of the Republic of the *optimates* and favoured the striking of a new balance between the aristocratic oligarchy on one hand, which was the *de facto* holder of all institutional power, and the plebeians on the other, as well as a dramatic reduction of the influence of horsemen; these, thanks to the power of cash, dominated both of the former categories.

The plan lays the foundations for a republic based on a balancing of the powers of the Senate, the magistrates and the popular assemblies (of centurions, curiates and tribunes), whose dignity

---

[20]   Cicero, *De lege agraria*.

[21]   M. Fini. *Op. cit.* p. 57.

had to be restored in addition to the actual powers that they had lost over time".[22]

Its powerful call to return to the original Republic is a call to times when all citizens, rich and poor, patricians and plebeians, could command respect. If someone was worthy of greater consideration, it was only because of his accomplishments (or at least those of his ancestors) in peacetime and in war – not because of what he owned and showed off. *Dignitas* was based on moral and not material values.

"Catiline is exceptional for his time. He is not a bourgeois, nor a plebeian, and does not identify with an aristocracy that no longer means (nor perceives itself) as a worthy élite. Catiline is an aristocrat of an aristocracy that has long disappeared; he is a patrician of the original times. His taking on the 'general cause of the unfortunate'[23] has nothing to do with class war, but precisely with his aristocratic nature. This is because he belongs to the genuine nobility, of courage and of soul, and not of money and privilege; of generosity towards the weak, the losers, the defeated. He is willing to meet his fate to the extreme and to face, at any price, his duties towards himself and towards others"[24].

In the Catilinarian Orations, Cicero stated that the conspirators were assassins, bandits, cheats, depraved. Sallust wrote much the same. It should be noted that the majority of Catiline's support consisted of Italic rural plebeians.

However, the conspirators also included some aristocrats and a few horsemen. Sallust names eleven senators.

Both Sallust and Cicero discuss in detail, with much horror, the mass participation of the Roman youth in Catiline's movement[25]. Sallust adds that these youth were certainly not poor: "They had every possibility to live in luxury and with every comfort, without

---

[22] M. Fini. *Op. cit.* p. 61. Author's translation.

[23] Sallust. *op. cit.* XXXV.

[24] M. Fini. *Op. cit.* p. 62. Author's translation.

[25] Cicero. *Pro Coelio.*

doing anything, and yet they preferred uncertainty to certainty, war to peace"[26].

In ancient Rome, the young aristocratic followers of Catiline had much to risk. Aulus Fulvius, a young aristocrat was captured on his way to Catiline's camp, arrested, and executed on the spot. The mandator was his own father[27], who declared "I did not raise him to fight for Catiline against the Nation, but to fight for the Nation against Catiline".

Among the conspirators was also Quintus Curius, of sound descent but who was notorious for his depravity, which caused him to be expelled from the Senate. For years, he had a relationship with a noblewoman, named Fulvia; due to his economic hardships, he soon was unable to be generous to her. Out of revenge, Fulvia began to spread around everything that he had told her about Catiline's conspiracy.

After the rallies had taken place and Marcus Tullius Cicero and Caius Antonius had been elected consuls, Catiline did not stay still. He tended traps of all sorts to Cicero, who was however no less vigilant and managed to avoid everyone. Ever since the beginning of his activity as consul, he had managed, through Fulvia, to learn of Catiline's plans.

Caius Cornelius (a Roman horseman) and Lucius Vargunteius, a senator, devised a plan to kill Cicero. One night, under the guise of visiting him to pay their respects, they went to his house together with many armed men. As soon as she knew of the danger to Cicero, Fulvia warned him of the impending attack and the perpetrators were unable to enter Cicero's house. In the meantime, Caius Manlius, an accomplice of Catiline, was gathering support among plebeians in Etruria.

When he learned of this double threat, Cicero became afraid. He realized that he no longer had the power to protect Rome from danger with his foresight alone, nor did he possess enough

---

26   Sallust. *op. cit.* XVII.

27   Id., XXXIV.

information on Manlius' forces or intentions. He thus chose to bring the issue to the attention of the Senate.

"In early June, when Lucius Caesar and Caius Figulus were consuls, Catiline began to make contact with individuals; he then exhorted and made promises, boasting of his revolutionary means and the great advantages that could derive from a conspiracy, which would be easy to achieve due to the weakness of the State. After performing his due checks, he gathered the most desperate and the bravest. His group included some senators, as well as many noblemen of the colonies and of the municipalities, and other nobles who supported his plan covertly, motivated not by a need for riches but by a hope for greater prestige."[28]

Catiline thus sent Manlius to Fiesole and the surrounding towns in Etruria; Septimius from Camerino to the Picenum area; Caius Julius to Apulia; and others yet in other places where he thought he could garner support. In the meantime, he had set several plans in motion in Rome: set traps to the consuls, station armed men in strategic locations, etc.[29]

"On the night of 20 October, Crassus, accompanied by the senators Marcus Marcellus and Scipio Metellus, went to Cicero's house with a pile of letters that he said had been delivered by a stranger that very evening. The letters were addressed to several members of the Senate and Crassus had only opened his. The letter was anonymous and warned that a massacre of the *optimates* was imminent, possibly even the next day, and begged Crassus to leave Rome immediately"[30].

"Who had written those mysterious letters? Crassus. Who had given him the information? Caesar.

On 22 October there was the hearing. Cicero handed the letters to their addressees and asked them to read them out loud to the assembly. This made a deep impression on those present".[31]

---

[28] Id., XVII.

[29] *Ibid.*

[30] Plutarch. Life of Cicero, 15. Author's translation.

[31] M. Fini. *Op. cit.* Author's translation.

Cicero added that he had information confirming the content of the letters. Although these were anonymous tip-offs, as is usually the case when the State is experiencing serious crises, the Senate issued a decree, a *Senatus Consultum Ultimum*, which is done only in case of grave dangers. The measure conferred upon the consuls full powers to act to avoid the State from suffering any harm.

For this purpose, it was established that if someone provided information on the conspiracy, he would have received in return freedom and 100,000 *sesterzii*, if he was a slave; if he was a free man, he would have received immunity and 200,000 *sesterzii*. It was also ordered to send groups of gladiators to Capua and other municipalities according to availability, and to distribute guards throughout Rome, under the coordination of minor magistrates".[32]

The citizens were deeply disturbed by these news. The atmosphere in the city changed drastically. All cheer and lightheartedness generated by a long period of peace quickly gave way to pervasive sadness. The consul had obliged all citizens of appropriate age to swear into the army. This was a sort of civil mobilization: in case of need, the consul would have resorted to this force.

Sallust tells that Catiline, with his ferocious spirit, persisted in his goals even though the defence forces had been alerted and he had been formally accused by Lucius Paulus upon mandate by the Senate, on the basis of the so-called *lex Plautia*, which imposed the death penalty or exile upon those who prevented the ordinary performance of state functions.

Catiline's arrest was therefore imminent. Yet he continued to walk around town, ostentatiously relaxed. However, he now carried a weapon with him.

Catiline chose to make the first move. He himself agrees to be taken prisoner at the home of Senator Marcus Lepidus until the situation is clarified. It was an ancient Roman custom for high-profile defendants to be held in pre-trial detention by an authoritative citizen, who would thus assume responsibility for them. However, Lepidus refused to accept him. Catiline, in a highly

---

[32] Sallust. *Op. cit.* XXX.

inflammatory gesture, went to Cicero's house. Terrified, Cicero locked himself at home.[33]

Catiline is finally accepted by M. Marcellus, a friend of his and perhaps one of the conspirators. Catiline continues to guide the conspiracy from his house.

The city is heavily armed and the strategic locations are checked. In addition, the aristocrats made two simple but effective moves. To keep the population under control, they organized extraordinary free distributions of wheat; then, to discredit the conspirators, they spread the rumour that their plans included the burning down of the city.

To confuse matters and pretend that he was innocent, and that it was all a plot against him, Catiline went to the Senate as usual. As he walked in, all the senators avoided him and nobody sat next to him. Catiline was alone. We can picture him as Cesare Maccari did in his famous painting "Cicero denounces Catiline": disdainful and proud, his body tense under his long toga as he listened to the consul's accusations without a word.[34]

Then consul Marcus Tullius, fearing Catiline and moved by disdain, gave a splendid oration defending the State. The oration was later writted and published.

The first of the four Catilinarian Orations pronounced by Cicero began with the famous sentence "When, O Catiline, do you mean to cease abusing our patience?".

The entire oration was an exhortation to Catiline to leave the city.[35] Why did Cicero not arrest Catiline on the spot? He had all the means to do so. On 20 October, the Senate had conferred upon him full powers; Cicero himself, in a passage of his oration, acknowledged that he should have taken measures "already twenty days ago".[36]

---

[33] Cicero. Catiline Orations I, 19.

[34] M. Fini. *Op. cit.* p. 100.

[35] Cicero. Catiline Orations I, 4.

[36] *Ibid.*

We can only surmise what Cicero's reasons were, as he never expressed them[37].

Perhaps, Cicero feared that dramatically arresting Catiline in the Senate would have sparked an uprising of the plebeians, even though the army was ready to intervene.

He may have preferred Catiline to leave the city. This would have allowed him to pass the issue on to Antonius Hybrida, who dealt with matters beyond the walls of Rome.

Arresting Catiline in the Senate would have posed some problems. What could be done with him after the arrest? A Roman citizen sentenced to death for a political crime still had the right to appeal to the people and be judged by it (and there was the possibility of appeal to the centurions' committees). This would have been much too risky.

Cicero may also have feared a physical confrontation, considering Catiline's disturbing countenance; he may also have been stopped by his own conscience. Indeed, Cicero had recently been granted Roman citizenship and did not have illustrious ancestors; he did not dare to personally arrest that great, proud and contemptuous patrician.

When Cicero finished his oration, Catiline, who was ready to refute all the accusations, assumed a humble expression and begged the senators to not consider him an enemy unless proof could be produced.

More specifically, he asked that they "not believe too easily all rumours against him; the family into which he was born, the lifestyle conducted since adolescence were such as to encourage every hope; they should not have thought that a patrician, equal to them, beloved to the Roman people for his own deeds and those of his ancestors, had to resort to destroying the Republic, when Marcus Tullius was watching over his safety".[38]

Catiline's speech was a moral affront to Cicero, because he recalled his provincial and lower middle-class origins. However, as told by

---

[37]   M. Fini. *Op. cit.* p. 102.

[38]   Sallust. *Op. cit.* XXXI.

Sallust, since "he added more insults"[39] a general protest broke out in the Senate. All senators were against him.

As Catiline continued to add insult upon insult, the senators began to label him a traitor. This made him furious and he exclaimed these words: "Since my enemies surround me and push me to ruin, I will douse the fire lit against me with a catastrophe"[40].

That very night, he left Rome for Etruria, where he reached Manlius's army.

What did Catiline want? What was his plan? He detached himself from Crassus and Caesar, whom he deemed unsuitable to support the people's cause, and recruits as conspirators men such as Lentulus and Antonius, who were ex-consuls. Men such as these did not lack freedom. What did Catiline reproach to the noble classes? Social injustice.

From Catiline's electoral speech for the elections held in 64 BCE: "Indeed, since the State has handed law and authority to a powerful few, even kings and tetrarchs have become their vassals, and peoples and nations pay taxes to them.

We, although brave and honest, noble and plebeians, are without influence, without authority, submitted to these people, who, in a republic worthy of its name, would fear us.

Thus they ran the State, manipulating for their own gain and that of their friends, favours, power, public offices and public funds; they left us with uncertainty, emargination, unfair trials, and poverty. For how much longer, then, will we stand such affronts? Is it not worthier to die courageously, than to spend passively and shamefully a miserable existence without honours, subjected to mockery and pride? In truth, thanks to the heavens, victory is in our hands, as we are vigorous and powerful, unlike them, who are worn out by time and riches. Now we must act; the rest will follow. These things, I hope, I will address with you as consul".[41]

---

[39]   *Ibid.*

[40]   *Ibid.*

[41]   *Ibid.*

Catiline promised that debts would be cancelled, that the wealthy would be banished and the conspirators would be appointed magistrates and priests and would receive riches.

In ancient Rome, the punishments for high treason were very severe.

The patriarchal laws of the time imposed the death penalty against those who threatened the State's safety.

Catiline went to Etruria to join Manlius; he was to remain there until his companions in Rome told him that they were ready to rebel. Precisely to allow affairs in Rome to be organized as well and as quickly as possible, Catiline decided to leave all of his men in the city and to leave for Etruria alone. This would have made people think, at least for some time, that he had gone into exile. He entrusted the leadership to Lentulus, a member of the *gens* Cornelia, which in the early days of the Republic had given rise to tens of consuls and hundreds of magistrates. Catiline left Rome that night in the company of three young men.[42]

Lentulus had been planning to take over Catiline as leader of the conspiracy. Instead of following his orders, then, Lentulus did as he wanted.

Lentulus hatched a grand plan which was, however, disproportionate to his forces. The date of the rebellion was set for the eve of the Saturnalia to be held on 16 December. The conspirators were to occupy strategic points in the city, started the insurrection, and killed the consul and other senators. Cetegus spurred the rebels to act fast, because the more time passed the more Catiline, hounded by the government's forces, was in danger. Cetegus did not agree to wait one more month until 16 December. He thought that a handful of men would be enough to assault the *Curia* and win the match.[43]

In addition, a serious misunderstanding arose between Catiline's followers in Rome and those in Etruria: Catiline was waiting for the insurrection to begin, before he would march on the city, while

---

[42]   Cicero. Catiline Orations, II, 4.

[43]   Sallust, *op. cit.* XLIII.

Lentulus and the others were waiting for Catiline to approach Rome to begin the insurrection. The two groups had difficulties in communicating. Indeed, for some time, the rebels who tried to reach Catiline's camp were systematically caught.

In the meantime, Lentulus, who was looking for reinforcements, had an idea. A few days before, two ambassadors of the Allobroges, a population from ancient Gaul, had come to Rome. The ambassadors were waiting to be received by the Roman government, to complain of the wrongs committed against the population by the Roman governor Lucius morena. Lentulus ordered Publius Umbrenus, a freedman who had spent much time with the Gauls and knew their language, to contact them. Umbrenus met them at the Forum and told them of the conspiracy and its aims. The Allobroges listened to him and then left. Consulting with one another, they agreed that the rebel group did not appear reliable and that it would have been better to reveal everything they knew to the Roman government, to ask for a reward. They thus spoke to Quintus Fabius Sanga, who, according to Roman tradition, sponsored their interests in the Senate. Sanga brought them to Cicero. The consul immediately understood that this was a unique opportunity to obtain the conclusive proof that he had long been searching for and that would have protected him from all challenges. He thus suggested that the Allobroges pretend to be extremely interested, so that they could understand how large the conspiracy was and, especially, obtain something in writing. The meeting took place. All of the main conspirators were there: Lentulus, Cetegus, Stailius, Cassius, Gabinius and Umbrenus. The Allobroges ask for a written document that they can bring back to their people. Lentulus, Cetegus and Statilius each write a letter – thus unwittingly signing their own death sentence. Only Cassius guesses the danger and leaves with an excuse: he would leave for Gaul immediately and negotiate directly with the Allobroges' chiefs.

Cassius immediately left the city and disappeared from history. Lentulus told the Allobroges to pass by Catiline's camp to confirm their commitments and to have him send some horsement.

He then entrusted Titus Volturcius, from Crotone, the task of bringing the Allobroges to the camp at Fiesole. Volturcius was also to inform Catiline that in Rome almost everything was ready for the rebellion and is waiting for him to reach the city. However, Cicero has already tended a trap at Ponte Milvio, where the expedition had to pass. The Allobroges were captured and the letters were confiscated.

It was the night of 2 December 63 BCE. Sallust writes that when Cicero learned of the news, he was seized with "great joy and great concern"[44]. Joy, because he finally had proof of the conspiracy; concern, for the same reason. He now had to decide the fate of the conspirators.

That very afternoon, Cicero summons the Senate.

The Senate was filled to overcapacity. Cicero introduced the praetor Flaccus. The latter produced a chest in which the confiscated letters were kept.

The letters were vague in content but the attempt to negotiate with a foreign power without involving the Senate, and their contact with Catiline, who at the time was already considered hostile, were enough to found the charge of high treason.

However, the so-called *lex Sempronia* was in force. Although this allowed for the death penalty, it prescribed that the last word be pronounced by committees of the population, which were to gather in the Roman Forum.

The decisive session was that of 5 December. The trial took place in an atmosphere of siege.

The Temple of Concord was chosen as the courtroom, because it was close to a rock wall and thus easy to defend if an attack were to happen. No possibility was to be discounted. Cicero had taken every possible precaution. Roman horsemen were posted at the two sides of the courtroom to bar entry, and others were sent on the *via Sacra* near the hill to the Capitol Hill.[45]

---

[44]   Id., XLVI.

[45]   I processi dell'età classica. Written under the direction of Franco Massara. Edizioni Ferni- Ginevra 1975. Pag. 51

Junius Silano, a "designated consul", spoke harshly of the seriousness of the crime, recalled the examples of the times of their ancestors, and concluded that the people charged were to be punished with "the utmost suffering". What did he mean by this? The death penalty, or exile and confiscation of all property? The second "designated consul" Murena thought that Silano intended the death penalty. He thus called for this to be imposed upon the conspirators. His request was seconded, one by one, by the main consular figures.

Caius Julius Caesar then stood, as Pontifex Maximus and "designated praetor" for the following year. To the great surprise of those present, Caesar expressly declares that he is contrary to the imposition of the death penalty upon the five conspirators. He orders that they be exiled to the most secure municipalities of Italy. In his *De coniuratione Catilinae*, Sallust writes that Caesar, when asked to speak by the consul, recalled those cases in which their ancestors, taming their inner turmoil, behaved wisely.

In the Macedonian war against King Perseus, Rhodes, which had become prosperous thanks to the Romans, became hostile towards Rome. When the war was over and the fate of Rhodes was to be decided, the ancestors avoided inflicting punishments, so that it would not be said that they had waged war for greed of money, rather than for the offence caused.

Likewise, during the Punic Wars, although the Carthaginians had committed terrible atrocities during the truces, the ancestors never took advantage of suitable circumstances to repay their deeds: they tried to choose the dignified course of action for themselves, not that which would have been appropriate against the Carthaginians, because one should not yield to resentment more than to honour."[46]

Silano explained that by "utmost suffering" he did not mean to speak of the death penalty, but rather of exile for life. He thus aligns with Caesar's proposal. As if it were not enough, the next orator, Quintus Cicero, the brother of Cicero, also agreed.

---

[46]   Id., LI.

The assembly is about to slide into a general recanting.

At this point, it was Cicero's turn to speak. He spoke calmly, enunciating each word clearly, dividing his sentences with long silences, in accordance with the art of rhetoric which he knew well. That was his profession. Indeed, Cicero came from the Forum. He had fought several cases and was well aware of the tricks of elocution. He studied in Greece and Asia, where he perfected his oratory skills. Cicero spoke that which will become known as the fourth Catiline Oration (63 BCE).

Caius Julius Caesar – said Cicero – knew very well that the *lex Sempronia*[47] applied to Roman citizens; he was also aware, however, that when one is an enemy of the Republic, he could certainly not be considered a citizen; the very person who drafted that law without a popular consultation had to pay the price of his attack upon the Republic.

Marcus Porcius Cato, descendant of the great censor Cato, was a model citizen.

Sallust described him thus[48]: "Cato tended towards modesty, decorum and especially austerity. He did not compete for wealth with the rich, for influence with the manipulators, but for courage with the brave, for reserve with the modest, for integrity with the honest. He preferred to be virtuous rather than to seem virtuous, and thus, the less he pursued glory the more he approached it".

Cato warned "Do not believe that our ancestors created this great Republic with weapons: if that were the case, it would be much more beautiful, in terms of allies, citizens, weapons, horses...No! Different were the means that made them great, and these means we possess no longer: laboriousness within Rome, authority based on justice outside; in assemblies, an independent spirit, free from manipulation and passions. Instead, what do we have? Love of luxury, greed, poverty in the public coffers, great wealth in private ones; we cherish our belongings but like to do nothing;

---

[47] If sentenced to death, Roman citizens could request a *provocation ad populum* (consultation of the people).

[48] Sallust, *op. cit.* LIV.

there is no longer any distinction between rascals and gentlemen; cheats grab the prizes due to the worthy. And we should not be surprised: each one of you decides only to benefit your own interests; at home you are slaves to pleasure, here to money and favours: this is why people think to seize upon a defenceless Republic".

Caesar's theory could have some foundation if the rebels' hideout was only in Rome. That would make things simple: the conspirators could be arrested and then exiled.

Cato says that the ancestors had left them one lesson: when the Republic is in danger, traitors can meet only one fate: death.

"It is twilight. The first shadows of the evening fall upon an exhausted, tense city. The Republic has experienced one of the most revolutionary days of its history. Under the Capitol Hill, everything is ready. Five men wait to be led there and put to death: Lentulus, Cetegus, Statilius, Gabinius and Caparius. The trial has just ended. The Senate has decided: may death be imposed upon these five wretches who, in Catiline's name, plotted against the State, its laws and its institutions."

Cicero, entrusted with having the punishments executed, was in a hurry. Indeed, a surprise attack by the friends of those sentenced could not be excluded yet.

He ordered the *triumviri capitales* to prepare all the necessary equipment, and then, followed by a great number of armed men and some senators, went to collect the prisoners. The group marched down the *via Sacra*, crossed the Forum, and reached the Mamertine prison.

The law required those sentenced to death to be led here to be strangled, one after the other.

In the meantime, in front of the prison, people were congregating in large groups. The consul, having exited the prison, found himself in front of a troubled crowd, which was agitated by various feelings, anxious to know the fate of the prisoners. Cicero hesitated for a moment, and then firmly raised a hand to ask for silence. He must give the people important information. *"Vixerunt"*, he says. "They lived" – and now they live no longer. The crowd fell silent for a moment, surprised. And then, suddenly, it burst into a great applause to salute the consul. The conspiracy was overcome. The Republic was safe.

Cicero slowly returned to his home. As he walked, towers and houses lit up. Men followed him and acclaimed him. For Cicero, this was a true apotheosis.

The poet Juvenal would write *"Roma patrem patriae Ciceronem libera dixit"*: "Free Rome called Cicero the father of the country".

The consul, visibly moved, looked back upon the proud, capricious and ungrateful city that one day gives glory, and the next day gives death.[49]

"After the camp heard the news that the conspiracy had been unmasked and that Lentulus, Cetegus and the others had been put to death, most of those who had been moved to participate, in the hope of gaining riches and out of a desire for revolution, disappeared; Catiline led those who had remained by his side towards the countryside of Pistoia, forcing them to march through rough mountains, to escape by secret paths to Gaul, on the other side of the Alps.

While Catiline's companions were being killed in the Mamertine prison, Catiline in Etruria was preparing the legions with which he would march on Rome. Two of these were already ready, providing him with about twenty thousand men. Of these, however only

---

[49] Indeed, after Caesar's death, Cicero assumed a key role. His political aims were clear: counting on the support of Octavian, he wished to rebuild a senatorial party. He was opposed by Antonius, who in the meantime had become the leader of the people: Cicero attacked him vehemently, pronouncing fourteen orations against him. However, Octavian had made a political deal with Antonius and Crassus. Cicero, included on the famous proscription lists, hid in his villa at Formia, but the mercenaries paid by the *triumviri* reached him as he was running away. They cut off his head and brought it to Antonius, who also ordered that his hands be cut off – the hands which had written the *Philippicae* against him – and to display hands and head in the Roman Forum. "In a society as was the Roman one, in which life was accounted for relatively and it was considered that it was death, and the way one faced it, that conclusively defined an existence." M. Fini. *Op. cit.* P. 29.

one-quarter had real weapons. The rest were armed with scythes or rods. Most of the men were in Fiesole, and many were once soldiers under Silla.

Catiline's plan was vast and apparently well-made. He kept relations with emissaries spread throughout the territory: in Capua, where there was a gladiator school; in Ostia, where there was a naval fleet; in Picenum, in Apulia, in the Gallia Transalpina, in Africa.

Everything had been prepared for the attack, but the execution of his five co-conspirators ruined his plans. In addition, news came from Fiesole that two armies, one under Metellus Celere and the other under the consul Caius Antonius, were marching quickly towards Etruria.

To avoid being clamped in, Catiline ordered to move towards the mountains near Pistoia and reach the territory of Gallia Transalpina. Metellus Celere, who had learned of the orders given by Catiline from his defectors, thus moved towards the mountains from which Catiline was to descend towards Gallia.

Behind Catiline was Antonius' army, which awaited the fugitives on the plains.

Catiline was thus caught between two fires: between the mountains and his enemies, without a chance to escape. He decided to wage battle anyway, closed in a narrow valley, between steep mountains.

After rallying his troops, Catiline ordered the ranks, had the clarions call, and ordered the horses to be led away, so that his troops could not escape, for better or worse.

Between Metellus Celere, who waited for him beyond the mountain passes, and Caius Antonius, who chased him under the Apennines, Catiline chose the latter. He chose to face he who was once his accomplice in plotting against Rome, against the Republic. However, the consul had remained in his tent, suffering from an attack of goiter. The legion was thus commanded by Marcus Petreius. When Petreius realized that the outcome of the battle was as yet undecided, he attempted one last strike: he launched the praetorian court in the middle of the enemy's ranks and, at the same time, ordered that they be surrounded on the sides.

For the rebels, it was the end. Catiline, seeing his army defeated, rushes where the fighting was most intense and died in battle. Sallust wrote "Only once the fight was over, could they understand the strength of the resolve of Catiline's soldiers". Petreius was unable to capture a single prisoner. Everyone had died in their place, after fighting and suffering blows to the chest.

"And yet, the Roman army did not obtain an easy victory. Indeed, many soldiers who had left the camp to scout the location or to grab weapons from the enemy, as they turned over the bodies of their dead opponents, found among these a friend, or a guest, or a relative; there were even those who recognized their own personal belongings. Thus, contrasting sentiments ran through the army: joy and sorrow, tears and rejoicing".[50]

It was the year 692 since Rome had been founded. Catiline's conspiracy had been conclusively quashed, drowned in blood.

*   *   *

It was a great and terrible event that certainly dominated public debate in Rome for a long time. Perhaps, those who had witnessed the event, and, two decades later, the readers of Sallust's brief essay, pondered the same questions that we ask ourselves two thousand years later. Was Catiline truly the ferocious and depraved monster depicted by Cicero and Sallust? If he had managed to carry out his plan legally, especially those aspects concerning particularly controversial issues (such as the cancellation of debts and returning civil rights to the children of proscribed individuals), could he have gone down in history as a wise reformer, rather than as a sinister revolutionary?

The bad habits of the leading classes, the privileges and abuses of the proconsuls and the exploitation of the provinces were not unknown to Sallust; however, he could not admit that social injustice could be remedied by the hand of extremists, with extreme acts, massacres, expropriations and robberies.

---

[50]   Sallust. *Op. cit.*, LXI.

What were the interior and exterior reasons that prompted Sallust to examine history, to revisit recent events?

Among the possible reasons were: their detachment from politics, the desire to become involved in a field in which important works were, as yet, scarce, the will to explain those deeds to his peers, to examine the social, economic and political environment in which a conspiracy of those dimensions could be organized, the social and cultural sphere to which Catiline and his companions belonged.

However, Sallust's aim is not only to report historical facts. His work implies a message: Rome's power cannot last if its sole valid historical justification comes to fail – moral superiority. Therefore, Rome must return to its rigid habits of yore.

The allusions were clear to his contemporaries.

A love for Rome, a severe condemnation of the conspirators, who also enjoy however a certain degree of understanding. Grief for the civil wars that threaten Rome, a shadow over them since Romulus killed his brother Remus.

Sallust had witnessed the war between Marius and Silla and that between Caesar and Pompey. As he wrote of Catiline, the long fight between Octavian and Antonius was just starting, a fight that would culminate in the battle of Actium.

Sallust was a follower of Caesar, who had come to Rome from a small Italic municipality. He counted no consuls among his ancestors and thus could not claim any *nobilitas*; he belonged to that active provincial bourgeoisie that, with Augustus, was to supplant the patricians' rule: Marius, and Cicero before him, were men of the same class and had the same mentality.

And yet, Sallust was conservative at heart. He observed the ethical code of the aristocratic sphere, the ancestral customs.

The revolution was a opaque and sterile tumult, a profane reality contrary to the sacred cosmos, which consisted of eternal values; of these, the most solid was the cult of the Republic.

Sallust's values were such that he hoped for certain changes in the Republic, and against others.

The discontent of the provinces' inhabitants, admitted by other authors, replicated the class hatred that burned within. Sallust, as would do later Lucan, Juvenal and Tacitus, sides with those protests and writes "from just and excellent as it once was, the government of Rome has become cruel and intolerable".

Sallust was willing to support protests as long as they respected the Constitution.

In absolving Cato of the "sin" of defending the privileged classes, Sallust implicitly acknowledged that the moral heritage of the *optimates* deserved to be preserved; disassociating Caesar from Catiline, he indicates him as the type of democrat that should govern – firmly intending to abolish inequities but well aware of his times and environment.

However, when he wrote, Sallust saw around him nothing but vengeful wrath: Cato, who committed suicide in the name of republican freedom; a few years later, he would see Julius Caesar die from twenty-three stab wounds. The two greatest men of his time had died to civil war.

Everything was submerged in darkness: in writing of them as if they were still alive and involved in a parliamentary debate, Sallust wrote their funeral elegy.

Perhaps, Augustus meditated upon these pages and understood that the stances of the two great men had to be combined, and thus sought to reconcile within his own person, the ideas of Cato and those of Caesar.

3

THE TRIAL OF GALILEO GALILEI

...It is not enough to look; it is necessary to look with eyes that want to see, that believe in what they see.

Galileo Galilei (Pisa 1564- Arcetri 1642).

From religion comes a man's purpose; from science, his power to achieve it. Sometimes people ask if religion and science are not opposed to one another. They are: in the sense that the thumb and fingers of my hands are opposed to one another. It is an opposition by means of which anything can be grasped.

Sir William Bragg (1862-1942), Nobel Prize in Physics in 1915 for creating the first X-ray spectroscope.

Before we discuss Galileo's trial, and to better understand the historical context in which he lived, it is useful to examine the cautious attitude that his predecessor Nicolaus Copernicus adopted towards his own peers.
Nicolaus Copernicus (1473-1543) had studied philosophy, astronomy and canon law. He had a deep knowledge of the ancient Greek authors, who were indeed a source of inspiration for him. Since 1595, he had been fascinated by the "heliocentric"

theory, according to which the Earth revolved around the Sun – which remains fixed in the center of the Solar System – and that the Earth rotated on its own axis. This theory cast doubt on the view that had been commonly accepted since ancient times, according to which the Earth was fixed at the centre of the universe, and the Sun and all other planets revolved around it. The development of this "geocentric" view peaked with Ptolemy, the last great astronomer of classical times, in 200 CE. Some followers of Pythagoras may have spoken of a "central fire" as early as 500 BCE, but the true predecessor of Copernicus was Aristachus of Samos, who lived in the third century BCE; it was he who outlined the basic elements of the heliocentric system. However, Aristarchus' ideas were not accepted and were soon forgotten. On the basis of Aristarchus's heliocentric hypothesis, Copernicus constructed a mathematical model that enabled the planetary motions to be calculated just as well as Ptolemy's model, if not better.

Copernicus was very guarded about his intellectual position. Rather reserved by nature, he was not particularly inclined to act as a revolutionary.

The new astronomical theories were widely condemned as they contradicted the Sacred Scriptures of Christianity. Luther denounced the theories as early as 1539 in especially virulent terms. Of Copernicus, he declared:

"that madman claims to wholly overwhelm astronomy, as established in the Scriptures, it is the Sun and not the Earth that Joshua commanded to stop".[51]

Copernicus was a prudent man, and thus was very careful to not publish his conclusions prematurely. He waited until 1512 to circulate among his friends a manuscript in which he summarized the new astronomical principles. Thanks to this pamphlet, his ideas spread throughout Europe. In 1533, Pope Clement VII learned of them and did not raise any objections. Indeed, high ecclesiastical officials encouraged Copernicus to publish his

---

[51] Jean-Pierre Lonchamp. *Il caso Galileo*. Edizioni Paoline. Turin, 1990. P. 20. Author's translation.

results. Copernicus tirelessly worked on a monumental oeuvre, a veritable six-volume encyclopedia of astronomy titled *De revolutionibus orbium coelestium* (The revolutions of the celestial bodies). Always extremely cautious and fearful of causing a scandal, he intentionally sought to delay its publication.

It was not until a young Protestant colleague, Reticus, enthusiastically insisted that Copernicus authorized the printing of a first compendium of the work in 1540: the Narratio Prima. Given the enormous success of this publication, he allowed *De revolutionibus orbium coelestium* to be printed; he received the first copy on his deathbed, in 1543. Some years later, Galileo Galilei (1564-1643), a mathematician, physicist, philosopher and astronomer, discovered the laws of isochronism from the slight movements of the pendulum he used to set watches. Galileo invented the thermometer and the hydrostatic balance; discovered the laws of weight; established the principles of modern dynamics; and in 1609 built the first astronomical telescope, with which he discovered the hilliness of the Moon's terrain, Saturn's rings, Jupiter's planets, Venus's phases and the sunspots.

In the space of only a few months, Galileo gathered a great deal of interesting information. He discovered that the Earth is no longer the only planet with a satellite (the Moon): indeed, Jupiter does too. Is Earth a planet, like all the others? Venus's phases were particularly instructive in this regard. The Moon has phases because of its revolution around the Earth, during which it also reflects the light from the Sun. Therefore, if Venus, as seen from Earth, also has phases, this can only be because it revolves around the Sun and reflects its light.

The success of the *sidereus nuncius* failed to charm the conservative spheres. Early criticisms focused on Galileo's use of the telescope. Some astronomers could not see anything with the instrument, because they were not familiar with it. Other detractors said that the stars discovered with it were fake images created by the instrument itself. Kepler too doubted whether Jupiter's satellites truly existed. To convince him, Galileo sent him a telescope that he had made himself. Kepler gathered his observations anew and, in 1610, confirmed Galileo's findings. Kepler also improved upon Galileo's telescope to obtain better enlargements of the objects observed, replacing the divergent lens with a convergent one. Thus, the first "modern" astronomical telescope was developed, and this basic form remains to this day.

In 1612, a campaign opposing Galileo began to take shape. The attack developed on two fronts: the university and the religious ones.

On 12 April 1615, Cardinal Bellarmino expressed his thoughts in a letter to Foscarini, a religious man and a friend of Galileo. The letter was supposed to serve as a last warning to all of Galileo's followers to behave cautiously:

"It appears to me that Your Person and Messr Galileo would do best to satisfy themselves with talking *ex suppositione*, or in terms of hypotheses. Because to say that it is supposed that the Earth moves and the Sun is still allows one to save appearances (the celestial phenomena), it is very well and does not entail any danger, and this is enough for mathematicians and astronomers. If there were to be a real scientific test, one could be led to review the interpretation of some passages of the Scriptures".

Well aware of the danger, Galileo nevertheless counterattacked with two very important letters: one to his friend Castelli (in December 1613) and the other to Cristina of Lorena (May 1615). The letter to Castelli summarized Galileo's ideas on the problems of Scriptural interpretation that arose due to the new astronomical theories. The letter to Cristina simply further developed the ideas contained in that to Castelli. Galileo summarized his main thesis in a formula (which was moreover reprised by Cardinal Baronio, the Vatican's librarian, according to whom, by means of the Bible, the "intention of the Holy Spirit" is "to teach us how to reach heaven, and not how heaven works".

Another character played a significant part in the dispute. This was Father Paolo Antonio Foscarini, whom we have already mentioned. Foscarini was a clergyman who subscribed to Copernicus' views, and tried to help Galileo by publishing a very long letter addressed to the Father General of his order: the pamphlet defended the heliocentric doctrine and sought to prove that the Scriptural passages used to argue against heliocentrism could also be given an interpretation that was compatible with Copernicus's ideas. Foscarini shared the opinion of the Spanish theologian Zuniga, who had affirmed this much thirty years ago.

Religion naturally felt threatened by this change. Some Biblical texts appeared to be irreconcilable with the new astronomical ideas. One of the passages that was invoked most often against Copernicus's theories is in the Book of Joshua:

"Joshua said to the Lord in the presence of Israel: "Sun, stand still over Gibeon, and you, moon, over the Valley of Aijalon.' So the sun stood still, and the moon stopped, till the nation avenged itself on its enemies [...] The sun stopped in the middle of the sky and delayed going down about a full day." (Joshua, 10: 12-13)

A passage from the Book of Job was also cited: "He speaks to the sun and it does not shine; he seals off the light of the stars." (Job, 9:7)

Galileo explained, however, that the passage confirmed the Copernican system: if we wished to interpret the miracle on the basis of the Ptolemaic doctrine accepted by the Church, the order "Sun, stop" should have yielded the exact opposite effect of that requested: the day would not have been longer, but rather four minutes shorter. To strictly observe the Ptolemaic system, Joshua should have said "Stop, *primum Mobile* [first moved]", because it is this ninth sky, with its rapid revolution, that transmits the East-West movement to the Sun and all other celestial bodies. By saying "Sun, stop", Joshua made a mistake according to the Ptolemaic system: on the Ptolemaic view, the Sun cannot stop, drawn into motion as it is by the *primum Mobile*, without throwing into disarray the balance of the heavens and provoke a cosmic disaster. For Galileo, therefore, it could be that the Sacred Scriptures could not be given a literal interpretation.

Galileo suggested interpreting Joshua's words according to the Copernican system. It was to be supposed that the Sun is at the centre of the Solar System and that it rotates on its own axis (as Galileo demonstrated in his *Letter on sunspots*); also, it had to be supposed that with this rotation, the Sun regulated planetary motion. Based on these assumptions, the words of the Jewish leader could make sense: "Sun, stop" would have stopped the entire planetary system and time, and Joshua could indeed have gained some hours of light and finish the battle. Ironically, precisely the passage drawn from Joshua's book to support the traditional view demonstrates the "falseness and impossibility of the Aristotelian and Ptolemaic systems, and actually agrees very well with the Copernican one".

Galileo then proposed to adopt Copernicus's and his view: thus, Joshua's words could make sense in scientific terms.

"Having discovered and demonstrated" that the Sun rotates upon its own axis "as do all other celestial bodies", and given that it is "much more likely and reasonable that the Sun, as the greatest instrument and minister of nature, almost the heart of the world, gives off – as it clearly does – not only light, but also movement to all planets... who cannot see that to stop the entire system, without altering the remaining relations between the planets and only lengthening the space and time of daylight, it is enough for the Sun to stop, as state the very words of the holy text? Therefore, this is how, without introducing any confusion between the [different] parts of the world and without altering the words of the Scripture, by stopping the Sun, daylight can be lengthened on Earth".

When was the heliocentric system demonstrated scientifically?

In 1686, Isaac Newton stated the law of universal attraction, which enabled him to justify the laws the govern planetary motion (Kepler's laws) and to construct a perfectly coherent planetary system. The earliest measurements of stellar parallax, which can be explained by the Earth's movement around the Sun, were made by Friedrich Bessel in 1837.

In 1851, the physicist Jean Bernard Léon Foucault proved that the Earth rotates on its own axis. He described his experiment in a famous and brief monograph titled *Demonstration physique du movement de rotation de la Terre au moyen du pendule.*

A pendulum necessarily oscillates in a fixed plane. If the Earth spins, the plane of oscillation must also spin. To verify this hypothesis, Foucault performed an experiment in Paris, at the Panthéon, with a 67-metre long steel cable, at one end of which he appended a sphere weighing 28 kilograms. To detect the movement of the oscillating plane, on a table he placed small mounds of sand that would be scratched as a pointed tip fixed under the sphere passed over them. It could be seen that those scratches moved progressively.

When Galileo was alive, the heliocentric system was only a working hypothesis: in modern terms, it was a "mathematical model" that enabled calculation of the position of planets through time, and nothing more.

In February 1632, he published *"Dialogo dove ne i congressi di quattro giornate si discorre sopra i due massimi sistemi del mondo, tolemaico e copernicano, proponendo indeterminatamente le ragioni filosofiche e naturali tanto per l'una quanto per l'altra parte"* [Dialogue over four days on the two chief world systems, Ptolemaic and Copernican, proposing the philosophical and natural reasons for one and the other].

This (very long) title promised a rigorously neutral exposition.

The Dialogue on the two greatest systems of the world features three characters conversing with one another. These dialogues take place over four "days", which constitute the four great parts of the book. The three characters are Salviati, Sagredo and Simplicio. Each character performs a specific role. Salviati is Galileo's spokesman. Sagredo raises intelligent questions and generally allows himself to be convinced by Salviati's exposition. Simplicio speaks for tradition, a disciple of Aristotle; his character is based on the figure of Simplicius, a forgotten mathematician and astronomer of the 6th century CE who commented on Euclid and Aristotle. Salviati and Sagredo were two friends of Galileo, who had both died a few years earlier.

Thanks to the skillful composition and subtle interplay of questions and answers, the Dialogue's readers could conclude that the

Copernican theory was vastly superior to that propounded by Ptolemy.

Galileo was summoned to the system of tribunals of the Roman Inquisition in September 1632; he was held there, but in a well-appointed apartment and not a prison cell.

To avoid entrusting the investigation to the Roman Inquisition, the Pope decided to appoint a special commission presided by his own nephew, Cardinal Barberini.

Various minor charges were made against Galileo: disrespect of the authors recognized by the Church; throwing ridicule on Ptolemy's hypotheses. The main charge, however, was that in writing the Dialogue, Galileo had violated the prohibition on defending the Copernican theory imposed upon him by Cardinal Bellarmino. It must be noted here that the principal charge was of a disciplinary nature – a violation of an ecclesiastical order, and not a doctrinal heresy.

The trial began on 12 April 1633. Galileo appeared before the judges three times.

On the morning of 22 June 1633, the last session of the trial took place. Galileo appeared before the panel of judges to hear the tribunal's judgment. The tribunal held that the publication of the Dialogue was an express violation of the injunction issued against the author on supporting or defending Copernicus's false and anti-Scriptural opinion.

Because Galileo had made himself a suspect of heresy by supporting a doctrine that was false and contrary to Scripture, he was asked to abjure, "with sincere heart and non-false faith", his mistakes and heresies. The Dialogue was placed on the List of Prohibited Books. Galileo received a jail sentence and had to submit to a penitential practice.

After the judgment was read, Galileo, on his knees and his hand placed upon the Gospel, recited the abjuration rite. After performing the sign of the Cross, he signed the abjuration certificate.

The jail term imposed upon Galileo actually consisted of home detention.

After the trial, Galileo stayed in Villa Medici for some time with the Florentine ambassador, and then in the palace of the Archbishop of Siena, who was his friend. Then, Galileo went to his countryside home, "The Jewel", at Arcetri, near Florence, and remained there until his death.

Here, Galileo received his disciples and in 1638 finished his masterpiece, in which he laid the foundations for a new study of mechanics. This work was titled *"Discorsi e dimostrazioni matematiche intorno a due nuove scienze attinenti alla meccanica ed ai movimenti locali"* [Discourses and Mathematical Demonstrations Relating to Two New Sciences].

Galileo died on 8 January 1642.

* * *

In 1616, Cardinal Bellarmino asked Galileo to "prove" the soundness of Copernicus's theory of astronomy.

Galileo used a method that is known today as the "hypothetico-deductive model". This method is based on the choice of a hypothesis or a model – for example, the heliocentric hypothesis – from which selected consequences can be compared with the results of observations: planetary motion, the phases of Venus, etc. Every successful comparison provides support to the model in question. The model's credibility rises as the support grows.

However, the models remain at the mercy of a comparison that could invalidate a certain prediction and thus cast doubt upon the model's validity. In the case of the Copernican model, none of the observations were such as to invalidate the model.

However, it must not be forgotten that in Galileo's time, the necessary perspective to place full confidence in the model he ardently defended was lacking.

History proved Galileo right, but his contemporaries could not possibly know it. Cardinal Bellarmino, who always advised Galileo to speak "in terms of hypothesis" almost instinctively adopted a very modern principle of scientific method; in his times, prudence was certainly justified.

In the Basilica of St. Maria Maggiore in Rome, the painter Lodovico Cardi (known as Cigoli), Galileo's friend, painted an image of the Virgin Mary at whose feet is a "scientific" moon, as discovered by Galileo.

If the conflict concerns issues relating to the natural world, the mistake is to be sought in the interpretation of the Bible; it is this interpretation that should be revisited, as the Word of God is to be revealed in the book of nature.

Indeed, questions on natural phenomena are not answered by the authority of Scripture or by Aristotle, but rather by means of "reasoned experiences" and "necessary demonstrations" – that is, by means of the mathematical-experimental method.

Galileo's story is often portrayed as a struggle between a group of conservative ecclesiastical figures and a scientist. However, this is a simplistic representation.

The Second Vatican Council confirmed that "methodical research in all branches of knowledge, provided it is carried out in a truly scientific manner and does not override moral laws, can never conflict with the faith, because the things of the world and the things of faith derive from the same God."

In his speech before the Pontifical Academy of the Sciences, in November 1979, Pope John Paul II stated that:

"I would like to confirm again the declarations of the Council on the autonomy of science in its function of research on the truth inscribed in creation by the finger of God."

Galileo's case left a deep and enduring mark on the public consciousness. Galileo became the symbol of science's struggles for emancipation, and is much more famous than the other illustrious personalities of those times: Kepler, Descartes, or Newton.

However, does entirely separating science from faith and morality make the former more authentic? Or does mankind "bend" science to the answers that it wishes to give, in a self-referential manner, in a challenge of omnipotence?

Galileo's case was exploited and used as a lens to interpret several issues which arose later in history.

Virginia Lalli

However, is it not equally obfuscating to support 1960s discourse on abortion without any consideration of the scientific discoveries on ultrasounds and prenatal life made in the 1980s and 1990s? Thus, the enduring conflict is between truth and science, because without the former, science is enslaved to a mere desire for omnipotence.

4

THE TRIAL OF OSCAR WILDE

Nowadays people know the price of everything and the value of nothing.

O. Wilde, *The Portrait of Dorian Grey*

Clergymen and people who use phrases without wisdom sometimes talk of suffering as a mystery. It is really a revelation. One discerns things one never discerned before. One approaches the whole of history from a different standpoint...

[N]othing in the whole world is meaningless, and suffering least of all. That something hidden away in my nature, like a treasure in a field, is Humility.

O. Wilde, *De profundis*

When Oscar Wilde (Dublino 1854 - Parigi 1900) was at the height of his fame, he sued the Marquess of Queensberry, the father of his young lover, Lord Alfred Douglas (also known as Bosie). Enraged by the persistent gossip on his son and Oscar Wilde, and after having unsuccessfully asked his son and Wilde to put an end to their friendship, on 18 February 1895, the Marquess of

Queensberry left a defamatory note, at Wilde's private members' club: "For Oscar Wilde posing as a sodomite."

For Bosie, that defamatory note was an opportunity to openly attack his father, with whom he was on acrimonious terms. He urged Wilde to bring the case before the courts, going against the advice of all of Wilde's friends.

Wilde thus sued the Marquess, who was arrested and brought to court. Wilde's lawyer withdrew the claim before the witnesses found by the Marquess's detectives could be called to testify, but it was already too late.

On the basis of the Marquess's defence, in which overwhelming proof against his counterpart was presented, Wilde was arrested for committing sodomy and gross indecency.

In two trials, Oscar Wilde and Alfred Taylor (a friend of Wilde's and a procurer of prostitutes) were sentenced to the maximum penalty: a jail term of two years and forced labour. Three years after finishing his jail term, Wilde died destitute in Paris.

At the time, Wilde's legal tribulations occupied the newspapers for several weeks and became a national case. It is no exaggeration to say that, despite Wilde's fame and acquaintances in high society and Parliament, he became the scapegoat for a category of people that had started to cause scandal in society. Having decided to wade into the murky waters of the criminal law, Wilde suffered the exemplary punishment that was to serve as a warning to all.

In the "Proceedings against Queensberry", lengthy consideration was given to the literary issue of Wilde's purportedly "immoral" writings (consisting in The Portrait of Dorian Gray, the Phrases and Philosophies for the Use of the Young and the letters to Lord Alfred Douglas) in addition to his alleged illicit relations. However, in the legal proceedings against Wilde, the youths who had spent time with him were called to testify. These were all young men of about eighteen years of age, handsome and of humble origins, to whom Wilde would give money and expensive gifts in return for sexual favours. Wilde admitted that he had had relations with them, but denied having sexual encounters with them.

Wilde was taken into custody in Reading Gaol on 25 May 1895. The genius had become despicable.

Wilde's exquisite collection of furniture and art objects was auctioned off. Many of his books were burnt. His dramatic works could no longer be played in theatres. Wilde petitioned the Home Secretary from jail with a request for mercy, deeply troubled for his own physical and mental health after thirteen months in solitary confinement.

"The petition of the above-named prisoner humbly sheweth that he does not desire to palliate in any way the terrible offences of which he was rightly found guilty, but to point out that such offences are forms of sexual madness and are recognized as such not merely by modern pathological science but by much modern legislation, notably in France, Austria, and Italy, where the laws affecting these misdemeanours have been repealed, on the ground that they are diseases to be cured by a physician, rather than crimes to be punished by a judge"[1].

"[h]is sentence may be remitted now, so that he may be taken abroad by his friends and may put himself under medical care so that the sexual insanity from which he suffers may be cured. He knows only too well that his career as a dramatist and writer is ended, and his name blotted from the scroll of English Literature, never to be replaced; that his children cannot bear that name again, and that an obscure life in some remote country is in store for him: he knows that, bankruptcy having come upon him, poverty of a most bitter kind awaits him, and that all the joy and beauty of existence is taken from him for ever; but at least in all his hopelessness he still clings to the hope that he will not have to pass directly from the common gaol to the common lunatic asylum. Dreadful as are the results of the prison system — a system so terrible that it hardens

---

[1]   The original English-language versions of the petition were taken from S. Karschay, *Degeneration, Normativity and the Gothic at the Fin de Siècle*, Palgrave Macmillan, Basingstoke, UK, 2015; and G. Brandreth, *Oscar Wilde and the Murders at Reading Gaol: Oscar Wilde Mystery*, Hachette Books, London, 2013.P. Orlandelli – P. Iorio (eds). *Imputato Oscar Wilde*. Stampa Alternativa, Viterbo, 2011. P. 262.

their hearts whose hearts it does not break, and brutalises those who have to carry it out no less than those who have to submit to it — yet at least amongst its aims is not the desire to wreck the human reason. Though it may not seek to make men better, yet it does not desire to drive them mad"[2].

"The petitioner is now keenly conscious of the fact that while the three years preceding his arrest were from the intellectual point of view the most brilliant years of his life (four plays from his pen having been produced on the stage with immense success, and played not merely in England, America and Australia, but in almost every European capital, and many books that excited much interest at home and abroad having been published), still that during the entire time he was suffering from the most horrible form of erotomania, which made him forget his wife and children, his high social position in London and Paris, his European distinction as an artist, the honour of his name and family, his very humanity itself, and left him the helpless prey of the most revolting passions, and of a gang of people who for their own profit ministered to him, and then drove him to hideous ruin.

"It is under the ceaseless apprehension lest this insanity, that displayed itself in monstrous sexual perversion before, may now extend to the entire nature and intellect, that the petitioner writes this appeal which he earnestly entreats may be at once considered. Horrible as all actual madness is, the terror of madness is no less appalling, and no less ruinous to the soul. [3] [...]

"[h]is chief terror that of madness, and his prayer that his long imprisonment may be considered, with its attendant ruin, a sufficient punishment, so that the imprisonment may be ended now, and not uselessly or vindictively prolonged till insanity has claimed soul as well as body as its prey, and brought it to the same degradation and the same shame."[4]

---

[2]   Id., P. 265.

[3]   Id., P. 263.

[4]   Id., p. 266.

The adjudicating panel did not find that Wilde's health gave cause for alarm and rejected his petition; however, it allowed him material for writing. He would later use this material to write "De Profundis" and the first pages of "The Ballad of Reading Gaol", as well as to compile a list of books that would be delivered to him. If Wilde had not been sent to jail, we may have never have had the chance to read "De Profundis", the letter to Lord Alfred Douglas in which Wilde traced the milestones of their "friendship"; after one year of detention, he was allowed to write the letter, on twenty large sheets of light blue paper that were given to him one at a time, thus making it impossible for him to reread what he had written on the previous sheets. In this letter, Wilde shed his cloak of success as an author to bare his soul, hanging onto the thread of his intelligence, his only lifeline to survive pain and despair, and that led him, unexpectedly, to admit and accept everythingthus dramatically approaching the chance to reveal the face of Christ. "De Profundis" is a poem on the pain of a soul made to rot by prison. Its pages bear witness, in distressing sequence, to all the emotions of a delicate soul before its dear yet lost freedom: despair, a wish for death, a powerful revolt against society; then charity, a spirit of fraternity, resignation, absolute humility, recognition of one's own mistakes and of the justice of penalty, compassion; and finally, the relief brought by faith and the horizon – appearing in the light of the pale dawn of hope – of a soul purified by pain.

Wilde enjoyed the chalice of pleasure to the utmost, but also drank to the last drop from the chalice of pain. In "De Profundis", his soul returned towards Christ very naturally, and in Christ found the peace he so futilely sought from mankind.

In the work, Wilde describes some of his moods as a prisoner and reflects on pain.

I have got to make everything that has happened to me good for me. The plank bed, the loathsome food, the hard ropes shredded into oakum till one's finger-tips grow dull with pain, the menial offices with which each day begins and finishes, the harsh orders that routine seems to necessitate, the dreadful dress that makes sorrow grotesque to look at, the silence, the solitude, the shame—each and all of these things I have to transform into a spiritual experience. There is not a single degradation of the body which I must not try and make into a spiritualising of the soul.

And, though at present my friends may find it a hard thing to believe, it is true none the less, that for them living in freedom and idleness and comfort it is more easy to learn the lessons of humility than it is for me, who begin the day by going down on my knees and washing the floor of my cell. For prison life with its endless privations and restrictions makes one rebellious. The most terrible thing about it is not that it breaks one's heart—hearts are made to be broken—but that it turns one's heart to stone. One sometimes feels that it is only with a front of brass and a lip of scorn that one can get through the day at all.

And he who is in a state of rebellion cannot receive grace, to use the phrase of which the Church is so fond—so rightly fond, I dare say—for in life as in art the mood of rebellion closes up the channels of the soul, and shuts out the airs of heaven. Yet I must learn these lessons here, if I am to learn them anywhere, and must be filled with joy if my feet are on the right road and my face set towards 'the gate which is called beautiful,' though I may fall many times in the mire and often in the mist go astray."

Lord Alfred Douglas threw the letter into the fireplace. Robert Ross, however, Wilde's friend and literary executor, had had it copied and published it in 1905, five years after Wilde's death, purged of all references to Lord Alfred.

"De Profundis" prepared the foundations for "The Ballad of Reading Gaol", the story of a soldier who is hanged for killing a woman. The man was executed in Reading Gaol while Wilde was detained there, and the event affected him deeply.

Wilde's petition to the Home Secretary after one year of detention is a chilling account of the effects that imprisonment had produced on him.

After the Ballad, Wilde was no longer able to write. He was ostracized from English society, bankrupt (all his possessions had been auctioned off to pay his creditors and legal fees), abandoned by his wife Constance[5], who died after the complications arising from a fall, deprived of his children (who had changed their surname to Holland and moved to Switzerland), and deprived of his audience.

The trial records were not made public, because they were considered offensive to public decorum. The most thorough account of the proceedings were published anonymously in London and in Paris in 1912 by the formidable bibliophile Christopher Millard, with the title "Oscar Wilde: Three Times Tried". The transcripts of the "Queensberry Trial" were recovered for the celebrations of the centenary of Wilde's death (1900-2000) and fully published in England in 2004 by Merlin Holland, Oscar Wilde's grandson.

Wilde had been charged with committing obscenities with male persons between 20 February 1892 and 22 October 1893. The same charge had been made against Alfred Taylor, Wilde's friend and notorious "intermediary". Before the Police Court, several young men, including Charles and William Parker, Alfred Wood, Sidney Mavor, Frederick Atkins, Edward Shelley, the waiters of the Savoy hotel and others appeared, confirming the statements made to Lord Queensberry's investigators. Wilde and Taylor were committed to trial and detained at Halloway Gaol until the end of the proceedings. In the meantime, a ban on performing Wilde's plays had been imposed and his books withdrawn from trade.

Wilde's lawyer had argued that the accusations were a conspiracy to ruin his client; that the evidence presented by the prosecution was unreliable; and that its main witnesses were a band of vile blackmailers.[6]

---

[5]   Constance Mary Lloyd (Dublin, 2 January 1858 – Genoa, 7 April 1898). After separating from her husband due to the scandal concerning his homosexuality, she died in Genoa in 1898, where she was buried in the Monumental Cemetery of Staglieno. Her grave contains no reference to Wilde.

[6]   Orlandelli – Iorio, *op. cit.*, p. 140.

The record shows that much of Wilde's testimony during the trial against Queensberry focused on that which Sir Edward Clarke defined "the literary part of the trial".

During Wilde's cross-examination on the subject of his written works – in particular, on his book titled "The Portrait of Dorian Gray" – it was sought to depict Wilde as a man without principle concerning relationships between men.

"The Portrait of Dorian Gray" is the story of a young, depraved man whose face does not reveal the depths of perversion to which he has descended; however, these are all borne by a portrait painted by an artist friend of his. "Do not confuse a writer with the characters that he has created", one may plead. If an imaginative author has included, in his novel, a consummate wrongdoer, and makes him speak words that are repulsive to humanity, he does not necessarily agree with them.

In the closing speech, Wilde's lawyer returns to the conspiracy and blackmail theory:

"I suggest to you, gentlemen, that your duty is simple and clear and that when you find a man who is assailed by tainted evidence entering the witness box, and for a third time giving a clear, coherent and lucid account of the transactions such as that which the accused has given today, I venture to say that that man is entitled to be believed against a horde of blackmailers such as you have seen [...] but it is important to remember that if blackmailers are to be listened to against the defendant in this case, then the profession of blackmailing will become a more deadly mischief than ever before. This trial seems to be operating as an act of indemnity for all the blackmailers of London."

"You must not act upon suspicion or prejudice, but upon an examination of the facts, gentlemen, and on the facts I respectfully urge that Mr Wilde is entitled to claim from you a verdict of acquittal. If upon an examination of the evidence you therefore feel it your duty to say that the charges against the prisoner have not been proved, then I am sure that you will be glad that the brilliant promise which has been clouded by these accusations, and the bright reputation which was so nearly quenched in the torrent of prejudice which a few weeks ago was sweeping through the press, have been saved by your verdict from absolute ruin; and that it leaves him, a distinguished man of letters and a brilliant Irishman, to live among us a life of honour and repute, and to give in the maturity of his genius gifts to our literature of which he has given only the promise in his early youth."[7]

But Mr Justice Wills will hand down a guilty verdict, and, to the defendants, says:

"Oscar Wilde and Alfred Taylor, the crime of which you have been convicted is so bad that one has to put stern restraint upon oneself to prevent oneself from describing, in language which I would rather not use, the sentiments which must rise to the breast of every man of honour who has heard the detail of these two terrible trials. That the jury have arrived at a correct verdict in this case, I cannot persuade myself to entertain the shadow of a doubt; and I hope, at all events, that those who sometimes imagine that a judge is half-hearted in the cause of decency and morality, because he takes care no prejudice shall enter into the case, may see that that is consistent at least with the utmost sense of indignation at the horrible charges brought home to both of you.

"It is no use for me to address you. People who can do these things must be dead to all sense of shame, and one cannot hope to produce any effect upon them. It is the worst case I have ever tried. That you, Taylor kept a kind of male brother it is impossible to doubt. And that you, Wilde, have been at the centre of a circle of extensive corruption of the most hideous kind among young men, it is equally impossible to doubt.

"I shall, under such circumstances, be expected to pass the severest sentence that the law allows. In my judgment it is totally inadequate for such a case as this. The sentence of the Court is that each of you be imprisoned and kept to hard labour for two years."

Exclamations and cries came from the public gathered in the courtroom.

Wilde replied: "And I? Can I not say anything, Your Honor?"

---

[7]   Id., p. 238.

The judge only waved his hand to the ushers, who quickly led the defendants out of the courtroom. The jury was dismissed and the court adjourned[1].

Upon completion of his jail term, Wilde moves to France, where he began to write "The Ballad of Reading Gaol", which he finished in Naples. The work was published anonymously in England (with Wilde's number as an inmate: C33) and gained unexpected success.

Wilde also wrote under the pen name of Sebastian Melmoth. Two of his letters on maltreatment in prisons were published by the Daily Chronicle.

In springtime 1900, Wilde went to Rome, where he was mesmerized by the beauty and richness of the religious ceremonies at the Vatican. His pleasure in assisting to such marvelous functions was such that he attended seven papal hearings. In May of the same year, he returned to Paris. Only a handful of friends helped him, and he spent his time drinking in cafès. He contracted meningitis due to a bout of tertiary syphilis.

He constantly suffered of migraines. On 10 October, he was operated and appeared to recover, but in November his health sharply deteriorated. On 29 November 1900 he was baptized. The next day, in the afternoon, he died in Paris. He was buried on 3 December in the cemetery of Bagneux.

On 20 July 1909, his remains were moved to the Père Lachaise cemetery, in the famous Art Déco sepulchre designed by the sculptor Jacob Epstein.

His epitaph reads: *Verbis meis addere nihil audebant es super illos stillebat eloquium meum"* (from the Book of Job, 22: "After my words they spoke not again, and my speech dropped upon them". The inscription is from the Ballad of Reading Gaol:

"And alien tears will fill for him/ Pity's long broken urn,/ For his mourners will be outcast men, / And outcast always mourn".

*   *   *

---

[1]   Id., p. 255.

The trial concerns the most fragile part of Oscar Wilde's life. During the trial, his brilliance – which was already abundantly clear from his written works – could not fail to emerge. The trial concerning specific acts of sodomy entrusted the prosecution with a simple task (asking of him "did you meet him and, if yes, where and why?; did you buy presents?; did you commit any indecent acts?") and exempted them from treading paths of abstraction.

The trial showed the artist in all his human fragility, forced to answer questions on gritty details, incapacitated from flying high on literary themes.

The trial "machine" sought procedural truth, and, since it concerned specific facts, only broached upon certain segments of the man's life, and not the man as a whole.

And yet even after the trial, Wilde did not lose his poetic streak. Rather, his circumstances became an opportunity for personal growth, reflection and artistic expression, as well as a personal path towards conversion.

During his incarceration, Wilde wrote "De Profundis" and the "Ballad in Reading Gaol". He sublimated his condition as detainee, which was no longer a personal moment but rather a broader experience to be shared: a testimony to a life lived in adversity, and not only a denouncement of his jail conditions.

Perhaps, when Wilde was called for judgment after death as a newly baptized man, he might have found a more indulgent judge.

5

THE TRIAL OF NICOLA SACCO (1891-1927) AND BARTOLOMEO VANZETTI (1888-1927)

The truth is that the judge is not a mechanism: he is not a calculating machine. He is a living man: and that function of detailing the law and applying it in individual cases, which can be represented, in vitro, *as a syllogism, is actually an synthesizing operation, performed in the heat of the moment, mysteriously, in the sealed cauldron of the spirit, where the mediation and welding between abstract law and actual fact requires, for their achievement, intuition and passion in a laborious conscience. To reduce the function of the judge to a pure syllogism means to impoverish it... parch it... desiccate it... Justice is something better: it is creation that flows from a live, sensitive, vigilant, human conscience.*

Piero Calamandrei (1889-1956)

Especially starting from the second half of the 1800s, the United States of America experienced massive immigration. Statistics show that between 1890 and 1914, about 14 million people (among whom an immense number of Italians) migrated to the United States from Europe. For many of these immigrants, life in the new country was not at all as easy as they had imagined in their homelands; this was particularly true in certain states, where public opinion viewed immigrants with extreme suspicion and they were effectively emarginated.

When the phenomenon of migration began on a vast scale, some of the most famous Italian exponents of the anarchist movement moved to the United States.

The anarchist movement originated towards the end of the 1700s. It called for the creation of individuals free from all external bonds, and based on his or her own autonomous activity alone. All manifestations of the State and political, legal and economic institutions were to be destroyed, through various means and plans –which did not exclude the use of violence.

This utopian ideology garnered the greatest support among the oppressed classes, who perceived this struggle as a sort of liberation.

The acts of violence perpetrated by members of the anarchist movement at the end of the 19th century, in the United States and other countries, were usually individual revolutionary attacks, which derived precisely from this mere illusion of being able to subvert the existing order with one's own strength.

The anarchists' main targets were especially monarchs, heads of State and representatives of the State. The institutions' responses were swift, consisting in violent repression of the anarchists; among the public, enmity towards the immigrants steadily grew.

On 6 September 1901, an anarchist killed the US President William McKinley, who was succeeded by Theodore Roosevelt.

In 1903, the US Government responded to the assassination by enacting the Immigration Act, which barred foreign anarchists from entering the United States.

The vile attacks only served to increase fear of the anarchist movement throughout the country. During Roosevelt's presidency, a number of federal laws were ratified to control the anarchic press; in this time, two young Italians, Nicola Sacco and Bartolomeo Vanzetti, decided to leave Italy for the United States.

South Braintree is a small industrial center about twenty kilometers south of Boston, Massachusetts. At 3 p.m. of Thursday 15 April

1920, Frederick A. Parmenter, a 45-year-old US citizen working as a cashier, and Alessandro Berardelli, a 44-year-old Italian bodyguard, left the headquarters of the Slate & Morrill shoe factory with two suitcases containing the weekly salaries of the factory's employees. In total, the suitcases held about US$16,000. The two walked down Pearl Street, South Braintree's main road, which hosted two shoe factories.

The pair walked past two men who, dressed in elegant dark suits and hats, were leaning against a fence and talking to each other, apparently ignoring them. Parmenter had to carry both suitcases, because Berardelli had to be armed and ready to defend him in case of danger.

A Buick furtively approached the scene. Only two people were aboard the seven-seater car: the driver and a man on the back seat. The driver stopped the car a small distance from the cashier and the bodyguard. He turned off the engine and remained hidden. A third man, serving as a lookout, hid behind a pile of bricks.

Parmenter and Berardelli went about their weekly ritual, which until that day had never encountered particular problems, and did not notice these unusual movements. However, the two men who had been leaning against the fence began to walk behind the two employees slowly, to avoid arousing suspicion, but then struck swiftly. One of them immediately attacked Berardelli, who, being armed, was the more dangerous of the two. The bodyguard tried to react but fear and shock paralyzed him.

In the meantime, clearly following a detailed plan, the second criminal began to shoot at the two employees. The Buick driver quickly emerged from the shadows, revved the car engine and drove at high speed towards the shooting. The shooters grabbed the cash-filled suitcases, threw them in the car and jumped in, along with the third man who was the lookout.

Then, the car sped towards a railroad level crossing that was about 100 meters away. At the time, the crossing was closed. One of the criminals ordered the operator of the crossing, Michael Le Vangie, to open the crossing, threatening him with a gun.

Le Vangie obeyed, terrified. The Buick crossed the railroad tracks, reached the main city and turned into a dense forest, thus escaping the police chasing it. The Buick was found there two days later, not far from the crime scene. Next to it, the police also found tyre tracks of a second car, which was most likely a Hudson Overland and appeared to drive off in another direction.

A long time passed before the true perpetrators of the horrible crime were found. Ultimately, two Italian men were accused.

The car, presumably a Buick or a Hudson Overland, led the Bridgewater Chief of Police Michael Stewart to suspect of Mike Boda, an Italian anarchist who owned a Hudson Overland.

On 17 April 1920, Boda brought his car to be repaired at the Johnsons' garage. Three days later, Stewart stopped the anarchist to question him, and then released him. Stewart suspected that he was one of the criminals involved in the shooting at South Braintree and decided to set a trap. Stewart visited the Johnsons and gave them precise instructions to inform him by telephone if an Italian man came to pick up the car.

A few evenings later, on 5 May 1920, Mike Boda and a friend of his, Riccardo Orciani, came to pick up the Overland. Other two Italian men were there with them: these were Nicola Sacco and Bartolomeo Vanzetti, who had walked all the way there to find a car that could help them in their efforts to destroy and hide anarchist writings, flyers and party pamphlets and to inform their peers of the risks for all of them.

Mrs. Johnson informed the police of the presence of suspicious "foreigners". Sacco and Vanzetti noticed what she did and quickly ran to catch a streetcar. However, a few policemen managed to enter the streetcar with them. The two Italians were brought to a police station.

Sacco and Vanzetti were not informed of the reasons for their arrest. They thought that it had to do with the raids against the "Reds" which at the time were becoming increasingly frequent. They were afraid of being deported from the United States because of their involvement with anarchist activities and this made them give confused answers, especially on the gun that they held with them.

Vanzetti was found to hold a fully loaded .38 Harrington and Richardson revolver and four shotgun cartridges. Sacco was found in possession of a loaded semi-automatic .32 Colt gun containing eight cartridges and other twenty-three loose cartridges.

Vanzetti had purchased the weapon to defend himself as he carried out his trade as a fishmonger, because in those times, robberies were very common indeed. Sacco had started to carry a gun when he found employment as a night guard at the Three-K factory.[2]

"The police thought that the car picked up by the two Italians was that used to commit the robbery and murders at South Braintree. At Brockton Police Station, immediately after the two men were taken into custody, they gave instinctive answers to the investigators' questions and false explanations on where and how they obtained the weapons. They also denied that they knew Boda and Orciani, even though the facts clearly showed otherwise. When questioned on their political leanings, they gave imprecise answers.

Mike Boda vanished and three days later travelled back to Italy, where he remained for the rest of his life.

For Sacco and Vanzetti, things looked dire from the outset. This was especially true for Sacco, whose semi-automatic gun was of the same caliber as that used to kill Berardelli.

On 6 May, the day after their arrest, Sacco and Vanzetti were brought before District Attorney Frederick G. Katzmann.

Immediately after the preliminary questioning, the DA organized a lineup (which was later held to violate Massachusetts law) with a number of eyewitnesses, whom the prosecution considered to be good and reliable citizens.

Sacco and Vanzetti were lined up in front of them and forced to perform the typical movements of a robber in action. Many of the eyewitnesses expressed serious doubts as to their identification.

---

[2]   J. Dos Passos. *Davanti la sedia elettrica*. Edizioni Spartaco. Santa Maria Capua Vetere (Caserta). 2007. P. 129.

Sacco and Vanzetti then understood that they had not been arrested for political reasons, but for robbery and murder. On the basis of simple conjectures on the presence of two cars, Michael Stewart had managed to have two Italian anarchists arrested. The evidence against them was weak but concrete."[3]

Although he had no evidence whatsoever, on 11 June 1920, DA Katzmann also charged Bartolomeo Vanzetti for another robbery that had taken place on 24 December 1919, in which some men in a car had unsuccessfully tried to assault the van carrying the wages of the employees of a shoe factory in Bridgewater. The culprits of that attack had not been identified and the investigation had been archived.

Bartolomeo Vanzetti had an alibi for that day, which was confirmed by several witnesses: he had been selling eels to the Italian community for their traditional Christmas dinner.

Unfortunately, the witnesses who testified for Vanzetti had serious difficulties with the English language: they were unable to understand it, let alone speak it correctly. It was necessary to rely on the services of an interpreter several times, which made it easy for Katzmann to diminish their declarations.

Despite the alibi, on 1 July 1920, after a summary trial, Vanzetti was found guilty and sentenced to 12 to 15 years of jail.

On 11 September 1920, Sacco and Vanzetti were charged with robbery for the Braintree shooting. Although the defence had applied for the trials to be separated, to avoid Vanzetti's previous sentence from influencing the jury, Katzmann managed to keep them together. As John Dos Passos wrote several years later in his autobiography, "If the man whom you are accusing has already been found guilty for a previous crime, then you're already halfway towards winning the case".[4]

---

[3]   G. Adducci. *Sacco e Vanzetti. Colpevoli o innocenti?* Serarcangeli. Rome. 2002. P. 27. Author's translation.

[4]   J. Dos Passos, *La bella vita*, Italian transl. by L. Angioletti, Palazzi Editore. Milan. 1969. P. 232. Author's translation.

To complicate the matter for the two Italians, on 16 September 1920, the anarchist movement reemerged. A bomb was detonated on Wall Street, which was already considered to be the country's economic core. The American press blamed the group led by Luigi Galleani, although it had no proof. Galleani was the editor of *Cronaca Sovversiva* – once a vital publication for Sacco and Vanzetti – and had published a manual on how to make a bomb. On 31 May 1921, the trial of Sacco and Vanzetti commenced before the Dedham courthouse, in Massachusetts.

The most emblematic representative of the jury was its president Walter R. Ripley, a warehouse worker, ex-police officer and fervent patriot. Every morning, when he entered the courtroom, he would pause before the flag of the United States and perform a conspicuous, symbolic salute. The other eleven jurors were not very different.

Fred H. Moore, a lawyer from California, was Sacco's defence attorney and head of the defence team. He was famous in Socialist circles for defending striking workers.

Vanzetti's defence attorney was J.P. Vahey. Well aware of the deep-seated prejudice commonly held against anarchists, Vahey wisely sought to steer the debate away from the political aspects, to avoid stirring ill will among the jurors.

However, Moore's brazen attitude towards the court and his rather aggressive manners when examining the texts, soon managed to evoke antipathy in Judge Thayer and the jurors.

He made a fatal mistake of strategy: he led the trial down the dangerous path of politics, which greatly favoured Katzmann's cross-examinations.

In addition, he failed to make valid arguments to discredit what could be considered the only credible piece of evidence against Nicola Sacco: the deadly bullet found in Berardelli's body was of the same caliber as that of the gun found in possession of the defendant. Katzman, instead, exploited this fact.

Sacco always resolutely denied any involvement in the murders of which he was accused. He maintained that on 15 April 1920, he had taken leave to apply for a passport at the Italian Consulate in Boston, as he wished to return to Italy. When he finished his business at the consulate, in the late afternoon, he returned to his home in Stoughton.

Katzmann summoned fewer witnesses than the defence. The defence team had called one hundred witnesses to refute the prosecution's accusations. The prosecution examined the various eyewitnesses, who declared that they were capable of identifying the two anarchists, or at least one of them, as the criminals who had killed Parmenter and Berardelli.

In fact, all of the eyewitnesses engaged in extremely vague and contradictory behaviour between the preliminary lineups with the two defendants and the actual trial, which took place one year after the lineups.

At trial, it was debated whether Sacco had used his Colt .32 to fire the shot that killed Berardelli, while Vanzetti – who did not take part in the shooting – waited in the car with the driver.

The most important witness was Mary Splaine, a woman who lived in Brockton and worked as a librarian.

Splaine stated that she had witnessed both the shooting and the criminals' escape from the second floor of the building located opposite the crime scene, which was several metres away from the railway crossing.

During the preliminary lineups at Brockton Police Station, which were also attended by DA Katzmann, Splaine did not identify Sacco and Vanzetti as members of the criminal gang. However, at trial, she declared that she was absolutely certain it was Sacco she had seen in the back seat of the escaping car.

It should be noted that when Splaine allegedly saw the criminal, the car was about twenty metres away from her and was driving away at a speed of about 40-50 kilometres per hour. Thus, she could not possibly have been able to observe the scene for more than three seconds. On 26 May 1920, during the preliminary hearing before the grand jury, Splaine's testimony was still rather vague, but certainly more conscientious: she avoided stating that the criminal whom she had seen for a few seconds, on a moving car over twenty metres away, was certainly Nicola Sacco. Thus, one year later, Splaine radically changed her testimony.

Suffice it to consider the sheer number of details she provided on the man whom she had seen in – to put it generously – somewhat unbelievable conditions.[5]

Some time later during the proceedings, Splaine stated that the differences in her depositions, given at a distance of one year from one another, were due to stenographical errors committed in transcribing her testimony.

Another witness called to the stand by the prosecution was Michael LeVangie, the operator of the railroad crossing near the shoe factory. LeVangie stated that on 15 April 1920, while the tragic robbery was taking place, he was near the crossing. He suddenly heard several explosions and at the same time, a car with several passengers sped towards him. One of them, seated on the left-hand side of the car, threatened him with a firearm and ordered him to open the crossing. LeVangie was terrified and immediately did as he was told. At trial, he testified that Vanzetti was the driver of the car – although it was well known that Vanzetti did not know how to drive.

Katzmann's ruthlessness emerged in this respect too. He admitted to the jury that the witness may have been mistaken, but still managed to show that the defendant could have been in the car anyway, sitting in a different seat. The DA thus managed to save a testimony that should have been discarded.

The two coroners who performed the autopsies on the bodies of Parmenter and Berardelli consigned all the bullets retrieved to the authorities, so that they could be used as evidence.

All the bullets removed from the two bodies were .32 in calibre. The bullet that caused Berardelli's death was labelled Bullet No. III, or indicated as the "fatal bullet", and was actually the only concrete piece of evidence in the hands of the prosecution.

---

[5]   G. Adducci. *Op. cit.* p. 41-42.

The testimony given by an ex-official of the Italian Consulate in Boston was particularly significant, as it provided Nicola Sacco with a rather credible alibi.

The official stated that at the time of the brutal murders, a great number of Italians, terrified by Palmer's raids, visited the Consulate every day to apply for a passport, with a view to returning to Italy. On 15 April 1920, Sacco had taken leave from work and was apparently one of these applicants: indeed, the ex-official declared under oath that he had met him in the early afternoon. If the jurors had given this testimony its appropriate significance, it would have certainly acquitted Sacco of the charge of first-degree murder. However, unfortunately, this was not the case.

Sacco always resolutely denied any involvement in the murders. He maintained that on 15 April 1920, he had taken leave to apply for a passport at the Italian Consulate in Boston and had returned home in the late afternoon. He confirmed that he had indeed gone to the Johnsons' house together with Vanzetti, Boda and Orciani on the evening when he fell prey to Stewart's trap. He explained to the court that his lies, his possession of a firearm without the requisite permit, and his conduct (which the authorities had deemed suspicious) were due only to his fear given the times, especially because he was an anarchist.

As for Vanzetti, the ballistics confirmed that he did not take part in the shooting. He was nevertheless accused of participating in an armed group with intent to rob and two murders – and these were capital offences.

During his deposition, Vanzetti declared that when the murders were committed, he was selling fish in Plymouth, as he did every day. Like Sacco, he too admitted that he had intentionally lied at the Brockton Police Station, possessed a gun without a proper permit, and had visited the Johnsons' house, but only because he was an anarchist, and the times were such that arrests and mysterious deaths of anarchists were common in the United States. He stated that he had visited the Johnsons' garage to urgently find a car to help him gather and destroy all the anarchist literature he could find, as these writings placed him and his companions in a highly compromising position. The revolver he carried originally belonged to Luigi Falzini, who had legally sold it to him a few months before; therefore, his conduct was not that of a person who was aware of being guilty, but only due to fear that his involvement with the anarchist movement would be discovered. As for the money stolen during the robbery, neither Sacco nor Vanzetti, nor indeed the anarchist movement, became wealthier after the crime.

The prosecution was aware from the very beginning that the evidence in its possession was weak and probably insufficient to secure a success at trial.

However, Katzmann's great act of cunning was to shift the focus of the trial from his futile evidence to the defendants' political and social backgrounds, thus stirring, with confrontational questions and speeches, ill will among the jurors towards the defendants.

Judge Webster Thayer's chief concern was proper observance of trial procedure. In his view, the trial was to be correct, not just – the rest were issues to be dealt with by the prosecution, defence and jury.[1] In the judgment with which he imposed the death penalty on the two Italians, Thayer stated that according to Massachusetts law, the judge should not decide upon the merits of the case: the only thing the judge can do is to examine the evidence.[2]

The statements made by Thayer outside the courtroom were even more indicative of his hostile (to say the least) attitude towards the two defendants.

G. Crocker, an eminent Boston lawyer, noted an emblematic statement of the judge, made during the trial: "We have the duty to protect ourselves from the Reds; there are already far too many in our country."

Katzmann knew that it could not be irrefutably proved that Bullet N. III had been shot by Sacco's gun; he was thus careful to avoid directly asking Proctor, the principal ballistics expert, whether the

---

[1]   Helmut Ortner. *Sacco e Vanzetti. Una tragedia americana.* Zambon. Verona. 1996. P. 89.

[2]   Id., p. 232.

examinations had yielded specific evidence that Bullet No. III was fired from that very gun.

Katzmann's questions to Proctor were very ambiguous, but the expert's answer was even more so: "it lends itself". Thus, Bullet No. III was apparently compatible with Sacco's firearm, and compatibility could be considered as a necessary, albeit insufficient, condition to prove that the bullet had been fired from that very gun.

According to another ballistics expert, Van Amburgh, there was further proof that Proctor had not captured: a tiny abrasion in the Colt .32's barrel and its corresponding trace on the bullets fired. He stated that this abrasion had marked the bullets with a long stripe.

Van Amburgh showed the abrasion to the jury. He set up equipment to enable the jury to view the minuscule mark, which was in any case very difficult to notice, given the jurors' inexperience. He even asked for a microscope, which was placed in front of the courtroom's window to provide better light for the jurors. Each of the twelve jurors went to see the bullets under the microscope.

It is doubtful whether the jurors were actually able to see anything – if, of course, there was anything to see at all. However, here too, Katzmann's persuasive abilities prevailed. At the end of the session, the jurors went home convinced that they had seen a microscopic and decisive abrasion in the barrel of a Colt .32[3].

To counter these accounts, the defence also called two ballistics experts. The first was James E. Burns, a ballistics engineer with thirty years of experience with the U.S. Cartridge Company.

Burns' examination was led by Jeremiah McAnarney, one of Vanzetti's defence attorneys.

When asked whether, in light of the marks left by the abrasions on other bullets fired from the semi-automatic Colt produced as evidence, he could state that the fatal bullet was effectively shot from Sacco's gun, he answered that he believed that this was not the case.

---

[3]   G. Adducci, *op. cit.* p. 81.

His opinion was based on the examination of eleven bullets fired from Sacco's gun.

The defence also called J.H. Fitzgerald to the witness stand. At the time, he was a tester at the Colt factory in Hartford. When asked for his view on whether Bullet No. III had been fired from the Colt .32, he answered that it had not been fired from that gun, because he did not believe that the marks left by the abrasion on Bullet No. III matched those on the other bullets shot from the same gun.

On 5 November 1923, about two years after the end of the trial, the new defence team of Sacco and Vanzetti (now led by the eminent attorney William Thompson), supported the fifth motion presented to Thayer to reopen the case with an affidavit issued by Proctor himself, in which he stated that he had never been able to find a single shred of evidence to convince him that Bullet No. III had certainly been fired from Sacco's gun. He apparently had stated as much to the DA and the DA's assistant. If he had been asked directly whether he had found any proof that the fatal bullet had been shot from Sacco's gun, he would have answered in the negative[4].

However, the jury appeared to place little weight on Proctor's deposition, preferring that given by Van Amburgh.

Sacco and Vanzetti had a clean criminal record, other than their registration as rather vociferous radical political activists.

At trial, emphasis should have been placed on the fact that people do not become professional robbers from one day to the other; rather, with them. The economic circumstances of Sacco and of his family did not change at all after the day of the murders, and the same was true for Vanzetti.

Furthermore, according to the police investigations, neither did the anarchist movement appear to receive large sums of cash in the days following the robbery.

On 14 July 1921, after a meeting in chambers that lasted just over half a day, the jury finally issued its verdict, declaring Sacco and Vanzetti guilty of the first-degree murders beyond any reasonable doubt.

---

[4]   Id., p. 84-85.

Thus began a long and tortuous battle of hope and appeals to prove the innocence of the two anarchists and save their lives.

From November 1921 and throughout the next five years, six supplementary motions for a retrial were submitted to Judge Thayer. However, he rejected all of them. During this period, as mentioned above, Sacco and Vanzetti's defence team was led by Attorney William G. Thompson, one of Boston's most famous lawyers. He was firmly convinced that the two anarchists were innocent and that the conduct engaged in by Katzmann and Judge Thayer at first instance had been greatly detrimental to the two defendants. Thompson began to defend them in March 1923. Attorney Fred H. Moore resigned in August 1924.

In the meantime, other circumstances had changed. Katzmann's mandate had ended in 1922. Harold P. Williams was named as his successor. A few months later, however, Williams resigned to pursue his career as District Attorney for the United States in the State of Massachusetts. Winfield M. Wilbar was appointed in his place and would be the DA in all proceedings that followed.

Thompson immediately understood that the best thing to do to prove Sacco and Vanzetti's innocence was to find the real perpetrators of the Braintree crime.

Thus, the sixth and final motion presented to Judge Thayer was based on the spontaneous confession made by Celestino F. Madeiros, presumably a member of the group that had carried out the bloody robbery at South Braintree on 15 April 1920. His written and sworn testimony was given on 28 June 1926 in Dedham Jail, where he too was detained pending the outcome of an appeal before the Supreme Court against the death sentence received for first-degree murder during another armed robbery. He had no political ideals or interests of any kind, aside from money that could be easily obtained.

However, Madeiros's confession gave rise to an unexpected complication: since he followed the customary "laws" of organized crime, he not only categorically refused to name the other members of the criminal group, but also did everything to prevent Thompson from finding out who they were.

Thompson, with only the geographical and temporal information and rough descriptions given by Madeiros, nevertheless managed to retrace the entire history of the ruthless gang.

From the archives of the Providence Police Department, he discovered that in 1920, a group of professional thieves was active and specialized in robbing freight trains (especially deliveries of shoes); the group was known as the Morelli gang. They targeted mainly deliveries from the Slater & Morrill and Rice & Hutchins shoe factories, certainly thanks to a tip-offs from an insider. Both factories were located in South Braintree, were close to each other and about one hundred metres from the railway. It was surely the same insider who told them about the cashier carrying the wages of Slater & Morrill employees. In the end, Attorney Thompson managed to discover the identities of the members of the ruthless group.

As for Bullet No. III, which had been fired from a Colt .32, Joe Morelli, the ringleader, owned such a gun, while the firearm usually used by Bill Mancini (another member of the group) was compatible with the bullets removed from the bodies of the two victims.

From the information gathered by the New Bedford police forces, it emerged that Mike Morelli (Joe's brother) owned a Buick car, which had been found in Mannley after the robbery. Those same police forces were firmly convinced that the South Braintree robbery had been committed by the Morelli gang, and immediately launched investigations on that basis. However, the inquiry was inexplicably closed soon after Sacco and Vanzetti were arrested.

On 9 April 1927, Thayer issued the death sentence against the two defendants. Thayer's last words were: "Thus establishes the law. And may God have mercy of your souls"[5].

Only Vanzetti signed the petition for a pardon submitted to the Governor of Massachusetts, then Alvan T. Fuller. Sacco, who had

---

[5] Dos Passos, *Davanti la sedia elettrica, op. cit.*, p. 121. Author's translation.

suffered greatly during his detention, had lost all faith and hope. He decided to follow his pride and refrain from asking for a pardon. On 3 August 1927, Fuller rejected the defendants' request, as he did not find sufficient reasons that called for an executive intervention on his part or justify a retrial. On 10 August, he set the date for the execution.

Nicola Sacco, thirty-six years old, and Bartolomeo Vanzetti, aged thirty-nine, were executed by electric chair in the night between 22 and 23 August 1927, after six years in jail.

Protests, demonstrations, rallies and vigils were held throughout the world: Paris, Geneva, Germany, London, Oporto, Buenos Aires, Mexico City and Sydney.[6]

In Bartolomeo Vanzetti's final speech to the court, he said:

"I would not wish to [anyone] what I have had to suffer for things that I am not guilty of [...] I have suffered more for my family and for my beloved than for myself; but I am so convinced to be right that if you could execute me two times and I could be reborn two other times, I would live again to do what I have done already. If it had not been for this thing, I might have lived out my life, talking at street corners to scorning men. I might have died, unmarked, unknown, a failure. Now we are not a failure. This is our career and our triumph. Never in our full life can we hope to do such work for tolerance, for justice, for man's understanding of man, as we do now by an accident... The last moment belongs to us – our agony is our triumph!".[7]

The Committee for the Defense of Sacco and Vanzetti was established in May 1920 thanks to the efforts of Aldino Felicani. Immediately after its inauguration, it opened an office in the heart of Boston, which Attorney Fred H. Moore, the lawyer originally chosen to defend the two anarchists, also joined.

In the same period, other two political organizations joined the committee to provide help. These were the Committee for Political

---

[6]   Id., p. 22.

[7]   G. Adducci, *op. cit.*, p. 125. English-language version taken from http://www. workersliberty.org/story/2010/06/22/last-speech-bartolomeo-vanzetti.

Victims of New York City and the Italian League for the Defense of Workers, whose headquarters were in Brooklyn.

Soon, the first public meetings were held. These were organized throughout the country to raise funds for the Committee. During these meetings, the most famous representatives of the anarchist movement of the time took to the stage, and some would tirelessly continue to give talks until the last day of the two Italians' lives. Among these were Elizabeth Gurley Flynn, a New York trade unionist who always attended the main US demonstrations for Sacco and Vanzetti; Arturo Giovannitti of New York, who then became Secretary of the Italian Chamber of Labour; and Carlo Tresca, an editor from New York.

"The calls to revise the trial multiplied. A vast movement of public opinion formed, not only in the United States but in the whole world, a movement that could count on the support of famous intellectuals such as Thomas Mann, Romain Rolland, HG Wells, Albert Einstein, Henry Barbusse, John Dewey and Upton Sinclair. Gaetano Salvemini, who was then exiled in a small town in Massachusetts, wrote to Camillo Bernieri, his ex-student at the University of Florence, that he had read an article written by Professor Felix Frankfurter of Harvard University, a "man of great intellect and highly noble moral conscience", who proved "with decisive evidence" that "the jurors sentenced the two defendants as two revolutionaries, rather than as guilty of the crime in question".[8]

The protest movement began to expand some months after the guilty verdict was issued, especially in Boston, Chicago, New York and San Francisco. In October 1921, they spread beyond the United States' borders to reach Europe and other continents.

In December 1925, the first issue of the Official Bulletin of the Committee for the Defense of Sacco and Vanzetti was released. The Bulletin provided regular information on the results of its activities to try and save the lives of the two anarchists.

---

[8]   *Gaetano Salvemini a Camillo Berneri, Chestnut Hill, Massachusetts, 29 febbraio 1927*, in A. Chessa – P.C. Masini (eds), C. Berneri, Epistolario inedito I, Archivio famiglia Berneri, Pistoia. 1980. P. 127-128.

Before Bartolomeo Vanzetti was led to the execution room, he briefly met with Thompson, who wished to remember him with these admirable words:

"In this closing scene the impression ... which had been gaining in my mind for three years, was deepened and confirmed --- that he was a man of powerful mind, and unselfish disposition, of seasoned character, and of devotion to high ideals. There was no sign of breaking down or of terror at approaching death. At parting he gave me a firm clasp of the hand, and a steady glance, which revealed unmistakably the depth of his feeling and the firmness of his self-control".

Soon before facing death, Vanzetti wrote a letter to Dante, Sacco's fourteen-year-old son.

"...remember always, Dante, in the play of happiness, don't you use all for yourself only, but down yourself just one step, at your side and help the weak ones that cry for help, help the prosecuted and the victim, because that are your better friends; they are the comrades that fight and fall as your father and Bartolo fought and fell yesterday for the conquest of the joy of freedom for all and the poor workers...

In 1977, to mark the fiftieth anniversary of the execution of Sacco and Vanzetti, Michael Dukakis, who was then the Governor of Massachusetts and a descendant of immigrants, reopened their case. Unlike his predecessors, Dukakis, after having the trial re-examined by his legal advisor Daniel Taylor, acknowledged for the first time the many abuses committed by the prosecution and Judge Webster Thayer. On these bases, the Governor finally issued a solemn proclamation recognizing that Sacco and Vanzetti had been denied a fair trial.[9]

*   *   *

In trials, it is necessary to tread a fine line between finding the culprit, who must be consigned to justice so that his wrongdoing

---

[9]   G. Adducci. *Op. cit.* p. 147.

may be proved by means of evidence, and finding the culprit because justice must be done.

The atmosphere in which Sacco and Vanzetti's trial took place was permeated by the fear of an anarchist-Communist revolution. Therefore, the innocence or the guilt of the two Italians was not actually a principal issue.

As ordinary crime increased in the United States in the aftermath of World War I, fears of an anarchist-Communist revolution, a revolution considered to be an indistinct rebellion against the established order, became widespread. The case of Sacco and Vanzetti unfolded against such a hostile backdrop, which was fostered by xenophobic ideologies (especially against Italians, among whom there were several anarchists) and class discrimination.

For the more reactionary parts of the population, the claims advanced by the trade unions and the struggles to improve working conditions – in which both Sacco and Vanzetti were involved – were considered subversive actions and were opposed as such.

This sparked off a set of fears that risked giving rise to explosive, uncontrolled reactions, to a veritable witch-hunt.

Indeed, those years were marked by a significant suspension of a number of civil rights.

Those who persecuted the "Reds" also had their reasons. Certain anarchist attacks were still very well alive to the mind of the citizens, such as the bomb placed on Wall Street and the explosive attacks against the home of the Minister of Justice in Washington D.C. These deeds discredited the arguments of those who believed anarchists and Communists to be especially *theorists* of dissent. In the history of the United States, two particular elements appear to develop side by side: a gain of individual civil liberties and a tendency to exasperate the sense of threat.

Finally, there was the issue of using violence or nonviolence as methods to advance the cause. Generally, there are two anarchist currents: one which endorses nonviolence and another that does not reject violence as an instrument of political affirmation.

While it is true that in a pamphlet of 1923, signed by both Sacco and Vanzetti, entitled *"Dateci o libertà o morte"* ("Give us freedom or death"), there may be a slightly ambiguous invitation to engage in violence, it is no less true that, if we consider the whole of Vanzetti's writings from prison, it could be said that in the Piedmontese anarchic movement the prevailing temperament was rather nonviolent: "The more I live, the more I learn, the more I am inclined to forgive, to be generous and to think that violence as such cannot solve the problems of life".

Attorney Thompson recalls that, during their last encounter, he told Vanzetti about "how from history it emerged that truth has no chance to affirm itself where violence is followed by counter-violence".

According to Anatole France, in his appeal to the people of the United States of 31 October 1921, Sacco and Vanzetti were sentenced for a crime of opinion.[10]

Eugene Debs (1855-1926), the founder of the American Railway Union and one of the most important figures in the history of trade unions in the United States, the two Italians were sentenced as "foreign unionist agitators".[11]

In any case, one thing is clear from the writings by Sacco and Vanzetti: their anarchist beliefs belie a sincere concern for emarginated people, a rejection of any form of exploitation that alienates individuals and a quest for a way of life that allows the greatest possible equality of opportunity to all.

This is the message that they left to us, and that we wish to remember. Sacco and Vanzetti died on 23 August 1927 in Dedham Jail, Massachusetts. The State of Massachusetts abolished the death penalty in 1984.

Today, 37 States still impose the death penalty, while 13 States have abolished it.

However, is the death penalty a true deterrent to crime?

---

[10] Dos Passos, Dos Passos, *Davanti la sedia elettrica, op. cit.,* p. 31.

[11] Id., p. 33.

According to data collected by Amnesty International,[12] in 2004, in the United States, the average rate of murders in States with the death penalty was of 5.71 every 100,000 inhabitants against the rate of 4.02 every 100,000 inhabitants in the States without the death penalty. In 2003, in Canada, 27 years after the country abolished the death penalty, the rate of murders fell by 44 per cent. The death penalty is a very convenient political option compared to truly effective programs to protect the population and prevent crime,[13] when it is instead necessary to address the real problems behind crime.

According to Amnesty International, a 1995 study performed in the United States found that only 1 per cent of police chiefs felt that a greater use of the death penalty was a priority in reducing violent crime, compared to 51 per cent who believed that the solution was reducing drug use and unemployment.

The death penalty can actually provoke further violence. Execution is the most severe penalty that a State can inflict upon an individual. Once criminals know that they have committed a capital crime, they no longer have any interest in refraining from further serious crimes to reduce their potential sentence.

For example, if the death penalty is imposed for armed robbery, the criminals have nothing to lose if they kill any other witnesses as they escape.

Police Deputy Commissioner Mark Shields declared: "In my experience working in Jamaica, it would be a complete and utter waste of time to say to these young men of violence that, if they kill, the likelihood is that they will be killed by the state, because they don't expect to live that long. They expect to die at the hand of a police officer or at another criminal's firearm".

It is clear that those who commit murder do not place any value on human life and thus cannot respect their own lives, nor those of others.

---

[12]   Amnesty International. *Dossier 2008 – La pena di morte. L'ultima punizione.*

[13]   J. Van Rooyen. *Il giudice penale e la condanna a morte: alcune osservazioni sulle opinioni del giudice Curlewis.* South Africa, 1991.

In addition, legal errors do occur: the death penalty may be imposed upon an innocent individual.

In his work entitled "Of Crimes and Punishments", Cesare Beccaria stated that "the punishment of death is pernicious to society, from the example of barbarity it affords. If the passions, or the necessity of war, have taught men to shed the blood of their fellow creatures, the laws, which are intended to moderate the ferocity of mankind, should not increase it by examples of barbarity, the more horrible as this punishment is usually attended with formal pageantry."

When public opinion requires violent crimes to be solved, the answer must never consist in further murders.

Marie Deans, whose mother-in-law was killed in 1972, stated:

"After a murder, the families of victims must deal with two things: a death and a crime. In that moment, the families need help to deal with their pain and support to heal their hearts and rebuild their lives.

By experience, we know that revenge is not the answer.

The answer is to reduce violence, not causing more death.

The answer is to support those who are afflicted by the loss of their dear ones, not in creating more grief in other families [by killing their relatives].

It's time to break the cycle of violence".

In addition, the death penalty causes trauma for the prison officials and guards involved in the executions, the grief of the families of the victims and of the prisoners put to death, and remorse on part of the defense lawyers, who may feel guilty of the death of their clients and of the involvement of other people brutalized by the process.

In "Of Crimes and Punishments", Cesare Beccaria condemns the death penalty: "Is it not absurd, that the laws, which detest and punish homicide, should, in order to prevent murder, publicly commit murder themselves? [...]

"That some societies only it either few in number, or for a very short time, abstained from the punishment of death, is rather favourable to my argument; for such is the fate of great truths, that their duration is only as a flash of lightning in the long and dark night of error.

[...]

"the voice of one philosopher is too weak to be heard amidst the clamours of a multitude, blindly influenced by custom; but there is a small number of sages scattered on the face of the earth, who will echo to me from the bottom of their hearts; and if these truths should happily force their way to the thrones of princes be it known to them, that they come attended with the secret wishes of all mankind".

6

THE NUREMBERG TRIALS

"War is hell", said General Sherman.

Before him, many had already thought the same, felt the same, suffered the same. Can war be dominated by mankind, or is war the master of man, and man its slaves? Unfortunately, law does not create paradise on Earth. But it remains the only art that can avoid the abyss of war."[14]

During World War II, it was with some hesitation – and pressure from the exiled governments that had settled in London – that the British Government began to address the issue of how to deal with the individuals who were mainly responsible for the atrocities committed by the Axis powers.

In January 1942, the nine exiled governments had established an inter-allied commission to punish the war crimes, which were considered to be among the main aims of the terrible conflict.

After the meeting between the British Prime Minister Winston Churchill and the US President Franklin Delano Roosevelt, in October 1942 the cooperation between Great Britain and United States was already sufficiently advanced for the two powers to publicize the creation of the "United Nations Commission for the Investigation of War Crimes".

---

[14] M. Walzer, *Guerre giuste e ingiuste*, Laterza, Rome-Bari, 2009, p. 41 ff. Author's translation.

"The next year, in 1943, the USSR and China were also involved in the consultations to decide upon how to deal with those who were guilty of war crimes.

The question of how to punish the high ranks of the National Socialist Party was also discussed in the talks between Stalin and Benes.

However, some individuals in the US and British governments also opposed the trial form, preferring rather more drastic means to punish the guilty. One of the most authoritative expressions of support for this position was made by the US Secretary of the Treasury Henry Morgenthau.

Morgenthau himself outlined a plan for Germany's radical deindustrialization and mass internment and forced labour for the Nazi rulers; he also advocated for publishing a list of war criminals, who were to be killed immediately once their identity had been ascertained.

Instead, the Secretary of War Henry Stimson and the Secretary of State Cordell Hull were in favour of a trial form. In September 1944, the head of the "Special Projects Branch" Murray Bernays drafted a Memorandum on the "Trial of European War Criminals", which later became the blueprint for the Nuremberg Trials.

Bernays was the first to formulate the charge of "conspiracy" against the Nazi leaders. However, Franklin D. Roosevelt and Winston Churchill still preferred the "Morgenthau plan".

The trial option became more popular after the "Morgenthau plan" was leaked to the press and generated widespread indignation, and when, after Roosevelt's death, the new President Harry S. Truman, a jurist, expressed his support for the trials. This happened in April 1945. A few days later, the USSR, Great Britain and France also agreed to the trials".[15]

Finally, at the Potsdam Conference, it was announced that a military tribunal would be established to judge the principal German war criminals. On 1 August 1945, recalling the Moscow Declaration, the representatives of the three Allied governments

---

[15]   M. Cattaruzza – I. Deak, *Il processo di Norimberga*. UTET, Turin, 2006, p. 3.

(Great Britain, United States and USSR) confirmed their intention to impose swift and just verdicts upon the guilty.

It was also hoped that the negotiations taking place in London, among delegates of the Four Powers to draft the statute for an International Military Tribunal, would soon produce an agreement. These Powers also believed that it was crucial to launch the trial as soon as possible. Finally, the London Agreement of 8 August 1945 established the Tribunal and set out its jurisdiction.

The International Military Tribunal was profoundly innovative, in terms of the practices adopted by the countries that had won the war towards those they had defeated.

The opening session took place in Berlin on 18 October 1945, but because the conditions in the German capital, which lay in ruins, were inadequate to the continuation of the trials, the seat of the proceedings was moved to Nuremberg; this city also held symbolic value, as its name was connected to the enactment of Hitler's racial laws.

Overall, the Nuremberg Trials successfully performed the tasks set by the Allied Powers. At the end of the cruelest war in history, it was absolutely necessary to sentence those who were guilty of war crimes and to mark, with their punishment, the end of an era; this would enable a catharsis that was to resonate deeply across the world. However, the fact that the Tribunal was a military tribunal also presented certain intractable issues: both the atrocities perpetrated and the genocide they were meant to pursue were simply incommensurable, with respect to the "war crimes" codified by international case law.

On 20 November 1945, the United States Attorney General Robert H. Jackson declared, in the solemn opening statement that marked the beginning of the first Nuremberg Trial, that:

"It is hard now to perceive in these miserable men as captives the power by which as Nazi leaders they once dominated much of the world and terrified most of it. Merely as individuals their fate is of little consequence to the world. [...]

We will show them to be living symbols of racial hatreds, of terrorism and violence, and of the arrogance and cruelty of power. They are symbols of fierce nationalisms and of militarism, of intrigue and war-making which have embroiled Europe generation after generation, crushing its manhood, destroying its homes, and impoverishing its life."[16]

The trials against the principal war criminals were followed by those against the doctors, lawyers and various economic bodies that were involved in the exploitation of forced labour in the concentration camps. Also, trials were held against the Minister of Foreign Affairs, the Commander-in-Chief of the Armed Forces, the Heads of the Reich's Security Services and other leading figures in the Nazi power structure who had been accused of crimes. All of these proceedings took place at Nuremberg.

The trials ended in April 1948. The number of death sentences imposed was far greater than those handed down in all similar proceedings held later: fourteen SS commanders had received the death penalty. Other parties were sentenced to long jail terms, while three were acquitted. Trials against war criminals were also held in Poland, the USSR, France and other territories that had been occupied by Germany; these led to thousands of death sentences being meted out, most of which were performed. The Nuremberg trials concerned the leaders of the Nazi Party and the highest officials of the SS and of the *Wehrmacht*.

Over one hundred thousand official documents were collected as evidence. The trial began on 14 November 1945 and ended on 1 October 1946, with hearings being held almost every day. The official documents had been systematically confiscated and archived by the Allied troops as they advanced through Germany, and were managed and kept in the Federal Record Center in Alexandria, VA, USA.

The shelves holding the documents of the German authorities, on the structure of the Nazi Party and on the various military claims were eight kilometers long. This immense set of material provided the bulk of the documents that were presented as evidence, and was marked with the name "Group 238".

---

[16] *Il processo di Norimberga* DVD, UTET. https://www.roberthjackson.org/speech-and-writing/opening-statement-before-the-international-military-tribunal/.

An incomplete collection of the documents was later published under the name of "Trial of the Major War Criminals before the International Military Tribunal: Nuremberg, 14 November 1945 – 1 October 1946".

The accusations fell under three main headings: crimes against peace, war crimes and crimes against humanity. The common theme of the various charges, defendants and institutions was the accusation that the defendants, "during a period of years preceding 8 May 1945, participated as leaders, organizers, instigators, or accomplices in the formulation or execution of a common plan or conspiracy to commit, or which involved the commission of Crimes against Peace, War Crimes, and Crimes against Humanity".

Significantly, at Nuremberg, no specific independent charge was made for the Holocaust. The mass extermination of the European Jews was addressed in the context of the crimes against humanity, together with the deportation of civilians to Germany for forced labour, the detention of political opponents in concentration camps and the deportation of Polish civilians from Warthegau to the General Governorate.

The fact that the first set of charges concerned crimes against peace reflected both the fact that the international tribunal had been created by the four victorious Powers, as well as the fact that the anti-Hitler coalition perceived the Third Reich as an expansionistic and militaristic power that could jeopardize the stability of the entire European region.

The main accusation was the conspiracy to provoke the world war; from this, the other charges flowed logically and chronologically. The Nuremberg Trials counted only 23 defendants and – even if the dozens of "secondary" trials are also considered – concerned only two hundred people.

The principal Nazi leaders were present. However, the main culprits – Adolf Hitler, Heinrich Himmler and Joseph Goebbels – were missing.

Albert Speer, an architect who had directed several Nazi celebrations, had been asked by Hitler to design a grandiose series of public works (among which the new building of the

Chancellery, completed in 1939), and later named Minister of Armaments, was one of the few who admitted their serious guilt. Speer was sentenced to a jail term of twenty years, which he served in the prison of Spandau, ending in 1966. Baldur von Schirach, head of the Hitler Youth and Reich Governor of Vienna, had received the same sentence and was also detained at Spandau (in his memoirs, he publicly regretted that he had not done more to oppose the concentration camps). Karl Donitz, Commander-in-Chief of the Navy between 1943 and 1945 whom Hitler (just before committing suicide) had designated as his successor, as well as the Head of State who signed the Reich's unconditional surrender, was sentenced to a jail term of ten years.

Franz von Papen, Reich Chancellor in 1932 and Hitler's Vice-Chancellor from 1933 to 1934, had worked on the Reich Concordat between Germany and the Holy See, thus helping Nazism to gain support in many conservative circles. He had resigned from government after the Night of the Long Knives (30 June 1934) after giving a speech at the University of Marburg in which he distanced himself from the regime, criticizing some of its violent aspects. At Nuremberg, von Papen was acquitted.

In 1947, when he was 68 years old, a German court sentenced him to eight years of forced labour, although he was granted clemency in 1949.

Among those who were put to trial and executed outside Germany for crimes such as treason, collaborating with the enemy and crimes against humanity, there was a surprisingly high number of heads of state and of government, general commanders and other high-level military and political officials.

Among the heads of state and/or government executed after World War II were those of Italy, France, Slovakia, Hungary, Romania, Bulgaria and Serbia.

During the trial, the defence was subject to a number of constraints. All of the defence lawyers were German and included some who had been members of the Nazi Party. The number of lawyers was equal to that of the defendants, but the defence had neither registry nor research clerking services. In comparison, the British staff comprised 170 employees and the US personnel numbered ten times that figure.

The German lawyers were granted very limited access to case documents and were denied access to the Allied Powers' archives – of which the prosecution and their assistants could make liberal use. The German lawyers were never given a chance to view Great Britain's secret documents on the invasion of Norway, although these constituted the foundation of the cases against Admirals Doenitz and Raeder for acts of aggression. The horrors committed by the Nazis against the Soviet prisoners bore significant weight on the formulation of the charges, but the defence could not discuss the maltreatments of German prisoners of war on part of the Soviets. And yet, millions of prisoners had died in both German and Soviet camps – and the practice of cannibalism was known in both. The bombings that almost razed Dresden and Hamburg to the ground could not be called into question, while the bombings of Warsaw, Rotterdam and Belgrade were examined in detail.

The Germans were originally charged with the mass killing of 925 Polish officials in Katyn forest, although the prosecution was already aware that the massacre had probably been committed by Soviet police forces. Later, upon the insistence of the Soviet Chief Prosecutor, Roman A. Rudenko, the number of Polish victims at Katyn was increased to 1,100. In addition, because the Soviets did not manage to provide any evidence at all against the defendants regarding Katyn, and some US officials had protested against such a miscarriage of justice, the Katyn issue was quietly removed from the charges and was not mentioned in the final judgment.

About forty-five years after Nuremberg, one of the last deeds of a dissolving Soviet Union was the admission that the Katyn massacre had been ordered by Stalin in 1940. It is estimated that 15,000 Polish officials, among whom 800 Jews, had been killed by the Soviets in Katyn and other sites.

One of the principles established at Nuremberg was that neither the prosecution nor the defence could call into question the legality of the proceedings. As a consequence, the Germans' insistent arguments that the Tribunal lacked any basis in international law, that the defendants could not be prosecuted for crimes that were not deemed such in law at the time they were committed, and that the Allied Forces had often committed the same crimes of which they were accusing the Germans, simply failed.

However, the court, which normally rejected *tu quoque* arguments as inapplicable admitted them in one case at least – that of Admiral Doenitz, who had been in charge of the *U-Boots* during the war. His lawyer successfully argued that the entire submarine war had in fact been imposed upon the Germans, and that the US Navy had performed the same type of submarine actions in the Pacific Ocean.

Telford Taylor concluded that "that if Doenitz and Raeder deserved to hang for sinking ships without warning, so did [the US Admiral Chester] Nimitz."

In his defence, Doenitz produced an affidavit written by Admiral Nimitz, which bore witness to the fact that the United States had engaged in indiscriminate war in the Pacific as a military tactic and that the US submarines did not help survivors when their safety was at risk.

Nevertheless, the tribunal found Doenitz guilty of crimes against peace and sentenced him to a jail term of ten years, served in the Spandau prison in West Berlin. Of all the sentences imposed during Nuremberg, that against Doenitz was probably the most controversial. Doenitz always argued that he did not do anything that his Allied counterparts did not do. Testifying to the divisive nature of the decision, several Allied officials wrote to Doenitz to express their regret for the trial's outcome.

The Auschwitz doctor Josef Mengele had fled to Argentina. He managed to escape because he had not been tattooed with the SS symbol. There was a 3 million dollar bounty on his head, and was wanted by the Mossad, the United States and the Simon Wiesenthal Center. However, his tranquil stay in Perón's country drew to an end in 1959, when the dictator was toppled. In the meantime, the German tribunals had started to accumulate evidence of his crimes. Mengele fled to Paraguay, and then Brazil.

In 1979, he drowned because of a heart attack near São Paulo, Brazil.

A US study conducted in 1990 re-enacted Mengele's experiments and showed that the Nazi doctor's research was conducted in the absence of any scientific methodology.

Nuremberg "imported" its judges from the victorious Powers. However, the tribunals set up at national level to adjudicate upon the wartime atrocities had to deal with a major problem: the majority of judges had collaborated with the enemy, or at least faithfully served the defunct and reviled regimes. In Austria, in 1945, almost all of the judges had been members of the Nazi Party. As a consequence, it was necessary to resort to non-professional judges – or those who had previously colluded.

"In the Nuremberg Trials, only the death penalty or a jail term could be imposed; instead, national courts could impose a wide range of sanctions. These included the death penalty, imprisonment, forced labour, a penalty for dishonour to the nation, loss of civil rights, monetary fines, or administrative sanctions such as expulsion from the country, parole, loss of the right to travel or choose one's place of residence, confiscation of all goods and loss of the right to a pension.

Rather unexpectedly, the most severe punishment was meted out in Norway, Denmark and the Netherlands, countries which, in the Western tradition, are considered as models of the heroic resistance to the German occupation and of the brave efforts to save the Jews. In Norway, after the war, over 90,000 people were put to trial – almost 4 percent of the population. As most of these were male adults, about one Norwegian out of eight was trialled for collaborating with the enemy. Almost the same proportions could be found in Denmark and the Netherlands."[17]

In France, almost 10,000 actual or alleged collaborationists were lynched in the last months of the war or during the Liberation; the same number of people was summarily executed in Italy.

---

[17]   M. Cattaruzza – I. Deak, *op. cit.*, p. 43. Author's translation.

In some countries, such as France, public prosecutors tended to prefer acting against actors, actresses, cabaret singers, journalists, writers, poets and philosophers. In Eastern Europe too (and thus not only in France), the women who were accused of entertaining German soldiers became targets of punitive raids; however, once their shaved hair grew back, they were generally reintegrated into society.

In 1960, Adolf Eichmann, the notorious Gestapo official, was captured, put to trial and executed.

After the war, Eichmann had fled to Argentina. However, in May 1960, the Israeli secret services kidnapped and secretly transferred him outside the Argentinian borders, handing him over to the Israeli police.

Eichmann was put to trial for "crimes against the Jewish people", crimes against humanity, war crimes and participation in a criminal organization. The trial was held in Jerusalem, and Eichmann engaged the services of a prominent German lawyer. Nevertheless, there could be little doubt on the trial's outcome. The arguments of the defence (that the court was not competent to adjudicate upon a German-Argentinian citizen; that Eichmann had not committed the crimes within the State of Israel, which, at the time, did not even exist; that the defendant was being trialled for *ex post facto* crimes; and that he had acted upon orders received from his superiors) were all rejected by the court, precisely as had happened in Nuremberg in 1946 when similar attempts were rejected by the International Military Tribunal.

Eichmann cooperated with his kidnappers, with the Israeli police and with the tribunal from the very beginning, seriously examining the archived document, explaining their meaning and clarifying the facts. However, in this way, he only proved the incommensurability of his own guilt. It was demonstrated that Eichmann was guilty of sadistic acts, that he hated the Jews and that he did much more than obey orders. As the war drew to an end, Eichmann still caused the death of thousands and thousands of people, even defying the orders of the Head of the SS Heinrich

Himmler, who by then hoped that he would be accepted by the Allied Forces.

Eichmann unsuccessfully appealed against his death sentence, which was executed on 1 June 1962. It was the only execution in the history of Israel.

On 23 March 1944, a sparse group of Communist partisans carried out an explosive attack in the centre of Rome, against a group of German military police. 33 Germans lost their lives in the attack, as well as 12-year-old Italian Pietro Zucchetti; many other people were injured. All of the partisans escaped unharmed – but the same could not be said of the civilians of Rome. The German Supreme Command decided to randomly seize and execute ten Italians for every German killed.

A total of 335 Italians, among whom generals, Resistance fighers, common criminals, innocent passers-by and Jews were killed in the massacre of the "Fosse Ardeatine".

In 1948, the Head of the Gestapo Herbert Kappler was put to trial in Rome and sentenced to death. The judgment was influenced by the fact that he had ordered not "only" 330 people to be killed, but had added five more, out of an "excess of zeal". Kappler admitted that when he realized that there were five more captives, he had ordered their execution so that nobody could ever bear witness to the cruelty.

However, Kappler's death sentence was quickly converted to life imprisonment. In 1977, he was allowed to evade from the prison. He died the following year in West Germany.

All of the partisans of via Rasella survived the war. None of them expressed any regret, because they had acted out of patriotism and to further the Socialist cause, in which they profoundly believed.

If we consider the exceptionally brutal nature of the Nazi system, it is difficult to imagine how informal military operations may have been avoided. In addition, the partisans – Yugoslavian, Russian, Polish, Greek, Italian and French – did succeed, if only to a limited extent, to keep the German military forces busy and thus hasten the end of the war. However, their actions wreaked terrible suffering upon local populations, because they exasperated the occupying forces and thus exacerbated their cruelty, and also because struggles against occupiers almost inevitably turns into civil war. The partisans of World War II fought against a ruthless regime; however, many of them also stole from and terrified the rural population, and killed partisans belonging to other groups and true or alleged collaborationists. The Nuremberg Trials did not address these problems, leaving the future generations to grapple with an increasingly intractable moral and political problem.

What concrete results did Nuremberg bring? The Trials introduced the concept of individual responsibility. They also emphasized that there is no such defence as simple execution of orders from above, nor that sovereign States possess absolute rights.

Today, there are fully operational international tribunals that intentionally follow the example of Nuremberg.

Due to the civil war and fratricidal massacres in ex-Yugoslavia, on 22 February 1993, the UN Security Council unanimously voted in favour of the establishment of an international tribunal "for the prosecution of persons responsible for serious violations of international humanitarian law committed in the territory of the former Yugoslavia since 1991". On the basis of the Nuremberg model, the tribunal is the first body of its kind since the end of World War II.

The establishment of a tribunal to prosecute the gross violations of human rights that took place in Yugoslavia was followed by the creation of special tribunals for the violations of human rights in Rwanda and Ghana. Then, for the first time in history, the newly-created International Criminal Court began to investigate the violations of human rights in the Darfur and in the Democratic Republic of the Congo.

Ironically, the great power that created and led the International Tribunal of Nuremberg, the United States, has yet to ratify the Statute of the International Criminal Court.

*   *   *

Other than being a tribunal of victors, the tribunal of Nuremberg was competent *ratione temporis*; in other words, it could only decide upon facts which occurred during World War II (1939-1945). This means that the earlier geopolitical affairs involving the same subjects could not be examined: the 1919 "peace" Treaty of Versailles imposed upon Germany after its defeat in World War I, the requisition of commodities and the payment of extremely high compensatory figures, "until, in November 1923, the dollar reached the astronomical exchange rate of 4.2 billion Deutschmarks"[18].

Chancellor Bruning had openly declared that Germany could no longer pay the compensation and that National Socialism was growing exponentially.

The rest is history.

In recent history and during the two World Wars, destructive escalations occurred in international relations, with mass killings, air raids and atomic bombs.

These "solutions" led to countless deaths and atrocious suffering. In particular, however, in symbolic terms, they marked the defeat of civilization, regardless of who may have won the war.

Indeed, civilization also means juridical alternatives to war that can be derived from prudence, wisdom and balancing combination of the various parties' interests.

This path, however, requires greater use of and investment and faith in the most human of resources, which are not however, for this reason, less practicable and capable of producing enduring peace.

According to Saint Thomas, politics is no more than the exercise of "prudence" – of virtue, which investigates upon and predisposes means in a just economy between relations and ends. This is so-called "political" prudence, which rulers must apply, but that must also be exercised by all citizens in their own lives, so as to

---

[18]   L. George. *La verità sulle riparazioni e sui debiti di guerra*. Mondadori. Verona, 1932. P. 114. Author's translation.

contribute to and collaborate in the development of the public good as aware and responsible actors.

Thus, the principles of sound politics are to be understood as responsibility in action for the common and universal good.

ABOUT THE AUTHOR

Virginia Lalli is an attorney called to the Bar of Rome.

She has spoken at several conferences on the subject of nascent life and maternity support.

Virginia Lalli is the author of Aborto, perché no? Risposte pro-life ad argomentazioni pro-choice (IF Press, 2013) and Women in Law (AuthorHouse, 2014).

She is currently studying toward a PhD in human rights at the University of Rome, La Sapienza, and leads a research group on bioethics at the Senate of the Italian Republic.

ABOUT THE TRANSLATOR

Sarah Pasetto completed her undergraduate and postgraduate law studies at King's College London. Other than her legal translation activity, she is also currently taking part in several research and teaching projects in public law and human rights.

Printed in the United States
By Bookmasters

REVENGE

AND

TARGETS

WALTER STEGRAM

authorHOUSE®

AuthorHouse™ UK
1663 Liberty Drive
Bloomington, IN 47403 USA
www.authorhouse.co.uk
Phone: 0800.197.4150

© 2016 Ken Margetts. All rights reserved.

*No part of this book may be reproduced, stored in a retrieval system, or
transmitted by any means without the written permission of the author.*

Published by AuthorHouse 01/13/2016

ISBN: 978-1-5049-9810-9 (sc)
ISBN: 978-1-5049-9811-6 (hc)
ISBN: 978-1-5049-9812-3 (e)

Print information available on the last page.

*Any people depicted in stock imagery provided by Thinkstock are models,
and such images are being used for illustrative purposes only.
Certain stock imagery © Thinkstock.*

This book is printed on acid-free paper.

*Because of the dynamic nature of the Internet, any web addresses or links contained in
this book may have changed since publication and may no longer be valid. The views
expressed in this work are solely those of the author and do not necessarily reflect the
views of the publisher, and the publisher hereby disclaims any responsibility for them.*

REVENGE

CHAPTER ONE

My life was full of danger, I was always in some conflict or other Even at school I was the one who had to climb the highest up the oak tree in the play ground. I would slide down the hill at the back of our house when the snow was down and many a time would end up in the busy road at the bottom closely missed by a car or bus. Fighting at school was a daily event and my mother was always being call to the heads office to discuss what to do with me, he don't Like the Asian kids she was told. But it was the other way around they didn't like me because I would not let them rule me like they did the other white boys. So as I grew up I mistrusted anyone who tried to rule me or take control of my life which made it hard for me to stick a job because if I thought I was right I would voice my opinion. I fell out with all my family over one silly thing or another so by then I had no one in the world to turn to or even love come to that My mother had her men my father his work and my sister her own life which didn't include me.

So at the age of fifteen I joined the army and started my life as a boy soldier in the Royal Artillery learning signals as a trade but also became a good shot with a rifle. For two years I faced up to the bully boys who ruled the barrack rooms and made most lads lives a misery to the extent that they would self harm or run away. But even though I did get a few beatings they gave up as they would know it was always going to be a fight to get anywhere with me. In the last year I got my rank up to corporal and had a good sergeant who too hated bulling and between us we turn our troop into a really good bunch, so good that we won champion troop in my final year and I received the Farren prize for the best soldier. Once I joined my regiment and was known as a very good sportsman Who got selected for the regiment rugby team and athletics team I was never picked on again. I held the records for the one hundred two hundred and four hundred meters plus the long jump title so I was a bit of a hero in sport. Also there was the battery bar sports darts and table football were among my best events. So has time went on I started to get my trust back for people they stop becoming the object of my fears that was until I was call to duty in Ireland.

On the streets of Belfast I soon returned to my mistrust for anyone And to survive that's how you had to be as no one could be trusted Many of the lads fell for the girls only to get murdered in some dark country lane trying to get their leg over's. Four tours made me harden to people but improved my rifle shot. Now you have got a bit of my background it brings me into my story, a story that starts two days after I left the army with nine years service under my belt. Walking around London not sure what I was going to do with the rest of my life window shopping grabbing a burger and a pint the things that you do when you have nothing else to do. I had been told to pop into the union jack club a place where you will find a lot of ex-soldiers and some still serving with nothing to do. As I entered I checked the notice boards which advertised a lot of jobs for us lads, one stood out Do you still fancy to travel ring number below and ask for Dave. Taking a pen out of my pocket I wrote the number on my fag packet I didn't know why as it didn't tell me what the job was about. A few beers a the bar later and a chat to some of the ex's I made tracks for the room I had rented for a few weeks. Walking those dark streets at night in London was not for the weak at heart as you meet up with all sorts of riffraff and that night was no exception.

I noticed the two fellows standing in a doorway as I passed and experience told me to watch myself so I was on alert when one asked me for a light for his fag. Stopping I drew the box of matches from my pocket and placed them in his hand, keep them I said I have more in the flat. Good came his reply and maybe you have some money to go with them too and with that he pulled a knife from his belt. Being alert is what saved me that night as he did not expect my next move, with a flat palmed hand at speed I pushed it upwards into his nose. I heard and felt his nose break and I followed up with a back hand chop to his throat, he went down like a sack of spuds. His friend who was not the fastest thing on the planet was slow to react and I had put two well aim punches into his face before he had made a move. I followed up with a kick to his groin which put him out the game but his partner had recovered and was swinging his knife at me with as much angry strength he could muster. He lunged at me and with a side step and a grab of his arm I used his strength against him spinning him off balance I knee him in the stomach as I twisted his arm. The knife dropped and in a flash I picked it up, I think the game is with me now I said to the two them, we wont forget this the one mouthed but as I lunged the knife in his direction he turned and ran and his mate was not far behind him. I took a detour to the flat so as to be sure that they where not following me, when I was sure I made my way in and locked the front door behind me. My own temper had cooled from the attack but I still felt angry that the incident had happened, why? couldn't people go about their business and leave others alone. With that thought in my head I noticed the phone number I had written down on my fag packet and remembered the reference to do you still want to travel. I could do with getting away from this crap I thought to myself and with that I went down to the phone in the hall at the foot of the stairs and dialled the number. It rang for awhile and just as I was about to give up it was answered, "Hallo" a voice rang out in a not to pleasant a fashion I then realised it was after midnight, I am so sorry I said I didn't realise the time I will call back in the morning, I am awake now so tell me what you want he replied. Hesitating I began to reply I saw your number in the union jack club and decided to give you a call, You ex mob he inquired? Yes I replied. Meet me in the jack club at ten ask anyone and they will tell you who I am and with that he hung up. Didn't sound to friendly I thought but then I had just awoke him from his sleep I also got grumpy when I get disturbed from my slumber and by a stranger must be worse. Going back to my room I decided to have a hot drink and put the kettle on the small gas ring that I had to use for all my cooking and hot water. This was another reason I needed to get out of this place I was living in a room with a bed a toilet and a sink with no hot water. The night dragged, sleep was a long time coming but when I did go off thoughts kept leaping into my head about the attack that had happened earlier. I awoke early and put two slices of bread into my toaster pushing down the leaver and watched it disappear into the fire which waited within the chambers. Walking to the sink I ran the tap and scooped up two handfuls of water throwing it into my face the cold was refreshing and help clear my head, I brushed my teeth with my finger and then filled

5

my small kettle and placed it on the ring after I had lit it. A spoonful of coffee went into my cup which still had the dregs in from the night before God I had let myself go. Pulling on a cleanest shirt I had I made to look some kind of decent so I didn't look like a bum who needed this job and would take any payment to do it. After breakfast I read the news paper that I found discarded in the street it was two days old but the news was all new to me.

It was all the same news though, a murder, government problems, the queen was visiting some commonwealth country in Africa and prices where going up on everything, England beat again at cricket and Villa beat Birmingham in the local derby. Toast eaten and coffee drunk I slipped on my top coat as it had started to rain and I would be walking to the club and off I set. I stepped outside and pulled my coat collar up tight it was not only wet the temperature had dropped a few degrees and the cold hit me like a fist in the face, it bit at my cheeks. It was a good hours walk to get to the club and then I would have some time to kill before my meeting with this Dave fellow, throwing my hand into my pocket I checked my cash situation. It was another two days before I received my unemployment check And the contents of my pocket told me my total cash was three pounds and sixty-five pence to last me. The cold made my eyes water as I walked on towards the club the damp and icy breeze chilled my bones oh god let me get a job I thought to myself as I continued down that miserable street. I entered the club as soon as I got there to get out of the cold and went through the same routine as normal reading the board but this time I had some time to kill so I picked up a news paper and sat reading. The club got a dozen papers each day for us to read but you was not aloud to take them away till they was closing, the crosswords were normally done very quickly but this morning I had got in early and was lucky to find one not done. Finishing the crossword I looked up at the clock it read nine fifty-five so I went to the reception area and ask if Dave was in the club? Not yet came the reply from the old boy sitting behind the desk but he is expected soon. He pointed to a door, if you wait in there with the others he will join you all soon you will find tea and coffee on the table. With the word others ran through my mind that meant there was more going for the job than just me and my heart sunk. Opening the door my heart sunk even feather there must have been about sixty or more men sitting around the room chatting and drinking tea and coffee. They all went silent as I walked in but the noise open up again once they realised that I was not Dave, moving to the table I pored myself a coffee and sat down. A few faces looked familiar as I searched the room with my gaze but I could not recall where I had seen anyone of them from, it could have been exercises in Germany or patrols' in the Belfast streets. The garrison towns of Minden or Dortmund etc it could be anyone of a hundred towns and city where British troops had been stationed. That I may have seen their faces while serving in that area. I was pulled away from my thoughts by the door opening and a tall. Well dressed man entered the room followed close behind him was a smaller man with a sharp looking face. Good morning gentlemen my name is Dave Beresford and I am a ex-Para from the first battalion, with me is Phillip Masters also from one Para. We have got you here today to recruit fifty men for a little job we have in Africa, I won't tell you anything about the job yet as we would like to talk to you all individually so Phil if you could give out the cards with the numbers on we will start the interviews. We have two interview room across the corridor Phil will be in room Five and I will be in room six, once your numbers call by the last man in you will come across to that room all clear? Everyone groaned back with a yes. The card Phil had handed me was number thirty-two so it was a long wait for me but even longer for some of the others, right if numbers one and two will follow us we will get started. The four men left the room and once more the buzz of chatter started work in Africa was the word on most lips wondering which part and working for which government. To me it made no difference to where or who I worked for I just needed the job with some good money in my pocket for a change it had been so long since I had been flush. It didn't seem long when the first two were back and called the next two to their interviews, after the interview you could leave and you would be informed if you had been successful, that was the information the first two gave us. Finally my turn came and I was call to room six so it was Dave who was going to interview me, knocking on the door the same voice from the phone last night called me in.

Dave shook my hand and offered me a seat, first I would like to apologize for the lateness of my call last night I told him I just didn't realise the time. You sounded a bit flustered he told me had you been running from something? No not really Id had a bit of bother in the street that's all, oh I see came his answer. He gave me a card to fill in with all my details including what regiment I had served in and what my job was, asking me questions as I filled the detail of my service. I will be getting details about you from that card have you any problems with me doing that ? I told him I had non. Then I will contact you in the next few days if you are successful we will arrange another interview this time more details will be given you About the job we require from you, with that he stood up shook my hand and asked if I would let number thirty-three or four they were next. Walking away from the club I felt empty as though that had been a wasted morning and that I was no nearer to a job now as I was when I got up this morning. Two days latter I was proven wrong, my landlady call me to tell me there was a call for me and it was Dave he would like to offer me a second interview and could I be at the club the next day at ten. My giro had just come that morning so after paying the landlady my rent for the next two week I decided to celebrate my good news with a pie and a pint in or local. Entering the bar I noticed Sue was serving behind the bar she was my favourite barmaid who had a bit of a crush on me but was a married woman with a dick head of a husband. Morning Ken she shouted be with you in a moment, I took a seat at the end of the bar so I could look at her long slender legs and spy on that amply cleavage as she bent to get the bottles. The bar wasn't very busy with just a few of the old boys that came in daily to have a few pints and a game of dominos, most were retired some had injuries from one accident or another. What would it be ? Sue asked when she had dun with the other customer, a pint of your best a hot pie and a squeeze of your tits I told her. This made the old boys chuckle and Sue went red but still had that smile on her face. You're a naughty boy she said but she smoothed down her blouse to show the shape of her chest better as she spoke and the lads all wolf whistled. She put my pint in front of me and went of to warm my pie, my thoughts went back to my next interview it sounded like I had got the job I couldn't wait till tomorrow to hear all the details of where we was going and for how much or how long. Still no work Ken? Sue asked as she came out the kitchen, I might have some news tomorrow I told her oh that's good anyone we know? No it will be over seas if I get it.

A sad look came to her face, so we will be losing you she inquired? only for a while I said not sure how long for, know more in the morning. How are you and that husband of yours getting on? Still drinking his money away is he? you know he works hard to earn it but he drinks it away without thinking what we could do with it she explained he's away now for a few days driving up to Scotland. You should have a fling I told her make him think about you for a change, you must be joking he would kill me if he saw me with another bloke let alone having a fling. Then you should get a bit on the side without him seeing you and you have some fun for a change, She returned to the kitchen and came back with a large pie and chips on the house she said in a voice that only I could hear and I get off in a hour with a empty house if you fancy coming round. I tell you I thought about it and it would have been her old mans fault but I could do without the aggravation at this moment in time so I kiss her on the cheek and told her I had a lot on and maybe another day. The disappointment on her face told me she really was hot for it but I wanted a clear head and no troubles that would stop me going on this trip should I get selected. Next day I was up early so I had a slow enjoyable breakfast of bacon and eggs, there would be no walking today I could afford the bus so I didn't leave the flat till nine thirty. Once at the club it was near to the time so I asked the old man if we was to wait in the same room for Dave and was told that was correct and that there was a few more already waiting. I crossed the floor and entered expecting to see around fifty more men but to my surprise there was only four, hi you made it back too ask one of the guys nearest to me yes I reply but where are the rest he said he wanted fifty I enquired? there was a lot of shoulder shrugging and nobody had a answer. We didn't have to wait long for the answer as Dave and Phil entered the room at that very moment and heard my question. The others have already been selected came the reply from Dave they were all combat troops but you four have a little more to offer so we needed to know a bit more about you, Ken you come with me first. I followed him to room six and took the seat he offered me, would you like a drink? No thank you I replied, ok lets get down to it he continued. I looked you up as I said I would and found some interesting things, first you were a very good signaller but most interesting was you were a crack shot number one in you regiment falling plate team. Yes I replied I enjoyed shooting I found it great fun, but could you shoot a person from a distance without thinking about it he asked me?. You mean a sniper I replied? Exactly he said, I don't know I said I was never called to fire my weapon in the four tours I did in Ireland but if I was called on to do so I would have fired. That's all I needed to know he said, I would like you to go to a friends farm for a week to do a bit of training and after that we will see how you have got on and I will tell you more of what this is all about. Ok that's fine I told him but I am a bit short on cash at the moment so how do I get to this friends? All expenses paid he replied Reaching into his pocket he pulled out a wad of notes and gave me one hundred pounds. That will cover your travel expenses plus buy you a few bits of clothes and here is fifty pounds spending money to keep you going your food and board is all covered. Have you any question? When do you want me down at this farm? Tonight came the answer and he passed me the address on some paper, I will ring my friend now and he will pick you up at the station In Norwich at seven tonight. There is a train about three and I think you have to change somewhere but you will find that out at the station he told me so you only have a few hours before you need to be at the station still want to go he asked?. Yes I replied, there will be working clothes boots weapon and anything you require waiting for you so I will say goodbye and I will see you in a week. With that we shock hands and he went back to the room were the others where waiting for their turn. Outside the club I stood for awhile and pondered over what had just happened if I wanted this job it was now in my hands to prove what I can do with a rifle and I was feeling very nerves about it.

Checking my watch, it was ten forty-five so I rushed back to my flat and paid the landlady another weeks rent that would keep the room an extra week after I come back from training. I put my few thing that I owned into a rucksack and set of to the town where I bought a few shirts and a pair of jeans I then made my way to the station got myself a return ticket to Norwich. I would have liked to pop in the pub to say goodbye to Sue but I had not got the time pity really I could have book a meeting with her for the week after next if her old man was out of town. Grabbing a coffee and a sandwich at the buffet I sat on the platform and waited for my train, I had brought a paper to read on the journey the first I had paid for in over a year. I watched people struggle down the platform with big heavy cases and looked down at my rucksack god what had I done with my life My total treasures lay in this small bag. Final I boarded the train and started off on my new adventure with money in my pocket and not a clue where I was going to end up. Once I found a seat and disposed of my rucksack on the rack above my head I took out the paper that Dave had given me, it had the name Roger and Mill farm and nothing else god help me if he don't meet me.

I stepped off the train and walked along the platform to the ticket gate where the guard punched my ticket and aloud me out into the station foyer which led to the street. About ten yards form the front doors a voice came from my left are you Ken the man asked? Yes I replied then you best follow me came back in a strong Norfolk accent. I followed the stranger to a dirty green land rover which was parked in the car park, throw your gear in the back and jump in the front he told me which I obliged without question. My name is Roger and that is all you need to know about me other than I used to train snipers for all the forces including the yanks when they needed me. You are going to spend a week with me on the farm and in that week I have got to push three months training into you so you had better learn fast any questions? Ur no was all I could say.

Tonight I will feed you but after that you eat what you find or kill because that will be the start of your training and it will end after seven days you ok with that? Again I just replied yes. The training will be fitness survival surveillance camouflage and patients and it all starts at five in the morning and that is on the dot be late once and I will fail you, do you understand? loud and clear I replied, good he said. Now I will get a few of the question you may have out of the way, Your going to Africa if you pass this training but I don't know which country or for how long. They will be paying you well but I don't know how much, is it going to be dangerous? Yes but if you learn well you will come home to spend your money. Dave told me that you are a very good shot so we start tomorrow by finding out how good any question? N o was all I said. I think the whole of the journey I didn't speak a sentence and he covered anything and everything I was going to ask and a lot more he did explain why he told me all these things was because there would be no time once we start to answer questions.

The farm house was a very traditional little cottage with barns and a milking shed with pen for the live stock, chickens scurried out the way as the land rover pulled into the yard. I was shown my room by the lady of the house, told me that there was a bowl and a jug of water for me to freshen up with so I still didn't have hot running water. Toilets down the hall she said if you need a bath we will boil you some water on the fire supper will be ready in half an hour and she was gone. Even though there was no running water the room was spotlessly clean with clean crisp sheets soft bed and a fire place with a log fire burning nicely a basket of log to one side. I freshened up in the cold water and went down stairs for my supper we have rabbit stew tonight I was told by Mary, Roger had informed me of her name as I came down the stairs into a lounge with another open fire letting off a warm glow in the room with two oil lamps. You don't have electricity here I asked Roger? Luxuries we don't need came the reply oil lamps log fires even the cooker is heated by logs burning below the ovens he informed me. What about Television? No we have a battery operated radio that we listen to each night or we read our books that's all we need don't need any fancy stuff. I make my own beer you can have a drop with you supper if you would like some, I hesitated at first but said yes to be polite. Rabbit stew was something my mom had told me about but I had never had it till this night and I must say it was a treat and home cook bread with a glass of Rogers homemade beer it was a feast fit for a king.

Eat up lad Roger said tomorrow you provide the food for the table or you go without we have plenty in our pot to see us through the week and he poured me another beer. Two more beers later I was feeling a bit light headed so I called it a night have you got a alarm clock I asked? No such thing in this home you learn to use your body clock you will need it where your going. I staggered up the stairs trying to think about my body clock but had not got a clue what it was and as soon as my head hit the pillow I was in a dream world. I was awoken by the crowing of a cockerel outside my window and the start of daylight shining in, looking at my watch four forty five I jumped out of bed my head was thumping but I washed my face and got into my clothes making my way downstairs hoping I was first up. I was out of luck Roger was waiting outside the door, morning he said with a smile on his face ready to start you training then? Yes I said pitifully and he passed me a twelve gage shotgun we start with this. I had never shot one before and told him that, well if you want to eat today you had better learn and fast. By the way I will tell you at the end of each day how I thing you have done, I will also tell you the reason for that curtain bit of training if you don't tell me first. By not telling me I will deduct points, you start each day with one hundred points at the end of the day under sixty is a fail so use your brain as well as you brawn and ability to be a good sniper you must use everything god gave you.

We crossed a dozen fields without saying a word then suddenly Roger stopped took aim and fired I didn't see what he shot at but when he walked over to the edge of the field and picked up a dead rabbit I knew I was in trouble. I thought I would get this one as you have walked past a hundred and not banged one he said sarcastically, we are not on a Sunday stroll you have to keep your eyes open ok? Ok I replied felling very angry at myself. I turned to walk and saw another rabbit bang I fired my gun and missed this happened four times I missed every shot and Roger started to laugh, ok I said what am I doing wrong? Rabbits run they don't reverse understand try shooting slightly in front of the target. I took the point and my next rabbit that I saw I aim slightly in front of it and fired as the gun clicked the rabbit took off but my pellets hit it as it went forward, you eat today Roger said with a smile. Roger got two more to my one so Mary had five for the pantry.

After some cheese and crackers I helped with some farm chores Mary milked the cows I feed the pigs and cleaned out the stables putting fresh hay down for the horses. Roger run a plough over a field till late afternoon then he took me back to the wood without the guns or any weapons at all. We just walked along and then he stopped me, stoop down be very quite and listen and tell me what you here and what direction you hear it from. Waiting for the noises I was making to settle down I tried to consecrate but found little interruptions like my breathing a cough A fly buzzing past me. Hold your breath Roger told me clear your mind of everything and listen, I did as I was told and soon I could hear movement to my left I said nothing and just pointed. Keeping really still I wait the noise got louder until I could see some fifty feet away a deer just walking slowly but very alert not yet aware of us but aware that something was about. Roger finally got to his feet and the deer bolted off in the opposite direction from us and was lost in seconds.

We started back to the farm it was very dark by now and I kept stumbling but Roger seemed so sure footed and I never saw him stagger once he seemed to glide along the floor. Rabbit stew was on the menu again that night but not the one we had got that day they had been hung to mature for another day. Roger offered me a beer but I declined the offer this evening. How do you think your day went young man? Roger asked me once we had finished supper, not sure I replied I didn't get off to a good start with the rabbits. Sixty five points you got so you was just in, but I did trick you a bit with the beer the night before, its not like the stuff you drink in your local its stronger and I knew it would have the effect that it did so I owe you five for that. Yes you lost points on the shooting as a sniper you will need to see everything that is happening around you everyone of those rabbits should be seen they could have had rifles aiming at you. Your fitness was good the work you did on the farm was first rate and you did a good job for a city slicker. Once you got your body under control you mastered the listening exercise when you are out there if you don't hear the enemy coming from a thousand yards you are in deep shit. Thank you for the lesson I told him everything we did today has now sunk in and I have learnt so much.

One thing I said to him how did you walk back so steady footed and I was all over the place? Ease he replied I was on the path you was walking on my new ploughed field, we both just rolled with laughter. I think I will call it a night I said and made for the stairs, by the way he said Harriet has been put in her pen tonight so you wont get a call in the morning, we smiled again good night and off I went. Not sure that it was the threat of failing or that my body clock had kicked in but I awoke again the next morning at four thirty and went down to find Roger waiting for me. Morning now we will see what you can do with these weapons and out of a bag he pulled a SLR and a M16 with the M20 grenade launcher attached. Where did you get these from i inquired? Ask no questions and I will tell you no lies he replied putting them both back in the bag and passed me a box full of ammo for them, you carry that he told me. We again crossed the fields this time I told him when I saw a animal even though we was not shooting them with the weapons we were carrying. He didn't indicate that he was pleased that I had done that but he also didn't show he was unpleased so I kept telling him. I know he didn't expect me to grab a weapon load it and pop off a round as a 7.62 round would make a mess of a rabbit or any other animal that I hit. We entered a quarry which looked like it had not been used in years, They used to get slate out of here many years ago the same stuff that the farm buildings are made of Roger told me but when I bought the land it came with it.

I want you to take up a position anywhere on that land fall behind some of the rocks and I will set up some targets for you to shoot at, I will make then different distances so I can really test you. Three zeroing rounds with each I inquired? Just one he said. After about thirty minutes he joined me at the firing point, I had spent the time getting the feel of each weapon and loading up the magazines. In your own time load Roger told me SLR first, I put the magazine onto the weapon, ready Roger shouted and I cocked the weapon and put up the back sight. One round a the target to the left of the shed aim at his heart he told me fire, I took aim at the manikin that he had standing about a thousand yards away and set my sight took aim again and fired. Roger look though a pair of glasses he had hug around his neck Two inches to the right of his heart he reported adjust your sight and take the same shot he told me. Bulls eye he announced after I had fired my next shot, see you don't need lots of rounds to zero in just a spotter and I am sure that's the way they will work in Africa. I followed the same procedure with the M16 one round at the target then followed Rogers adjustment before firing the next round with the same result bulls eye. The next hour was spent firing at the targets Roger called and the spot that he wished me to hit but now I got no result just a target change and the area he wish me to hit.

Finally he said lets get some breakfast, I cleared both weapons and asked him to check that they were safe, that's fine here he told me but when you get there you will keep a round in the breach at all times understand? Yes I do just like Ireland. The proceeded follow as it did the day before more farm work after breakfast with the horse boxes cleaning and the pig pens all the heavy dirty work while Roger drove his tractor around the fields. It was late afternoon when I finished the work and I went to the cottage to get a drink, I must admit I was feeling a bit with the smell of horse and pig shit clinging to me. Mary do you think I could have a bath tonight? Yes she said I will get it in by the fire and put you some water on for you and Roger has left a note on the table. Picking up the note I just knew what it was going to say and I was right it just said "supper". I collected the shotgun from its rack and headed out across the fields My luck was in and in the second field I bagged two pheasant and carried them in very proud of myself. Mary looked at me with horror as I put them on the table, out of season for those Roger said from the doorway but you was not to know hang them up Mary we will have them in a week or so.

Supper was potatoes and vegetables with some large cuts of pork covered in gravy, boy I was so hungry that I wolfed it down. Mary has put the tin bath in the sitting room by the fire and the water is nearly hot so after tea you can take your bath. Thank you I said but I hope I want be putting you out, not at all Roger replied as a matter of fact when you have jumped out I will have one too. Once I had finished my supper I washed the dishes while Mary filled my bath with the hot water from the stove fire, its nice and hot now so when you are ready it will be just right thank you I told her and went and fetched my soap and towel. The lounge was empty when I came down so I undressed and was just getting in when Mary and Roger came in, oh my god I said rather loudly and tried to cover my manhood. What's up son said Roger as Mary sat in her chair and took out a book and started reading, your not shy are you? Well yes I am a bit I replied. No shyness on a farm Roger told me, Mary have I got the same things this young man as got? yes she said without looking up from her book but his is bigger, you cheeky monkey he told her and they both laugh. I eased down into the water and after that my shyness was gone even though I'm sure I saw Mary sneaking a peep once or twice. I suppose you would like to know how you did today? Well I scored you seventy today your shooting was one hundred percent you can certainly fire a weapon. You lost some score by not checking out your area even though you took my word for it that this was my land you should always and I mean always check out the ground you will be working in. The people you will be looking out for will have snipers too and you don't want to walk in one of their traps now do you? I take your point I told him start as I mean to go on, exactly. Your last point lost was shooting those birds, don't bring attention to yourself if there is any doubt don't take the shot that is also the philosophy for any danger by taking the shot, if you cannot get the shot in without endangering yourself don't take the shot there will be another day. Day three started very much like the first two days, out for five only this time Roger gave me a sheet of cam net and told me to go into the wood and make a hide he would then see if he could find me. Off I went he was going to give me an hour to hide then try to find me, if he didn't I was to get back for my farm work at midday. I also had to take some food with me as I would not be back for breakfast I was to help myself out the kitchen. Helping myself to some biscuits that Mary had baked plus some cheese and a canteen of water to drink

I set off I ran most of the way more to keep me fit but also to give me more time at the hide.

Once in the woods I took my time to find the ideal place, somewhere with natural cover where I could blend in by using the camouflage netting and the surroundings. I found the spot under some bushes with a bit of a hollow in the ground which I could lie in and cover the netting over me, I pull bits of branch and dead leaves over the netting to brake up my body shape and make it look natural. I lay there for thirty minutes doing the breathing trick that Roger had taught me on day one, sounds were coming in from all direction birds breeze in the trees and the odd animal running around. I pulled a biscuit from my pocket and a small lump of the cheese and ate them both without crunching the biscuit and I did it in a way that I didn't make any movement that could be detected. Another ten minutes passed and then a voice rang out from behind me come out your under the bush, the voice was Rogers how the hell had he found me. I stood up and he came across from behind a tree were he had been hiding, you must have followed me I told him? me cheat never you left to many clues if I had been the enemy you would have been dead now. How did you know I asked? I will show you first you left foot marks everywhere you bushed against branches on the bushes and disturbed their natural shape. You pick a decent spot then spoilt it by putting wet leaves over your cam net the leaves would have been dry as the damp would not have got to them and the biggest error was your choice of food to bring cheese can be smelt from a long distance. Two other points under bushes is ok but get in deeper and make sure you have a clear view to make a shot, finally if someone calls out like I did don't step out like a school boy who has been caught stay put it could be a trick.

Every point he made was right and my head sunk to the floor, don't be to hard on yourself he told me this is part of the exercise that I have to teach you nobody as ever got it right first time. You don't have to bring any food home tonight you are staying out here in a hide that you are going to find somewhere that you can observe the farm live off the land move without being seen and not be found when I come looking for you in the morning do you think you can do that? you bet I can after that cock up I just did. Ok lets get some proper breakfast and get the farm work done before you get yourself together for the night. We walked back to the farm and I washed myself down before I had some bacon and eggs and a large mug of tea, I started my usual jobs and spent the time thinking about that coming night. It was while I was cleaning out the stables that I had my idea for my nights exercise and I planned it very carefully there was no way he was going to find me in the morning. After we had finished the work Roger sat me down at the table to go over some of the points that I would need to show him in tonight's exercise and prove that I had carried them out. Point one you will need to eat off the land so you must show me the food that you had found, point two I will be doing five different things through out the night too prove you have stayed awake you will tell me what you saw. Three, you will be carrying your rifle with you and using your night scope I wont to know how many times you see me and at what times You would have taken the shot, ok so far? Yes I replied. Finally by morning I will be hunting you till twelve noon so see if you can last that long if you do, make your way back to the farm and I will make sure Mary has some food for you. At six it was dark and without any meal I was sent off with my rifle, sight, and cam net also one contaner of water as the ground water around was polluted. I made my way out towards the woods leaving as many boot marks as I could and once in the trees I took my boots off. Hanging my boots around my neck I walked into the sallow stream just inside the woods and followed it around till It became level with the back of the barn. The stream had a stoney bottem so would not show any footprints plus by morning any mud I distured at the bottom would be washed away and clear. Moving to the edge of the bushes I used my night sight to peep out towards the farm buildings, the farm house was obscured by the barn so I could get in close without being seen. The ground was very hard and didn't sink when I put my bare foot on it so I took long strides and stayed on the very grasse bits to shield my feet from stones that may cut into them.

A blood trail was ease to follow so I took my steps very slow and carefully so as not to get any damage and give the game away in the morning. Once at the barn I slid along the floor till I reached the large pile of straw and horse droppings that I had piled up that day. I found the edge of the sacking that I had burried under the shit and strew and wriggled underneath it making sure that nothing fell off to show the sack. Once I was happy that my hide was well coverd I poked a little hole to my front so I could just see out with my night sight. Scanning around the farm I took note of the main areas and any blined spots but overall I could see every area very well I could see Roger moving around in the living room and Mary bringing him a hot drink. I pulled up the little plastic bag of goodies that I had stashed inside the sack earlier that day it contained some apples that I had took from the tree in Marys garden and two sweeds that I got out the field. A pen knife from out the tool box and some string made up my tools for the night, in my pocket I pulled out a small tourch which I had painted the face red using some of Marys nail polish to stop the glow. With the sting I tied some sacking and straw around the barral of the rifle to hide the shinny metal and to blend in with the hay stack.

My watch told me it was nine oclock I had been setting up for three hours and know all was ready for my long stay in this smelly But comfortable hide. I had dressed for the cold even though it was a warm evening but I knew that the night would bring a drop in temprature also in my pocket was a large piece of plastic which I had cut off the bag which contained the horses oats to cover me if it rained. Rain it did just after eleven I watched the light go out in the house but knew Roger had not gone to bed as I could see the glow of his pipe as he sucked on it to draw the taste of his favorite brand which Mary called old socks. Imade note of all the timings so I could tell him when and at what time he did things throughout the night. As I said the rain came it was very fine at first then it got heavier and around midnight it was throwing it down, my bit of plastic kept my upper body dry but I could feel my lower legs starting to get wet I kept flexing my muscles so that they would not stiffen up. Just then the back door opened and Roger stood in the doorway in the dark but I could see him as clear as day with the night scope. One moment later and he had gone closing the door behind him, I made a note of the time that would have been my first clear shot at him. There was one good thing about the rain it would clear any tracks that I had made making it harder for Roger to track me in the morning. Tiredness was now becoming my enemy and with little to do but watch the scope I could feel my eyes closing so I took out my knife and cut a apple in two and started to eat. Light on in second bedroom Roger at the window ten seconds light off shot two at one thirty seven rain still heavy all these were notes on my paper. I watched a fox come into the yard with a rabbit in his mouth it just passed through without stopping oblivious to the fact I was there just getting some food back for her young. A movement in the garden revelled Roger standing by the wall looking out over the dark fields, he stood there for no more than a few seconds but long enough for shot number three at three ten.

The rain had died down to just a drizzle my legs were now very cold but I could still move them and I rubbed the tops to keep my circulation going. My eye were getting sore now with the strain of the sight and the tiredness but I kept going knowing that the day before I had dropped points I was not going to drop any today. Four minutes passed four again Roger appears at the back door shot number four another entry onto my little note pad. The final time I saw Roger in the house that long dark night I nearly missed him, he was standing looking out the attic window I had not anticipated him going up there and I just had him in my sight long enough to claim shot five.

Five o'clock that was and soon after the kitchen light came on and I saw Mary starting her daily chores, by five thirty she was collecting the eggs from the hen house. Six oclock she was boiling up some washing on the stove in a big tin bath there was no sign of Roger not until six thirty when he came out shot gun in hand and marched down the field in the direction I had set off in. I could just see him disapper into the woods he was then out of sight I took that opportunity to close my eyes and have a doze, I don't know how long I was off but I came too with a sarttle. Mary was cleaning out the Horses and was throwing the hay onto the pile ontop of me just far enough away from my little spy hole not to bloke my view. Roger was checking the building still looking for me and he came across to were Mary was working and checked the stabbles. I think that lads run off he told her I cannot find a track or anything down in the woods, the rain washed away any marks he made in the dirt. He wouldn't leave with your gun would he she inquired? No I don't think so but he has found a good hide somewhere I was expecting him back when that rain came down. They moved away together which was a good job as I needed to move my legs they were numb, I glanced at my watch twelve twenty four the exercise was over.

I Backed out off my hide and tried to stand up but my legs wouldn't hold me and I fell, sitting on the ground I rubbed my legs as hard as I could to get the blood moving again. I finally managed to get to my feet a walk to the back door, Roger opened it and I fell in into his arms, They got me to a chair and sat me down. Mary pulled off my wet trousers and rubbed my legs with a dry towel Roger got me a drop o whisky and rapped a blanket over me God lad you almost killed yourself out there with that rain and temprature he told me. After a nice warm and a bite to eat I read my notes to Roger and he confimed that all my sightings and timings were correct, a pat on the back told me he was happy. After you have had some sleep we will go out and shoot that rifle and see how you handle it he told me, it is the same as the one you will be using in Africa. Sleep came ease and it was around four in the afternoon when I climbed down the stairs and was meet at the bottom by Mary. Roger said to meet him at the quarry when you get up he will be waiting with your rifle and could you bring a few targets out the barn with you. I meet Roger in the quarry he had been busy making some make sift situations with windows and vehicles walls of brick and a small building he had put some targets in a few mine went in the rest.

Now we will do the same as the other day but I wont all head shots and from a longer distance ok with that he asked? Fine I told him and moved to the far end of the quarry. Three standing shots first he shouted and stood back a the side looking through his glasses, in your own time he called one zeroing round followed by three shots. Taking a good stance I aimed at the target in the car with no windscreen bang the rifle recoil hit my shoulder hard but I held it firm, good shot don't change your sight he called to me again. The next three shots hit the same target cutting his head in two leaving one half on the floor of the car, nice shooting now try the crouch position and put three in the next target. After about an hour of shooting all called a halt and rejoined me yes you can really shoot he said you hit every target where they needed to be hit and not one stray. Tomorrow we will spend a hour with a silencer so you get used to the extra weight on the barrel, you will more than likely use one a lot in Africa Roger explained now lets get some supper will be dark soon. On the way back he gave me the points for the day, you got ninty five today which made up your poor start yesterday morning but today the shooting was excellent and your night exercise was as good as it could be well done. In the morning we start with a run carrying full pack and weapon followed by the firing with the silencer and by the way you don't need to get any supper tonight Mary is cooking them rabits you got the other day. I was proud of my days work and I knew that Roger was impressed with what I had done I just hoped the next three days would be just as good for me. Another feast for a king awaited us included a bath I still smell like one of the horses, rifle had to be cleaned and then back to bed good night both I said climbing the stairs. That night I slept like a log and awoke with plenty of time to wash and get dressed in a full combat uniform that Roger had kitted me out with before it was time to run. A rucksack waited for me down stairs full of bricks and two ammo pouches full of ammo all attached to dp webbing straps. My rifle was now slung across my front with a rifle sling a water bottle was attached to my belt, god if anyone see's me they will think world war three has started I told Roger. You my not carry this much in Africa but you will need to be fit enough if you do, so today we test your fitness are you ready to go he asked me? Yes lets do it I replied. Roger ran beside me in a vest and a pair of fatige bottems with dms boots and for his age he had kept himself fit with a well trimmed body just like the pti's back in the old days that took us for all our fitness training. We crossed the fields which where soft from the night before rain fall And crossed the stream which came up to my kness with the extra water.

Through the woods and passed the quarry till we hit a tarmaced road, this road takes into Norwich Roger informed me but we will be turning back before we get that far. Roger called the pace and we walked for two miles then ran a mile and had a sprint for two hundred yards then started our next two mile walk and this is how we went for most of that morning. Ten miles out we took a restand Roger explained what he had install for me next, the rest of the day you will carry on with your farm work he told me but I will be out setting up your exercise for tonight with some friends of mine. All that you have learen't this week will be put into practise tonight he told me so remember everything from day one till now. I had kept myself fit after I had come out the army but I was sure glad to see the farm gates after that run, the pain in my back from carrying that load was like a knife being twisted. There was not a muscle in my body that didn't ache and I now knew that there was no rest for me I was to clean the pigs and horses. Mary gave me some rub that she uses for the horses to help ease the pain and I must say it worked, I finished my work and went and banged a brace of rabbits for another meal. Roger was missing all day but arrived home for his tea and gave me my instructions for the night ahead of me which would start with me being dropped off about five miles away. I was to make my own way back without rogers friends spotting me then get to the quarry make a hide and take out four targets throughout the night. Roger would set up the targets and try to see or hear me taking my shots, you will have your night scope and your silencer fitted to the rifle. After we have discovered the targets have been hit we will be coming to look for you if we find you at anytime in this exercise you will fail and be sent back to London. So remember all what I have told you and use it all to get through this exercise he told me and don't forget to travel light tonight as you will when you are out in Africa on one of these missions. We ate tea and I went to my room to get ready putting together a small rucksack containing cam net ammo two apples and my silencer. I had learen't by my mistake of how cold my legs got when I was under the hay so I put on another pair of light wight trousers under my combat one's. My combat jacket which was water proofed was put on next and I filled the pockets with things that would come in handy compass penknife etc etc.

I blacked my face and hands hiding any light flesh that might be showing and sat waiting for Roger to call me to go. At nine thirty he called me down for some last minute instructions, I want you to pass this exercise he told me and I know that you can do it so don't let me down. We didn't say much more as he drove me to my drop off point just that the exercise starts ten minutes after he dropped me off and good luck. I watched him drive away and go out of sight before I took out my pocket tourch and checked my barrings on the compass, I had used it most of the day on our run and made note that the farm was in a north eastly direction from where I was. Leaving the road I entered the edge of a grassy medow and stayed close to the bushy edges, I knew that following the road back would mean certain capture. Moving from field to field I checked that the way was clear before in moved on into another one and checked my barring after I had moved through three fields. The road had move at lest one field distance away from me and I could see from my cover the head lights of car travelling along it And noticed if they stopped. They to could be using night scopes so I just layed low once they stopped and didn't move until they moved away well out of my range. My legs still ached from the morning run but they was a lot better than what they would have been if I had not used Marys horse rub It had realy loosened them up. I tried to keep to the unworked edges of the ploughed field as the rain had made the soil sticky and heavy to walk on. Once I had been walking for about one hour I picked up the tree line of the woods close to the farm, here I changed my direction and made a wide sweep around to come in from the far end of the quarry.

Removing my boots so as not to make large foot prints I moved on slowly brushing any marks behind me so I would not leave a trail for Roger and his friends to pick up on. The top of the quarry was stoney with bits of broken slate so to get to near the edge could cause bits to fall and give away my position so I stayed back from edge. Using the scope I servayed the land on top of the quarry, one end had the roadway in which had been used for the lorries and machinery to enter and leave. One side was steep and ragged edged which I would say was the side they had worked all them years ago to remove the slate. Two side's were high but were covered in bushes trees and brambles They made good but obvious places to make a hide so I disregarded them as places for my hide I would need somewhere that Roger would not think of. Moving round to the trees on the left side of the quarry I took a sneaky peep with caution as not to be seen down into that vast hole using my night scope. I didn't see any movement and nothing of any targets so I thought that Roger and his friends were still out looking for me, I noticed that there was a rocky area up one side of the road in which my give me the shelter I was looking for. I made my way around to the area and dropped down gently as not to disturb anything or kick up any dust, surrounded by large rocks and stones gave me a whole cavern of hides were I could hide unseen And even see in to the quarry. Some bushes had grown in between some of the rocks and I found a spot where I could lay down under a rock which give me all round cover and a clump of bushes that I could place my rifle without it being seen. Just as I had finished setting up I saw the landrover enter the quarry and park near to one of the old buildings and soon after a second arrived. Any sign Roger asked the two men the got out of the vehicle? No came the reply we covered the whole area that you told us and never saw a thing not so much as a track.

Well he will be some were here now so take a look around the quarry while I set up the targets. I hope this lads as good as you think he is I don't want him thinking im a target a big tall lad in a lumber jacket told Roger, Told you he can shoot a flea of a flies bollock if he needed to came the replie from Roger which gave the thinner man out the group a great deal of amusement. Roger opened the hut and pulled out four targets and I watched as he put the first one in a make shift gun tower before returning for the second. The two other men went down to the far end of the quarry starting from the middle one went left the other right and walked right around the lower edge of the base looking in any spots that may hide a sniper. I kept a close watch on the two while Roger worked out where to put his dummy targets, he had made some realistic looking places To stand them, some could only just be seen. At first it looked as though this spot I had picked had been made for the position of the targets but then I could see that two of them would be hit easer from a different angle than that of mine but from here I could still hit them. By now both men had reached the road out of the quarry and walked up to the top, passing by me some twenty feet below and only glancing up towards the rocks, they then joined Roger at the hut. Deciding to wait a few hours before taking a shot I settled down for a long night watching Roger and his friends sitting in their vehicals and checking the targets every so often. There was not a cloud in the sky this evening so the stars shone big and bright so I could see the shape of the landrovers without the night scope and also any movement that the men made. Around two-thirty I took my shots starting with the tower target, bring the centre of his head into the cross wires of my sight I squeezed the trigger. With the silencer on the end of the barrel the sound was like a release of flatulent wind which lasted for I fraction of a second Silent but deadly I thought. Checking Roger and his crew there was no movement, checking the target revealed a large hole in the head.

Moving across to the next target I lined up my sight and fired again checking Roger and friends, nothing no movement no sound Three targets latter I had done my work. I settled for the rest of the night watching and waiting for the men to discover the mess I had made of their targets and it came about four when the thin guy checked the targets. I heard him call Roger he as got everyone of them plumb in the head you was right this lads good, Yes replied Roger now lets see if we can catch him he is out there somewhere. One set off in one rover Roger and the big guy started checking around the area and they looked very close to me but I was safe. I lay low for the best part of the morning and watched each one of the group come and go from the quarry and saw them checking both sides of the woods at the top of the quarry. My area around my hide was checked on two occations but never close to reveal my hide, eventually Roger called a halt to the ecercise by telling me to make my way back to the farm. I watched them drive off in both vehicals but didn't make a move till I was sure it was not a trick by Roger but eventually I scrambled out of my hole and headed back to the farm. As I entered the farm house I was greeted by Roger, well done he told me you completed the exercise without detection and hit all your targets.

Its nice to have a student who listened to what I told him and put it all to practise on his final exercise he continued but I have another day I told him. Tomorrow will be a map reading exercise which we will do in the house plus the gear you will be taking to Africa will be arriving so you will need to try it all on. But how did they know that I had not failed I asked him? Because I knew you would pass and ordered it yesterday while I was out. Thank you for everything I told him I learnt so much in the last few days I thought a few times I was going to land on my arse, that reminds me he said talking about landing on your arse when did you jump last?. Four years ago I told him from a Dekota for a bit of fun with some mates why do you ask? You will be having a couple tomorrow afternoon iv been asked to arrange it he told me. No work that day I was given the rest of the day off after cleaning my gear and putting it away followed by a nice cooked breakfast and then some well earned kip. The next morning I helped Mary clean out the horses and pigs before doing some map reading that I found easy but I had always been good at it. Towards noon a van pulled up and about four carboard boxies were delivered to the farm, good said Roger this is your gear and ripped off the enverlope stuck onto the box marked one. Now you open the boxies and check off the kit as I read it out he told me. Two pairs of rubber boots. Box1. Four pairs of light fatigue trousers. Box 2. Four pairs of shorts. (jungle). Box 2. Four pair jungle green vests. Box 2. Six pairs jungle green socks. Box 2. One set of dp webbing. Box 3. Four pair of shortsleeve shirts. Box 3. Four pairs under shorts. Box 3. One ground sheet.(poncho style). Box 4. Two jungle green bush hats. Box 4. One cam light weight bush jacket. Box 4. You will need to try this gear on before you leave as once you go from here you wont be able to change any of it Roger told me. Everything fitted fine I told Roger after trying it all on but what do I put it in? I wont get it in my rucksack, try this he said throwing me a brand new kit bag. After a spot of lunch he drove me out to a small airfield which was for private members only and waiting for us was a small single engin aircraft that Roger owned. You going to fly it I asked ? in a bit of a nervous way, you bet I am he replied got over two thousend flying hours in this baby don't you trust me?.

I took a large intake of breath before I answered then said yes of cause I do, good go to the office and get a parachute and I will check the switches and controls. Once fitted I was back out by the plane, climb in he told me just finishing off my checks before we take off. I closed my eyes as we sped along the short runway and we was soon up in the air, do I really need to do this for the work I am going to do I asked? don't know he said but you might so its worth doing it. We reached a altitude of two thousend feet, now open the door as I cut the engine and jump he told me I did has I was told and soon I could feel the strapes pulling at my sholders as I glided down. I landed with a roll as I had been taught and rolled up my chute And waited for him to land and take me up for a second time. That night was my last night that I would ever see Roger and Mary so I envited them for a meal and a drink down at the village local as a thank you for their hospitality. The place was just as you would picture a village local with horse brasses everywhere old plows and tools hanging on the walls toby jugs on the shelf above the bar and a busty barmaid. We ordered our meals and Roger and myself had the local ale but Mary had a shandy, its nice to come out for a change she told me the farm can keep us very busy when there are crops in the field. Roger also seemed to enjoy the brake he knew everyone there and it had been a long time since he had seen them. It was not long before an old sing song was going Mary had a good vioce and Roger could bash the old spoons to most tunes. Then a bit of a jig was going I was hanging onto the barmaid while Roger and Mary plus four other couples spun around the floor to the home made music. With nothing happening the next day I let the beer flow and was informed by Roger that Dave would not be here till around noon so I had time to recover. Why would he becoming here I asked, well he will explain your job then if your happy you will be gone by the morrow he told me, as quick as that I asked? Yes as quick as that.

I had not thought about how soon, but I had nothing to go back to so what the worry and I let the night take its toll. Not remembering going to bed I awoke with the heaviest of heads that I had had for a long time, the room just spun and spun. Making my way across the room to the wash bowl I poured the water over my head to try to help clear the throbbing it felt good at first cold running over the heat but as I dried my hair the pain shot back. I dressed very slowly trying not to move my head to much and once my clothes were on I attempted the stairs, down one step at a time each one adding pain with the bump. Good morning Mary said as I made it to ground level I managed to get a morning back to her, breakfast she asked in a cheerful voice no thanks just a black coffee I replied and sunk into the nearest arm chair. You had a good night last night she shouted from the kitchen, don't remember much about it I told her was I really bad? No you was dancing mostly with the barmaid till you passed out and it was a good job you did you was asking her to marry you. "What" I shouted making my head hurt, yes you did and it was good for you that Roger picked you up because I think she was going to except your proposil. Where is Roger now I asked? He out in the fields with the tractor pulling up the cabbages, my heart told me I should go and help but my head wouldn't let me. I will just have my coffee and the go out and do my chores I told her, to late all done hours ago she replied its qauter to twelve. Dave was arriving at one thirty and I had only just got up, you should have give me a call Mary its only fair that I should help around the place. You would be lucky if you made it to the barn yet alone clean it out she replied with a chucle, that was a good night she repeated as she went about her cooking. I drank my coffee and could feel my head was starting to ease but not enough for me to get up and try to move around, another coffee Mary ask and some toast it will help soak up some of that alcohol That you drunk last night? Ok I will give it a try. Dave arrived a hour later pulling up outside the front door in a flash BMW car, he kissed Mary on the cheek as he entered, how's our boys today he asked her? Well Roger is fine but Ken over indulged with the local brew last night and he is in the living room feeling the worse for it.

I goodnight then he said to her? You bet she replied again with that cheeky smile I'll bring you a cup of tea in leaving Dave to enter the room on h8is own. Ihave been hearing nothing but good stuff about you he said once he had patted me on the shoulder, Roger has told me that you are the best trainee he as ever had. I would'nt say that I said he kept me on my toes and what he showed me made a lot of sense once he explained I answered. Maybe so but he tells me that he as never seen anyone as good as you when it comes to shooting a rifle, better than he was. So Roger was a marksman? The best around in his day

Dave replied he as taken shots for some of the biggest countries in the world including America who have some good shots of their own. Mary brought his tea and left the room closing the door behind her now down to businness first I will explain what it is all about and where. We would like to send you to Chad to do a little job for some world banker that are investing some money into the countries oil program. They are a bit worried that some rebel groups who are againt the countries leader will try to stop their plans. You will go out there today, if you agree to go into the trouble areas and take out any of the leaders who are stirring up trouble for those bankers. They stand to lose big bucks if these rebels succeed so they are willing to pay for your services generously but I will talk about the money side later. You will fly from Luton airport to Lisbon were you will meet up with the rest of the team, Are they the fifty that were picked at the club I asked? Only the four at your last meeting the others are going to another job I have. If you had fail here I would have used you on that other job as a signalier but I think you are just right for this job. Phillip or phil as you will call him will be going with you and he will be body guarding the countries leaders with the four lads, you will be sniping the area's that they go taking down any trouble. You will travel by boat to Marroco were you will pick up your weapons and fly on across the Shara into the north of the country to the airport at Bandai. You will then travel by road down to the capital N'Djamena where you will meet the Agent that has been sent by the money men to take care of your needs and pass on all the information he gets. What do you think so far he asked me? It sounds dangerous so I hope the money is good I answered, it will be and all tax free he continued. Chad has its own army and they don't like the idea of you lads being there but the bankers are insisting that if the money is going to be invested you will have to be there but don't ruffle the armys fethers try to aviod them as much as you can. There are a great number of rebel groups some are talkers and will put their point across a table but there are a few that will fight for what they wont. Your pay will be $30,000 a month paid into an account in your name for you to come home to, any money you need out there will be given to you by the agent this is extra to the thirty thousand. Well what do you say he asked me? What times my flight I replied.

CHAPTER TWO

I sat looking out of the window of the aircraft at white fluffy clouds Which looked snowy white with the sun on them, the captain had announced that we was now flying at thirty thousend feet over the bay of Biscay. Thirty thousend was a figure in my mind, twenty-five thousand pounds a month more then I had earned in any year before but had I done the right thing?. I had thought about it all the way to the airport with Dave but then the money came in and I just sat there and said nothing even when we went to buy my ticket and he asked me if I was ok with the deal I just said yes. Danger was with me again but this time there was a lot of money involved and that made a lot more difference to the times before when I put my life on the line. Closing my eyes I dozed off trying to clear all thoughts out my head and to shake off the headace that was a reminder of the night before when I had enjoyed my self so much. I found it hard to say goodbye to Mary and Roger they had become like family which I would never forget, a kiss on the cheek from Mary and a harty hand shake from Roger sent me off on this new adventure. I dreamed of the night before dancing and drinking with the locals and the barmaid getting very close to me pushing out her ample tits. Could you fastern your seatbelt sir please we are coming into land the stewardess told me as she shook me awake, Her face red and her eyes bulging at the sight of my large errection pushing up my trousers with some discomfort. Thank you was all I said and was glad she moved away so I could ajust my trousers to hide the offending sight, she made a few trips passed my seat before she finaly sat for landing. The touch down was smoth and soon we had stopped at the air terminal were we disembarked from the aircraft as I passed the the stewardess at the door she just smiled and said im sure you had a good flight.

I collected my gear from the baggage area and passed though passport control and customs before I went out into the large reception area hoping to find someone waiting for me. Phillip stood by a news paper kiosk and walked to me as I came into view of him, nice trip he asked me? Yes it was fine I told him I slept most of it. Dave said on the phone to me that you was a little worse for the night before partying, not idle way to travel with an hangover is it he asked ? Not really I answered. Leaving me with my kitbag he picked up my small suitcase and told me to follow him outside where he called a taxi gave the driver the case and jumped in. We have got two nights here before we set of by boat to Morroco so you will be able to sight see tomorrow and let yourself go tonight. We arrived at the hotel Regal where I found the rest of the lads sitting arround the pool drinking large glasses of beer playing cards. Phillip booked me in and the porter took my bags to my room while phillip introduced me to the guys as we had never relly introduced ourselves just saying hi and odd comments. Guys this is Ken nickname Brummie he is the shooter in the group A man we will all rely on very much to watch our arses phillip told them and they all said hi. Im Bill said the lad with a large beard nickname blast work with explosives and disposel. A tall lad with a scotish accent spoke next im Hamish nickname jock hand to hand combat expert love the knife he grinned. Next came the lad I had spoke to before at the club, im Tony from Newcastle nickname Gordie weapons expert. And finally came a mighty looking man six foot five tall with musles on his musles a real power house, im Don nickname tiny hand to hand combat expert also good with a baseball bat he to gave me a bit of a smile. As you all know my name is Phillip but as from now you will call me Phil, leader of this little group and what I say go's if you have any problems you bring them to me. As you have all arrived today from different airports and come straight here to the hotel you would not have got any local money so I will give you some to get you through the next two days. You are free to spend till midnight tomorrow night at your leisure but stay out of trouble and don't get into anything that would jepadise the job that we have to do in Chad. Tuesday at 05.30hrs we board a boat will take us to Morroco and once there we will go to a wearhouse on the jetty and collect our weapon, from there we will travel by truck to a private airfield where a transporter plane will fly us onto Chad. Then the long journey over the desert which we will do in three stages sleeping under canvers at night till we reach the capital as anyone got any questions about these travel arrangements? There was no reply. Good then gentlemen enjoy your stay in Lisburn and Phill was gone. We spent the rest of the day around the pool with the exception of me slipping out to buy some swimwear so I could enter the pool.

The beer flowed that evening and we chatted till late talking about our units in the army and where we went on tours. Next morning we discided to tour the city and see some sights taking on board a few beers as we went along, shopping was for little Keepsakes to remind us of this place which was a beautiful city. We found a club which we dicided we would use that night so it was back to the hotel for a dip in the pool a bite to eat and change into something appropriate for that evening. We all made a vow that like cindrella we would all be back at the hotel before midnight as we had that early morning boat trip to start our adventure. We arrived at the club early about seven-thirty but it was still full of young people, heading to the bar we ordered five beers at incredible prices and moved to a table still free. The dance floor was shiney and the room dark except for a few wall lights and the spinning globe of mirrows in the center of the floor being hit with a few spotlights imaging squire patterns around the room. Another beer and the lads hit the dance floor spliting up pairs of girls to dance with they was making sure that none of the women was attached to any men as they didn't wont any aggro this night. Jock soon had the girls flocking around him, he had put on a kilt with no underwear and the girls were sqealing as he twarled and jigged about. Tiny had his party piece too, he had lifted one girl on each of is upper arms and was spinning them around like a carousal exposing there panties as they went round but they loved every moment of it. Gordie and myself just sat watching the fun and keeping a close eye on the local lads to make sure there was no underhand planing going on but all seemed calm. Blast had found some sort of gambling game going in another room and was going to watch so he said but later that evening reappeared with a fist full of money. Soon the night was over and we all arrived back before midnight as we had promised we would to find Phil drinking at the bar so we had one for the road on phil and all went of to bed. Early the next morning the night porter phoned our rooms to let us know it was time to rise and breakfast would be ready in twenty minutes. I through my kitbag with the others in the reception area but decided to keep my small suitcase with me as I kept most of my money in it and didn't trust the hotel staff. The lads all sat at a large dining table, there was trays of assorted food placed around the middle and a side table contaned cereals and milk pots of tea and coffee plus juice. There was hams cheeses three types of bread bacon eggs fryed scambled boiled and poached, hash browns suasages beans tomatoes fryed bread and toast, mushrooms. God phil it looks like the last supper tiny said as we all sat down to eat, It may be the last English style food we have so tuck in and enjoy phil told us all. It was four thirty in the morning and I had never ate such a large meal at that time but I tucked in like the rest even making bacon and suasage sandwiches for later in the day. We finally reached the port and found the boat that was going to take us across to Morroco, it was not a large boat but it was comfortable the sort you would go out in to have a day out fishing. There was a small deck with lots of fishing rods stuck into brackets along the sides, a door lead you into a well furnished cabin which we could all sit in. Ether side of the door on the deck was a stair case leading to a upper deck with all the equiptment to run the boat radar, radio, steering wheel etc, A large window to watch where you was going and a sunbathing deck finished the tour. The sea was like a lilly pond but Tiny was sea sick after only a mile and with the size of the breakfast he had eaten he stayed with his head over the side the whole crossing.

The rest of us lads were fine and spent our time chatting about things back home and what they had done all except Phil who remained very quite. There was something about Phil I was not sure about, he seemed to be a loner who loved the power of command, he would watch you as you moved around but never spoke unless it was to tell you something or give a order. He was ex-para but nobody knew him and he never talked about his army days, but he must have been there as Dave had told us he had and had quite a good record, but I didn't trust him. We finally reached the port and said our thanks and goodbyes to the captain and his one crew member, Tiny was first ashore and made out that he had been sleeping and not barking up over the side but we all knew better. Phil told us to wait while he sorted out the customs for us I watched as he passed a wade of notes to the officer and we passed through without trouble. We walked along to a large wearhouse with our kit over our shoulders, the heat was burning my body through my shirt and I had been wise to wear shorts. Outside the wearhouse was parked a three tonner and Phil instructed us to load our kit on which we did laying it right up front of the truck, under the seats was alredy loaded with tents field stoves spare diesel water and food Right lads follow me Phil called and lead the way into the wearhouse, the inside looked bigger than the outside and it was full of alsorts of army equipment trucks, jeeps boxies of ammo boxies of weaponry rations you name it it was in there. We continued to follow Phil who must have been here before as he knew all the turns around the equipment we stopped at a large counter which reminded me of the qm stores back at my old camp. Right you will be collecting your weapons from here as well as your flack jackets and other weaponry so make sure you collect it all he growled at us. I was called first and given a American sniper rifle a silencer two scopes one normal one night a belt with a knife and sheth and a revolver ammo will be on the truck I was told. A small webbing rucksack was given to me to put all the small equipment in and I slung the rifle over my shoulder. Once all the lads had recived all their personal eqipment we were given some extra weaponry that we may need to be with us incase we needed it RPG's, C4, grenades etc.

Once we hand all the gear stowed on the truck Phil introduced us to Mustafa who was going to drive us to the airfield which was a hour and half away. Driving through the town was a whole new nightmare and we could see why Mustafa was driving, at time's we just crawled along for the traffic was so heavy. Car bikes animals they would all cut across you there was no such thing as right of way and as you was moving so slow people would jump on the tailgate trying to flog you something or anything. But once we was out on the open road we got our foot down and hit every pot hole there was our backsides were batterd black and blue and of course Phil sat in a soft seat in the front grinning at our discomfort. The other times when the traffic was slow, traders would jump on the tailgate and try to sell us a whole array of different items from handbags to carpets etc. We turned into a small field of dry dusty sand, this cannot be the airfield Blast asked there is not a runway, but airfield it was and down the far end of the field stood a tiny hut with a wind sock blowing about on its roof. There was no sign of an aircraft but there was a ground crew of two aging gents and a body of an old fuel tanker which must contain the fuel for the aircraft. Phil got down from the truck and spoke to the old men and was informed that the aircraft would be back soon as he had gone out to spray some land that had been taken over by locast in the night and the boss was asked to save the mans crop.

Right lads he told us get all the kit down and put it in a pile just here so we can get it aboard the plane when it arrives, if you want to smoke after you have unloded move well away from the fuel tank. With our work finished we all sat on the ground about a hundred feet from the tank, the truck had left us and started its return journey, got a fag Brummie asked gordie mine are in the bottom of my rucksack. This was a comment that I had heared meny times befor by someone who will smoke yours and save his it was very common in the army but I passed him one. Thanks mate you are a life saver he told me lighting the ciggy and taking a large draw on it, you attached back in blighty he asked me? No not me I said never got the time to find the right girl what about you?. Yes got a wife and three kids all girls he told me, one of the reasons I came on this caper two get some money to keep them all plus a break from all the nagging. We both laughed, im sure you don't mean that I told him, no she's not a bad old stick she must be some good to put up with me, we expressed more laughter. Anyone else got a family I asked? The only other one with family was Jock and he two girls and his wife, what do they think of you being here I asked them both don't they mind. Mine thinks im in the bookes Gordie announced to more giggles and Jock just said she don't know I told her I was going to look for a job in the south.

That finished the conversation about families as the sound of the aircraft approcing made us all get up and walk back to our kit. The aircraft landed and taxed close to the fuel tank so he could be refuelled, an old dekota a very old dekota that was dusty and rusty with markings that had wore off. Its wings were covered with red dust and the nose and windscreen had the splattered bodies of insects all over it, Should be on our way soon the pilot shouted down to us from the cockpit, if you get your kit on while we refuel and clean the windscreen we sould be ready by then. We all looked at each other with open mouths, is that thing safe Jock commented them bankers don't spend to much on transport do they, its about low profile Phil stepped in if we turned up in a flashy jet people would wont to know who we are. With the kit aboard we all found ourselves a seat and strapped in, The seating was still along the sides of the aircraft facing in just had it had been fitted for the day the lads used to jump from it. There was a stonge smell of a chemical which gave you a nasty taste in your mouth but we was told we would soon get used to it. I don't think we will get a wee bonny lassie on this flight Jock commented we will be lucky to get a drink Tiny barked, only whats in your bottles Phil again butted in now stop moaning. The engines started up one by one with the same spluter and cough that they always did in my days in the army but this time it seemed to be choking the life out of its self.

I thought about getting off but before I could move we were taxing down the runway (dirt track) then we picked up speed and with a few bumps the front lifted and we was in the air. Nobody moved a inch for a long time they just held onto anything they could hold but after a while when we could hear the purr of the engines we all settled down. You lot have been spoilt Phil shouted over the noise, in the old days we always travelled this way not those fancy 747's or any other jets. I looked him in the eye and saw him get uncomfortable for he knew that I was a bit older than him and was in service first and knew better than what he was saying. He changed the subject quickly, I would try and get some sleep the road is rough where we go to next and there is a lot of it and with that he spred himself along the bench seat. Myself and gordie followed suite but the others decided to play cards and settled in another area so as not to wake us with their sqabbles. A few bumps and engine nosies disturbed my sleep but all told I slept well with no bad dreams or thoughts of back home awaking me. Soon I felt the lightest of touches, we land in ten minutes Phils voice whispered in my ear and he was gone not wonting to look me in the face. My trust for him had already gone and I think he knew that I knew he was a bullshiter that he was never in the army or not in the mob he said he was and one day I would challenge him. The landing was no better than the take off the airfield was not one of the best that I had been on but was better than the one we had took off from. We stepped out of the aircraft onto Chad soil in a town called Bardai which was in the north of the country awaiting for us was two trucks and a guide to take us across the desert.

It is going to take us the best part of three days to reach the capital N'djamena Phil told us as we loaded the kit onto the trucks So make yourselves comfy in the trucks he grinned. Why couldn't we have landed in the capital I asked him with a glare of suspicion in my eyes?

Well even though the Chad heads of state know we are coming nobody else do's he explained. Even here there are reble eyes watching us but we hope they will think we are a group of exploreres or archiologist looking for relics for the museums of the world. If they look at Tiny they will think he is a relic from the past Jock said with a large grin on his face until Tiny threw a mess tin at him. Only joking wee man Jock said retreating into the back of a truck, stop mucking about and finish loading them trucks Phil growled I want us on our way as soon as the guide arrives. It was plain to see that Phil was going to be a right stick in the mud and a real control freak who will be making life hard for us. The guide arrived in a jeep and we watched as Phil threw his gear in the back of it, nice comfy ride he as got himself said Gordie? Yes I agreed more like a Rupert every time he opens his mouth. Once the trucks were loaded Phil gave one more order before we moved off Tiny you drive the first truck with Gordie in the cab seat Brummie you in the back, Blast you drive the second truck with Jock next to you. Keep a close distance to us and follow us everywhere we drive the sand out there can swollow a truck of this weight and with that he jumped into the jeep. We moved off from the landing strip up to a gate manned by government troops who acknowledged the guide and waved us through Without any show of passports or paper work. As we drove through the town I saw the rough living of the people, it was a hard life here in the north of the country where not much crops would grow and only certain animals could servive. I made myself comfy in the back of the truck using the tents to make a matteress but the heat of the sun made it very hot and sticky under the canvers but I think it would have been worse out in the open. Soon the town had gone and we was now travelling along a dirt road with sand finding its way through every opening in the truck canvas Making breathing very hard for me, I tied a cravate around my mouth to keep the sand out.

It became clear to me why I had been put in the rear of the truck. Looking out the rear of the truck I could see how dry the land was we were now crossing the area that was called Borkou ennedi tibesti An area that was bigger than the whole of France. There was some life in this area but we would be lucky to see it outside of the villages, vegetetion ranged from grass/shrub steppe to thorny, open savanna. This Saharan zone averaged less than 200mm of rainfall annually and the livestock was mostly small ruminants and camels. I had managed to pick up a African history book at the airport shop in England and was now reading as much as I could about Chad and its surrounding countries that land lock it. Gordie poked his head through the canvas at the front of the truck you ok he asked? Yes I replied its just the dust its choking me, I will try to tighten the straps this side but to do the other side we will need to stop, no don't stop we can do that side later I told him. With the one side fixed it did help keep the dust down and the other side was not to bad, it was the last thing I wanted was to stop and let Phil know that I was having trouble by his making. With the dust flying around not so thick I managed to brush the heavy stuff of my clothes and make myself a bit more comfortable but it still felt gritty around my face and neck. We finally reached our first night stop at a village called Zouar Phil raced from the jeep to watch me climb down from the back of the truck, you ok he said? with a bit of disapointment in his voice Im fine I replied slept well except for the bumps. The angery look on his face told me that from now on I would need to keep an eye on him as he was gunning for me but I dicided to get at him first. We was told to make camp and put up the tents, Phil once more had got himself a comfy hut were he would be out of the sand when it blowed about and got under your tent flaps. A fire was lite and a few of the locals came to talk to us and offer a type of bread they had made it was while I was cleaning my weapon I noticed Phil taking a strole and decided to follow him. He made his way to a hut were he stopped and looked about him then went in closeing a cloth sheet behind him so nobody could see in. I made my way closer and heard voices but couldn't make out what they were saying but to get closer would give me no escape if he came out suddenly so I watched for a while and then returned to the lads for a brew hoping that soon I would find out what he was up to. I had remembered what Roger had tought me and cleared my tracks in the sand so he wouldn't see that someone had followed him but when he returned the look he gave me was as if he knew. Brummie you take first watch as you got plenty of rest in the back of the truck two on then tiny will releave you for a meal, Blast next then jock and Gordie, why do we need to lookout for the villagers seem real friendly I asked. This bunch of desert rats I wouldn't trust them as far as I could throw them he replied they would cut your throat in your sleep, well you seem to have some friends here I pushed, what do you mean he ventured, well I just saw you go into a hut over there and you was chatting to someone.

You spying on me he screamed, no on the contre I was doing what you have just told us to do I was watching your ass after all we are all in a strange country are we not. He looked at me with a wild look in his eye and he knew he needed to say something as the lads were now as interested as I was, I was here once before a few years ago when they had a bit of trouble with there own people. And I piped in, and nothing I just did a little job for them and I don't wish to talk about it so brummie get on watch and you other get your food. With that he walked to his hut and again pulled down the cloth so he couldn't be seen, you got his back up there Brummie whats going on Jock asked? Not sure but something don't smell nice I told him and went off on petrol around our camp site. I made sure that the rest of the night that I slept with my weapon right beside me but we never saw or heared Phil again not even for his meal that the lads had cooked. The next morning he left his hut and came over to were I was breaking down my tent, I think me and you have started off on the wrong foot lets start again and try to be friends he said, I would pefer not to I replied as I don't like desert rats ether, I could kill you for that he said then stopped his advance at the sight of my gun Now look we need to get on as we must work together so lets forget all this and go and earn some money what do you say? he tried to coxs me, next time you force me to get you in my sights I will kill you I told him and walked away. With the trucks reloaded we was ready to go Gordie you take the rear of the truck today let Brummie go in the cab was Phils instructions and with that we boarded and set off. Today was a lot nicer day no wind so we could see the track a lot easer and Gordie popped his head by my side window to chat, don't know what you said to Phil but this morning he as been plesent to everyone, it was ease I said I just told him I would kill him. Gordie just grinned and moved back into the truck, you didn't realy tell him that did you Tiny questioned yes I did and best thing is he knows I would do it. Phil stayed away from me the rest of that day and when we stopped at our second night stop he just gave orders to Tiny to sort out the guard duties and to make sure I was on a late one. Faya Largeau was a bit larger village it was like a capital village of this area and what I noticed was that the people spoke more French than any other language but that too was a language I was not very good at. Blast on the other hand was fluant and had the locals eating out his hand, one took a shine to blast and kept tapping him and asking questions, Im not to sure but I think he wants me to come home with him to shag his wife. In your dreams I told him he will get you back there and put one up your arse, the lads all went into fits of laughter and Blast just sent the bloke packing without another word.

I looked over towards phils tent and he was standing there listening to the fun and I know he would liked to have joined in but took one look at me and retired through the flaps and went to bed. Faya Largeau was the region capital so there was a few more people about the place plus herds of camels which was the best form of transport in this area as they needed little water. Gordie and myself went for a stroll around after our meal and we couldn't beleave that people could live in such hard conditions, it was so dry and so hot even in the evening it felt like the sun was on you till later and the temprature seemed to drop. Even a few degrees made it feel colder, What you going to do with all that money when you get it Gordie asked in a casual way? I haven't give it a thought yet I told him I think I will get it first What about you? Im going to buy an house he told me and settle down, sounds good I said, whats with you and Phil he asked out of the blue we have all noticed that you two don't get on to well. I don't fully know I said but there is something strange about him he don't seem to be like the rest of us, What do you mean he asked? Well I don't think he was ever a para but I may be wrong. Dave said he was and I beleve that he was in the para's Gordie informed me, but did they serve together or is Phil pulling the wool over Dave too, but why would he do that? To be in command of this group maybe I told him.

I don't know he said I will keep my eyes open and see if I notice anything and let you know, yes you do that and tell the rest of the lads we just don't get on I don't want them sniffing around it may alert him if he is up to something. I pulled my late duty watching that Phil never left is tent which he didn't maybe I am barking up the wrong tree I thought to myself but we will see. We set off the next day to cover the longest part of our journey we would be staying in a village in the Kanem area at a place called Salai. I noticed that as we moved south so the land got a bit greener and a few more people were out on the tracks and roads, rain was in the air we was going to have a storm and boy did we have a storm. Moisture that had been building up in the high land to the north had moved down with the air flow and was now going to deposit it on the land. We reached our destination and erected our tents just before the storm hit, it was early evening and the sky got very dark, flashes could be seen in the distance as we erected the tents. Keep the gear well coverd Phil told us I have seen this before and it can get very wet and muddy, back the trucks tail gate to tail gate with a canvers over the gape between them that should keep the rain out of the backs. A loud crack of thunder informed us that the storm was here and then the heavens opened up with rain falling like bullets from the dark sky. Soon the dry land was soaked and muddy pools were forming all around us in our tents, people and animals struggled to run to shelter in the mud and the flashes lite up the whole sky like shearch lights. We managed to get a brew on and had a meal of biscutes and tinned cheese from our compo rations there would be no cooked meal tonight.

The storm went on for a few hours and even when the rain stopped the thunder could be heared in the distance and it continued through the night till first light. To our surprise next morning the rain had soaked away into the dry soil just leaving a few muddy puddles here and there but every thing looked a lot greener with grass showing in parts. We will be pushing on non stop today I want to reach N'djamena by early evening Phil informed us so get a good breakfast and I want a volanter to make up a meal as we are going along to keep us going. We will have one stop for a pee so empty as much out now as you can, the meal can be handed out at that break, Why the rush I asked? We are to start working tomorrow he stated and we will need a good rest tonight in real beds, and I want you on the ball in the morning. With food finished and tents packed away we started out 06.30hrs each truck starting first time which surprised me with there age. I had climbed into the back of the first truck and open a ration box and found a few tins of bully beef and compo marg so with the bread that the villagers had given us I made up sandwichs. We had some powdered lemon so I added water and made a drink for them all, it was not perfect but it would fill the gape till the main meal that evening. Four hours into the journey we enter the area called Hadjer Lamis which was a much greener area with crops growing all over woodlands and a lot more people and traffic on the road. Stopping on the outskirts of Massakory which was the area capital we took our piss break and I handed out the food and drink, Phil thanked me for making the food but it broke his heart to have to say it. The lads found the drink very refreshing and said it was just what they needed to break the thirst, Tiny asked if I had a beer as that was the only thing that broke his thirst. We was now in the area which was near to lake Chad so we was seeing more rivers and streams and after last nights storm they were swollen and pushing through with some speed.

The roads were a lot better and we could put our foot down a bit harder so it was not long before we was on the main road to the capital and near to the end of this journey. 17.00hrs we reached our goal and pulled up outside a army barracks, Phil chatted with the guard who call for his sargent who called his officer who finaly rang someone to confirm that we should be here. We was showen to a large hut where we was to bunk for the time we was there, unload all the gear less the tents Phil told us we wont need them again he said to a load cheer from the lads. What about the trucks Blast asked are we going to use them? No was the reply we will have one jeep plus other transport but not sure yet of what that will be Phil confirmed. Inside the hut was quit homely, there was five beds spaced out around the room one corner had a kitchen area and though a door was a shower/wc room and another small room which was Phils bunk. We each claimed a bed and a locker and stowed away our gear Jock got a brew on and Phil rejoined us to give us the low down on the place and the orders for the next day. Right you can see that we have been given this hut to ourselves as that's the way the milatry here want it, like I said before they don't like us here but they need the world banks money to invest in the oil project so here we are. The head of state one Idriss Deby and his government are not liked and rebels are trying to oust them out, because all the deals have been made with this government they need us to protect there interest. If anything should happen to this man the world banks stand to lose a lot of money, and if they don't the banks will make a large profit from the oil I said with a snarl. That's true Phil confirmed but that's not for us to judge we are here to do a job and get paid the politics we can leave to the polititians. Now around the camp we cannot use any of there facilities that's why we have our own kitchen we will cook for ourselves, fresh supples will be given to us every two days. If and when we get time off it will be spent here or down town, with a warning that if you go down town you do so as a group individualy you would not be safe is that understood, we all nodded. So there are no bars on camp that we can get a drink asked Tiny? At the moment no but I will see what I can do. With that he told us to get a meal on the go and he would be back soon, whats in the larder? Jock asked looking down at the compo boxies.

Well let me see said blast reading the contents of each box, box (x) has chicken supreme as main meal processed cheese and biscutes as another meal and oatmeal biscute for a breakfast meals for four men he continued. Box (y) contained a main meal of Irish stew, box (a) had a main meal of salmon in white sauce, and finally box (z) had corn beef and vegitables in a gravy. We all screwed up our faces at the thought of any of those meals but our pallets was saved as a knock on the door reveled two cooks carring a pot of steaming food and two more men with a tea earn. We thanked them in Blasts best French and they left us to it, not telling us what it was, well the tea is fine Gordie said pouring himself a cup after finding some mugs in the kitchen area. I grabbed some metel plates from the same area and filled one with the hot food, well I said there is meat in it and some veg but don't ask me what they are, I took a small bit on the spoon and tasted it.

It was rice in flavour but it was nice I grabbed a chunk of the bread they had brought with the meal and started to tuck in, soon the others followed and all got stuck in. Phil returned with two more men in tow carrying four crates of tiger ale which they put down and left, so the answer to my question was no then Phil Tiny asked? that's correct but they said they will surply us with anything we require I am just to leave a note with the gaurds as we go out every day. Whats the food like Phil inquired? Its good I answered but we don't know what it is, best not know Jock piped in that way it wont harm anyone. It was Tiny that almost spoit the meal by asking do they have rats here, don't know was the answer but if you find a tail keep it to yourself we don't wish to know I told him. Tiny tucked into seconds and thirds so it must have been fine and the rest of us seemed very content once the meal was over. Our hosts had trried to hide their lack of welcome by leaving a lot of books and magazines mostly in French but some in English and I found one all about Chad past history and geography. I lay on my bunk with two bottles of tiger and started reading the book, Chad always seemed to have its troubles from way back in time and most of it was it was land locked with six other countries. To the north was Libya to the east was Sudan, west was Niger and Nigeria southwest was the Cameroon and south was Cental African Republic. In the early days before air travel inports would have to come across land and most were exposed to robbers and extorsion by the other contries that charged them for crossing their land. There was also the elements that they faced from the long journies they had to travel to get to the bigger cities. N'djamena is 1,100 kilometers northeast of the Atlantic ocean, Abeche which is a major city to the east is 2,650 kilometers from the Red sea and Faya Largeau which is northern in the middle of the sahara desert is 1,550 kilometers from the Mediterranean. Chad stretches from 1,800 kilometers from its most northen tip to its southen boarders and averages a width of 800 kilometers, with an over all area of 1,284,000sq kilometers nearly twich the size of France. I gave the lads all the figuers that I had just read, hope we never have to walk Jock commented I hope we are not asked to visit the beach came from Gordie, Tiny asked how many pubs there was, blast couldn't give a shit.

Phil said there are some good points there as we may have to cover a lot of this country doing our duty for the government, we maybe ask to go where there are troubles could effect the welfare of the oil supples all I know is that the drilling is down south of here. Do you know what we are doing tomorrow Gordie asked? Yes we are to meet our transport at the gate by seven thirty to escort a convey of diplomats to a meeting in the centre of the city.

Brummie you will be out at six to sweep the route and find a vantage point were you can watch and cover the entrance to the building. Transport will be at the gate for you and our agent will give you all the information you will need to carry out your task, I glanced at him if Gordie had not asked the question when was you going to tell us this information I growed at him. In about an hours time when you had had a few beers to settle you in was anything wronge with that he growled back at me, I rolled over and turned my back on him. I sensed his movement towards me but his voice gave him away, iv had enough of you he shouted and made a dive in my direction but not fast enough I spun and planted a foot squire on his jaw sending him spinning into the lockers. I sprang up from my bed and grabbed him by his hair swinging his head back towards me and planted a left cross which contacted on his nose and we heard the bone break. Down he went like a sack of spuds with blood trickling down his cheek, he coughed trying to get some air into his lungs, before I could continue my attack Tiny grabbed me and pulled me away. This is no good he shouted we all have to live together and we need you both to do this job so for the sake of the rest jack it. Tiny's words pulled me from my anger and I had to admit it was not good for the others this constent bickering between us. Ok mate im cool now, just needed to get it out my system but I want to know what mob he was in? it was not the para's. Phil picked himself up of the floor with gordie and Jocks help and wiped his face, is that whats bugging you he said to me, well it will have to bug you more as I am not saying nothing. Dave told me you are the best there is other wise I would send you home now so all I want from you is to do your job and not stop the others earning and at the end if you want a piece of me we will do it. With his comment about the others earning had put them in a mood against me and they showed it with there comments. Ihave come to earn some cash and im sure I am not going to let anyone stop me getting it came from Blast and the others nodded in agreement. I turned and lay back on my bunk but knew in my heart that this was not over but if I wanted to get on with the lads I would have to let things rest for now.

Phil retired to his room and the rest just went into another corner to play cards and there was a lot of whispering but nothing I could hear so I set my watch for the morning alarm and went for a shower. Phil was cleaning himself up as I entered but nothing was said, looking back towards the door I could see Tiny standing watching to make sure nothing kicked of again. I didn't sleep well so I was awake before the alarm call, passing the time cleaning my weapon and dressing in the gear I would wear for that day I finally slipped out the door to meet the agent.

At the gate was a old banger waiting with a american spoken person in the drivers seat, get in he told me put your rifle case in the back you wont need it yet. My name is Tim Grant he told me as I sat down in the passangers seat, they call me Brummie I told him, do I call you mr Grant or tim please call me Tim. Iam going to show you the route that the cars will take and I will let you tell me the weak spots so I can get them coverd is that ok, that's fine I said remembering what Roger had told me. The journey will take them about forty-five minutes he told me so there is a large area to cover but we have the men to do it just your expertise is needed. We started from the gates of a government building that was well covered with guards and camera's nobody would try anything here so we moved on down the route. Moter escorts will stop all traffic at major junctions he told me so we should not have to slow down, at one junction there was work going on at a building put some men on the scaflding I told him That would be a place where I would take a shoot lots of escape routes. He put in a radio call to request that that would be done with the effect as now, men were sent straight away. The whole of the route was planned like this so we had every angle covered, but when we reached the hall were the meeting was taking place there was a group of demonstraters. What the hell is this I asked him?, these are from a group that think the money for the pipe line would be better spent on schools and hospitals we are trying to prove to them that they will get them things but they are armless. What do you mean armless I queried? They have been shearched For weapons and they will be kept well back behind the barriers Tim confirmed. I told him to stop the car at the front entrance so I could look for the position that I would like to be and get set up in plenty of time you have about three hours before they get here he told me.

That's cutting it close I told him I will have to find a spot check that nobody spys on me by moving around and then set up in readiness for their arrival, ok buddy you do your thing. Has I was about to move from the vehical he handed me a small radio, your friends will be on the same freqence and so will I so any trouble give us a call. I wondered around for about thirty minutes after seeing where I wonted to be after just five, I finally made my way up to a position on the building across the street from the hall using a outside stair well to get to the roof. I called Tim to let him know that I was in position and he asked me where, that's my information I told him. But what if any of my men see you they may take a shot at you? don't worry they wont see me I told him.

Opening my case I removed each part of my snipper rifle as I needed to assemble it ending with the sight and the silencer, I finally hide the case were it couldn't be seen and settled in my position. I checked the arch of fire and discovered that I could cover the whole of the area that I needed to including a bit more. I put the cross sections onto the head of one of the demontraters And sqeezed the trigger slowly, not loaded but it would have been a sweet shot if it had have been. Checking my watch I noticed that I had a full hour before the arrival of the deligations so I just settled back and watched the movements of the people below me. It was about half an hour later when my radio crackled and a voice came across the airways, it was Phil calling all stations for a radio check, Tim had given me a call sign of one bravo. One bravo ok over I call softly into the radio mike and heard each of the lads confirm their status by saying their call sign and ok over Phil finished with an ok out which told us had received all our calls. Even if they had not had call signs I would have known who was answering out of our lads they all had strong accents and that would of told me. Phil came back on the radio, one bravo this is nine are you in position over? I smiled at the fact he had a call sign of nine that was the commanding officers call sign in the mob. One bravo affirmative over, good he continued we sould be in your vicinity in about ten repeat ten minutes so make sure you are alert and ready for us out.

That made them twenty minutes early, I wondered why but never asked just raised my rifle up to my face so I could see through the sight down towards the ground level and watched for their approach. Everything seemed calm all the troops were in place, demostraters well surrounded a quick glance around the roof tops of the other building showed the other sniper belgoing to the army alert and ready if needed. A red carpet had been rolled out along the walk way and up the steps leading into the building, honour guards stood awaiting their salute at the top section. There was six on each side and I scanned their faces though the rifle sight, each of them looked the part except for one, standing to attention they all looked the way you would expect them to stand but this one was different. He looked nervous he was sweating and I could see a slight tremble in his shoulders just at that moment a car pulled up and out got all the lads moving to stations that would cover the arrivals. Phil stood ready to open the door of the next car that pulled up that of Idriss Deby the leader of the present government in Chad. Has he moved forward up the red carpet I put my sight back onto the nervous soldier, his hand had moved from the precent position and was bringing the rifle to the firing position. Ihad no time to warn anyone on the radio as this was a split second reaction I just aimed and squeezed the trigger and I just felt the kick of my rifle. I checked my aim and fired again both rounds hit there target, one In the throut the second in the fore head and the soldier went down like a sack of spuds. Now all hell let loose screaming from the women shouts from the men our lads grabbed Mr Deby and rushed him into the building and out of harms way, The demontraters were all running away as the police and troops charged them with battons and tear gas.

Hello nine this is one bravo, target was making a move with his weapon had to take the shot over, roger that you will need to vacate your position and make to find your agent friend who will get you back to HQ Phil informed me. Keeping down low I moved away from the edge of the building stripping my weapon down as I went and made my way down the outer stairs to the street level. I turned the corner and headed towards the area that Tim had dropped me off only to be meet by a group of milatry police who pointed their weapons at me. I didn't understand what they was saying but their actions and aggression told me I needed to lay on the floor and not move which I complide to their order. One stepped up and opened my case and once he saw my rifle all hell broke lose, I was hit and kicked until I lost conscousness. I came to in a hospital ward with a doctor and two nurses taking care of me, what the hell happened I ask but nobody answered my question. Each area the nurses touched gave me great pain and I could taste blood in my mouth and my nose was blocked with dry blood. Brummie a voice called out from the other side of the room, it was Gordie silly question but how do you feel? Like I have been kicked by a herd of stampeding bulls I replied to him. I noticed that Tim was standing beside him, what the hell happen I said? The milatry police didn't see what had happened and they thought that you had tried to assasinate Mr Deby. I have an appolage here from their commanding officer he sends is regrets and hopes that you will recover soon, you also have a message from Mr Deby who sends his many thanks to you and his looking forward to decorating you. The soldier you killed was a member of the rebels but which group was not known he had kill a soldier and stole his uniform so as to take his place in the guard of honour. A number of people saw his action but were not able to responed as quick as you did so well done, Tim reached out to shake my hand but the pain made me dicline. The other lads were here but you was out so they told me to tell you that they will pop in later, what about Phil I asked did he come down? No he said he had to write a report. Funny thing was the milatry police said they was told by one of our guards that it was a sniper that had taken a shot at Mr Deby and pointed them in the direction after the shooting.

I contacted Phil within seconds of making that shot and it was him that told me to come down, Brummie I know you don't get on but he wouldn't line you up for this beating, you think not I answered. Tim looked at me is there something I should know he asked? No I replied just a mis-understanding. What do's this doctor think is the matter with me and how long will I be layed up? He spoke to the doctor then replied to me. You don't have any broken bones just some bad brusing around the ribs and face a few nights rest and you will be out in a day or two. With that I did start to feel tired, what happened to my rifle I asked closing my eyes and feeling really drowse, its safe was all I heard then I was gone, the doc had given me something to help me sleep. For two days I rested and all the lads came to visit me all except Phil, the brusing was now really coming out and my ribs were a blacky blue purple if there was such a colour. I had got a couple of stiches in my left eye that I had not notice when I had first awoke but now they had a large dressing covering them. You can leave tomorrow Tim told me when he came to visit me again They say that you must not do anything to heavy and you must have the stiches out in another ten days. That's good news I need to get back to work I told him I have a few things I need to clear up, well it will be another week before you will be able to move around so just take the rest until then Tim told me. It was midday once the doc checked me and let me go he gave me some pain killers which I was grateful for and wished them all thanks and a goodbye. Tim collected me and took me back to the barracks were I was greeted by the lads who had got a day off and were going into town you feel up to coming? Tiny asked me or are you to worn out from shaging those nurses?.

The pain I was in I couldn't raise to a wank I told him yet alone a fuck, you lads get yourselves off I will see you later and have a good time for me, bring me a few beers. An hour later and Phil entered the billet, oh, your back then he said I was going to come and see you but work got a bit heavy. Do you mean you was going to come and look at the handy work that you did by telling them milatry police I was a sniper trying for Mr Deby life, I don't know what you mean he said I didn't tell anyone anything. His face went red, I think it would be better if I sent you home he said you will need some rest for a while, you try and send me home and I will kill you as you sleep I told him. There is something not right about you and I am going to find out what it is and if it puts any of us in danger I will kill you. He looked at me with a sickly smile as if he knew that what I was saying I would do, you have got nothing on me he barked now get off my back before I his words were interrupted by Tim entering.

Just the man I want he said to Phil, the day after tomorrow we need to set up a op at a site by lake Chad we need two men, Phil couldn't get it out of his mouth quick enough take Brummie and Gordie they are mates. Will you be up to it Brummie you should be resting for another week at lest he told me, no I will be fine I said tell me what it is about. All the while we talked I never took my eyes off Phil and he did the same to me, after Tim had finished he asked me again if I was up for it and I told him if I don't do it Phil was going to send me home. Not on your nelly Tim said you cannot go home you are going to receive a award from Mr Deby once we can arrange a date he wants to shake your hand, it was just a thought Phil pipped in to save his shame of being over riden. Another thing Tim said I have never seen two rounds hit a target as fast and as accurate as those did my report will state that to the bankers and they will insist he stays.

Phils face got redder and redder ok he snapped he stays like I said it was just a thought and with that he left the room, I don't know whats going on with you two but if you have any trouble let me know Tim winked then he left the room. Over the next twenty-four hours plans were made of how Gordie and myself would travel and the cover story we would have if stopped and questioned by any of the locals to the area. Phil made sure he had a input into work as he told Tim these two men are on our pay roll and sould get paid for work they do, Tim told him this was an extra job that had been requested and we would be paid by him. But never the less Phil sat in at all our planning, do they need one of our vehicals he asked? No Tim replied they will use a range rover suppled by the water authorities as they will be acting as water consultants. You will keep your weapons concealed and only use them if it is absolutely nessasery too, Tim warned us, there are local troops in the area but they will not be told of your presence as we don't what anyone to let it out the bag.

The government had had a tip off that there was to be a meeting of a few different rebel groups in the area of the lake, we was to try and find out when and where this meeting was to be by talking and listening to the locals. You will have a radio in your vehical so you will be in contact at all times and I would like a report every evening to let me know your progress and news of any rebel plans. You will set of at six in the morning with another group of maintanace men who are checking some pipe line that we are installing to transfere some water to a plant of ours so good luck. At six the next day with Gordie at the wheel we set off behind two works trucks carring pipes and other materials needed to build this pipeline. Heading north easterly out of N'Djamena we followed the river Chari on route to lake Chad about fifty-five kilometers away, the river was one thousend two hundred kilometers long and ran from its oragin in the mountains of the central African republic.

In the rainy season it floods its banks and turns the ground to mud but in a few days it as all dryed up and soon returns to normal leavels leaving the land coverd in vegetation. We was inform that some rain was expected so we needed to get to the lake before the rain fell and cut off this road for a few days. Geordie was his normal fun self on the trip up to the lake and never once showed any concern for the job ahead, we became real mates talking about our school days and where we grew up as kids. We arrived at the lake around noon after we had stopped to repair a puncher on one of the trucks plus a few calls of nature. What a sight meet us this was truly a place of beauty with hundreds and hundreds of flocking birds landing from every direction, one of the locals told us in his best English that there was over one hundred and fifty different species of birds that lived around the lake. We pitched up our tent and made a brew before going to the waters edge and taking samples of the water so we would be seen to be doing our job, a few locals came to watch but nothing with a weapon. The locals came over very friendly and gave us some fish they had caught earlier that morning so supper was a treat that first night. Our companions left us that next morning and headed to the sight where they was laying the pipeline, by now the rain was falling steady at first then it fell like buckets. We stood watching as the kids jumped up and down with excitement we also watched the lake rise a couple of meters and knew then why we was told to camp higher up the bank. The land around us soon started to flood and we was left stranded on a island surrounded by water with no safe place to walk without sinking in the mud so we just stayed near the vehical and tent. There is one good thing I told Gordie there will not be any meetings around here till the rain stops, yes he agreed but if they move it somewhere else we will be stuck here.

The night passed and the rain had stopped soon the sun was burning the wet ground and steam was lifting high into the air like a giant steam bath that you would see in Turkey. Once the water had cleared the local kids were back with fish that we paid them for and we found the we was starting to understand there lingo a lot more now but it was more actions than words. One young man in his early teens spoke a reasonable amount of English and told us that they was going to make some good money the next day as many men are coming to the lake so they would sell plenty of fish. I glanced at Gordie, this was the news we were waiting for, so no fish for me tomorrow I asked the lad? No he replied we have to catch them down the bank a bit more to be near to men he pointed. That was as good as showing us were the meeting will be and for how long we have no fish I continued to question without giving to much away. One maybe two days but no worry we will come back as soon as men go he told me with enthusiasm and we bring you big fish from up that end of lake. The rest of the day we took more water samples and went through the motions of testing the water as we would do if we was experts on water pullution. That night we called Tim and told him what we had learen't, so have you seen anybody there yet? No not yet but we are going to break camp and move up stream in the morning I told him and once we make contact we will inform you. That's good but be careful these people don't mess about they also don't take prisoners especially spys, I am reading you load and clear I expressed we will be careful. We pulled the tent down at first light and set off about five kilometers feather round the lake till we noticed a small gathering of me with camels.

We made camp about four hundred meters away from their camp and started work collecting water samples, it was not long before we had company and a real band of cut-throats they looked. What are you doing here we was asked by what looked like a well to do young man who was more like an European than African except for his cloths. We have been asked by your government to run tests on your water to see if there are no impurities or bacterias thet could hurt your heaths I told him very professionally. We work for world water Gordie continued, we go all over the world testing waters to see if they are drinkable, last month we was in the Amazon rain forest and found a stream that had that much acid in it that it would have burn't out your throat. You could see the man was not all that interested, we would like it if you would test your water back that way he told us pointing back the way we come. But we need to take sample in different areas I started till five weapons came out from under there clothing and where pointed in our direction, fine I said we will leave and without another word pulled down the tent. Them our boys Gordie said? as we was driving back the way we came, not a doubt I told him, get on the radio and let Tim know While I find a place we can hide and watch them.

We found a bit of high land just north of the lake which looked down on the rebels camp site I parked the van off the road and we walked to a area which was thick with grass and thorny bushes. It was not comfy but it gave us enough cover to watch and not be seen. I got gordie to stay with the van while I crawled out to the edge of the cover so I could look down towards the lake and see what was going on. A few more had arrived at the site now and I could count about fifty milling around a large fire they had lit and in the middle was a few of the children trying to sell their fish. I noticed the young teenager that had given me the information about the group standing in the centre of the largest group doing some real hard selling, he was putting up a good argument to get the right price when the same man that had moved me approached him. Words were exchanged before this brute of a man grabbed the fish and slapped the face of the young man who went down clutching his face. He hit the floor only to spring back up and try to get back his fish again the man hit him only this time it was a punch, you are mine I said to myself feeling my anger surge up in my body. Once more the lad got back on his feet and tried to retrive his goods but this time the brute had lost his patience and pulled a knife and plunged it into the lads chest twice. The young mans face twisted and he clutched at his wound and let out a scream of pain that even Gordie heared back at the van, then he dropped to the floor dead. If I had got my rifle with me I know brain matter would have been spread all over the ground surrounding that brute but I knew that would have compromised the situation. Making my way back to the vehical I felt so empty inside a few days ago I had killed my first person and that had given me a shock but today I wanted to kill that man so badly I could dry to do it. Brummie" what happened Gordie asked in a conserned voice? That bastard killed that teenage boy I replied and I'm going to kill him.

You cannot do anything now he told me, Tim is on his way here with a hundred government troops to lock them all up. Did you manage to speak to Tim personally? No it was Phil he passed my message on and called me back with Tims answer. God I don't like that I said and rushed back towards to edge of the cover to see what was going on below, I was not surprised to see that the tents had been pulled and the fire put out. Most of the rebels were speeding off in all directions only a handful was still there loading there camels until they to was on their way and soon out of sight. The lads body had been buried on the shore you could just make out where the ground had been disturbed and the brute was well gone, I stood up and walked back to Gordie. They was tipped off I said they've all gone, Phil" I said I think he told them, that don't make sense why would he do that he is here to help protect against the rebel groups like we are Gordie insisted. They may of got the wind up about killing the kid and scarpperd Maybe I said but I still smell a rat. Tim arrived with the troops to the disapointment we had to tell him, he ordered the body to be dug up and taken back to his village to be buried by his family. I will send out a few patrols to pick up any individuals on the roads but the chances of getting any of them will be slim they will hide in the desert and wait till another day.

Tim I asked did Phil seem concerned when he gave you the message was there any sign that this was a good bit of news?, no not really he replied he just said you had made a contact and told me were you was. Do you think he is up to something? No it may just be me but I will be watching him from now on and I will let you know if I find out anything. We stayed around for two more days but nothing happened it was as if everyone stayed away from that part of the lake except the kids selling the fish they always came around. We returned to N'Djamena and to the duties that we was being paid for and for a few weeks nothing happened except I was called to meet president Idriss Deby who awarded me a gallentry medal for saving his life. Phil spent as little time as he could around me and only made conversation when he had to but that suited the books as I wanted as little to do with him as I could. The rest of us bonded well, the lads just ignored what was going on with me and Phil and just got on with the job. News came one day that there was some trouble kicking off in the east of the country in a place called Adre which was on the Sudan boarder. This was the latest raid of a few which the Chad's blamed on Sudan They blamed them for formenting unrest along the border and protecting rebel groups from Chad in their country. About two hundred men from the garrison were sent and we was asked to go with them for a birds eye view of what some of the new rebel groups forming in Chad looked like. Full kit Phil shouted from his room as we all packed to go, weapons and ammo to carry, grenades one box plus some semtex for demolition Jobs rations for four days.

The Chad army will supply us with any other ammo we might need he told us so don't over load yourselves with it. With that we boarded a aircraft and flew to Abeche were we was trucked to the trouble area at night so the rebels wouldn't know of the build up of the army waiting for them. I made myself a job of watching Phil and keeping a close watch when he was near a radio but he did have a cell phone that worked sometimes but not always to weaker signal. We was positioned near a radio tower Blast set up some trip mines across our front while Jock set up a machine gun post at the front gate Tiny set up another on the roof. Phil myself and Gordie plus Blast with his switchs set up a firing point along the front door. Now don't forget the government troops are in charge of this oparation and we only get involved if we are attacked, this radio tower is a important asset for this part of the country.

Don't fire till I give the order Phil continued, we don't want any mistakes and bystanders getting hurt watch for government troops they may run across your line of fire. Why didn't the troops protect this station I asked looking at him with a suspicious frown? They have been tipped off that the attack is coming down the road from the north and have deploded all their men to counter that attack. The answer was lodgic with the size of the force they had sent, Chads army was stretched with all the trouble spots and new groups that were forming every day against them but this didn't seem right. Don't worry you will be safe here Phil said to me with a smirk on his face, I know you are used to hiding and not being seen when you fight. I felt my blood boil but didn't take the bait he was throwing at me I just put a clip into my rifle and pointed it in his direction, this time he went red and looked nervous and moved as if to check Blasts had set his charges right. God you two really hate each other Gordie said when he was out of hear distance, yes I replied but there is something strange about this set up I don't like the feeling im getting but I don't know why. Twenty minutes later we found out why, from a distance we heard the noise of vehicals aproching, there engins was roaring with the speed they was doing. They are coming from over the boarder I shouted and they are coming our way take cover, remember Phil shouted don't fire till I give the order, don't foget to give it I commented load enough for him to hear what I had said.

Soon they came into view arround seventeen vehicals with men hanging out windows or loaded onto the back of trucks all armmed and screaming anti government curses. Each one of us cocked our weapon putting a round into the chamber in readiness of what was to come, I glanced at Phil who looked as if he was ready to run but seeing my look made him stay. Two vehicals headed towards the gates and Phil looked again at me Blast I shouted let them have it throw the switch Phil as if in a startle repeated my order. The first explosion sent the front car high into the air bodies fell from the windows and car parts littered the ground as they returned to earth. Fire at will Phil commanded with another glance at me before he discharged his weapon in the direction of the enemy or as near as it looked. My first round hit the driver of the second vehical making it swerve to a halt and tip the contents of the back onto the road, our two machine guns made light work of the rebels as they rose to their feet. The other trucks drove around in circles peppering builds as they past but it was obvious that the tower was what they was after. Forming a blockade using the trucks they stopped one behind the other and used the cover of the trucks to fire at us. It got so heavy Jock had to retreat from the gate and form again along side us which gave them a chance to move closer to their goal Phil jumped to his feet and shouted I will get help and was off before I could stop him.

I didn't have time to notice which way he had ran as I was now busy knocking down rebels as they came through the gate at us. Tiny sprayed the front row of charging men, bodies were flung backwards into the second group of chargers giving us time to reload our weapons. Shit Gordie shouted this is getting dangerous how many are there Just keep knocking them down I told him over the noise or you wont be here tomorrow to talk about it. We was pinned down now by now only Tiny could move to help us from being over run and he did that job with expertise taking down row by row as they ran towards us. Then more vehicals arrived but to our delight they were government troops and soon the rebels headed off back towards the boarder with the troops following them. I picked myself up of the floor as did the others all covered in sweat and mentally and physically exhausted, we had all made it without a scratch but only just and no thanks to Phil.

CHAPTER THREE

Once we arrived back at the barracks there was no sign of Phil he had disapered, the only reason we were alive was that the troops had heard the fight we was putting up and came to help. I told you he was up to something I address the lads in our room, he was just a chicken shit Tiny said that's all, he was more than that I think he lead us into that attack. You cannot be sure Jock challenged me he may have lost his nerve and ran off we was all shitting ourselves was we not? Yes I admitted but I think he knew that attack was coming and tried to get out before it started but I stopped him. That's true Gordie said I witnessed that, but I am still not sure that he knew about the attack on the radio tower. Well I think it all stinks of shit I told them and nobody will change my mind, what about you Blast you have not said much? I wish to keep my thoughts to myself at the moment he replied but if he don't return we need to let Dave know. Tim arrived at that moment, well done lads he said I hear you did well, the army are reporting that the rebels lost over three hundred men and your position acconted for half of them.

That's about right I said but it nearly cost us our lives we was not surposed to be in the fight unless we bumped into some rebels while in that area instead that was the main force we encountered. Well we will investigate what went wrong but at lest your safe. Tiny told Tim that Phil was awol and that he needed to contact Dave so Tim took him to his office so he could use his phone. Thirty minutes later he was back, Dave told me to tell you to take over Blast as you was a sargent in the mob and we are to carry on getting our instructions for Tim. Iwill do it, but the first one of you that steps out of line I will kick shit out of you and send you home have you all got that, we all said yes as we knew he could do it. Tim wanted a report of what happened and I was given the job to write it, Blast told me to tell it as it was but to leave out my thoughts on Phil, if the bankers think we have trouble in our ranks they could pull out of our deal with Dave. I had to admit I also needed this job so I just told it as it was just reporting that Phil had gone missing. We had two days off before we had to escort president Deby to his next engagement so we hit the town and let our hair down Tim even joined us. Tiny had found out about a knocking shop were the girls was something to look at white girls not blacks they all came from France and spoke good English. Gordie Tim and myself decined and went to find a bar were we could get a cold beer or two and sit and relax, Tim took over the paymaster job that Phil had been doing and he gave us all some funds.

We found a nice little place and ordered some beers before we sat at a table in the window and watched the comings and goings in the street. You two know each other a long time Tim asked? No we both said, we meet at the meeting for this job Gordie replied, we were in different units in the mob I continued so we never bumped into each other but I dare say that our paths crossed somewhere out there. Tim told us that he had never done any milatry service he was always working in the diplomatic department and spent some time in Vietnam working with the heads of state. He came from Kansas but didn't sound like your normal yank and was not as arrogant nether he was a real nice fellow. Has we chatted I glanced out the window towards the club where the lads had decided to go for the girls, I noticed a few shady men standing on the corner looking in the direction of the club. One looked like the brute that kill the boy at lake Chad and I dived for the door without a word to the others. I hit the street at few speed and noticed the other man with him was Phil but before I got to the road an explosion knocked me of my feet and forced me up against the wall of a shop. Dazed I got to my feet to find Gordie and Tim helping me up, god the lads I shouted to them but I didn't hear their reply because of the ringing in my ears. Crossing the street we burst into the large ballroom with the remains of the bar in one corner smoldering with broken glass covering the counter bodies littered the floor some burning some moaning some with limbs missing and some dead.

We checked the bodies but could not see our guys anywhere, we thought the worst as there was many that was so badly mutilated that we would not know who they were. Then the large frame of Tiny came from out of a door he was carrying the limp body of a young woman who was dripping blood from a wound in her back. He was in a daze and all he kept saying was she was on top of me when it went up, her body had taken the blast and saved his life but she was dead with a hole torn from her back. Where are the others I shouted at him but got no response so I ran through the door he had emerged from and went looking for Jock and Blast. Blast was helping injured people when I found him a nasty cut to his face was all I could see and he confirmed that he was fine, what about Jock I said? He is in there he pointed. The explosives had been thrown into the rest room from the open window just as Jock was taking a leak he got the full force of it and there was very little you could tell that it was him except for his curly red hair. It was Phil I told them once Jocks body had been taken away to the hospital morgue that was what was left of it, "Don't" Tiny said I don't wont to hear this now and he walked away leaving the rest of us watching him go. To the lads they just thought that I was suffering from the blast and making up stores that I had seen Phil and I couldn't make them belive that I had seen him. Tim organised the sending home of Jocks body but we had a little service together to say goodbye before his remains left, it was and will be one of the saddest days of my life.

It was also the day that I vowed that I would kill Phil on sight if and when I saw him again. The team went about there work in a none to joyful mood after that day, we got two replacements for Phil and Jock a young captain call Simon who took over the team and another ex-para called john. Dave had spoke to us all over the phone and expressed his condolences for Jock but said nothing about Phil and I never mentioned his name again in front of the lads. Tim would still allocate our jobs but Simon would give us all the details and were each of the team was expected to be on the set day of a escort or a stackout. Each time we went out on a job I was looking at every face watching every person that looked anything like the brute or Phil I just knew that where ever they was I was going to kill them. Sitting in our room one night Simon entered and told us to gather around as he needed to talk over a job with us, it's a very special job he told us. President Deby was going out to the site where the oil pipeline is going to be started and he is going to travel the length of it till. Do's that mean we are going into the

Cameroon I asked? No the president is only going as far as the boarder with Cameroon but we have to cover his route and make sure its safe.

The pipe line will run from the oil fields in Doba and head south crossing into Cameroon, then on to Kribi a sea port in the Cameroon there it will be stored and then shipped around the world. As you know this development has been partly financed by the world bank and is backed by US oil giants ExxonMobil and Chevron and Malaysias Petronas.

The bank as put up £2.2 bn while the oil companies a cool £2.3 bn Geordie let out a long whistle, So if we get it wrong a lot of big people are going to come down on us hard Simon expressed. You also are aware that the rebles in this country wont to over throw this government and stopping this pipeline would put a lot of pressure on President and would make him have to stand down so we will have to watch the pipe line as well. How are we going to do that Tiny asked there is only six of us? The government is setting up stations along the areas the pipe line will travel patrolled by land-rovers day and night until the route has been surveyed and the work begins one of you will be stationed at each of them sites. Your jobs will be to set up the patrols and plan where it will be best to deploy your troops that will be with you, we are going to give the army orders Blast asked? No not quite you will work alongside their officers who have been told to work with you.

Brummie while the president is travelling from one site to another you will move forward ahead of him to check out the site's Tim is going to be your transport. You will leave each site as soon as the president arrives unless there is a problem and then you deal with it ok, ok I replied. Now the president will have is own body-guards so we wont have that duty but we will watch the area that he is moving around and remove anything that looks like trouble is that clear? There was a big shout of yes sir from us all. There was a lot more chatter in the billet that night with everyone excited about the task ahead of them, equipment was cleaned and packed into our rucksack weapons were also cleaned and oiled. Two types of ammo was loaded into my ammo pouches eight millimeter for my pistol and seven point six two for my rifle I also sharped my knife which was put into its scabered.

Finally finished I ask if anyone wanted a drink and nobody turned down a beer but Simon told us that two was our limit that night so I knocked the tops of two bottles each. John joined myself and Gordie at the table while Tiny and Blast sprawled on their beds reading some wank mags that Tiny had picked up from some black market character in the town. John told us about his time in the para's and places that he had been his family and why he had decided to jion up with us. His wife had been messing about with a mate of his and when he found out he had beat shit out of both of them. He had put them both in hospital and he decided that there was nothing there for him to hang around for so he answered Dave's ad and here he was away from all the troubles of home.

We chatted for a few hours it was good as there had been little talk since Jocks death but all the while we chatted I could not get Phil out of my mind and what I would do when I see him. The night passed and it was soon time for us to get ready to go we loaded our kit onto the truck which was taking the lads to their stations my kit was taken by Gordie who had pull the strew to give him the last of the stations the place where I would end up at the end of Deby's tour. Tim arrived to drive me to the first of the stations so I would be ready for when the President arrived and the area would be as clear as I could make it.

On route we chatted about this and that keeping our eyes peeled looking for any sign of trouble, I do belive you saw Phil he told me out of the blue but it will take a lot for the others to come around to beliving you. Well thank you for telling me that I have stopped talking about that day when Jock was killed the others seem to think that I was concoused by the explosion and seeing things. Do you think there was a chance of that he inquired? No I said in a sturn voice I saw him before the explosion and was making towards him when the bomb went off, then we need to keep our eyes well open as he knows most of our movements.

We arrived at the oil fields in Doba where the president would arrive first to watch the first pipes laided, it was full of people mostly oil workers but there was people from the world press and many delegates from other countries. This is not going to be easy I told Tim there are to many areas to cover, don't worry we have the area that are not so open and more likely to recive an attack, the main areas are well protected with troops that will keep the crowds at a safe distance. Snipers I stated, that's our job we will check every roof over looking the site Tim told me, "How" I asked with a bit of fear in my vioce If we take that high roof there we will be able to see onto the roofs in the area, any one moving will be seen. We have radios to warn the ground troops and there will be two helicopters flying around from the time he arrives till the time he leaves. My heart slowed back to normal with the news of air support it was now looking like a routine job where if they see anything they would inform me and I would take the shot. You said we in that sentence are you coming on the roof with mei ask? Yes another pair of eyes will help but a marksman I am not so you will still have to take the shot if I see anything. I will be glad to have you abroad I told him but don't you carry any weapon I have not noticed one?

Only this and he reached towards the back of his waistband coverd by his jacket and pulled out a Smith & Wessen m&p 9c with a 12 round magazine. Good at close range but not very good at distance I told him, that's why I told you im no marksman but at close range im like Billy the kid and with that he spun his weapon on his finger.

That gave me a big smile, this man was a real friend and had a good sence of fun but was also deadly when needed in a tight situation. I got out of the jeep and looked around, I will be up there I told Tim and pointed to the roof of a large building ok I will park the car and join you in a while he told me pulling away once I had got my gear out of the rear. On the roof I found a spot where I could see all the other roofs in the area plus any roads that came into the oil works, the ground was covered with soldiers searching builds and stores for any danger. Tim arrived a few moments after I did and was soon scanning around with his binoculars, nothing suspicious down there at the moment he reported. I assembled my rifle and connected my day sight on to the top of the barrel picking the front door of the main building I focused the sight till it was clear to look through. After making a scan I told Tim that there was a hundred places that the rebels could hide down there and I hoped the troops were searching the area well. Who has got this position he enquired? Blast will have the job once we all pull out I replied, He as got a large area to cover with his patrols Tim continued I hope they have given him enough troops. We kept the area scanned and nothing was seen to cause any alarm so once the Presidents party pulled up I made my report to Simon and then moved off to the second location with Tim.

This location was about eight kilometers from the first there was no town just a few buildings for the machinery and some huts for the troops all infenced to make a compound. A trench had been dug where the pipe had been layed it was just waiting to be covered over with the earth and this was tobe started once the president arrived. At that moment nothing was being done the workmen were just standing around smoking by their bulldozers and diggers but the troops which John would be working with looked a lot more alert and were checking papers and id's of everyone. Tim found a spot to park and I unloaded my M21 rifle from his car boot while tim reported to the soldiers who we were and got the thumbs up to be there. I looked around and decided to set up near the edge of the trench looking across towards the wooded area on the far side away from the compond this would give me a view of all the open area.

Icould see where the work was going to be done and the approach to the compond from all angles there was only one blind spot but Tim had that covered. We studed the area but again there was no sign of anything, I watched the President arrive this time is convouy was larger with big vans of the world press following behind the milatry escort. Tim picked me up in the vehicle and we set off to our next destination as fast as we could as the president was not spending much time at these smaller out posts. Who has the pleasure of this site Tim asked me? Site three that's Tiny I replied, he as got the short straw Tim continued, out of all the sites this is the most vunerable it is surrounded by thick woods outside the compond.

The entrance in and out is down a lane with trees either side which are thick and have lots of hiding places, the land was very moist no good for digging so they left the trees to soak up the water. As we approached I felt very uncomfortable this was a good place for snipers and ambushes, today the track was lined with troops but in future there will only be a small detachment. There is one thing Tim explained those trees are not easy to walk through they are very close to each other and have large thorns growing from the branches. It would not be easy to tip-toe through them without making a sound or getting snagged Tim continued his explanation. Drop me off here I told him, I want to walk the woods to see what I can see and if I can get around in there, hold the presidents convoy up a little till I get back. I disappeared into the woods and walked along towards the compound inside the tree area, struggling to pass through the trees but did manage to do it with a scrach or two and a sqeeze. It was about five minutes into my patrol that I notice a figure crouched beside a tree just in front of me, he was dark skinned but I could not see him clearly due to the darkness of the woods.

I eased my revolver from its holster after leaning my rifle against a tree I tried to focus on the figure but it was hard with the darkness of the woods I couldn't tell if it was male or female. Looking towards the road I could just make out a few soldiers lining the route and called out to them and the next thing a round hit the tree beside me and the figure was now on the move. The person scurried into the woods finding the going rough but it was also rough for me, I managed to get off three rounds at a form but was not sure I hit anything. I was now joined by two soldiers who challenged me and this aloud the sniper to escape, they had picked up my rifle and took my revolver off me and pushed me out off the trees to the road. The last row of trees before the road I was pushed that hard that I stumbled and hit a low branch and a thorn pierced my cheek. Tim raced to my rescue before the soldiers could do any more damage and ticked off the officer about his men then ordered them to send in some patrols to search the woods. Keep still he told me that thorn has broke off and has gone into your mouth, he put two fingers into my mouth and held the other side in his other hand snapping it in the middle and removed one end from my mouth and the other from my outer cheek.

The taste of blood filled my mouth, It has left a small hole he told me but it will heal in a few days just keep it clean and don't let it get infected they will give you a jab back at camp. Lets move on I said it will be fine till I get back to base just then the Presidents car pulled up beside me were I sat and the window was wound down. Tim approached the vehicle and gave a report of what had happened.

Then the presidents face appered at the opening and I pressed myself close to block any sniper fire. I here that once again you have filed an attempt on my life he started, sir I interrupted it is not safe here and

I beg you to close your window and get your driver to pull away to a safer area, very well but I wish to thank you later and with that he was gone. After briefing Tiny about the area, Simon went forward and took the serch of the next site while I got some treatment on my face, that site is Gordies I told Tim as we drove passed the compound to the next location which was to be my base. Now you have drawn the long straw Tim told me, your site is in one of the larger villages down here and has shops and bars and you can hire a lady or two if you want the pipe workers love it down here. The compound was a bit smaller than our base camp back in N'Djamena and had more workforce than any of the others.

This workforce would run the pipeline all the way through to the coast in the Cameroon and build the holding tanks and pump houses. The streets of the village was crowded it was market day and all the stores were doing a roaring traded with home grown products and a lot of exports including Coca-cola. This village reminded me of the old gold rush towns in America what ever you could make a buck on was being sold including old western cars and vans. The president car is not coming this way but entering the compound via a side enterance so we need not panick about this area Tim informed me. We headed across town towards our destination passing some ladies standing by the roadside "Hi" Timmy one shouted you have some time for me today, Tims face went a good shade of red said nothing and drove on. We drove up and down the road to the compound gate and could see nothing of danger on that route, troops covered over two thousend meters ether side of the road and the street was very quiet so this route had not been advertised. What do they expect me to do here I asked Tim?

The streets are full of people every side of the compound an attack could come from anywhere and we would have no warning. That's why this section was built first, the pipe is buried deep under this road, in the compound is a pumping station and that would be the rebels target and that's where we need you Tim told me. Your job here will be to test the weak areas of the compound and use the troops to sercure them. You have a large force here so you can make this location very safe, one armed car leaves the compound every five minuets and heads back to Gordies site and the same happends his end so throughout the night a lot of traffic travels this road. So as you see the pipeline is safe it's the pumping station that is your priorate Tim instructed me, with that we pulled up at a building and both got out. The president will be having a good look around this site so we will need to stay a little longer that water tower looks a good spot to view over the site what do you think? Yes it looks fine I agreed and removed my rifle from the boot.

I clicked on my radio and informed Simon that we was in postion And ready for the President to arrive, road well guarded and compound is safe I told him. You can stay there now he informed me, I will be racing on to the base site to set up my defences so you and Tim can stay at your site. I was glad to hear that and rogered the message, my face was sore from the thorn and I could taste blood again so I could realy do with a doctors attention and was told that there was one on site. Tim didn't stay and went on to the last site commenting that Simon was not his boss and he had his own orders to follow.

From the top of the tower I could see all four corners of the compound and once the president arrived nobody was allowed to enter any of the gates. Simon called me on the radio to inform me that he was now leaving the President and moving on to his location leaving me responsible for Mr Deby's security. I watched painfully through my sight all movements around the area but I saw nothing that looked like a threat to the president.

The soldiers on the ground were doing a grand job keeping people away I noticed a quick smack with a baton moved anyone who protested their orders or did not obay. One hour later and it was over the President's car pulled away to his final destination at base site were he will have a tour and then make a speech before going to a lunchen with all the heads of the development and some of the backers. Once I was free from my duties I found the site doctor a French chap who spoke perfect English and got him to look at my cheek, you will need a jab he told me and got me to drop my denims. Your face will swell for a few days he told me so keep it clean and take these anti-biotics they will kill any bacteria that as entered your blood but if you start feeling un-well come back to me. I left his office and made my way to the front gate to inspect the security around that area and to talk to the officer in charge of the site who had his office in a hut to the side of the guard house.

We walked the perimiter of the site making note's of any weak spots and anywhere that we found any damage to the double fence that went around the site.

The officer who I called jimmy as his real name was not in my languge bracket was very helpful and didn't seem to mind me being there to help out. He took in all of my advice and even inputted some of his own thoughts to the movements of his troops and their best use. As I said there was a double fence around the site and the gape between the two fences was wide enough for a landrover to drive between so we set up a twenty minute vehicle patrol at night. We would also keep the road patrols to and from Gordies site to stop any tampering with the pipe line as it was layed. The pump house's on site were completed and the pipes in had been laid for a hundred yards outside the compound, they were ten feet under ground so once buried would take some digging up but it could happen so the patrols stayed. We worked out how many men we would need to run the operation and found we had plenty of troops to do the job so we split them into three groups.

Group one would take on the morning duties group two would do the night duties and group three would be on rest/stanby. Happy with my days work I made my way to the works canteen for a bite to eat as I was now very hungrey and I tucked into a stew like dish without knowing what I was eating but enjoyed every bit Except for the pain in my mouth as I ate. On the wall of the canteen was a plan of the site showing where everything was so I soon found my hut and got my head down. Jimmy awoke me next morning knocking on my door, He had been called down south to meet up with his commanding officer so would I watch the site with his men while he was gone.

Dressing and grabbing a coffee as I passed the canteen I took up residents in his office checking the maps and plans of where the pipes were being layed. I worked out the distances from this site to the two other sites nearest to me and worked out the time it should take a vehicle travelling at a set speed to reach its destination. By doing this we should be able to know where each vehicle is at a said time so if they run into trouble we could get to them asap. Each day the equiptment had to be taken out of the site yard and driven down to the job site and a patrol of men had to escort and stay with them all day I could now see why we had so many men. All day I had site forman managers and workers coming along requesting escorts for this job or that job I was glad it was only for a day I had to do this it was so easy being a sniper. One job that I did get done was to install more landline phones around the inside fence so that patrols could call in as they passed or report any breaches. Once Jimmy got back I was worn out again but I needed to do one last perimeter check befor I handed over to the night officer, I walked the full site checking the gaurdes plus the new phones I had got installed once happy all was well I turned in.

Alarm bells ringing awoke me in the early hours and I grabed my pistol and ran out the door to be meet with the smell of smoke and a glow in the sky made by flames. I reached the gate house to see the gaurds running out with a hand pulled fire tender to tackle a blaze in a house just outside the compound, "stop" I screamed at the top of my vioce "stop" with that a sargent ordered his men to stop. Where are you going I asked him?, to fight the fire he replied, and leaving your post open to every rebel that's around to sneak in and distroy the site. His head dropped sorry sir but there could be people in there so I didn't think, yes that could be but it could also be an ambush a trick to get you off site. Did you notice anyone around since the fire started? no screams or people running around not even anyone from the area out to put the fire out, no sir he replid again, that's because it's a trap I continued the people have been warned there is none there.

Its outside our site nothing to do with our job so turn off that alarm and stand the men down I told him, he looked daggers at me but called his men in. Now alert your men that there could be rebels in the area and tell them to be double alert, I will be in the tower so warn them that im there I don't want anyone shooting at me, yes sir he said and was gone.

I collected my rifle and climbed the steep steps to the tower watching for movement as I went, crouching low as not to be seen from below keeping out of the light created by the fire. By now the build was in full flame it lit up the whole area around it but lerking in the shadows I could see dark shapes with faces that lite up when a flame flickered in that direction. I noticed that no-one was panicking or rushing about as they would if they wanted to save the building or its contents or even persons that maybe inside this said ambush confirmed when the light picked up a man with a Ak47 across his body waiting for some action. Taking aim I located his head and for a split second it was as if time stood still and I fired.

The stillness soon passed as shadows became running figures as the shock of seeing one of their friends heads cracked open like a water melon and the contence splater everyone stood by him. I never got chance of a second shot as within seconds they were gone lost in the darkness of the other buildings and away into the streets between houses and vehicles.

Making my way down I bumped into Jimmy who had gone to the other gate to check his men after the sargent had told him what I had said, you was right it was an ambush and I hope my men have learned something from you tonight, if they don't it will be them laying out there instead of a rebel I told him.

The next day when the body was recoverd we found that it was a wanted rebel who was not knowen to be in this area. So for the next few days things were quite nothing reportable happened but I still felt un-easy about that man being in a area that he was not normaly in it smelt of trouble. Tim arrived back a few days later and we dicided to go out for a drink, you fancy some company he asked there is a place I know where the girls good for your moral. Yes I replied but are they good for your pecker, he laughed don't worry theres a camp doctor that can sort anything like that out, lets just drink I said. Two stiff shots of whisky later I was telling him of my suspicions, it smells I told him they are calling in troops for an attack on the place I am almost sure of it. But you have plenty of men he replied, yes but look at them some would run at the first sight of action most are just young men who are wet behind the ears. But they have you, that shot you took plus the one that saved the President as given you quite a name, what do you mean I asked? They are calling you argent renard the silver fox. Why would they call me that? Well in these parts they have a fox that is a grayish silver and he is cunning and strikes without being seen and that's what they say about you, your never seen but you strike fast and accriate.

I felt quite chuffed that I had been given a nick name other than Brummie it was like being made a part of the tribe a chief even with all the respect that go's with the title. But back to my suspicions about the attack I told him, they are seeing men that don't come from this area but are known to be active else where but they don't lift them. It is the same here as it is in England they have to be proven that they are rebles before they get arrested, but is harder here as the volume of people is a lot greater to check. What about Phil and his partner I call the brute I asked him as anyone seen them around here? If we can get some news on those two we would know for deffernt that something was going down. I will tell you what Tim said there are a few ladies that owe me a favour so I will go do some snooping around see what I can find out and with that he was gone.

I looked around the bar and I could tell you that there was some realy shady characters stood around drinking and some had their eyes on me I was very pleased that the sargent from the fire walked in with a few of his men for a drink. I will buy this round I told the barman and the men gratfuly excepted, sir I would like to thank you for what you did, if I had taken the men out there to that fire I could have gotten them killed.

How did you know that it was an ambush he asked me? Well sometimes you have this get feeling and that was one of those moments. Yes but how do you get this feeling he pushed for the answer I don't know I replied but I think experience comes into play, watching for signs. You see nobody was rushing to put the fire out only you and your men that made me think that something strange was about to take place and I had to stop you.

We had a few more drinks and the locals stayed clear of us, even though the sargent was off duty he still carried a revolver and a large baton as did his men. Tim arrived back about an hour later looking like the cat that got the cream, you don't need to tell me what you have been doing I told him, all I the line of duty he replied with a smile. Anyway the young lady that I was with said she had a man in her place two nights ago and he sounds like Phil from her discription. He was talking to another man about attacking the site but stopped when he noticed her near to them so she do'snt know when the attack will take place but she will keep her ears open. God Tim we could do with all the lads here not just me I told him, you was put here because we knew this was the main target, if they get those pump houses it will put us back months. You can bring these troops around to be a top unit with your skills and the respect they will now give you after that fire incedent. You can use the troops anyway you would like to protect that site, get the plans tomorrow and build your defences in anticipation of the attack and don't worry back up is only a radio call away. We had a few more drinks and then left at the same time as the sargent and his men did jumping into the back of their truck instead of driving back in the jeep (wise move we found out later).

The next few day I made changes to a lot of the areas of the site, at the gate I built a chicane made with sandbags making it hard for any vehical to drive straight through the site without slowing right down. We put sandbags across the building doorways so it would be hard to lob granades into the buildings plus we could put men behind like a fort rampard. More machine guns were placed around the site to strengthen areas that I felt were weak and we also tightened up the gate checks on the civilian staff that enter each day to work.

Tim came round to the site so often now I thought he was moving in it really shocked him when he heared that is car exploded when one of the camp troopers went to collect it for him. That could have been us he kept saying for hours after the incident and also became more sercur when he went into the centre to talk to his lady informer. It was a few days on when he returned all excited with new from his snitch, she had heard two men talking about the attack that was about to take place on the pumping station on Friday which was in two days time. They had noticed her near to them and stopped the conversation so she didn't get the full details she just kept dancing as if she had heard nothing. We have two days to make sure we are ready I told tim, should I call the others in he asked? No it will leave them to weak. The men we have should cover any attack you told me that yourself I reminded him, yes I know but that was before, he stopped in mid sentence. That was before your car was bombed I snapped at him, it could have been in the car it could have been in the club it could be right now from a sniper in the woods if they wont you they will get you.

The IRA tought me that in Irland, so stop worring about it and get on with what you do best, track the bastards down before they get you. Tim's face glowed red with anger and he walked away and I heard the word bastard repeted a few times. He would get over it I did when I was shit scared and a sargent gave me my pet talk, we will mourn you get drunk piss on your grave and forget you, was what he told me and it made me so angry that I forgot about being scared. I now got all the officers together and told them my news, Jimmy instructed his officers to brief their men and for the next two night to confined them to camp.

The next morning we practiced with all the warning systems we had to alert everyone of an attack and the position they would take up in the case of such an attack. Tim had come round and was glad to lend a hand making sure that all position were well stocked with ammo and water. They may see us practising Jimmy told me, that's good I replied it may stop them attacking if they know we are strong and ready.

On Friday morning we stood too at 04.30hr and stayed in our position till 09.00hrs when I told Jimmy to get a third of his force to the cookhouse for breakfast followed by a second third till they have all been fed. I finally got them to stand down around midday as nothing had happened around the time that I thought it would, but there was a strange feeling in the air. A lot of the workforce had not turned up for work, the streets had no market traders working, it was as if the word had gone out that something was about to happen. Around 15.30hr just as the change over was about to happen a truck approached the main gate I was on the water tower watching out over the town when I noticed the truck slowing down at the gate. The guard approached the drivers side of the cab and he was accompanied by two riflemen who was spaced out on ether side of the road watching the sides of the truck.

A split second and up went the front of the canopy of the truck and four men with machine guns opened up on the guards, not knowing what hit them the three men were killed instantly. The machine gunner on the guardhouse roof opened up with his weapon forceing the men at the back of the truck to dive for cover but the driver and his mate were not so lucky rounds smashed into the glass and pepered their bodies with holes. The alarm was sounded around the camp and men were running in all directions to reach their positions. Just as this was happening so a small army seemed to come out of every nuke and crannie charging towards the main gate firing wildly as they came. They must have missed our preperation for this attack as they just charged in like a wild riot without a care in the world for their own safty. They over run the gate house and streamed in every direction down the site roads heading for the major buildings, I took down two of the leading runs heading for the first pumping station. Two of Jimmys men had joined me setting up a machine gun they let go with the first burst sending the whole front row of the attackers flying backwards the way they came with limbs torn from their bodies.

All of the soldiers had hid behind the sand bags and as the attackers got near they let them have it, the same happened at every building they ran to they got close then bang they were hit with grenades bullits and rockets. I saw a man with a RPGand took a fast aim and fire, the round hit him near to his neck and I saw his throat rip open and a great cloud of blood burst into the air as he fell. It was then that I saw the brute hacking at the machine gunner that had been on the gate house roof I snapped of a shot which must have ripped a scar across his right cheek. Dam I said to myself as he ran behind the truck for cover, only nicked him I explain to the men by my side even the fox can miss. The site was now in a state of panick the attackers had abandend their explosives and was running for what ever escape route they could find even trying to climb the fence. They got picked off by the men on the roofs and were left dangling on the wire a great number escaped though the main gate while my crew had a jam in their weapon.

In this moment as the crowd run past the brute made his escape using their bodies as a shield for himself I got off a couple of shots but could not get a clear shot at him. He ran towards the woods and that was were I saw Phil waiting in the trees calling for his buddy to come that way to him, I raised my rifle but again he was gone. There was a mass escape into the woods just as gordie arrived down the road with his men, Tim had called him in a hope to cut off the rebles retreat.

But even though gordies men went into the woods after the rebels only a few were captured other choose to die and once again no mention of Phil so I said nothing. You look like you had a good scrap Gordie commented once he arrived beside me? Yes I replied the lads did a good job, I second that said Tim as he joined us and it is all down to you he told me. Your training and strategy was what give them rebels a bloody nose and I don't think they will be back soon Tim continued I can see another medel coming your way from the president and maybe a reward from the money lenders for saving their assets. Jimmy arrived with us at that moment and anounced that we had only lost seven men with four with minor wounds, the enemy had lost over one hundred dead. No wounded or captured I said? Only the once that your friend captured in the woods he said with a large smile on his face I could feel my blood boil I would never kill a wounded man never, Tim could see my feelings and pulled me away this is their country let them deal with things their way he told me, yes I said but I don't have to like it, lets have a drink the rounds on me Tim said and we headed to the mess. Gordie had one drink with us then had to leave while me and Tim let the beers and whisky flow till we both needed to be carried back to our rooms were we slept sound for the rest of the night.

The next morning over black coffee I told Tim about the brute and the scar he would have on his face that I gave him I also mentioned Phil but told him that Gordie had not seen him so do not mention it to the lads. I left the canteen to do my rounds and was surprised to see that everything had been cleaned up, no blood no bodies no sign there had been a battle. The gate house had been rebuilt and all damage had been repaired, a group of passing soldiers gave me a salute and I heared the word Renard come from one of them The Fox.

I had got over my anger of the wounded and prisoners but I was still jumping mad at missing both the brute and Phil. Tim was right about the medel and I was given the highest order of military medel in Chad and given the freedom of the country not that I would ever visit it much once our work was done. I had asked for the soldier on the roof of the guard house to recive a award and he to got his gong for his bravery that cost him his life. That battle also caused the rebels a great number of loses, men power weapons and face, nobody wonted to follow them while the army had now got so strong. We was no longer needed on pipeline duty so we was sent back to escort duty and boarder patrols we was ordered to try to find were the weapons were coming into the country from. This was a better job for us as we worked as a team again and I got to do some sniping with Gordie spotting for me.

Our first patrol took us to the east of the country very close to the boarder with Sudan were most of the known rebels were hiding and since our battle at the pumping station not many had been seen or even reported anywhere in Chad. We stayed in a small boarder camp with about fifty soldiers who spent about a month here before they were releaved to go home and see their families, we was to spend six weeks here before we was to return for another escort duty with the president. The camp was the closest to the Sudan boarder and the most crossed area from the east with camel travelers crossing daily to bring their goods to the markets in Chad. Mine fields covered a large area on etheir side of the road coming from Sudan but there was always people getting through cut fences told us this. People on foot was not that much trouble to us as they couldn't carry many guns or ammo but it was the large trucks and animal convoys that we had to search for the heavy loads of weapons.

The days were long the nights were longer on this job but we worked hard to complete the duty we had been asked to do, but not one day did I not think of getting Phil in my sight and I knew it would not be here. Simon entered our hut one morning to tell us of a problem that had happened a few kilometers north of our position, someone is cutting the wire up there and when they go to check the mined field they are getting injured he told us. We have been asked to go up and see what we can find out so pack your kit and get aboard the truck that will be outside in one hour grab some breakfast if you have not already its going to be a long day. One hour later we were all on the truck heading north, Myself and Gordie took the tail gate seats while the rest seat inside playing cards. It was very hot and we had all decided to wear white tee-shirts with light combat trousers nice to keep cool but the mosquitoes loved the show of flesh it was like a invertation to a free meal. I heard Simon talking to Tim about extending our tour here Gordie said to me in a low voice so the others didn't hear him, you sure I replied yes straight up no bull shit.

I didn't care how long we stayed at that moment I didn't want to leave until I put a bullit in that bastard Phil, we must be doing a good job I replied with my face show nothing of my desire to go home as well. The truck pulled up at a boarder crossing check point and Simon jumped down from the cab, right get your kit and follow me he shouted up to us and with in a minute we were all ambeling behind him towards a small hut which was going to be home for a few days. Right once you have settled in I want the following done by the following people Simon told us, Tiny you and John will set up a machine-gun post at the side of the hut so as to repel an crashers who try to cross the boarder. Brummie you and Gordie will find a good hide for yourselfs and you will watch the area were the wire is always getting cut sleep by day watch by night ok? Yes sir we both replied. Blast and myself will go and look at the mined field and make safe any faults plus lay any new one's that are required everyone know what they are doing ? Yes sir came the shout from the whole group. Simon came and told us where the area he wanted us to watch was and gave us instruction to fire on any persons trying to cross with heavy boxies or weapons he also said that we could be out there two days and two nights so take dry rations with us. We made ourselves ready black and green cam paint covered our faces necks and hands, light-wieght cam jackets were covered with Camaflarge netting which will get the local growth pulled into it once we start to go into it.

My rifle was coverd in sacking which will also get covered with the local brush and leafes once we pick our spot, once ready we set off taking a wide trail away from our area so we could come in without being seen. We crawled over a hundred yards in thick undergrowth till we found a spot which we could see the mine field without being seen ourselves and set up my weapon while Gordie watched through his day sight. With my weapon now well cammed up I focused my sight onto the area in front of me now im ready I told myself checking that we were both coverd with the local brush.

The day was long and hot and we took it in turns to sleep as we also had to watch out for the local insects and spiders that had nasty bites and we didn, t forget the snakes most of them would be out at night when it was cooler and more meals for them to catch now they would be soaking up the sun. Most of our comunication to each other was by hand signal and we seemed to get it off to a tee, till night fell and then it would be taps on our sleaves and a point. Gordie pulled out his night scope from its bag and checked the area while I flipped the end of my sight and it changed to night vision the area looked a light green a figure would show black. It was around one-thirty when Gordie tapped my sleave and I looked in the direction of his finger, a black figure approced the mine field from the Sudan side carrying a large heavy sack and I mean heavy.

We watched him as he stepped slowly into the mine field prodding with a sharp instrament stopping when he located a mine then what he did was highly dangerous but very effective. From his bag he would pull out a heavy rock and place it on the mine which would activate it but it wouldn't exploded untill the weight was taken off it so anyone following him would have a path marked with rock safe as long as they didn't touch the rocks. Now we could see why people was getting hurt they were moving the rocks and the mine would jump up and blow up.

These were anti-personal mines, once you trod on one they would activate the detinature and once you stepped off it would spring into the air about two to three feet and explode blowing your legs off if you was tall or your nuts if you was short, not nice kit. Once he had cleared a path the man went back and signalled his friends that it was safe to cross. Like as if from out of the ground six more figures appeared carrying weapon boxies long and heavy two men to each box, I took aim Gordie indicated one hundred and fifty yards.

They were in a close line so I decided to drop the second man which I did with ease knocking the top of his head off and as he fell the box fell onto a rock which sent up the mine and it blow. The explosion took down the mans partner plus the front man of the second box carrier who in turn dropped his box hit another rock which exploded taking down the next pair. Only the last carrier turned and ran but my next shot hit him in the back and threw him out of the mine field, the only one to escape was the path maker he was faster than a rabbit. The injured men now screamed from their wounds, Gordie put up a flare to light up the area, and what a sight we had once the flare sent down its light the five bodies in the field had limbs lying near to them but not attached the ground was stained with blood only two were moving,

Soon troops arrived from the boarder detachment and before we could get to the fence a volley of shots rang out and the rebels were dead. Simon arrived just as I was about to club the officer on the head with my rifle butt, stand down Brummie he shouted to me but Simon they didn't need to kill them we could have got some info out of them. I agree he said but they are the law here we just do a job for them now yours is done here so both of you back to the hut, anger burned in my chest but I turned away and Gordie followed close behind me.

The other lads had stood too when we got back and we got a big question game off Tiny, what happened he said? And lucky for me Gordie took over the explination, Brummie was great he fire two shots and got six blokes he told them. I just enterd the hut a went and lay on my pit, if we had got them to talk we my have got some information about Phil I thought to myself, again I was thinking about Phil was I getting paranoid was I getting obsessed with killing that bastard?. I awoke early the next morning and explained to Simon about the rocks and told him not to move any that he saw laying about, good job you told me early there is a team going in to recover the bodies I will inform them and well done that was a good job last night. With the job completed we was sent back to the city to continue escort duties something the lads were pleased about as they could get out for a drink and some fun when off duty.

I also enjoyed my nights off but could not relax and was always looking around the room to see if I could see Phil or his buddy also having a night off from their evil doings but no such luck they were well away from our nightouts. I recived my second medel from the President and the freedom of the city was also instoled on me a honour I would never use once I left this place as I would never come back. Days turned into weeks and nothing happened that fight at the pumping station and the incedent at the boarder crossing had seamed to knock the stuffing out of the rebels but we knew that this could be a lull before the storm. Simon turned up in his shorts and told us we was going for a run one morning to stop us getting out of shape it got the cobwebs out. The very next day we were called into action, half the regiment was to go up north to the very airport that we arrived at as it had been attacked and taken over by the rebels.

It will take us days to get up there Tiny said as we was getting all our kit ready to go, it took us three days when we arrived he continued, not this time Tim replied as he entered the room your going up in choppers. Simon entered and confirmed what Tim had said, travel light just your light combat dress flak jackets weapon and helmet everything else will be waiting up there for us.

Outside in five he told us as he walked back outside with a small pack and his revolver holstered in his shoulder holster, Fuck me shouted Blast this sounds as if it could be big, maybe we might win some medels this time, I ignord the comment I think Blast was not having a go I just think he really was looking for some action. We boarded the aircraft and was soon airborne heading north at a low altitude first looking at the lush green land crossing over the river then onto much drier land with just its camel trails show that somebody had been there. Right lads listern up called Simon over the noise of the engine this is what I know of the situation, the rebels entered the airport around three oclock this morning and attacked the control tower and hangers.

They took a lot of staff hostage so we will not be going in all guns blazing it will be a tactical assult to try to save the lives of the staff But don't worry you will see action this time as the President has stated that he will not be held to ransum and expects the conflict to be over before the day is over. There are some heavy tanks in the area so we will have some back up from those also we have air support if we need it but with the low tollerance we will still try to get in and recover the staff without lose of life. Tim looked at me then back at Simon, it sounds as if we have been given the job to rescue the hostages he commented from his dark corner of the aircraft. Well yes Simon replied I convinced the President that we could go in and get them out and I know we can do it, if there is anyone that disagrees speak up we can always get you replaced.

Nobody spoke a word so I said I think we should look at the situation first then make up our minds, the lads all nodded in agreement yes let's check it out first said Tiny who was sitting next to Simon I mean we don't have to be to rash he continued. Fine said Simon we will check out the situation and decided then if we can do it or not. Not another word was spoken the rest of the flight only to call for check of weapons, I had put my sniper rifle in its carrying bag and had a M16 slung across my chest so if I get into a close contact fight I would have the right weapon.

My sniper rifle will be used for long range firing, taking out of guards or rebels that are a threat to hostage lives. We landed about a mile from the airport and could hear small arms fire and the sound of the odd explosion so we knew that this was going to be a real stand off with the rebels. Moveing to a holding area we was given the low down of the situation by a major who could speak no English so Tim had to translate to us what he was saying. The rebels hold all the main buildings and have taken over the control tower, they have the hostages in the main terminal and are using them as a shield to provent us attacking the building. There is heavy fighting going on on the approach road to the airport But there are no milatry personal on the airport its self. The rebels have driven petrol tankers used to fill the aircraft onto the runway preventing a landing of troops we can only presume that these are rigged with explosives to blow if anyone trys to move them.

They have machine guns mounted on all the roofs and are well equipt with RPG's to take out any of our heavy equiptment Tim continued and all roads into the airport are heavily mined. They seamed to have thought of everything I piped up how do we get into the place? Tim relayed my message to the major who made a reply, it seems that we cannot get in without getting noticed Tim repeated the words. Ok Simon came in, first we do a reccy of the perimeter fence find a way in, then we will have to work out how we can get close then enter that main building.

We split into three teams, Myself Geordie plus two of the majors men made up team one, team two consisted of Tim John Tiny plus to soldier and the last team which had the explosive experts of Simon Blast plus two of the majors explosives men. We will all search the perimiter looking for a good entery which will keep us out of the rebels eyes, some where we will have cover and can get close to that main terminal building Simon told us. We moved of in two directions with our patrol taking the left end of the runway the explosive lads took the middle with Tims team taking the right.

A frontal assault was out of the question as we would be mowed down by the mass of rebels putting up a frontal action already and doing a good job pinning down the government troops. Out side the perimiter fence the earth sloped down away from it so we was able to stand without being seen from any of the buildings but to get a good look you needed to crawl on your belly to prevent being observed. There was plenty of holes in the fence but once inside you would not find cover so our patrol went back to our assembly point to wait and see what the others had found. Tims team returned with the same result but Simon return with news of a possibility, there is a gape in the fence and in front of it is one of the tankers on the runway Simon repoted.

From that tanker you can only be seen by two rebels on the roof manning a machine gun if we can take them out we could get across to the main building. Then how do we get in to the building Tim asked? We will have to cross that bridge when we get there as there is no visable view from the tanker to any doors except the departure doors which have guards and could be wired. Sound very risky said Tiny, it is replied Simon but I don't see any other way to get any where near that building. So we made a plan to at lest get to the building, Brummie we will need you to take out those two men, then using the blind spot we will run across to the building and search for anyway of entry I will get the major to put some of his men on the bank to give us covering fire should it go pear shape.

I slung my M16 over my shoulder and carried my M21 sniper rifle across my body so as to be ready to take those shots when I was told. Geordie was to spot for me so he carried the special looking glasses which gave you a accreat distance from you to target, I must say that today I felt very nervous this shot will hold a lot of peoples lives at risk, hit and it could work out miss and the hostages could be murdered. We made our way through the fence and crawled on our bellies to the truck, there was just myself Geordie and Blast, while I set up for my shot Blast checked the truck over for explosives. Once Blast had defused the two devices that he found on the truck I took up my position with Geordie by my side with the spotter glasses.

Taking a look through my rifle sight I focosed on the first figure who was standing looking out over the airfield with the machine gun just below him on its mount his partner was about a foot from him to his left smoking a ciggy. One thousand yards Geordie told me and I set my sight accordingly, I needed to fire and get of the second shot as fast as I could so I could take down the two of them without them getting off warnings not a easy shot. A small trickle of sweat ran down my face just missing my left eye I stopped and wiped it away and started my set up again. Geordie knew not to speak now as this was now my consentration time one distraction could put me off target and blow the whole thing. I brought the sight up to my right eye and and stedded the weapon into my shoulder with the round in the chamber I release the safty catch with my right thumb. I had the target in view he had not moved, cross section on his head and I fired moving to the next target in one movement again a head shot I swear I saw the first gaurds blood splater onto the seconds man face as I fire and a hit before he knew what had happened.

Both men down I had done the job, Geordie had watched through his glasses what a shot he gasped that second one would have won you a coconut on the fair he stated. We signalled to the others and one by one they crawled across to us until there was six then we ran from the cover of the truck to the build reaching without any challenge. Once we was all at the building we spead out and looked for a way in without being seen and we fould it in a fire door which had one of those push bars on the inside to open.

Now if this had been Gatwick this door would have been alarmed but here in Chad security didn't seem to matter so it was easy to push Tinys thin bladed knife into the gape in the closer and push Up the bar door opened. Inside the door we found a stairwell to our right which lead up to the roof Simon indicated to John to take four of majors men onto the roof and set up a defencive area. The rest of us moved forward slowly towards the main hall reaching a door with a glass window in the top, slowly Simon took a peep in and after a few seconds he stupped down to whisper to us all. The hostages are all sat on the floor in the middle of the main hall at lest two of them are wired up with explosives, there are six rebels watching over them two near to the hostages and the other four are spread around the room. I don't know if this door is wired but the front doors are and there is a lot of explosives laying about on the ground and tables. Simon frowned as he continued, as you go through this door in front of us are what looks like checkin counters so we have some cover but with the two wired I don't think we could take down the rebels before they would blow the place up.

Blast checked around the door, there don't appear to be any wires he said but im not sure, I would say not said Simon as this was the root to the roof it would be used to releave those men on the roof. Blast opened the door very slowly and to our relief there was no loud bangs, one by one we crawled behind the counter which had a small gape at the bottom which we could see out. There was about twenty-five hostages most looked like cleaners with at least two air traffic controlers a few security men and the rest were airport workers. The noise of the fighting outside had stopped and everything looked a lot more relaxed the rebels who were wearing black ski masks which just showed there eyes and mouths light up a few smokes and some grab a bite to eat. One who seemed to be in control spoke out to the two nearest to the hostages, Tim whisperd he as told them to get some food and then change over with the men on the roof. This would mean they would pass us so everyone got right under the counter and prayed they would not be seen, Tiny and Geordie I want you two to follow them out and take care of them slip into the clothes of the men on the roof before returning I have a plan Simon Told them.

Watching the other four while we waited till Tiny and Geordie returned they came into the room with masked faces and sat on the end of the counter smoking. One of the majors men stayed close so he could answer any of the question that the rebels would tell Tiny and partner to do but at first it seemed they was happy to let them smoke. Simon whispered instructions to them as we watched the rest, I wont you to walk over towards the hostages and with your fingers confirm how many are wired and then we need to see who is holding the trigger switch to set them off.

What if they ask any questions? We will just all open up and let them have it and hope for the best, again to risky said Tim what if I leave the room and Tiny comes after me and brings me back as a hostage that escaped. We could get close to the hostages and maybe the one with the triggers would come forward and Tiny could jump him, sounds better than my plan said Simon lets do it. Waiting a few seconds and then Tim jumped up and ran to the door Tiny reacted very fast and got to him before he could open it using his body to shield Tims just incase one of the rebels open up. Tiny and Geordie dragged Tim towards the hostages and one of the rebels shouted out, he does not recognise me Tim told Tiny then made a smart answer for Tiny. I was hiding there all the time he shouted to the rebel who was now very close to them, he was so busy watching Tim that he didn't give the lads a second glance. Simon got us all ready and as soon as Tiny saw the switch and knocked it from the rebels hand we all jumped up and open fire on the three remaining rebels.

Tiny put two rounds into the man now reeling back holding his arm and Geordie gave him two more to make sure he had nothing hidden under his robes he was dead before he hit the floor. The other three was jerked from one side to the other as rounds entered their bodies and blood spater sprayed in all directions till they hit the floor dead. Blast waisted no time and calmed the hostages with Tim talking their lingo they were soon quite, he went to work removing the explosive device off the two hostages that had been carrying them. Simon and the majors explosive experts worked on the devices around the building making them all safe while the rest of us made defensive barriers.

With the fighting outside at a lull they was bound to have heard the noise that had come from the inside of the building and a attack was inevitable.

They didn't disapoint us first of all they sent in a Rpg rocket that exploded as it hit the main door frame smashing every window around it and covering us with flying glass. Get the hostages out into the back the way we came shouted Simon. All the devices have been defused but a hit by one of those rockets would make a mess of this building and us shouted blast, Brummie see if you can get the bastard firing that Rpg. I raced to the roof as fast as my legs would take me, the lads up there was under heavy fire some coming from the control tower but my first priority was to get that launcher. I kept down low and made my way to the front wall of the building taking a look down offerd a chance for some one to take a snap shot at me the round hit the wall about a foot to my left.

Imoved about ten foot to my left to change my position so mister pot shot would not have the same shot again I glanced over and saw the man with the launcher standing ready to take his shot. I snapped my rifle up and took a shot, it didn't serprise me that I missed but it made the man take cover and gave me a chance to mark his position. Calling one of the majors men over to me I instructed him in the best way I could to go up to my left about ten foot and start firing down and I would do the rest. The man followed out my instructions and once the rebels returned fire I made my move I raised up rifle at the ready and out popped my man under the cover of the fire and wham I put one between his eyes. He spun around as the bullet knocked him back and he lounched the rocket straight up in the air now what go's up must come down and it was heading back into the rebels strong hold. Bodies were flying in every direction as they ran to escape the rocket this gave our lads on the roof a opportunity to open up at easy targets and the lads on the ground floor let rip too. The Major brought his troops forward from outside the airport and soon the whole thing was over with heavy losses for the rebels and lots of captures which the Major assured us that they would be put in a prison and not shot.

This time the rewards for this battle went to us all and not just me even though I was praised for the shot on the rocket man, a large parade went through the steets of the capital and the words for silver fox were chanted from street to street. There was little doing for the next few weeks the rebels had not taken such loses before and the weapons were none replacable so we had a peaceful time. Dave Beresford sent a message congratulating us for a job well done and informed Simon that he maybe pulling me out of this contract to help with another he had and he would let us know in a day or two. In a way I was happy about the news but I was also unhappy that I never got a chance to get Phil.

CHAPTER FOUR

A week passed and still we received no orders from Dave until a message came through that a flight had been booked for me to fly home on Wednesday afternoon three days from now. I started to put together my things and get them ready for my trip home but on the Monday we was called out to trouble in the city.

A demonstration had got over heated and was close to a riot so out we went and back to the same building that I had took my first life when I had got here fourteen months ago. Geordie spotted for me this time as there was so many to watch in this mob and a weapon could be missed in the crowds. Then came the surprise, o my god its "Phil" Geordie screamed out and pointed to a general area of the street and sure as I was standing here there was Phil standing in the crowd. I pulled my rifle into my shoulder and took up a firing position, looking through the sight I cannot get a clear shot I called out to Geordie. Every time I had him some one would get in front or he would move swiftly to one side or the other, he knows you're here said Geordie I wonder could this be a trap to get you.

I lowerd my rifle, could be I replied with me out the way he would be safe to go about his dirty work with me around he would need to look over his shoulder I'v already had two shots at him or his mate. While Geordie watched the mob and Phil I moved back to the stairs from which we climbed to get up here and I was not surprised to see three men making their way up.

I had left my sniper rifle with Geordie and brought my M16 so I could use automatic fire if needed, just as the first man rounded the top flight of stairs I let him have it. Three rounds left my muzzel and hammered into the mans chest knocking him backwards and over the low cement wall that finished off the staircase. Taking the two men behind him by surprise they turned to run and let fly with a few wild rounds of their own nothing coming close to me so I let go with another burst of my own. This time my rounds hit the walls and the floor all around them but nothing hit etheir one of them, they made the ground very quickly and I ran back for my rifle. Geordie watched the back of the building, nothing this way he called they must be making for the crowd I raised my rifle and watched through the sight and sure as Geordie had said it I saw them join the riot.

I followed their movement they too weaved from place to place to stop me having a clear shot but this time I anticipated one mans movement and fired hitting him on the side of the head. The whole street panicked and has the man fell to the floor people ran in all directions to get off the street and find safty. That ended the riot the place was clear in a few moments just a few bodies of injured that had been knocked over in the stamped and of cause the body of the man I had tagged. Geordie beat me down to the street to check the body of the man that fell from the top, three neat little holes could be seen on his chest and a lot of blood. One in the heart and one for each lung Geordie said if you ment that that was some shooting, I smiled at him I always mean it I replied even though this time I was not sure if it was not luck. While Geordie cleared up the explanation to the soldiers I continued around the corner into the main street where my second man was lying face down in a large pool of blood.

I rolled his body over and even though the round had made a mess of his head I could still see that it was the brute that had kill the kid that day at the lake. I looked around as if to see if Phil was anywhere to be seen but he was gone well away and now his plan had failed he would continue to run and hide as far away from Chad as he could. The government saw the brute as the leader of the rebels and decided that we had done our job and done it well so with a big pay check they released us from our contracts and sent us all home on that Wednesday flight that I was already booked on. The trip home was long and tiring but we finaly landed at Gatwick and was met by Dave who shook our hands and thanked us for a job well done and told us that our money was in the bank.

Dave also told me that Mary, Rogers wife was very ill in hospital and would I like a few days to visit them in Norfalk as they had only given her a short time to live. I told him that I would go, good there is a train at two you can get some sleep while you are travelling up there stay a few nights but you must be at the club by Monday so I can fill you in on your next job. I didn't sleep on the train up to Norwich I had to many things on my mind with Mary being ill Phil escaping from my clutches again and the new job.

It was late afternoon by the time I arrived at the main station so I decided to go straight to the hospital, giving the taxi driver the instructions that dave had given me for the private clinic we set off. I dropped my bag off in reception on arrival and soon found the room that the receptionist had told me to go to, there I found Roger sitting in a chair with his head in his hands. Hello my mate he said as he looked up and noticed me, you could see he had been crying and he tried hard to hide it, were is she I asked and how is she doing. She is not good it's just a matter of time he told me. What is the matter I asked feeling a tear well up in my eyes. Cancer he replied she had a small lump in one of her breast's they tried to remove it but it had spread to fast for them to do any thing. What about cymo I asked again with urgency in my voice? It's to late the cancer is to advanced to save her. Just then a nurse came in to the room and announce you can go into your wife now she is already for you.

Roger lead me by my arm towards a door and we entered, Mary was sitting in a large arm chair with a shawl rapped around her shoulders and a blanket across her lap magazines lay on a table beside her and a large vase of flowers. She looked weak but she smiled when she saw me, her face pale and drawn her eyes had black rings around them and there seemed to be no flesh on her bones.

My she spoke what a sun-tan you been on your holidays or something? you could say that I said and winked at her and gave her a kiss on her cheek my arms seemed black next to her flesh she was that pale. I am glad you have come she said I need some one to make him go home and get some rest he as been here for two nights already sitting in a chair, don't worry about that said Roger lets get you right first and then I will get some sleep. We spent some time just talking but I could see that she was tired and needed to rest so when the nurse came in and said we should let her rest I grabed Rogers arm and lead him out.

She is going to need you when she gets home so its no good you making yourself ill I told him lets get some rest, I cannot leave the hospital he replied something may happen.

There is a hotel just down the road lets book in and get some rest as I am prity bushed myself I told him we can leave a message where we are and they will call the hotel if there is any change. Reluctently he gave in and we left the hospital and walk the few hundred yards to the hotel, two single room I told the night porter and fillrd in the register we may get a call from the hospital up the road could you make sure we get it straight away.

The porter gave us two keys which I gave one to Roger room 4 I told him and would you like some food?, I am afrade our kitchens are closed for the night sir the porter said but I could make you some sandwichs, that will do finr I said plus some tea. Our rooms were on the first floor so we were soon at the doors, look im next door so if you need me just tap on the wall I said and open his door for him, im glad you're here he said and entered the room closing the door behind him. I entered room 5 and made for the bath room and washed my face and brushed my teeth using the complimentary brush and paste and just as I finished there was a knock on the door. The porter stood outside with a try full of sandwiches and a pot of tea, I knocked on your friends door but got no answer he informed me. I took the tray off him and slipped him a tip don't worry he is so tired he has probable dropped of to sleep I told the man and wished him good night.

Eating some sandwiches and drinking some tea made me feel better. I don't know when but at sometime I lay on the top of my bed and must have dropped off and I was awoken at six the next morning with a banging on my door. Something is wrong Roger told me as I opened the door the hospital have rang the porter buzzed my room I grabbed my coat and we was on our way only stopping to tell the porter to keep our rooms open. We made the hospital in two minuetes flat and once we reached the room where Mary was we were meet by the nurse, she had a bad night she told us and we don't think she has long so we thought that we would call you, thank you I said as Roger pushed passed and sat beside his wife holding her hand.

What will I do he asked me with a tear in his eye I have never loved anyone like I have loved this woman she is my world I have nothing without her. I was lost for words all I could do was squeeze his shoulder and try to comfort him, Mary never awoke and just silently drifted to her death there was no pain and I swear that at that moment she looked very young again. I left him in her room and went to phone Dave and let him know what had happened and told him that I was taking a few days off too stay with Roger and help sort things, that's fine he told me under the circumstance but I should have had you on the new job tomorrow. I will ring the client he continued and tell him the score and if he don't except that I will send someone else we can always change you over later, give my condolenses to Roger tell him I will speak to him in a day or two and with that he hung up.

They gave Roger sometime with Mary before they took her body down to the mortary were it would be collected by a undertaker to make ready for her funeral in a week or so. I took Roger back to the hotel and spent the day just sitting around talking about their passed and how they meet and things they did in their life together.

It was not until the evening that we got a bite to eat I persuaded him to take a walk and popped into a local café where I ordered him a mixed grill whice he hardly touched. He was in a world of his own and I just had to sit there and do nothing but be his mate, just out of the blue he asked me about the mission in Chad. I told him what had happened and showed him my decorations which I had in the inside pocket of my jacket, I told him about Phil and how nobody belived me until Geordie had seen him at the end of our tour. Did you say that Dave knew about all this he asked me? Yes I replied he sent out the replacment in Simon and I phoned him to tell him that I had seen him twice working with the rebels "why" I asked?.

Well last week when I was in London sorting out some things for Mary I saw Phil and Dave come out of a club both were the worse for drink and looked like good friends to me not someone who had crossed his boss. Are you sure I ask ?, yes I tried to cross the road to talk to them but they saw me and jumped into a cab I just thought that it was funny but never took a lot of notice. What was going on I thought had Roger made a mistake or was there something that I needed to find out, I dicided that I would make a phone call to Chad and ask Roger to excuss me for a moment. I found a phone in the café and dialled the number Tim had given me when I was leaving to keep in touch with him, it rang and rang but there was no answer, he must have been on a patrol I will ring again later from the hotel I told myself.

I went back to the table and Roger was now very inqesitive there is something not right there Brummie he queried something smells what do you think? I will answer that once I make that call to Chad. How well do you know Dave and Phil I asked him? don't know much about Phil meet him once on a call to Dave was just told he was in the para's and had a rank of staff sargent but Dave I'v known a long time. He was in the mob the sametime as me he was a major and we did some tour of the provence together.

He had some trouble about money missing from the mess which he denide all knowledge of it but resined his commission instead of going for a court marshell. The next thing I know I had been out the Army for twelve months and I get a phone call asking me to do a job which as you know im doing it training marksmen to serrive. How long have you been doing the job? Coming on three years now he replied, and anything like this happened before ? No nothing. What about Phil when did he come on the scene?. He as been around for three years but took more on in the last eighteen months. Dave told us that Phil had spent sometime in Chad before I think that's the conection I told Roger but I cannot work it out yet but I will. We left the café and went back to the hotel, I asked the porter to get me Tims number in Chad and gave him the number I will be in room four I told him.

On entering Rogers room I made for the drinks cabinet and picked up to minutures of whisky, I don't know about you but I need this I told him and I was pleased to hear him say he needed one too. Afew minutes later the phone rang and the porter informed me that nobody was answering the phone ok leave it I will try again tomorrow I told him and wished him goodnight.

I think we emptied the minuture cabinet but it was just what Roger needed he fell asleep and stayed there all night. The next day all the arrangments were made to get Mary's body removed to their local undertaker so after a spot of breakfast which Roger ate a little we booked out and made for the station to catch a local train. One hour later we stood on the platform of the local station making our way to the exit, I don't think I could face the farm Roger told me, ok but what about the animals they will need feeding wont they? No the farmer down the road as got it coverd. What do you wont to do?, I will pop in the funaral director to make some arrangements you go make your call and its ten know looking at his watch meet you at the pub in a hour. I found a call box in the street and rang the operator to help me connect and Tim answered first ring, hi" Tim its Brummie, hello got back safe then he said. Yes I replied timmy listern when Phil went awol you did tell Dave that he had didn't you? Yes of course he replied you know he sent Simon and John to replace him and Jock. So just to be clear Dave knew that Phil had run off? Yes and I also told him later that you had seen him with the rebels, that's all I wanted to know I told him I will ring you soon to explain this conversation.

My mind was now pounding I couldn't think straight what was going on? I decided to ring Dave. Hello boss I said its Brummie just got to Rogers village just thought I would let you know that I am staying for the funaral so it will be ten days or so before I see you that ok, fine he said I am sending the rest of the boys out tomorrow on their next assignment you can follow later.

By the way you have not seen Phil around the city have you as a friend thought he saw him a few weeks back, I wish I had he told me sounding very cool I would have kicked his arse he continued. Fine I said trying to sound convinced I will ring again soon, are you staying at the farm he asked me? Yes was all I replied, see you soon then he said and rung off. I meet back up with Roger who was tucking into one of the pubs pies I will take one of those I told the barmaid and bring us two pints of local brew as well. I am glad to see you eating I told him are you feeling any better for eating he just nodded his head with a mouthful of pie. Mary will be cremated in nine days he told me I have seen the vicar and we can start out from the church were we will have a short service there then the main service will be held at the crem.

Roger was looking a bit better I think with him doing something and not just sitting around had took his mind of sue death a little. You get through on your call he asked? Yes and I got the answer I wonted and then I called Dave and asked him if he had saw Phil Which he told me if he had he would have kicked his arse.

He is sending the lads off tomorrow and wonts me to join them when I am finished here, he seemed concerned with where I was staying, Strange Roger said yes very strange I agreed but right now I am ready for this pie and the pint that the young lady is bring me. She placed the pie in front of me followed by the two pints of ale did you have a good time last time I saw you she asked, don't know I said did we?. She went redder than the cross on an ambulance and skurrid back to the bar giggling to herself, well if you don't remember I not going to tell you.

For the first time in three days I saw Roger smile, I think she is dead keen on you he told me, she is not a bad looker I said and what a body, by the way that night I didn't did I? don't ask me he said I was drunk too. Oh my god I cannot ask her and if I cannot remember she will think that I don't care and just used her. Don't worry they are a strong string these Norfolk girls thick skins and as hard as nails you wont hurt her feelings.

What do I say I asked him? You really wont to know well watch this, "Emma" he just said when he as drunk this pint and eat his pie he would like what he had the last time. She blushed again and shouted back we close at three he can wait for me and I will take him back to my place.

There you go all fixed, I cannot leave you I told him you can and you will I have things to do anyway so you go and enjoy. It had been a long time since I had had anything like sex so I was a bit nervous when she took me into her house but I didn't need to be as soon as she put her bag down she came to me. See anything you like she said leaning forward showing me down the front of her blouse at those ample soft mounds of flesh that formed her breasts. She undid her buttons very slow exposing more flesh as she went until she reached her black bra by then the blouse was off and she was reaching around her back to undo her bra. It must have been longer than I had thought because as she removed her bra my whole body shaked and my mouth just cupped onto those big errect nipples and they felt so hard just like the aniseed balls I used to suck when I was a kid. I felt her back arch up and there was a little moune as she sat on my lap faceing me and pushing herself towards my manhood. Pulling my jumper over my head she exposed my sunburnt skin, my were have we been to get a tan like that she said? Tell you later I said and slowly pushed my hand up her leg until it reached the soft material of her panties and the fleshy lips that they coverd.

This time there was a sqeal and a surge forward had my finger pushing her panties inside her soaking wet pussy ang the first of her many orgasams. I am not sure how long it took us to get undressed but we was on the bed kissing and foundling for such a long time, then she lowerd her head down and my whole world went into a spasm. The sensations was like I had never felt before each touch of her lips on my helmet my me almost orgasem, she pushed the length Of my shaft as far as she could down her throat.

Her seliva made my manhood so wet, it was throbbing and harder than I could ever remember it being, my hand touched her pussy and again got that urgent thrust of anticipation this time I couldn't hold back and rolled her onto her back. Her legs parted and I moved my body forward until I felt the tip of my manhood hit a slight resistance but to wet to stop me opening that hot little love passage. This time her back arched so much that my manhood went in hard right up to its full length and she screamed with pleasure and dug her long nails into my back.

We moved into a steady rock which made my manhood rub her tight moist walls of her pussy and soon the build up was to great and I felt my manhood explode into her as I felt her orgasem run down my shaft and spill out onto my balls so wet and so hot. I kissed her and just held her there with my throbbing manhood still deep in her pussy and she was still gushing out, how was that compered to last time she said? Wonderful I said much better, you liar she said you fell asleep last time before we got undressed. We just rolled around in fits and kissed and made love again till it was time for her to open up the pub for the evening shift and I needed to make my way back to the farm, see you soon I said yes if you don't leave for some other country, no I wont. Roger was seating in the kitchen when I got back drinking tea and looking at some pictures of him and Mary on different holidays or around the farm with the animals.

I didn't expect you back tonight he said did you have a good time? Yes this time I did and you knew that I didn't do anything last time didn't you. I don't know what your talking about he said with a grin, She is a nice girl I told him one that I think I could settle down with if I was not doing the job that I do. I have sat here thinking about that, now that I'm on my own I was thinking about what I wont to do and I thought about you. Ya what about me I moved to the teapot as I was talking and poured myself some tea, well you wont work for Dave any more so why not work here with me.

What me a farmer it would send me crazy, no not farming we could have our own school for snipers and charge the countries that wish to hire our men he continued. You could teach them how to shoot and I would teach them the tricks just the way you had to learn, it sounds great but I have something to find out and do first. I know all about that but you are not in Chad now you cannot go about killing people like you did there the laws stop you here so I think you should wait till the time is right then take your revenge.

I cannot do that Roger to meny people have been hurt now somebody has to pay for what they did. We talked on till late evening and until we were both falling to sleep as we talked, im going to call it a night I said am I in the same room as I was before? Yes he replied I'v aired the bedding so it should be warm in there. With that I said goodnight and made my way to my room leaving Roger to lock the doors and put away the cups we had used. The energy I had used that afternoon and the lateness of the night took its toll and I was soon tucked up in bed and sound a sleep in no time and didn't even hear Roger go to his room. I don't know how long I had slept but I awoke to what I thought was a noise down stairs and got out of bed straight away and crept down the stairs.

I was met by Roger at the bottom who put his hand to my lips to stop me from talking and whisperd there is someone around outside I can hear things moving and the animals are restless. I held my nine milimeter pistol up so he could make it out by feeling it in the dark, that's ok close up but these are better for longer range and he pushed a double barrel shot gun into my arms. Crawl on the floor to the front window while I go to the back door and if you see anything blast them and don't worry about the window.

I moved slowly around the furniture till I was under the window sill and took a slow peek, it was dark but a full moon gave the yard some light and cast shadows of the buildings around the farm but I saw nothing that would alarm me.

I stayed close to the window till Roger returned, who ever it was have gone he said turning on the light, are you sure you heared something I asked him?. As sure as my Mary is laying in the morgue down town he said, when you have been at this game as long as I you will know when you hear movement or not even when you sleep. We will see at first light there will be telling signs that I will know and after my training I hope that you will know, and with that he wondered into the kitchen and made a brew as we would not sleep no more that night. We talked about what happened in Chad and how Phil had switched sides half way through our tour and how is move had cost the life of Jock. I felt the burning inside me as I mentioned his name and the disire I had to kill him grew stonger with every word of his dirty tricks, it was as if he was trying to lead the rebels to a all out war I told Roger why he would want to do that I don't know.

You can garentee that there is something in it for him Roger replied and it mybe that Dave is a lot more involved than you expect, are you sure that's not just you trying to lure me away from him so we can set up this business together?. Roger gave me a stare that told me that he was hurt by what I had said, that decisions is yours he barked and there is no rush to make it. Daylight was now lighting the room and he beckond me to join him in the yard, so where would you start to look he ssked me? A spot where I would leased stand a chance of being noticed I replied. Good he said now look around a the spots where someone could watch the house but it would be hard for us to spot them, the barn I said you could stand back and look out without being seen, lets look he replied. We marched across to the barn which only had one half of the door remaining as the wind had blown it down I year ago and Roger had not got round to replacing it. Inside was parked the tractor and other farm equiptment and at the for end sheltered from the elements was kept hay seeds and animal feeds. I strolled to the rear of the tractor which was about ten foot inside the barn and looked out, I can see both doors to the house from here I said so this would be a good place to watch from and in the dark you wouldn't see this far into the building from the house.

Roger looked down at the ground around the tractor, yes who ever it was stood here he said picking up a butt end of a ciggy and pointed to an area of the floor that had some loose seeds that had been stood on and pushed down into the earthy floor. Park drive Roger told me looking at the ciggy, do you know anyone who smokes that brand?, not really I replied could belong to anyone Well it don't belong to me or Mary he confirmed we don't smoke.

I helped Roger with his farm cores and then went off to the village as I had arranged to meet Emma and go into Norwich for the rest of the day. Do you want to drive she asked me as we got to her old Mini she's old but she gets me around, no I replied I will just injoy the view glancing down at Emma's short skit which I knew would show off her charms in that low driving seat. Your cheeky you are she said but made a great display of gusset as she settled into the drivers seat, are you sure you need to go to Norwich I asked with my manhood twitching in my pants. Yes we do she replied and you can wait till we get back for that I have the night off from the pub so you have got me all night. With that we set off down the country lanes at a speed that Donaled Cambell would have used for his warm up run for his land speed record. We didn't say much just a glance now and then and a smile which was enough to tell me this girl was something special and that I had not had the feelings for anyone like I felt right then. About thirty minutes into the journey Emma said, that car behind us as been with us since we left the village and he as kept up with my speed if I didn't know better I would say he was following us. I held my position and just glanced into the mirrow without making her feel alarmed, he must be going to Norwich too I told her, yes maybe but I don't recognise the car at all he is not from the village, maybe on holiday I told her.

For the rest of the journey I watched the rear view mirrow until we reached the city, take the next left I told her "why" just to check out the fellow behind I told her. But why would somebody follow us she inquired don't know but take the next left. We rounded the next corner and a few seconds later the car behind us followed, ok now take the next right and pull up about twenty yards on the right side of the street. She did has I instructed her and we pulled up, a few seconds later the car also turned into the same street and when they realised we had stop made a effert to pull over but there was not enough distance to keep him away from us. The car a ford Cortina came to a halt in the middle of the street close enough for me to see the passengers inside, they were both black and dressed in multi-coloured shirts the type you see Caribbean people wearing.

They soon realised that we was on to them and the driver though the car into reverse and backed out the street and was gone in no time. What was all that about Emma ask me, don't know I replied maybe they are after someone and mistook us for them, could be she agreed but it seems a bit spooky. We found a parking spot in the city centre and went off shopping I checked about but didn't see the Cortina again that day but spent the day alert for any trouble. Shopping is not my favourite past time but watching Emma rummage through the different shops buy alsorts of clothes and especially the underwear were she made sure I was agreeing with her purchases to the amusement of the shop assistant. We drove home without any sight of our friends but I made sure that my nine milimeter was close to hand without Emma noticing it. I had got it tucked down the back of my waist band and when we had left the car I had hid it in the door rack so it couldn't be seen but now it was under my leg out of sight.

Emma cooked a meal and after the washing up we made love but I told her I was not happy to leave Roger on his own to long and I would be going home later.

About ten-thirty Emma gave me her car keys so I wouldn't have to walk back to the farm and I kissed her goodnight with a promise that I would meet her after work the next day. I followed the road from the village and headed for the farm as I got closer to were I had to turn into the yard I slowed down and killed my lights.

Everything seemed fine as I rolled the car up along side Rogers landrover and has I got out I glanced around the yard not seeing to much but listening for any sounds there was non.

Roger was just moping up the last bit of gravy off his plate when I went in, again he told me he was not expecting me back that night but once I told him about the Cortina he seemed glad I came back.

Ok, I wont us to do a night visual tonight and watch the barn area in particular if you set up outside I will keep a movement going around the house so as to keep anyone watching interested. Roger gave me one of his rifles only use it if they fire first if you can use this and he handed me a canon automatic camara with a zoom lense.

Lets try and see who as been out there and what they are after Roger continued I don't like these bastards stalking me like this so lets go and don't forget if you shoot aim to make them flesh wounds.

I moved slowly along the walls of the house trying to keep to the shadows and crossed the yard to an area were I could get a good view into the barn with the night sight. Covering myself with cam netting after I was sure nobody was around watching me I settled down for my wait, it was strange to be back here doing the things that Roger had tought but this time it was for real. I checked my night sight into the dark barn enterance and could see as far back as the back wall the tractor showed up a light green with a slight shine off the paintwork. Skimming around the yard I identified each object that I knew was there, bushes water barrels the feeding troughs for the pigs. As I moved back towards my start point I picked up Rogers shadow in the window he had drawn the curtains and the light from his lamp was throwing his shadow onto it.

Moving back to the barn door I relaxed and took a glance at my watch face and pressed the winder and the face lite for a second, twelve thirty that was the time it showed. I started my scan again but as I did I saw a figure move across the middle of the barn followed by a second and then a third, three of them I thought to myself. I looked towards the house and not only did I see Roger moving around the room I could makeout the silhouette of a head above the chair back one of Rogers tricks I guessed. Looking back towards the barn I noticed two of the figures had rasied there rifles up into the shooting position and without stalling for a moment I chose my target and fired. There was a scream of pain as my round ripped into the flesh of my targets hand causing his weapon to jump up and fire into the air, his partener got off a snap shot which broke the window. I knew Roger was fine as he retured two shots from the broken glass almost immediately towards the barn.

My target had hit the floor holding his injuried hand the others dived for cover behind the tractor, I placed a few shots very close to their hiding place and they was off like two rabbits out the back of the barn and gone. I shouted to the wounded man not to move or I would put another bullet in him at first he thought about it but I took the heel of his shoe and he just flopped to a sitting position with his hands up in the air. By this time Roger was out of the building and covering my prisoner but he said after that he could hear the other two stumbling about in the dark and sent a shot off in their direction.

That will keep them running he said as I joined him, now you get to your feet and don't make any funny moves he told the fellow sitting on the floor. He will make a few funny moves I told Roger I shot his shoe up so he wont walk that good in those shoes, Roger laughed and poked the man with his gun pushing him towards the house. Once inside we sat the man down and tied up his legs and arms to a chair Roger took a look at his hand, not bad he commented he will have a scare to remember you by but he wont loose any of his fingers. I looked at the face in front of me but it didn't ring any bells I had never seen him before, Who are you I demanded and what are you here for. Silence he said nothing so Roger sqeezed his bad hand and his face contorted with pain, I ask you again who are you and what are you doing here?.

This time Roger held his hand out as if he was going to hit it with his rifle, ok ok the man shouted I'll talk my name is Trevor Jenkins And I was sent to do a job on both of you. Who sent you said Roger and who were the two lads with you? Those two are mates of mine we was approced in the pub by two men they didn't say there names but gave us some dough.

They told us we would get more when the job was done and we had to give them a number so they could ring us to find out how we got on he continued in his cockney accsent. Now listern I wont you to discribe these men to us and think very carefully about it, if you do well we may let you go if not I will hand you over to my police friends. First he described Phil right down to his sunburnt skin and then he described Dave so now I knew that they are both involved in what ever the scam is and they both now see me as a threat. Ok we want you to take that call and tell them that it was a success and that you had killed the both of us and get to your mates and tell them to say the same if they are contacted. Whats in it for me he asked? Well we are experts at eliminating people and im sure you and your friends do not wish to be added to our list we don't mind a few free hits it keeps us in practise Roger told him. Besides I said you will get the extra money off the two that hired you if they think you did the job they paid you to do.

Nodding he said can I go now I will need to catch up with my friends befor they reach London and give the wrong information away, its going to be a long hard walk in those shoes but it will be a reminder of how good a shot we are we could have killed you now "get" Roger pushed him out the door.

Fancy sending a bunch of amateurs to do a job like that I told Roger as he closed the door behind the wounded man you better take a look at this befor you call them amatures. He lead me into the sitting room and there sitting on the settee was the mannequin that he had used to make the shooter think it was me, it had a hole in the back of its head. Jesus that was some snap shot I said if it had have been me I would have been pushing up the daisys soon I commented trying not to make any comments which would refer to Mary's funeral soon. That's why I let him go Roger said he was not your every day villain that you pick up in a bar those guys were ex mob and very well trained but this time we were better. I don't understand I said why didn't we just plug the guy and be done with it? Because my dear friend they will be back and next time they will be stronger and a lot more sharper than today. But I still don't understand why we let him go?, well as he was talking to us his eyes were clocking to see the weapons we had so he could go back to his friends and tell them our strenghs and weaknesses.

But what he didn't know was what we have in here and he pulled a book on the book shelve and the whole case open to reveal a doorway behind it. We entered into a dark room and Roger switched on the light, the walls were covered in all types of firearms, rifles handguns grenades knifes c4 landmines rpg's and lots more that could supply a army. But what can we do with all this equipment? I asked the laws of the land will not permit us to have a gun battle with a gang of hit me.

What the law don't know will not hurt them Roger replied and after we deal with this lot we both go after Dave and Phil, but Phil is mine I want him really bad I told him. We didn't expect anymore trouble that night but we took it in turns to get some sleep which was not a lot as we stayed on the settee so as to be close to each other if we got the call.

Roger went out at first light to check the area was safe while I cook us some breakfast, all clear he announced has he returned they must be licking their wounds after last night.

After we ate our food we went out and tended the live stock it was mild so Roger let them loose into the fields, they will be a good early warning if anyone disturbs them tonight roger explained. We then set about fortifying the farm buildings weapons were placed in areas that we could cover any approach by undisirables. Roger layed mines in areas that we was at our weakest but made sure nothing would set them off by accident after all we didn't want to kill the postman. Once the work was finished I set off to see Emma, we had arranged to have a meal together at the pub then spend the afternoon having some fun around the country side taking in the views. I told Roger that I would make it back before dark so as to be ready for anything that night may bring. Emma was serving behind the bar when I entered the pub, the rooms were very full with people having there lunches. A river ran by the village and it was full of holiday boat people who parked up on the jetties and used the pub for refreshments and this day was a very busy day for visiters.

I pointed to a free table in the corner and Emma acknowledged indicating that she would join me soon, there was two girls waiting on the tables and one brought me a pint of beer that Emma had poured for me. I looked around the room at the faces of the people but there was non that looked like hired hit men or anyone that was not there for a good time if anything the groups were having lots of fun.

It was a good hour before Emma managed to join me and she approached the table with two meals on large plates, I took the liberty of grabbing us both a meal I hope you like what I got you. At that moment I was so hunger I would have ate a raw cow, but I must say that home made steak pie with potatoes and vegitables was just the ticket. You are very busy today I said is there some reason that so many are on the river today? Yes she replied it's the start of the hoilday season and it always starts with a boat race up the river. Again I glanced around the room at all the faces, some of the men looked the part with their captains caps and polo neck sweaters other just look like day trippers out with their picknick baskets.

The women looked stunning in their summer frocks and flat shoes with ribbens and bows in their bonnets, some wore shorts and some had leggings on. What are you looking at Emma asked me with a cheeky grin on her face, I hope you don't want to sail off with some of those girls, no I said squeezing her leg under the table. After we had eaten our meal we sat chatting about the pub and other things about the village and I used this conversation to ask her about a few things. I expect you get a few strangers around this time of the year I stated were would they stay if they stayed over for a few nights? Well we have three rooms in the pub that we let out and then there is two more bed and breakfasts down the road but most people stay at the country view hotel on the outskirts of the village.

Why are you so interested you are not looking for anywhere to stay are? No I was just interested in were you could stay if you was visiting here as it seems very popular. Well the people with boats stay on the river but like I said there are places to stay she said starting to look suspicious, another drink I asked changing the conversation very quickly. What time do you get off work Emma? Oh I will be late today as it is so busy I promised Dad that I would work over after lunch. That's ok I told her

I don't wont to upset your dad after all he does own the establisment and you don't know we maybe related some day. Are you preposing to me she said? No but I may want to some day and I want to beable to be friends with your dad, she leaned over and kissed me. Listern I have promised Roger that I will be back early tonight so once you go back to work I will go a take a stroll around the village and I will see you tomorrow is that ok? Sure I don't think I will get away till after closing time tonight and im going to be tired so I think that will suit me too.

We kissed again and she went back to work leaving me to finish my drink, it was then that I notice a man standing at the bar who was not there last time I looked. He was tall about six two with dark hair and very broad shoulders his clothes didn't match those of the boat people and he was not dressed like a local more like a gangster. He watched Emma walk from our table and then glanced at me turning away as I looked back at him, he necked his drink and walked out the door. I rushed to pay my bill only to find that Emma had covered it so I followed the man out of the door only to find no sign of him. I hurried to the bridge to see if he was on the toll path but he was not with any of the others that were sitting on the bank. Making my way to the main street I checked the shops and the post office but still there was no sign of the man I moved down the street to the first bed and breakfast but the door was closed and I could see nobody in the lower windows.

I upped my pace as I walked but still there was no sign of the man until a car passed and there he was in the driving seat looking at me as he passed. The car was soon out of my sight, why had I not checked the pub carpark that's were his car must have been. There was no good crying over spilt milk I thought and made my way back to the farm to tell Roger what I had seen, he may have just been a passer by he told me once I had explained. This man was no sightseer he noticed me and he was gone and the look he gave me has he passed was that of a man out to get you. Well if they come again we will be ready for them Roger said and this time there will be no prisoners, but Roger we cannot fight a war here this is England there are laws. Yes my good man and the laws stink when a man cannot live safe in his home and can be punished for defending himself from riffraff like the guys that are coming here, well bollocks to the law.

If we don't get them they are going to take us down and they wont worry about the law Roger continued, but the bodies I asked how do we explain the bodies. Don't worry I have friends who will take care of that side and you don't need to know anything about it, lets just say that the pigs will be fed well the next day and Roger smiled. Things went very quite for the next few days we had no sightings of the tall man or anyone else come to that, that was until the day of Mary's funeral. I think the whole village turned out to see her off and people that had come from other parts of the country all filled the church that day. I sat next to Rogers sister who sat next to Roger she was the only family he had left now as his perants had died many years ago and were buried in this church yard as was Mary's mom and dad. Roger had decided to rest her body in with her family and it was when we stood around her grave that I noticed two men stearing over the wall.

Emma was standing beside me holding my hand and she noticed my glance and told me later that I squeezed her hand so hard it hurt her fingers, whats the matter she asked me?. Nothing I told her just a face I thought I knew and it was it was Phil but at that moment I couldn't do anything about it I was saying goodbye to a friend. I took another glance in Phils direction but he was gone, I didn't say nothing to Roger until we was at the wake and I had him alone without any friends around him. Are you sure it was him he asked? Positive I replied I would know that bastard anywhere his face will be in my mind even when I get him. Then tonight we must be on the alert, they will think after the sorrow of today we will be off guard but we will have a surprise for them and tonight you may get your man, Rogers words sunk into my skull tonight you may get your man.

With our traps set we took up position outside of the house, Roger went up into the loft of the barn, this gave him the full view of the back door of the house and all the rear buildings. I took up my position under the hay as I had done in my training days when Roger had been hunting me, from there I had full view of the front of the house and the yard up to the barn.

The smell made me feel sick at first but my nostrils soon got used to it the biggest problem I had was it was a warm night and the horse muck was very warm to so I was getting very hot under my cover. After three hours I was at boiling point but I stayed as still as I could in that sticky temprature. Checking my night scope I picked up every movement and I was surprised to see the diffrwant visiters that we had to the yard of a night. Fox, badger, rabbits, and rats all paid us a call that night but at three in the morning I noticed my biggest movement a dark figure appered in my scope.

The figure stayed close to the bushes at first but came out to look at the rear door moving close as if to inspect it. This man was a decoy, testing the area to see if we was laying in wait for them I just let him move around and watched him, he sneaked up to the kitchen window and sneaked a glance. At that moment I heard a faint rustle about a yard from where I lay someone was walking close to me and had trod on the hay making a crushing sound as the hay pressed together.

I held my breath as a figure appered from the side of my view and walked slowly into the yard till he was fully in front of me, the full moon outlined his frame and I could see this was a big man. He moved closer to the building until he had joined his friend at the back door, I moved the safty catch to the ready position on my weapon and line the big guy up for my first shot. Just then there was a almighty bang from my blindside of the building someone had tripped Rogers trap and let out a scream, the two in front of me hit the dirt. Gun fire was coming from the front of the house and Roger was returning it from the barn, the two men in front of me got to their feet but kept close to the wall one went to the left with his back to me the other came to the right facing me. I lined up my sight on the nearest man and fired hitting him in the head and has he fell he fired a round into the ground, this made the second man spin around to face me but was unable to see were my shot had come from so again he pressed himself up against the wall.

He fired two random shots wild hoping for a hit but one hit the wall of the pigsty and the other past by me heading out into the field. I took aim at the second man just as he decided to make it back to the bushes and he was half way across when my round hit him in the chest knocking him sidewards to the ground. More explosions came from around the far side of the building and a lot more shouting flashes from the barn told me Roger was still incountering the enemy but nothing more came my way.

Then silence fell for a few moments it was as if nothing had happened I waited there was no way I was going to move till I knew it was safe to do so Roger had told me that. I could hear moaning coming from the front side but no firing or shouting was to be heared now, there was some light coming from a fire I could see the flickering of flames but not see the fire. Then I heared a car engine start up some distance away and the squeel of the tires as they raced off on the tarmac of the road. Roger came to the corner of the barn and gave me the all clear and I crawled out from under the hay and walked over to the two bodies laying on the ground. The tall guy was the man I had seen at the bar that day my round had hit him near his right temple and had took the left half of his face away the best part of his brain lay in the dirt.

The second guy I had hit just under his right arm the round had smashed his ribs and travelled through his right lung and punchered his heart. I moved around to the front of the house to find the fire was in a oil drum that Roger kept for his tractor fuel, he also had two bodies one had been hit by a round from Rogers rifle and was as dead as a dodo.

The second had been caught by Rogers make shift device and was still alive but very badley chewed up the bandage on his hand gave his identity away Roger walked over and put two rounds in his head at close range. How many you get he asked me? Two the same I replied non of them were Phil, no I didn't see him this side of the house so he didn't come or stayed at the car Roger informed me. What we going to do with the bodies I asked him? I'v just got to make a phone call in the morning and these will be sorted now give me a hand and we will get them in the barn till day-break. After we had put all the bodies into the barn and Roger had thrown a cover over them we checked the area to make sure no-one was lurking around.

Let's get a bit of shut eye he told me I'll take first watch I will wake you in a few hours time, surprisingly my head hit the pillow and I was gone and Roger never did wake me up. When I did finally wake it was getting on for noon, I looked out the window and Roger was out in the field driving his tractor. I washed and dressed and went down and found a pot of coffee on the stove with a note saying some bacon and eggs in the larder help yourself.

After breakfast I made my way out to the barn just as Roger was pulling into the yard, why didn't you wake me? I shouted over the noise of the engine. I wouldn't have slept he answered me now Mary has gone I don't think I will sleep that much again, I nodded in understanding but knew that he should get some rest. I wandered into the barn and to my surprise there was no bodies, Were are they I asked with my eyes? By now they will be pigs swill Roger said. He explained that his friend about four miles away came and picked the bodies up early this morning and took them back to his farm where he mashes up offel and bones for pig swill then sells it to the local farmers to feed the pigs.

So that's the end of them boys and nobody will ever no that they were here and im sure Dave and his mob wont report them missing will they? Roger said. I don't surpose they will I replied, here let me help you with the live stock I expect they need feeding? They do I spent the first part of the morning getting rid of the devices that I made so we are all safe now. Once the work was done we sat down to have tea and Roger went over his plan for the future, I will keep the farm going but not as much as before he told me. We will recrute some lads from the mob and train them up to go fight in trouble spots around the world, pay them a good wage but make a good living ourselves by supplying them. We will train them well and make them a ellite force so all the money countries will come to us for our men. I want you to be my partner so you will not need to go out again on any missions you can just train up all the crack shots.

What about funds to get us started I asked him? we will need more equiptment than you have in that room I pointed to the wall and contacts you will need to know people I continued. Don't worry I have some money put away and Mary just left me a nest egg, I will sell the part of the farm I don't need to help with the running costs to start. Once the money comes in we will take out the running costs and then the wages and the rest will be ours. I need a bit of time to think it over I told him, but if I do come in I have a few bob that I earned in Chad and didn't spend that go's Into the kitty too. Do you have to see Emma tonight he asked? me once we shook hands on the possible deal, I think I had better I was surpose to call in this morning. With that I got my coat and headed off to the village, it was a lovely early evening with a light early evening sky a royal blue with a few stars just starting to show.

I entered the main street and headed towards the pub still searching The area for signs of any trouble but there was non to be seen.

Emma's dad stood at the bar as I entered and he didn't look to pleased, where have you two been he stated making the four customers in the room turn their heads and stare. She was surpose to be back on duty at six and she didn't turn up he continued, im sorry I said I don't know what you are talking about I told him I have not seen her today. His face dropped and he explained that when I had not turned up she had told him that she was going to come to Rogers farm to see if I was alright and that she would be back for six. I felt my heart beat speed up and a sick feeling move from my stomace to my throat, I had to do some work for Roger I told him and that's why I have arrived now to see her. So where can she be he said its not like her to miss a shift without telling us, I don't know but I will make a search of the area give me the names of her friends I told him never mind that im coming with you and he called his wife to cover the bar.

Close the kitchen if you get to busy he told her im going to look for our Emma she may be hurt somewhere. A few of the local lads where just coming in and when they heared the news they came out with us. She was heading towards Rogers farm Tony Emma's dad told them so there are only two ways so you two take the road way and we will walk the river tow path. The word river made me shudder what if she as fell in went through my mind but all the while we looked I knew that Phil and Dave was involved some how. As we walked the tow path we checked every boat to see if anyone had seen her, it was dark now and the face's that came to the doors where dark in the cabin lights but nobody had seen her that was until we came to the last boat moored up.

It was one of the holiday makers that used the area a lot and knew Emma well from the nights they used the pub. She went passed us about three they told us and stopped to talk to a man about a hundred yards further up the tow path, did he grab her I asked feeling that sick feeling in the back of my throat. No he seemed to ask her something and then they went through the hedge and climb into a car which I could only see the roof becoase of the hedge. "What colour" I asked my voice now showing anger? It was green but I couldn't be sure of that the sun was in my eyes. I have got to get back to the pub I told Tony and make a call, Who has got her Tony asked me you know something and you an't saying, I could be wrong just let me check I told him and with that ran back to the pub.

Once in the bar I went to the public phone, took out the paper Dave had given me with his number on and dieled the number, it rang for a long time then it was answered. Nobody spoke not until I asked is that you Dave, Brummie a voice came back which was not Dave's it was Phils, I have been expecting you to call he said we have your young lady here. His reply tore into my chest and this time I was sick, We couldn't get you at the farm but we hold all the cards now he continued, you are making a lot of trouble for us and now it will stop if you want to see her alive again.

You bastard you harm one hair on her head and I will search the world looking for you and when I find you, He cut me short of my threat. You are in no position to threaten me at this moment I can do what ever I ljke to her and there is nothing you can do to stop me so you had better listern and shut the fuck up. We wont you to stop your little quest at getting me or Dave in return we will be out of the country and out of your life, as soon as we have reached our destination we will contacted you and let you know where you can find the girl. What if I tell you bollocks I said then we kill the girl after having some fun with her and fly out anyway and you will have to search for us and that could take you a life time. I leaned back on the booth wall and could not get my breath, how can I trust you I said ?

You will just have to he replied now listern we have a flight out of here in a few hours and in that time we don't want to see you or Roger anywhere near this address. You killed some of our best men last night but we have more and they will be keeping an eye on us and if you turn up here before nine a.m tomorrow they will kill your girl. Now do we have a deal or do I start removing her cloths and have some fun it would take you a good while to get here and im sure I could have a lot of fun before I would need to leave.

I could feel the tears running down my cheeks as I answered him I will not move from here till daybreak I told him and another thing no police if my lads see so much as one bobby taking interest in this place and I cut her throat and run and with that he hung up. I turned to find Emma's mom and dad standing behind me, who's got her Tony asked? with sadness in his voice.

They are dangerous men I told them but if we do as they tell us she will be fine, are you one hundred percent sure of that her mom said?. I didn't answer straight away as I needed to think, Phil was a barstard that had killed before for no reason and he had sent people to their deaths with no conscience so why would he spare Emma. I don't know I told them, well who are they and what do they want Tony ask? The answer was simple they want me to stay off their backs while they escape to were ever they are going.

They both looked at me puzzled, so this is about you Tony said with anger in his voice? I just nodded, if anything happens to my girl I swear I will kill you he told me now lets call the police. We cannot do that I told them they will kill her for certain if they see the police anywhere near their place and I have only been once so im not sure where it is. Can I please ask you to wait till the morning and see if the call comes in telling us where she is, will you do that for me? They both just gave me a nod.

I need to go back to the farm and speak to Roger so I will be back at first light to wait with you for that call and with that I left heading back to Roger as fast as my legs would let me. Once I reached the farm I explained everything to Roger and he was as shocked as we all was but his mind started planing what to do. They don't want us there until nine so I can see two reasons for that, one that is the time they reach their destination, two they could have set an ambush for us and that is the time they now know you will get there looking for Emma. So what do I do? "we "go now and make it before they can get away and kill Emma. Why do you think he will kill her? I asked with more tears running down my cheeks, because you have put a spanner in his works and to him this will be pay back for the money he has lost and the men you have killed that would have cost him more money. What he said made sence so we got some kit together and loaded Rogers jeep it would take us some time to reach London but it will be faster than waiting for the next train.

Has Roger drove we made plans of what to do when we got there now we don't wont a gun battle he told me as that would bring the police before we got into the building. We will watch for a while to see where the gaurds are then take them out one at a time with these and he pulled out two long thin bladed knives from the glove compartment. Then we will enter the building and take care of anyone in there lets hope Dave and Phil are still there and Emma is still alive he looked at his watch we should be there for about three thirty. We spent the journey down to London making plans on how to get into Dave's apartment and what the surrounding area looked like if we meet trouble. Roger had handed me a nine milimeter pistol with two magazines with nine rounds in each, also he handed me a silencer to fit the barrel if we meet any trouble we will need to keep it quiet. Tony was determing to come so Roger told him to drive the car and not get involved with the rescue, but its my daughter he had demanded but Roger told him harshly that if he got in the way it could cost Emma her life.

That did the trick and Tony said he would stay with the car incase we got into trouble. It was three thirty six when we reached the outskirts of London and it took us about four minutes to arrive two streets down from Dave's street and his swanky apartment block. Now Tony you wait here and if you see or hear anything get out of here and go for the police but you told me that, Roger stopped him mid-sentence, if we get into trouble we could all be dead so just do it. Roger and I climbed from the car and made our way to the corner keeping close to the wall as not to make any shadows.

Peeping around the corner we could see Dave's apartment block about one hundred yards up on the other side of the street, it was a old Victorian building squire in shape with a flat roof iron railings ran across the front with steps leading up to a main front door in the centre of the building.

We will need to cross the street to get to the other side and have a look around the back Roger told me Hopefully we may find a better way in.

Use the parked cars as cover he told me and keep your eyes open at the front of the building I will go first Roger told me and just as he was about to go someone lit a ciggy in the car parked across the street from

Dave's block. Dam said Roger with those street lamps they would have seen me crossing the road and at this time of the morning who would it be out and about?. How can we get near the place with those men in the car and god knows how many are hiding in hedges and alley-ways all around the building. What if we get Tony to drive past with us in the back and once we have passed the car we could slide out behind a parked car that would put us on the right side of the street I suggested.

That might work they wont know Tony's face so he might be a person on a early sift going off to work for all they will know, lets try it, we went back to the car and gave Tony instructions of what we wanted him to do. Just drive past at a normal speed we told him and don't look at the cars just incase there was more than one and when we are about seventy yards away slow down and we will roll out behind the parked cars. We hid ourselves low in the back of the car and Tony pulled way keeping his speed to the limit and he whispered that he was just coming up to the building. Has he got close he noticed two men step out from the doorway at the top of the steps and Tony just drove on as if he had not got a care in the world which must have been hard for him to do.

He slowed the car down a bit further on and and Roger was up door open and out like a rabbit and I was not far behind him, Tony kept at a slow speed so the door would not fly wide open and bang a parked car.

Roger and I lay flat on the floor looking under the car we was behind untill we was sure that nobody had seen us and then Roger crossed the pavement and into a garden I followed a moment later.

We climbed a gate and made our way round to the back gardens were we climbed each fence and wall until we reached the garden that belonged to Dave's apartment block. Carefully we peered over the wall into the garden, Two men stood near the rear gate talking as if there was nothing to fear but soon they would find out that their security was far from adequate. Roger indicated what we was going to do and I readied myself to carryout the movement that would take down these two men with the utmost silence.

Roger scratched the wall with a stone he had picked up off the ground and both men stopped talking and indicated with hand movement were the noise was coming from.

Slowly they moved towards the wall and when they was close myself and Roger sprung like two gazelles over the wall and landed two heavy blows to each of their heads.

Both went out like sleeping babies and after removing their weapons we dragged their bodies into a out-building and put a heavy roller up against the door locking them in.

We made our way to the rear entrance and found the door unlocked, entering we headed for the staircase not risking the lift up to the third floor we climbed the stairs with caution.

Checking each of the landings as we went we meet no opposition and finaly reached Dave's apartment door which was slightly open.

I smell a rat Roger whispered to me but I was keen to find Emma and slide into the room and moved slowly down a dark corridor heading towards a room with a light on.

Roger was now beside me and indicated to be careful, I glanced through the door but saw nobody Roger again indicated to be careful So again I pulled my weapon from my waist-band and made it ready for trouble. I entered the room and made a sercure sweep with my weapon paning around the room it was empty I then checked the kitchen and the two bedrooms they to were also empty. Once we were sure that the apartment was empty we started to search for any clues to where Emma my be and that's when I found the letter. I had opened the door of a writing bureau and just lying on there was a note which read, We knew you would come so we have left a little surprise for you, you didn't need to come down here you should have checked the water for the girl bye bye "boom".

"Get out of here "I shouted to Roger who was checking the other side of the room and without question he dived for the door and was out the front door in a shake. I only made it to the hall before the blast knocked me over and I must have fell unconscious becouse the next thing I knew was I was in the car with Roger and Tony heading out of London. You alright Roger asked me? Apart from a large headace Im fine I replied checking myself over for cuts. We was lucky the bomb had been put near to the window and most of the blast had gone that way and the hall wall had save you from death he continued. I ran back after the blast and dragged you out, Dave's man had all scampered off so tony drove to the front and helped me out with you before the police arrived. I read the note Tony stated you still had it in your hand when we lifted you do you think my Emma is dead, I don't know I replied I just don't know.

Anger took over and he shouted if you two had not got her mixed up in this lot she would be safe at home now and then tears ran down his cheeks and Roger just leaned over and sqeezed his arm, we don't know yet she may be ok.

We drove as fast as we could in the early morning traffic keen to get back to Norfolk keen to get back to the river to search for Emma.

My head was still pounding from the explosion, you alright Roger asked noticing me holding my head, yes just a thick head I told him. You were lucky he repeated that bomb was for you, yes I agreed they are trying to get me now befor I get them. That bomb was triggered to go off as soon as we opened the door with a timer set to a limit so we would be right were they wanted us befor it went off Roger stated thank god you found that letter as fast as you did. Tony breaked hard at that very moment and broke our conversation, steady Roger told him we have just escaped death once we don't want to do it again for a while or bring the police to us carring these weapons on board.

Tony growled something back and continued to drive a little slower this time but still faster than the speed of that road. I closed my eyes and that helped to clear my head a bit but I couldn't stop thinking about Emma, what had them bastards done to her and where would we find her. I don't know if I blacked out or I fell asleep but a heavy jolt brought me to my senses as Tony pulled up on the pub car park and jumped out of the car. We made for the river without going into the pub, where are we going to start Roger said?.

There were very few boats moored along the bank that morning so we decided to split up Roger would take the left bank Tony would cross the bridge and take the right bank and I would check the basin. Once I reach the basin I could see about ten boats some had covers over them so I checked them first. Undoing the ropes I pulled back the covers one by one but found nothing, most of the boats were being repaired so they had there engines out on the bank or had tackle up ready to lift them.

One took my eye it was low in the water looked like it had taken in water so I made for that and as I got near I could hear a faint tapping sound. Climbing on board I went down the stair way to a small galley area the tapping was coming from down below this area so I lifted a inspection hatch and lowered myself down. There was a lot of water down there but the boat had been put on blocks so it would sink no lower and there in the corner just out of the water on a pile of ropes was Emma. She had been tied and gagged her clothes were torn and dirty there was a cut near her left eye she was just about alive. I was going to need help to get her out so I untied her and wiped her face with my handkerchief to remove some of the blood she was not awear I was there so I climebed out and ran to get Roger and Tony.

Both followed me into the basin and down into the bottem of the boat Tony removed his coat and coverd her body then we all lifted her Up into the galley and out onto the deck. We carried her to the pub and rang for a ambulance which took about thirty minutes to arrive in that time Emma just lay on her bed in a coma state of shock not moving and not speaking. Tony's wife went with the ambulance and Tony followed in the car not allowing myself or Roger to go, you did this he told us now stay away. I had never in my life felt so gutted as I felt at that moment I loved that girl and through me she had suffered this terrible ordeal and I could do nothing about it.

Roger patted me on the back, he is angree now he said just give them time and it will all sort itself out, Im going to get them bastards I told him if it's the last thing I do, no he replied we are going to get them. The rest of that morning we phoned around some friends of Rogers calling in favours one worked at Luton airport and he could check the first flights out that day and passenger information, information that could get him the sack but he owed Roger big time. The hospital wouldn't give me any information about Emma so we had to wait till Tony and his wife came home, he was still not in the best of moods with us but his wife told us more. Emma had been raped and was suffering from shock the hospital said it could take a while befor she came out of her world that she was in but they said she would recover from her injuries.

I put my arms around Emma's mom and told her that I loved Emma and I was going to put things right, please tell Emma that I am sorry and that I will be back soon.

It will take some time for this to heal she told me but once it do's you will both be happy together again and she kissed my cheek, and don't worry Tony will come round soon. Roger got the call back from his friend about noon, Dave had used his real name when he booked his flight to Paris that morning but he was travelling with a Mr Alan Walker, they had a connecting flight booked to take them onto Tunisia and then by charter plane into Libya at nine o'clock that morning.

They was trying to hide in Gaddaffi country but I was going to follow and kill them both. I made arrangements for myself and Roger to fly out that evening to Lisbon and then get a connecting flight to Tunisia we would have to make arrangement when we get there of how to get into Libya. We cannot take any weapons with us Roger told me we will have to find a contact there to buy some, fine I replied but first I need to ask Tony if I can see Emma.

Tony had calmed down by this time and he was more interested in me getting the men who were responsible for Emma being hurt and gave me his blessing to see here later before we left on our flight. The hospital was close to the airport at Luton so we packed a few things and set of in Tony's car he would drive down with his wife in her car and pick it up from the airport the next day. Emma was in a side ward keeping her away from the other patients So as not to get her embarrassed by the staring eyes and the unwanted questions. I had not noticed her face when we had got her up to the ambulance.

They had really beat on her, her eyes were black and there was a cut on her cheek which had been made by a ring. Scratches all over arms and legs were they had held her to stop her struggling and alarge red mark were the gag had been on her mouth. She didn't speak she just dropped her head in shame, don't do that I said you have nothing to be ashamed of and I held her hand and kissed her on the forehead. I have to go away for a while but as soon as I get back we will go away for a break, America or Jamaca some where hot so you can rest. She looked me full in the face and said you are going after them aren't you? This time I dropped my head, they have to be sorted I told her I wont rest untill they are put away, or dead she finished my sentence.

Yes I said if it comes to that then yes, and I will have to lay here not knowing if you are dead or alive don't you think I have been hurt enough?. Emma there are men in Chad that will not be coming home I must do it for them too. As tears ran down her face I kissed her again and turned away leaving here there alone with her sorrow but I knew that I must do it or those two would get men killed again. Roger had been busy calling in some favours and had arranged for some weapons to be waiting for us in Tunisia plus he had got us a lift on a cargo flight that travels daily into Libya and was not ever serched so we will get our weapons in. We had six hours before the flight so we grabbed a bite as we may not get a good meal for a while and we needed a couple of hours sleep at lest but we would get that on the plane.

Outside the hospital was a flower stand so I got Emma some roses and sent them up with one of the nurses to tell here that I will come back and we will have that trip plus I loved her very much.

I just had time two buy a few things in the airport shops befor it was time for us to board the aircraft, thing like shorts and t-shirts so we could look like tourists when we reach Libya.

On the aircraft Roger told me what his friend had said about Dave and Phil, they had offered him a partnership in their cunning operation but he had turned them down.

But why would they offer him a shear of their bussiness I asked him? Because he is one of the biggest gun dealers in Europe Roger stated and they need guns. He continued to tell me what it was all about during that flight to Lisburn and when he had finished it now all made sense. They were offering troubled countries a supply of men to help fight the rebels but at the same time they were supplying the rebels with arms and ammunition. They had made themselves the best of both worlds by keeping the troubles going they got paid for having the man power out there and they were paid well by the rebels for the weapons.

The bastards never had any thought for the men they were sending to there deaths or the wives and kids that would lose their husbands and dads I told Roger and he just nodded in agreement. And that's where you come in he continued you done such a good job in Chad that the rebels give up there fight and the president didn't need you no more and the rebels didn't want any weapons. Makes sense I commented, yes but Phil broke away to try to keep the rebels going only for you to cover every move he made and that's why they are trying to kill you. Well now they can watch their own backs because I am going to rip both of their hearts out and stuff them down their throats.

Roger had a smile on his face, what are you grinning at I asked him? I was just thinking how good I have taught you, your now almost as good as me.

I must confess continued Roger I was offered a partnership with them too but only to train snipers I didn't know about the rest of the dealing and I promise you that. We arrived at Lisburn to find our connection had been cancelled till the next morning so we booked in at the airport hotel and got our heads down for the night. I didn't sleep well I kept thinking of Emma so I finaly got up and phoned the hospital to ask how she was and all I was told was that she was comfortable.

After a hearty breakfast we arrived back in the departure lounge and boarded our flight to Tunisia and I slept most of the flight only waking to hear the wheels of the aircraft being lowered for landing. I will need to contacted the contact Roger told me as we left the airport you wait over there in that little café while I poke around looking for his place and order me a coffee but not that small cup black shit they drink here. I made myself comfy in one of the out side tables and waited with our coffees till he returned which was only a few moments later. Found him he said, our flight has gone today so again we need to wait till tomorrow but he has a room for us and he will get us to the private airfield in the morning to get our flight. The weapons are in the room so we can check them out he continued there is even a place we can go to fire them to make sure they work ok and we have not been off loaded with some scrap. All these delays were starting to piss me off but I knew that I was going to get those two bastards even if it took me my lifetime finding them. The room was basic with two single beds that were at lest clean that's more than I can say for the rest of the room it needed a womens touch to put it back into shape. Dust was thick on the furniture and the windows had never seen a water bucket but it was only for one night and I didn't think I would sleep anyway.

Saffi Rogers friend from the past and our host for that night pulled up a floor board and pulled out two sniper rifles and two pistols from beneath. I have only twenty rounds for the rifles he told us but there are thirty rounds each for the hand guns, fine Roger told him we should only need two for the rifles anyway. The weapon were new and still in the makers grease, so I got down to cleaning both rifles while Roger tackled the hand guns. First I cleaned the American M21 it took a 7.62 round and was light to handle, good for a shot of around seven hundred and fifty meters. This one had a five round mag but you could get a ten or twenty round mag for them, this weapon had seen some action around the world.

The next rifle was a Dragunov svd a weapon I had never seen befor yet alone fired one, also took a 7.62 round and was effective up to 8 hundred meter with a max range of 1500 meter with a scope and a ten round mag. We will need some more ammo for these if we are going to test them. Saffi acknowledged my request and took off to find some more ammo for the rifles returning thirty minutes later with fifty more rounds. Both the hand guns were Beretta 92fs models 9mm with a 15 round mag, these have never been fired Roger commented Saffi nodded his head been under floor for a long time I forgot they was there till yesterday he told us. They were soon clean and oiled so Saffi got out his old van which looked like a butter tub on wheels but it got us to were we needed to go even though it sounded like we left the gearbox on the dusty road more than once. Finaly we reached a quite little spot were there was no buildings or any sign of life, here is good said Saffi no peoples and ran down a length of the road with a arm full of bottles and placed them on bits of wall that was still standing.

I decided to fire the Dragunov first, taking aim I squeezed the trigger the round hit the wall about nine inches below the bottle. Making the adjustment to the sight I pushed another round into the chamber and lined up my sight on the target, this time the round hit the bottle near the neck leaving the body standing on the wall.

Another adjustment to the sight and this time the bottle flew into pieces as the round hit it full on, Two rounds later and two more smashed bottles I was happy with that weapon.

I went through the same procedure with the M21 doing the adjustments were needed until I was happy that that weapon too was up to the standad I needed to hit a target from a distance.

Saffi had set up a small range to test both the hand guns which Roger did the testing and both were very good hitting his targets first time without adjustments.

Content with our evenings work we went back into the city center and found a place to eat after we made the weapons safe back at Saffi's the we found a little bar full of holiday makers.

After a few beers we went back to our room, what are your plans asked Roger once we settled down on the top of our beds, what do you mean I asked we are going to kill those two bastards that hurt my girl.

Yes I know that bit but what are you going to do once its all over, I will marry Emma if she will have me and settle down. What about my plan to go into business together? We can do that but I will not go out to other countries and fight their wars I will just train men how to shoot I told him. That's fine by me he said but sometime we may have to go to the country to strike up a deal for the hire of the men or arrange weapons? We will cross that bridge once we come to it.

I slept a lot better that night and awoke refreshed I even ate some chicken cuscus that Saffi had prepared for breakfast. All the weapon got packed into some package cases a we set off to the airfield were we boarded the plane to Libya. Roger had told Saffi to start getting some weapons together as we my call on him in the future to supply us with some big orders and he told us that he would always do business with us. The flight was just one and a half hours and once on the ground we only saw a few of Gaddaffi's guards checking some of the aircraft but ours was not approached. Saffi had arranged everything including transport there was a landrover waiting for us and with the weapon on board we drove off out the gate and headed towards Tripoli were we knew that's where Dave and Phil would head.

The large sea port with its industrial connections and terrorist links would be to much of a chance for them to turn away from.

We drove around the streets looking like lost tourests but keeping our eyes open for anything that might look a bit shady or any clues to were we may find our targets. We found a run down hotel by the docks which offered cheap rooms for sailors to bring back the ladies for a night of pleasure before they sailed off to some country that were still dealing with Libya. Roger was very good at finding things out so while I was sorting out the weapons in our room he went to chat to some of the locals and see if he could get any clues to were Dave and Phil could be. The first day passed with no news of any Englishmen arriving in the area but on the evening we had found a bar which was very shady.

Full of seaman both cargo ships and fishermen were to be found in this establishment rogues and pirates the lot of them all here to watch the dancing girls who rotated their belly-buttons and moved to the music and offered plenty of after services to get their hads on the sailors money. We found ourselves a seat close to the dance floor and a waiter came and took our order which was two cold beers.

A bowl of dried fruit was placed on the table, even though this place was rough it did have some style and the service was pretty good. The place was not that well lite with only a few lights around the room but the centre of the room was best lite as this was the dance floor and this was where the girls earned their money.

Our drinks arrived and we sat back to watch the show, two girls came spinning in from out of a dark corner both wearing seqined panties with a satin bra like top bare midrifts see through nylon trousers covered the panties which were split down the sides showing their fleshy legs.

Both girls had a ample cleavage which looked like it was going to fall out of that red satin bra top. Roger was not paying that much attention to the girls he was surveying the room to see if there was anyone doing any businness most people selling stuff in a place like this are normally good for information.

One of the girls got close to our table and Roger pushed some money into her waistband this made her dance a lot more closer to us after that so I followed suite and put a note in the other dancers waistband. The waiter returned to our table with two more beers and asked if we would like to order any food so we took the menu as a tourest would and made a order of lamb and vegetables with cous-cous. Roger had seen some dealing going on over in one corner of the room so headed over to see if he could do some dealing and maybe get some information that may help us.

The dancers were now getting to the climax of their dance and were shaking their bodies in a frenze that would worry a doctor if they were lying in a hospital bed bed here it just made the audience clap and jump for joy. Our meals arrived at the table just as Roger returned and the dancers took a break, well did you find anything out? Maybe was his answer as he spooned in a mouthful of food. I'm so hungry he told me as he chewed his meal but I was to impatient to eat I wanted to hear his news, tell me what you heard I pressed him. Two English men have hired a warehouse on the docks not to far from here.

The man said there was guards all around and they was not Gaddaffis troops they had no uniforms on. Roger took another mouthful of food, well lets go I said raising from my seat, sit down eat your meal and wait as soon as the fellow has finished his dealing he is going to show us the warehouse. I sat back down and tried to eat but I was so keen to get out and find this place it had took away my hunger and I just watched for the man to see when is dealing was finished. Finally the man beckoned us to follow him and we followed him out the door and into the street which was still full of traders selling their goods and seamen looking for a sexy lady for the night.

CHAPTER FIVE

We rushed along the crowded streets trying to keep up with the dealer it was obvious that he was keen to go back to his work and earn his living.

Soon he stopped and spoke to Roger and pointed in a direction which then Roger gave him a small amount of notes and he was gone.

We have to go down this alley and we will be at the docks Roger told me, the warehouse will be just to our right once we hit the dock road there will be a gate with a guard.

In no time we were looking across the road at the warehouse which was fenced off with only one gate to enter or exit, it had its own docking bay which would accomadate at lest three cargo ships. Six cranes on rails ran along the dock but only one ship was docked and that sat low in the water so it was loaded to sail or waiting to be unloaded and stored into the warehouse.

We hid ourselves behind some small rowing boats that had been turned upside down on the jetti just outside the compond close enough to see into the warehouse if the doors opened, we could also watch the guards patrol the area.

How are we going to get in there I asked Roger? We are not going to yet he replid, first we will watch the place to see if this is where Dave and Phil are operating from, once we have established that we then make our plans.

This time I had to agree there was no pointing going in half cocked and getting ourselves into trouble that would be a waste of time. We started a six hour watch till we were sure that this was the place, I started the watch and roger went back to our room to get some rest before he relived me. Nothing happened on my first watch but I was able to observe the guard movements and change overs, if we was going to enter that dock it would have to be at night. At three in the morning Roger relived me and I told him the guards movement so he could establish if the pattern changed at all throughout the night.

Well I was so tired that I had no sooner put my head down and I was gone and I was awoken some hours later by Roger coming into the room, what are you doing here I said thinking something was wrong. I have seen everything that we needto know and he began to tellme of the things he had seen at the dockside. Around seven thirty they started emptying the ship first there was creates that went into the warehouse weapons by the looks of them Then came boxies of medical supplies and other UK products that have been boycotted by the europain countries.

At nine a dozen lorries arrived to take away these supplies with a escort of Gaddaffi's finest with a high ranking officer to make sure all went well and guess who arrived in tow with him ? Dave and Phil but they didn't leave. What do you mean they didn't leave I shouted at him? I mean they are still there inside the warehouse checking those creates. Lets go I said making a grab for my weapon, now just wait a moment he said if we go barging in there we are going to get killed lets just cool down a moment and work this out. Iknow you are angry and you want their lives but I have trained you better than that lets make a plan and stick to it. I knew he was right so I sat back down and listened to what he said, I have drawn a map of the dock showing fences craines guard positions and weak spots where I think we can get in. Here is the main gate he pointed to a spot on his make shift drawing there is always one guard there checking everyone in and out.

Next we have one guard at the first warehouse door he is in contact with the gate man all the time and there is one other guard on the first craine looking down on them both again he has a radio to talk to them and anyone else that is listening. The two men on the ground will be easy for us to knock down but the guy on the tower craine will be hard without tipping off the rest of Dave's men. We studied the map which was rough but very accrete he had not missed any detail as of what I could remember, maybe we could swim from that other warehouse across from their dock. That could work if we could take down that tower guard first without alerting the other two, then hit them both together.

Ok Roger said you go back and keep watch I will get some sleep then join you there, Phil and Dave were both there when I left so just watch for them if they leave with no escort we may be able to get them on the road. I made my way back to our position behind the boats without being seen and watched the warehouse doors, twice they opened but there was no sign of them two. After three hours Roger joined me and we watched together, Roger had obtained a pair of binoculars and when I asked of where he had got them he just said don't ask.

Has we watched the ship cast off from the dock and sailed still with cargo onboard bound for god knows were after doing its law breaking drop here in Lybia. Now we could see more of the dock and there was a set of steps from just below the water line leading up onto the dock used for small moter launches like these we are hiding behined Roger informed me. But what a stroke of luck lets just pray no othere ships dock today or we may have to swim between the ship and shore and that was dangerous we could get crushed between the ships hull and the dock wall. Time was now moving towards night and still we had not seen Phil or Dave but just as it was getting dark somebody turned up at the gate, it looks like a delivery of food Roger said.

Well the guards have got to eat I told him, yes but it means they are staying that could mean so is Dave and co. The guard made the call and two other men with weapon came out of the warehouse door to collect it and this time we saw a glimps of Dave closing the door.

My heart pounded at seeing him that was the thing we had come here for and I hoped we would soon be putting an end to their lives. We now set about planning what we was going to do to get over there without being seen and how to take out the guards to clear the way for us to get to those warehouse doors. While we planned the guards changed allowing the men that had been on duty to get their food so now we could see how many different Faces we see that would tell us ruffly how many we would be facing. Roger went and got the weapons which we assembled there on the dockside leaving there cases hide under the boats, I put plastic bags over each end of each rifle to keep the water out. It was now very dark but the docking area was lite up by flood lighting on the walls of the warehouse so we could see everything on the shore and all the guards were very obvious to us. We sneaked around to the warehouse across the way from the one that Dave and Phil were in and slowly entered the water by climbing down the step ladders beside a large ship that was about to be emptyed the following morning. There was a watchman but he was sat in his hut watching what sounded like football on the television and stuffing his face with some delights from home.

Both Roger and I had stripped down to our trousers removing our shoes trying to make ourselves as light as we could in the water our weapons straped around our shoulders. The swim was about one hundred and fifty yards, not far you may say but the current was strong with the turning tide and it was hard to swim trying to keep the weapons dry. Finally we reached the ladders on the other side of the dock, Roger signalled to me to go first and I climbed till I was half way and then stripped the plastic off my weapon looking down Roger was doing the same. It was hard to hold onto the vertical ladder and tear the bags off but we managed to achieve it and remain silent as we did it.

From my pocket and waistband I pull out the silencer that was part of the rifles kit which I had put in a plastic bag pushed into my pocket and threded the knot through my waistband.

I needed both my hands to screw the silencer on, Roger had saw my struggle and climb up close to my feet and held my rifle with one hand while he hung on with his other his rifle dangled from his neck. I hooked my left arm around the step while holding my rifle barrel with my left hand and screwed the silencer on with the right. Finally I put the magazine onto the weapon and slowly forced a round into the chamber I was now ready. I made my way up to the top of the ladder and took a peep over the top to see where the guards were, the man at the gate was watching a lady of the night some distance up the road. The man at the warehouse doors was leaning on a oil drum smoking a ciggy and the man on the crane was doing the same only he was leaning over the rails with his weapon resting on the same rail as his foot. One of the things that worried us was who to take down first, the man on the crane may fall and the noise of his body hiting the ground would alert the others.

If I could hit him in a part of his throat that would stop him sreaming out and would kill him in a few seconds we could drop the other two before they knew what hit them. I indicated to Roger that I was taking the man on the crane he nodded and pointed to the door man, hooking one arm each into the same step we stood back to back and aimed our rifles. My night sight located the man on the crane and I sqeezed the trigger slowly feeling the kick as the round left my weapon, at the same time Rogers weapon had targeted the man at the door. Both targets were knocked back and sidewards mine cluched his throat as he fell to the steel floor his weapon remained still resting on the rail. Roger's man just went back onto his bottem then his head flung backwards and hit the floor his weapon clattered as It hit the ground But by then it was to late for the man on the gate has I had swung my rifle around and put a round in the back of his head.

For a moment everything was silent, all of the bodies lay still and no mouning was to be heard. Climbing onto the deck area with caution we moved to the doors and I put my ear close to listern to what was going on inside, Roger kept a search of the area around us with his rifle to make sure nobody was outside that we had missed. Ther was sounds of talking but it was coming from a distance from the doors so I open the small door in the centre of the main large door and peeped in. There was a stacker truck just to the side of the door and a rack of shelving which went up high almost to the roof this was used to stack large boxies and was full. I open the door a little wider and stepped in closely followed by Roger and we both kept close to the large door until we reached the high shelves and it hid us from any glancing eyes.

This part of the warehouse was well lite and we could see that the cargo of weapons had been stacked on the center of the floor in about the middle of the floor area. Towards the rear of the warehouse it was darker and I could just make out more shelving that was high up to the roof which stretched the length of the warehouse.

129

Roger tapped my arm and indicated to a opening in the middle of the shelving nearest to us and we walked towards it keeping close to the shelving for cover. I peeped into the opening to find a row of offices behond the shelves and a staircase leading up to more offices above, two were lite up but the one's on the ground had no lights switched on.

The voices that I had heard outside the door were louder now it sounded like there was a card game being played in one of the rooms above and somebody was a sore loser. Roger indicated that he was going to look around to make sure nobody was down on this level with us, just then one of the office doors opened and Phil's voice rang out "keep it down you four me and the boss are trying to do some work".

A muffled reply came back and the door was closed again, you four were words that told me a lot we were looking at six upstairs and as long as Roger didn't find anymore that was what we were up against. I settled close the the shelving waiting Rogers return and reloaded my rifle and checked my pistol to make sure of no problem when I needed it. Roger returned and whispered not a soul anywhere on the ground level, I told him what I had heared and he came up with the same answer that I had "six" I nodded. We made a plan to climb up the stairs one behind the other this time Roger would lead and duck passed the first office window and make his way to the second office door. I would stay low outside the first office till he was ready and then at the same time kick open the doors and catch them cold. All went to plan except just as Roger reached the door it opened and ther stood a tall man who was about to use the toilet staring face to face at Roger "what the fuck" was all I heared then a shot. A hail of rounds came from the second office window as Roger went low and race towards me and the stairs, "move he said" and I moved down the stairs and back to the opening in the shelving.

By now shots followed us from the first office door and window we was now in a gun battle and they had the upper ground. Roger reloaded his weapon after pumping rounds wildly behind us to keep their heads down while we found cover, what now he said to me?. Live or die we will have to continue to fight I told him, if we swim they would get us in the water and if we stay here they only have to wait for Gaddaffi's men he replied. There was no attempt to follow us down the stairs but rounds kept hitting the racking above our heads, cover me I said and ran across to the crates in the middle of the floor.

A crowbar lay conveniently on top of one box which had been opened and I found the box that we needed Exposives I made myself a device using the materials I had and fired up a fuse using my lighter. Let's get out of here I shouted and ran to the door turning to cover Roger as he ran towards me with gun fire hot on his heels, one of Dave's men showed himself just a fraction to much and I put a round in his head. We cleared the door and were half way to the water when the device went off, it blow the warehouse doors clean off and then a number of explosions kept the display going like bonfire night when I was a kid. To my surprise Dave, Phil and his two remaning men came running out from the now blazing warehouse shooting in all directions trying hard to take us down. Roger and myself just lay on the floor facing the oncoming men but then they split but all firing in our direction ment we was getting cross fire and I saw Roger take a hit in his arm. I took aim and brought down one man then swung my rifle the other way to take down a second but by now one had reached the craine area and was lost from sight the final one was heading for a jeep near to the gate.

I snapped off a fast shot which hit the man around his legs making him fall, Are you badly hurt I asked Roger? No he replied its just a scratch I will be able to stop the bleeding go see which one you got he said indicating to the body crawling along the floor. The mans revolver was lying on the floor as I approached him and he made a grab for it but I was faster and kicked it away and turned him over Dave I said my voice sounding disappointed. Yes he said and he has got away again just as he spoke the noise of a moterboat leaving filled the air a heard Roger let off a shot but his chance of hitting anything where slim.

The army will be here soon that gunfire and explosion will bring them all so you had better run if you don't want them to catch you. Not until you tell me why you had to do that to my girl she had done nothing to you. Not me he said I told Phil not to hurt her that's the truth, but you never helped her by stopping him and you was to blame for the death of Jock.

My leg he cryed its bad im bleeding to death you have got to help me, I will I said and put two rounds from his pistol into his head one down Emma and one to go. I made my way back to Roger he was standing now and looking at the body was that Dave he inquired yes I answered, you showed him no murcy he said did they show Emma any, guess not he agreed. The sirens were coming towards us from some distance now, throw the rifle into the water he told me and lets get out of here. With the rifles gone we moved faster out of the gate and across to the built up area just before a mass of trucks fire engines and police turn into the yard where the warehouse was now blazing.

We cannot return to our room they will be checking everyone that is a stranger to the area and if we get arrested they will not treat us nice you can bet on that Roger told me. Lets get out of this city and then re-plan what we do next, I agree I told him but can you walk far with that wound?

I will walk back to England if we needed to he replied. Using the side streets we ducked and dived our way out of the city till finally after a couple of hours we found ourselves out of the city and on a dusty old track that lead to God knows were but we walked along it till we could see no building We took a rest and I checked Rogers arm, he had lost a lot of blood and it had run down his sleeve and onto his trousers making an awful mess which we needed to clean off.

His wound was as he had said it was only a flesh wound but it had gouged a deep grove across his forarm it would need a stich or three but where would we get it looked at out here. I stopped the bleeding by wrapping my t-shirt around it and we continued down the track till we reached a small building which looked like a goat hearders house.

You need to rest I told Roger shall we take a chance and see if anyone will help us? well we still have our pistols so if they do get nasty we can defend ourselves he replied. I knocked on the door then looked at my watch, gee its two fifteen in the morning they will all be in bed but to my surprise the door opened. My friend is hurt I said to the woman standing on the inside of the door but she didn't understand so Roger moved forward so she could see by the light of her candle. When she saw the blood she moved to one side and beckoned us in doors and went to get some water off the stove fire.

The house was small with only three rooms, one was this living area which had a few chickens and a few baby goats wondering around.

The second room which had no door on was a sleeping area and the third was like a kitchen come washroom come storeroom. While she bathed Rogers arm I took a look around there didn't seem to be anyone else in the building but then a baby cried and she went into the bedroom to tend it. Where do you think her husband is at this time it's a bit late to be out with the boys, I have no husband came her voice from the doorway of the room see stood holding a baby just a few months old.

My man was killed a year ago when some of Gaddaffi's men drove up and started argueing with him over something that I know not what and he spit at them and was shot dead.

After that it was my turn and they took it in turns to rape me and the child is the out come, she paused in her story, I was going to kill the child but I thought that it was not the childs fault and he was part of me. Your English is good I told her and she dropped her head my man was English he told me the words of your country so that someday if we went back I could talk to people.

Now I live alone with my baby on this small farm and twenty goats and a dozen chickens which keeps us alive. How do you buy food Roger asked her? goats milk and eggs she answered twice a week I go to the market to sell and buy that's how we live. Take off those clothes she told Roger I will wash them and get them dry, but it is time to sleep I told her not wash clothes, this is market day I must collect the eggs and milk the goats before I can get money to buy the food. Don't worry today you will have money so you can forget selling and just buy your needs I told her, and passed her a wade of notes.

Her eyes opened wide with the shock of seeing that much money, this is more than I get I one year she told me I cannot take that much for little work. You have already done good work for use but there is one thing we would ask you to do tomorrow, how do you get to market with your goods I asked her? by cart she replied I walk and the goat pulls the small cart.

We would like you to go to our room and collect our clothes for us but you must be careful and don't get caught and if you do that I will pay you a lot more. That is all you ask me to do she replied ?, that's all I repeated then I will do this thing she said, good then go get some sleep we will take the floor here. The rest of the night was long with the hard floor and the animals disturbance we didn't get much sleep but still the woman was up before us and she had washed Rogers shirt and trousers.

There are some of my mans clothes she told Roger pointing to a box in the corner of the room, Roger was a bit embarressed to get up with just his boxers on but she turned away as not to notice. We gave her the address of the rooming house and we was surprised that she knew of it, I used to live very near there she told us and went off without another word, don't forget our passports was the last word I said to her before she was gone.

We cleaned our hand guns while she was away and made sure they were loaded we didn't want to be caught napping if anything went wrong with her pick up. Roger watched the road leading to the house but it was quite with only one old lorry passing going south and that was full of sacks. We watched the baby while she was gone and he was a cheerful little fellow not crying but just laying in his bed playing with his toes.

Here she is Roger call a few hours later and she is smiling like a Cheshire cat that got all the cream and when she entered we could see why, there was things for the baby and plenty of food for the whole family chickens and goats included. She had not only got all our gear she had picked up all the spair ammo as well, the police went in as I was moving away she told us they didn't notice me at all.

Roger gave her more money and said be careful how you spend it or you may bring the police down on you wanting to know where you got it she jumped in the air and hugged us both. She went to preper us all a meal while we discussed our next move, where do you think he would go I asked Roger? Well I would have made for somewhere I felt safe he replied. Maybe Chad. I don't think so I said he has lost his surport there and besides he would have to cross a lot of dersert to get to the border. Well that boat would not have seen him across the Med to Europe if anything he would have turned back in to the nearest port, what about Giddaffi would he shelter him?.

Possible but why would he now he has his supplies? He could do the deal on his own with the ship's capitan. So where I said?, He must have money or accsess to it so he could travel anywhere but he will need to get to a airport and he will not use the one we arrived at for fear we would be watching. I think he will jump on a ship maybe work as a crew member until he reaches a safe port, that idea sounded right but how can we find out?

Back to the docks Roger said and let's see what is leaving and what has gone. Again we waited till night fall before we moved and after saying good bye to our new friend we got on our way, she had made us some food for our travels and later we would be grateful for it. As we arrived in the city we noticed that there was a lot of excitement close to the docks and we stop close to a group of men who were dancing and shouting, seems like a celabration of some sort I whispered to Roger, yes lets take advantage of it he told me.

Soon with the cover of the carnaval atmosphire we was back at the waters edge looking at six ships loaded and waiting for high tide to sail to there destinations. We stopped two passing seaman heading back to their ship which was waiting, where are you bound for Roger asked them, we are old friends the one told us but we travel on different ships. I am on that one there he pointed to a large Norwegain cargo ship and we are taking supplies to Argentina and I am on that one over there his friend said and that is going to Cuba.

Why do you ask are you looking for a job they inquired, we could be I answered but I don't know where I would like to travel to. How many have left today Roger asked, Nobody as moved since the fire the one answered, we have been waiting since yesterday for the state troops to check our ships and they finished checking one hour ago. The news was music to our ears it ment Phil was still here some-where, well thank you for your time I told the men, that ok they said we are the captains of those two ships and we are both looking for new hands if you change

135

your minds. Have you took any new hands in the last few days Roger asked? in a polite manner as not to sound to inquisitive, yes I have taken two locals but my friend has taken on four all from different countries.

That was a greater interest to us because that was the ship that was going to Cuba, give us a few moments to discuss it over and we will make up our minds we told them, fine you will find us in that office there the one pointed. Once we get our clearence papers we will be on our way so don't leave it two long and with that they walked away. Well Roger said do we take a chance he is on that ship or do we search and maybe let him get away?or we could split up and take a ship each both are docking in Madira to pick up some cargos I replied.

That will give you one whole day and a half to find him Roger said and if you don't find him on board by then? I go to Cuba I replied.

What if he is on board my ship he inquired? Then you kill him and be on the docks in Madira so I can see you and I will jump ship. The decision was made and we went to the office to find the captains and book on board their ships with me taking the Cuban voyage while Roger would board the ship to Argentina. Gentlemen we will expect you to complete the round trip and you will not be pay until the night before we dock back here, you will need to hand over your passports to each of us so we can clear you at all ports we stop at. I handed over my documents and climbed the gangway up onto the deck with a wave to Roger has I went and I watched him board his ship.

A crew member showed me to the crews quarters and I stowed my bag onto my bunk, is this the only quarters for the crew I asked him? This is the main one but the engine room have there bunks near the engines incase they have any break downs.

The senior crew members have their quarters one deck up above this one close to the galley and the captains cabin.

We all share the same galley except the captain who eats in his cabin, meal times are staggered hands on duty get fed when they come off watch there is always food on the go.

You have been assigned to me and we are on the main deck watch. Your duty starts now as we are getting ready to sail there is plenty of thing that must get done so watch me and you will learn ok he said ok I replied. I had never worked as hard as I did in that hour before we sailed tying up ropes which we had pulled up from the side and making everything on deck that should be tied down tied down. Once we were under way Hans my new friend told me we can now eat as we would be on deck watch at night fall for four hours then if we was lucky we would get five hours sleep.

I entered the mess room with a little caution just incase Phil was sitting having his food but there was no sign of him disapointment must have showen on my face as Hans noticed it, something the matter he asked ? No I replied and went forward and collected my dinner.

The food was good and very welcoming after the long day we had spent after leaving the goat farm, it was hot and was a little spicy but it went down a treat with a mug of coffee. After my meal I took a stroll back on deck and looked back from the stern to see Rogers ship about a mile behind us, it didn't seem to be travelling as fast as we were.

Hans joined me on deck and handed me some water proof clothing oil skins, and a cunky roll neck jumper, you will need these he said it gets wet up here and very cold at night so go put them on and report back here when your done.

This was the chance I had been waiting for a chance to check around the ship and try and find Phil.

I wonder along each deck looking into rooms until I found myself down in the engine room were there was a great number of men stoking the boiler and oiling all the moving parts.

I saw no sign of Phil at first then a group of men came along and the engineer shouted his orders to relieve the watch so they could eat And has they made for the steps I noticed Phil. I ducked into a small control room until he had passed and then followed at a distance, "you" a voice behind me rang out what are you doing down here?. Lost sir I said as I looked back to see the captain coming towards me where should you be he inquired? I was making for my bunk sir to put these clothes on but I must have come down to low.

He looked at me with a stare of disbelief but did not say as much, you need to go up two decks and you will find you quarters near the bow of the ship in that corridor.

You will need to hurry you are expected to releive the deck crew anytime now yes sir I said and hurried up the steps to our deck and changed into my all weather gear.

Things had changed on deck once I got out there the waves were hitting the ship with some force and the wind was blowing hard, spray hit my face and made my eyes sting with the salt, it even became very cold but that was the water hitting you.

Hans screamed at me to put on a safty line which allowed us to walk along part of the deck until we came to another tie then we needed unhook and hook the other side of the tie.

Water now came over the deck and made it hard to keep upright but I watched Hans and he made it look easy, we need to get to that life boat and tie down the weather sheet that as come loose he shouted over the wind.

I put my thumb up to acknowlage and off we went towards the boat which I could now see the ropes and tarpaulin now flapping in the wind threatening to fly over board.

I grabbed the corner of the sheet first and pulled it down while Hans grabbed the rope and hooked it under a rim on the boat and pulled it which pulled the sheet down to cover the boat.

Tying off now made the whole thing secure, and we went around the whole deck doing the same thing securing items that had come lose.

By the time my watch was over I ached all over and I was frozen to the bone Hans made a indecation for a drink and we went inside.

The wind had dropped now and the ship was moving a lot steadier, you did well out there Hans told me not bad for someone who was doing it for the first time.

You could tell I said? Yes you are not the first to climb on a ship to get away from something or to look for something he added but that is your business but just watch me and you will be ok.

It was now my rest time but I needed to find Phil and hopefully do the job I came to do so again I went below towards the engine room and this time Phil was there.

There was about six otheres working along side him so I couldn't just do him and stuff his body in one of the burners I would have to wait till he came on deck.

I kept close to the pipes going around the decks I didn't want him to see me even though there was nowhere to go there was a lot of hiding places on a ship and I didn't fancy having to search the bilges looking for him.

My luck was in one of the engine room staff came passed me and asked what I was doing so I told him I was waiting for my mate who was in the engine room. What time do they change over shift I asked him? Not for another two hours he replied but if you hang on they will be sending two at a time up on deck for a smoke break you may get to see him then. Phil smoked like a steam train so I knew he wouldn't pass up a chance for a fag so I went back on deck and watched the doorway that he would come through to reach the deck. Twenty minutes passed and two sets of two came up for a quick fag but no sign of Phil, then just as I was about to give up out he came with another member of his team. They lit up a fag each and leaned on the rails looking out over the sea which at the moment was very calm.

I had a burning inside me it was built up anger awaiting to be released I kept thinking if only that other man was not with him I could just push him over that rail and he would be gone.

Instead I would have to make a plan of how to get him and try before we docked that evening in Madira or I would be making the full trip to

Cuba. Once Phil and his mate had gone back to work I made my way to my bunk to try and get some sleep but after one hour I got up and went for some coffee and breakfast as sleep evaded me. Hans was still up and sat drinking his coffee, you no sleep he asked me as I joined him at the table, no things on my mind at the moment. You should try he said we are back on duty in four hours and the forcast is for a heavy sea once we pass Gibralter into the Atlantic so you will be tired and trying to stand up on a wet deck.

He had been telling me when I was back on shift but I had not seen any rotas telling me when my sifts were so I asked him, they are on the wall in our quarters all sections change at the same time. The only one's that differ from ours is the engine room and they are two hours different, why is that I asked? Well im not sure but I think it's because at night they only have a small watch who cover all night then two day teams take over.

That team finish in another hour and they have the rest of the day off, sounds good to me I said, no not really it's a shit duty you work all night and sleep most of the day I like ours better. We both made for our bunks and managed to get some sleep before we was awoke by the ship rocking to and frow, looks like another storm hit us Hans said we may as well get ready there is only twenty minutes before our shift. Again I dressed in my storm weather clothing and made my way up to the upper deck and as I opened the outer door I was hit by a wave which knocked me back into the corridor wall. What till the ship rises Hans called and we both moved out at the same time hooking on our safty lines as we went out.

We checked all the lashings and made sure nothing had broke lose This was not just any storm it was a gale and a half there was times when we was up to our waists in sea water as if the whole ship was under water. Once we had done our checks we re-entered the outer door and locked it shut behind us feeling safe on the inside of the ship and we watched the waves crash against the outer wall of the upper deck. Then the Capitans voice came over the intercom, This is your capitan speaking due to the storm we have had to alter coarse and head into the waves to stop the chance of over turning. I need all crew members on duty to check that portholes and water tight doors are closed, try to secure all lose items of equiptment to stop it rolling around the decks capitan out he signed off. Hans pulled at my arm, lets start on the lower decks and work our way back up, this is my chance I thought, I will catch up with you I just need to get something from my locker I told him and sped off.

Reaching my bunk I opened my kit bag and pulled out the which I had wrapped my hand gun in, I quickly checked it and pushed it into my waist-band of my jeans under my all weather top.

I found Hans stacking life jackets into a cupboard which its door had flow open and deposited the jackets on the floor, closing the door he pushed a chain with a crabs claw on it to secure it closed.

This is the sort of things we will find he said so be carefull not to get hit by things fulling out of top lockers. We made our way towards the engine room, the watch should be making sure that things are safe down here Hans said but they do miss things mainly tools which can do some damage if they hit you or parts of the electrical eqiupment.

This shift has just come on duty so they will not know if the last shirt as left things laying about he continued. The ship was realy rolling around now and there was loud bangs as the bow crashed down into the sea after the waves had lifted it, it took me all my time to stand yet alone work but some how I managed to follow Hans.

My plan was to try to get near to Phil sleeping and put a bullet into his head, I had worked out that the capitan wouldn't like the port police snooping around his ship so he may just throw the body overboard. But the chance never came as the Capitans vioce blasted out from the intercom, all hands to the upper deck our sister ship is in trouble and needs our help, a great amount of bodies appered from all directions. We reached the top deck in double quick time to be meet by the first mate who explained the situation to us, the engines have shut down and she is adrift.

We will try to bring most of the crew onboard our ship but it means we will have to turn into the wind and waves which is not a easy task but once the manuver is complete everyone out on deck propering climbing lines.

Turning in a gale was so dangerous, if a large wave hit us the ship could turn over but the chance was worth taking if it saved the lives of the other crew for they had no chance drifting the way they were.

Our captain was a old sea dog and had been in situations like this before so everyone had faith in him to pull this manoeuvre off.

We felt the ship rise and turn a full 360 on top of a wave and as the wave went down so the ship dived down with it a loud crash told us that the ship had nosed into the sea and we was all throwen forward.

I picked myself up off the floor just as the bow lifted back up out of the water back to its normal trim, he had done it he had turned the ship, damage reports the captains voice once again came over the inter-com. With the wind behind us now the ship seemed to fly along and soon we could see the dark shadow of our sister ship lying in the water taking the hits that the waves were throwing at her. Her captain was holding her bow to the wind but how we did not know but if she turned the waves would beat her side and over she would go. What we didn't know till late was that the engines were just ticking over enough to keep here steady but not enough to give her forward thrust for her to move to far. We all made our way to the outer deck and started making ready to throw climbing nets over the side just incase her crew abandon ship, I think we knew that it would be very hard if not impossible to row in these conditions.

Waves were lashing onto our deck and the spray was icey cold salt in our eyes made it hard to see but nobody left there post or complained. At that moment tragedy struck and their ship seemed to turn slightly and a wave hit her side on and she went over onto her starboard side and lay there for a few moments before she turn fully over. It was a horrible to see it was obvious that there was not enough power to keep her straight and the waves to strong to stop her floundering. I prayed that Roger was safe but I knew anyone still on that ship would soon perish as they were now under water, We all watched in shock as the hull moved around in the water thr props now still as the engine had failed.

Everything that we could recognise was now under the water just this big large belly like a dead whale was all that we could see. Then somebody shouted there and was pointing to a spot in the sea to our amazment we could just make out two small boats with men fighting with the oars to keep her into the wind. Slowly we move towards them the wave crashing on the rear of our ship trying to push us along but our engines were now in reverse to slow us down. The small boat were now along side our ship being bummed into our hull and tossed up and down as the waves hit, quickly the net was lowered and men started to climb.

The waves were that strong that twice the net was pulled away from the hull and then crashed back tossing two poor souls into the sea to their deaths.

But now we had men near the rail and we reached out to help them onboard tired cold wet they was all suffering and finding it hard to climb the rowing had taken there energy. Rogers face appered just below me and I grabbed his shirt coller and pulled just as another pair of hands grabbed his arm and pulled him over the rail. He lay flat on his back like a captured fish his eyes closed but alive I raised my head to thank the other person but then shock hit us both I was looking into Phils face and he into mine. For a second we did nothing then he jumped back along the deck and away from me, I thought about my gun but didn't go for it as I watched Phil disapper into the ship.

With both boats empty we watched as the sister ship sank never to be seen again and taking with her twenty two lives. I got Roger down to my bunk and dried him off after a change of clothes and a hot drink he told us how the captain had got them to abandon ship as he knew that the ship would go down but before all the boats could get away it happened.

I whispered to Roger as he drank his hot coco Phil is onboard and he now knows we are here as well as a matter a fact he helped me pull you aboard.

He did what Roger shouted out blowing a large mouthful of his drink down the neck of his crew mate sitting in front of him.

I explained to him what happened once I had calmed him down, what do we do now we cannot just gun him down he will be waiting for us. We wont do anything yet I told him I have to finish my duty and then we will decide what we are going to do mean while you keep your eyes open and don't let him get the drop on you.

I made my way back to Hans on deck who had been covering for me while I was looking after Roger, your friend is he ok he asked me on my return? He is fine I replied.

We pulled up the nets that was hanging over the side and stowed them away and returned to our safe haven inside.

We wont be docking on time he explained to me the Captain is taking the ship fether north so he doe's not have to attempt that turn again so it will be twelve hours late docking.

The storm was dying down by the time my shift ended, the wave were still hitting the deck but they was not as fierce now but they was still to heavy for the captain to try to turn.

By now I was exhausted and went to my bunk, Roger was curled up under the blankets so I left him sleeping and hit a empty bunk below him and I to was soon in the world of sleep. I was awoken again by Hans come on buddy he shouted time for our shift just got time for breakfast, I rolled out of my bunk and pulled on a pair of jeans and a t-shirt.

That's all you will need today Hans told me it a lovely day outside the captain turned the ship six hours ago and we should be docking in two and a half more. I nudged Rogers bunk, come on mate lets get some chow, there was no movement I nudged him again still no response, I pulled back the blanket and stepped back with the shock. Roger lay there his eyes wide open with a mass of blood soaked clothes around his upper chest his thoat had been cut from ear to ear. Hans looked at me and said who would do this? I know who I cryed and reached under my pillow for my gun, wait Hans cried don't do anything you will regret later my friend. I wont regret it I shouted back running down the corridor and headed for the engine room with my gun fully exposed to one and all.

Leaving Hans ringing the bridge to inform the captain of what had happened and what I was about to do. My blood was boiling I knew that I was going about this all wrong but I didn't give a shit Phil had now killed my best friend more than that he had killed my family. I hit the stairs to the engine room and a shot rang out hitting a steam pipe above my head but ricochet off and hit the wall and flattend down. People were shouting and diving for cover I fired two rounds into the air to get them to move away from me but one poor lad ran in front of me and was hit by a burst of gun fire from Phil.

You have nine lives Brummie Phil shouted I have tried so had to kill you but you just don't lay down, I lay down last night you bastard and you missed me again I was under roger.

Fuck I heard him curse you did it again, but this time you are on a ship with nowhere to run so this time it ends here I told him.

I wont you both to lay down your weapons and surrender to me the voice was that of the captains behind me, captain stay out of this this man killed my friend in cold blood I am giving him a chance I shouted back to the captain. Captain this man is mad he as been chasing me for a long time because he thinks I did his girl some harm Phil cried.

You will both lay down your arms or both die here as I have four armed crew men here with orders to fire if you raise any more threats towards anyone so please lay down your arms.

I felt the pain of frustration but put down my weapon as did Phil and he ran to the captain begging for protection from me. He was good he knew all the tricks and he used them to worm his way into favour with the captain, did you kill his friend the captain asked him? Yes but he pulled the knife on me and he was killed in the fight. But his thoat was cut the captain said, I was scared that the two of them was going to get me so I killed the one so I could hide from this one but he found me.

That's a load of shit I told the captain this man raped my girlfriend and left her to drowned plus he is responsible for the deaths of men he hired to do him a job. We will let the police decide what this is all about but we have just under two hours before we dock so I am going to lock you both in separate rooms till I can get the police to sort this out. You in here he said to me indicating a door and once inside it was locked behind me, Captain I heared Han's voice this man killed that crew man he is the one that should be locked away.

They are both going to be locked away until the police take them away and that's my final word on this matter now lock this one in there till we dock. I would like to talk with this one so wait outside while I ask a few questions and the captain closed the door behind phil and himself. I had stood listening by my door but now I could hear nothing only Hans moving around outside in the corridor but lucky for me he was listening at the door of the room the Captain and Phil had entered.

There was nothing I could do at that moment in time so I lay on the bunk and tried to plan what I did next, I must escape from this situation and get off this ship. Soon I could hear the Captain back in the corridor and he ordered Hans to lock Phils door, there is no need for a guard down here he told Hans they are going no where and he walked away.

Hans had heared every word that the Captain had said to Phil so he stayed close by until he was sure the captain had gone then he doubled back and unlocked my door.

Putting his finger to his lips to tell me to remain silent he beckoned me out of the room and placed my pistol in my hand, once out he relocked the door.

Two strides across the deck and I was at Phil's door my heart beating fast for my revenge but Hans grabbed my arm and lead me away to a place were he could speak to me.

I don't know the full story but the Captain is in on it he told me, I heared him talking about getting some more work off Phil as it paid good money.

They was also talking of how they will get rid of you over the side once they are on their way to Cuba, you where not going to leave that room until they would have come late tonight killed you and throwen your body into the sea.

It will be awhile before anyone will enter that room so we can arrange away to get you ashore and safe before they notice and what about Rogers body?.

It was sacked up weighted and throwen over the side ten minutes ago he informed me the Captain has about ten crew men that are loyal to him so that's why I stopped you from going in and shooting that man you would never get off this ship alive.

I cannot let him escape me again it could take me years to find him if I ever did I cannot take that chance you will have to let me into his room. And what about me he said my life will be in danger after you have gone? You could leave the ship with me and you could get another ship and do the same job. Getting another ship will be easy but going home would not, the Captain come's from the same area as I do so he could get people to look out for me and my family. I started to see the problem that I could course him and after what happened to Emily I just didn't wish to get anyone else involved but I just couldn't let Phil get away. My passport I said out aloud the Captain has still got it and I will need it to check into the authoritise, I know were he keeps them I will try and get it for you now stay here and hide.

I watched him go down the corridor and then vanish into the maze of twistes and turns that form the inside structure of the ship. My anger had stopped me thinking about my lose of a friend and now I was thinking of Roger how close we had got in such a short time. Tears filled my eyes and a pain burned in my chest like I was having a heart attack, this was grief something I had never felt before a pain I couldn't cope with and I cied openly right there where I stood. My friend had gone and I had not had the chance to say goodbye and my mined told me that they were not going to get away with this Checking my weapon I moved in the direction of the cabin that Phil had been put in.

I stood for a second then opened the door, Phil stood by a table pouring a drink from a bottle of whisky he had not noticed me at first then his face went white as his glance picked me up and the gun pointing at him.

Now wait he told me don't be to hasty, lets have a drink and try to work this out, I noticed his gun was laying on the table about two foot from his reach.

I will give you one chance I told him grab your weapon, I won't he replied your not a murderier you won't kill me in cold blood.

I heared someone comeing down the corridor and knew I had to do something now or I never would get the chance again.

This is for what you did to Emily and the lads and at that moment he knew I was going to fire and went for his gun, I fired two rounds before he got his hand on the weapon.

One round hit him in the chest and one went into his stomach the forch knocked him backwards and he went down to the floor with his back leaning against the chair. Blood poured from both wounds he had not got long to live, you need to try that girl out he said in his dying breath she was a nice fuck and his head slumped and he died. The door opened and Hans stood starring at Phils body, sorry my friend but this will save you and I hit him with the butt of my weapon on the head and he fell to the floor.

I moved Hans inside the room and picked up my passport that had dropped from his hand then made my escape along the corridor away from the sound of people advancing towards my location. I now needed to escape this ship and get to the authorities befor the captain got to them and told his vergen of the story which would make me a murderer of both Roger and Phil. I made my way to the top deck and stepped out into the fresh air, I could see the harbour wall very clear now just about one mile away I thought about swimming but I didn't have the energy.

There was some cargo on deck which was to be unloaded in Madira I managed to hide between some of the crates, crew members were not running around like I expected them to be but why they should be searching for me. After a short while I heard the captains voice, stow that body in the cabin away till we can dispose of it at sea the other guy must have swam for it but I don't think he will be telling any stories to the police we could turn it round so easy. I took a peep from my hiding place and noticed he was talking to.

Two of his crew and in the back ground I could see Hans with a towel to his head sitting on the steps up to the bridge. Looking around at the cargo I noticed some inflamable drums of oil I had an idea of how to get off the ship so the authorities would not find me suspicious when I went ashore.

I waited till the deck was clear except for Hans, I gave a little whistle and he spotted my wave and crossed over to the cargo I was hiding behind. Sorry about that smack on the head but I had to make it look like you had not helped me, well it worked he said the captain never asked me any questions.

He thinks you jumped me in your cabin and made me take you to the man you killed then knocked me out and he has offered me a bonus when we get to Cuba if I keep my mouth shut. But you don't really wont to travel any further with this lot do you I asked him?, well no he replied but I need the pay for my family back home. Don't worry I told him I will make sure you get your money even if I pay you myself I told him now listern to my plan and spent a few moments telling him what I was going to do. Now you get me the things I need and get back soon and off he went with my instructions in his head and I started to do my work. First I put a small hole in the oil drum so it leaked out very slowly Then I stuffed the towel that Hans was using into the hole. We was very close to the port now so I had to move fast, Hans returned with two life jackets and a box of matches, I lite a match and threw it into the puddle of oil on the floor.

This stuff was more inflamable than I imagined and whoosh it went up like a bonfire soaked in petrol spreading to the other cargo in seconds soon a big part of the deck was ablaze. I slipped on the coat that Hans had fetched me and pulled on the life jacket, "fire" "fire" we shouted and soon there was a great number of the crew on deck tackling the blaze. I mingled in with the others fighting the fire which was getting out of control, two launches came along side spraying water and a voice came over a speaker, we must tow you out of the port to protect it from danger of explosions. By now the upper deck was ablaze and the crew had to withdraw from that deck or risk getting burnt to death, I waited after they had all gone knowing that the captain would come and check the fire for himself. I didnt wait long he came out of the same door as I had and stood on the deck observing the fire by now there was nobody fighting the flames just the two boats spraying the deck.

All the deck hands were forward securing a rope for the tug to tow the ship out of the harbour so there was nobody watching us, Captain I said pushing my gun into his ribs. His hands went up as he saw the weapon, please he said don't kill me I was just doing as I was told, no I said you was doing what you was getting paid for and it cost the life of my friend. The sweat was pouring from his brow and I don't think it was the heat of the fire, I have money he said lots of it its yours if you don't kill me.

I have a family he begged they need me please don't kill me, Did you think about my friends family when you through is body over board I snarled at him.

Look the money is in my cabin take it its yours just let me go and I will say nothing to anyone about you killing that man after all he was a pig I didn't like him.

I smiled no but you liked his blood money, no it was just businness that's all I was paid for work nothing else please you must believe Me I would not have done you harm, just then there was a large explosion which knocked us both back. I got to my feet fast and it was good that I did has the captain was come towards me with a blade in his hand and shouting for help, I punched out at him with my left hand and caught him around the temple and he fell backwards. He tried to get to his feet again but a part of the crain we used to load and unload the ship fell on him and he lay there lifeless, I pushed his body into the fire and watched it burn for a while then walked towards the hand rail and climbed over to jump. Now I don't need to leave this ship a voice from behind me spoke. No Hans I said but if you go down to the captains cabin you will find the money he owes you plus a bonus there should be enough there to keep your family for a long time.

With that I jumped into the water which was cool after the heat of the flames which I had aloud to lick at my face just enough to blister the skin a bit but nothing to disfigure me.

A week later I was discharged from hospital and was boarding a plane to take me back home to Emily who I had spoke to on the phone from my hospital bed.

The fire on the ship had been put out and the damage was minor so she continued her journey to Cuba and the new Captain was a very happy rich man.

Once home I settled down with Emily and never went to fight again we had three kids and I made sure they had all the love that any kid would wont from there dad.

The end

TARGETS

CHAPTER ONE
HIT NUMBER ONE

Five full magazines for my 9mm pistol were slid into my leather shoulder holster which also held the weapon its self. Getting ready for these hits was as hard preparing as it was doing the job. My rifle had been cleaned and was ready for action three rounds attached to my belt. I always took three even though one round will do the job and the rifle was then dumped you could say it was habit. My orders had come in the mail as normal, half the pay had been put in my bank the rest went in on completion of the hit. I had been hired by some goverment agency but i never knew which one, thats the way they wanted it, it suited me too. It meant if i fucked the hit up i couldn't say who had hired me, it also meant i had no one to turn to for help.

Normally i work alone but this was a heavy shit hit, drugs Baron and his mob, so i had called on three of my old army buddies to help. Bret had been a green beret in Nam, one of the most deadliest killing machines i had ever seen second only to me. Danny another green beret, nicknamed sniffer as he could find your target before any blood hound. Cole was the last member of our group, he had forgot more about explosives than most ever learn in a life time he had been in the Engineers. Has i said this job we was working together, i would need a few distractions so i could escape once i had made the hit. my name is Will ex navy seal sniper, weapons, expert in hand to hand combat. We all live in differnt parts of the states but not one of us know were the other lives its safer that way. when i need the lads i post a message in the national paper with a code word that lets them know they are needed. We have a place where we meet, if they are not there in two days they are not coming but that has never happened yet. The war in Vietnam had took its toll on us all, not one of us could settle back into normal life when we came home so a few words in the right ears and I started my trade. The lads followed suite and got in touch, once we got established we all moved homes for security and started our cleaning up of bad men.

We continued checking our equipment, this time we were carrying a great amount as we would be out for about two weeks. It would take us this time to find the mobs camp which is somewhere in Colombia make our plans to do the hit and escape. Rations, ammo, explosives, and our weapons would need to be taken, the weight distributed around the four of us. Each man would carry an amount of each item so if we get split the hit could be completed as we would have the equipment needed to do so. There was not much conversation going on at this time the lads just went about their business packing the equipment away on there persons.

Each man would carry a small rucksack with rations and explosives as the content, Cole was packing them all to make them safe. Detonators had to be packed safe so they did get damaged nothing was left to chance it was done by the book. Lads I said to catch their attention, we have about another four hours before we reach our drop off point so once you are ready try to get some sleep. It is going to be a long night and you won't get a rest later I continued. With a nod they all agreed and soon they had all settled down in whatever comfort they could find in the hull of that boat. She was an old Columbian fishing boat which would get us close to land without too many eyes. But we would leave her about a mile off shore and make for one of the estuary in the rubber boat we had on board. Going in at night would make less chance of being spotted. News of four white Americans riding into town dressed in army fatigues armed and carrying explosives just my not look right. So the still of the night was our aim, to not be seen and find a hideout where we could observe.

This operation will only succeed if we stay out of sight, find our target do the hit and get out without anyone knowing that we were there. The vibration of the engine soon had me drifting into a sleep but soon came the dream that always came the blood the screams the bodies. "Will" I was awaked with a shake, you're having a bad one, my eyes focused on Danny's face, you ok he asked. Fine I replied just fighting old wars I told him. You too he replied back, I never go a night without one nightmare of Nam. I checked the time, twenty minutes to drop off, wake the others I told Danny it's time to get ready. Soon we were all on deck cam paint faces took away the glare from the distant port which we could see about a mile away. We lowered the boat into the water and one by one we climbed down into it and fired up our outboard engine. The noise it made was drown out by the large boat engine, we moved along side for a while then turned and headed for a river estuary which we had choose earlier that day from a map of the coast line.

Once we were on the river we headed for the left bank away from the lights of the town Lonca and carried on down the river with the tide. It was three in the morning but we could still hear people talking on the far bank we kept close to the near side bank under the overhanging trees. Cutting the engine and getting out the paddles we rowed now to kill the noise of the engine, four hours we had set to reach our operating area and set up camp. The river Sinu was a very busy river with boats coming up and down from many towns inland, used to carry goods to the sea ports were it would be shipped to buyers around the world. The city of Medellin was ahead of us but we would have left the river a good time before we reached that our target was ten kilometers to the north of the city. There was good cloud cover tonight so we blended in with the river and tree cover, just the noise of the wild could be heard. Humidity was high and the river felt cool on my hand as I dipped it in the water, mosquitoes buzzed around us chancing a meal every now and then. A boat engine was heard and we pull up close to a overhanging branch, a long flat boat passed full of something I could not make out. It looked like three hills of grain standing high along the length of the boat the pump squirted water out as it passed us making a splash as it hit the river.

The wake lifted our small vessel high in the water almost dumping us on the bank, soon it was calm again we moved on. Two rowed while two sat back resting then we would change over, this is how we traveled one hour rowing one hour rest. No sleep was had, we had to stay alert all the time watching and listening. Cole I whispered in the dark, yes he replied as he carried on rowing with Bret, just after this bend in the river find a place to pull in we are now in our working area I told him. Ok he replied, five minutes later we were dragging the boat ashore covering it with foliage to hide and moved inland. When you have been on a boat for so long your legs take a bit of time to work as normal, mine at that moment didn't feel like mine and the others where the same. Now we looked for a base, some where we could use as a base to work from and stay hidden from all eyes. Searching for about one hour we finally came across a spot where the trees had grown close together with undergrowth filling the gapes making it hard to squeeze passed.

Each branch had over-lapped each other making a very good roof with big leaves sheltering us from rain. Dead leaves covered the floor making soft beds, we checked the area north south east and west and found no sign of life within a two mile radius. Daylight had broken so we settled down to get some sleep two hours guard duty each though out the day would give us rest. I took first watch, using the time to check the equipment we had brought with us. We will return to the base every night so rations can stay at base I thought to myself, just carry one day's rations.

Ammo each man to carry as much as he can carry, explosives split between us one quarter to each man he can take what he needs. Light cam nets light ground sheet, also each would carry his weapons. There would be some heavy tarrain to go through so we needed to travel as light as we dare, I made a mental list in my mind. Cole would have his rucksake with explosives and mine's in, his detonators will be on his hip bag. He has, like the other's a M16 rifle which weighs 3.26kg plus the ammo. M1911 pistol with ammo. So he had the most weight, followed by myself who would carry my rifle which is a M40 {a1} sniper rifle, pistol, ammo, and rations two scope's for my rifle. Danny carry's his rifle, pistol, and ammo for both his weapons, days rations plus a scope has he is my spotter. Bret would be very light, rifle pistol a collection of knives and his rations will all he will carry. On Bret's rifle he had attached a M203 grenade launcher which only weighed 3.4lb. The boxes of ammo we had brought with us will stay at base till we needed it. I woke Danny up to take over from me and got my head down, I slept for six hour till it was my watch again. Cole had been busy sorting out our hide, he had also made a meal from cheese and dry biscuits. Sorry no coffee he told me but the water's like wine we both smiled at the remark the water was from the river with a purifying tablet in it.

I checked the perimeter not a sole to be seen or heard closing the entrance again with loose brush I returned to Cole who had not moved from the spot. Not tired I asked? No I will grab some later before it gets dark he replied, I explained what I had decided about the supplies and he agreed. That makes sense its better than carrying it around from place to place he told me. Yes but once we have done our homework and found the target we may have to move closer. Spending the rest of daylight cleaning and checking our weapons making sure they wouldn't let us down when we needed them. It soon approached the time for us to leave the base and go search for the target, faces painted and final kit check was done no mistake would be made. An envelope had been sent to my post office box, when I opened it there was a picture of my target plus the area that he could be found but nothing on where or when. So we would have to search the area till we found his home, then plan how we can get away after we hit the target.

I could go in find him shoot him and run but that would mean hiding out for days while his men searched for us. Every move would be life risking so I liked time to plan the hit, getting us all out is my main priority. It had been decided that the first night we would go out in two groups, Bret with Cole and me and Danny. Danny would spot for me on the night I take the shot he will also watch my backside as we get out of the area. Cole would lay the explosives were they would be most useful and would fire some by hand control. Bret would be Cole's minder keeping watch while Cole laid his explosives, dealing with any unwelcome visitors. There was a big area to cover it could take us days just to find his home then days watching his movement to find the right place to take him down. Bret and Cole left first leaving the hide the disappeared into the dark we would not see them again till just before first light when we will all return. Walking though the forest took us two hours until we reach the first plantation in an opening. Danny moved forward across a field of grape vines I followed about fifty yards behind him. Once we reach the end of the crop there was a road that lead up to a group of buildings. Danny waited for me on the edge of the crop, I will go in and take a look you wait here he whispered and moved off towards the building keeping close to the vines. From were I lay I could make out four buildings, one was a barn another was just to its right was a stable the doors all closed.

To the left and about a hundred yards from the barn was the main building and a row of garages was to the left of that. Who ever lived here had some money as this was a rich man's home, my heart pounded had we found our target first time. I got my answer some thirty minutes later when Danny arrived back with me. There is a family in there he told me, no guards no gun's just a farmer with his wife and six kids. We moved on into the dark hoping we would be in luck soon, again Danny took the lead another two hours past before we arrived at the outskirts on a small village.

This time we sheared the work load with Danny going to the left while I took the right. Both of us took the rear of the buildings there was still people about on the one road that went through the middle of the village. There were twelve small buildings which were homes two stores and a canteen which had four men in drinking. I stood in a gap between the supply store and the canteen looking through a small window. These men were just farmers ending their day with a drink no weapons nothing that would make them a drugs barons bodyguards. I made my way back to the area we had started, Danny was already there, nothing but workers and families he said. I agreed with him and checked my watch, its one in the morning we will go on for another hour then head back to base. One hour later we was making our way back to base, no luck nothing found to help us find our man. On the hike back we stayed close together observing the area and watching our steps we didn't need any injuries so I paced the path while Danny secured the area. What is the name of this hombre you are targeting? Danny asked.

The name is not always with a picture from the government agency but this time it was, Domingo Silva I told him. Nice name he replied sounds rich doesn't it? Well with the money he has made from the drugs he must be loaded. But little did I know that he had another source of income which also made him a packet I would find this out later. Making it back just before daylight we joined the other two who had no luck either. We told each other about our nights work and lack of luck in find any clues to where we would find Dimingo, then we settle down for our days rest. That evening we moved north and south with same result no luck and that result went on for another two nights after that without any clues to where we would find him.

On the fifth night we went out earlier and covered the ground that we had covered the first night. Discussing with the lads the lack of clues to our targets where abouts resulted in this decision to go earlier to cover more ground. This time when Danny and I reached the village there was a lot of activity, people singing and dancing kids playing. There was music coming from the canteen, this is some kind of festival I whispered to Danny as we peared out from our hide. He just nodded at me, food was being brought to tables in the street women were chatting fun was being had so much fun no one saw us cross the road. Slipping away into the dark with the music fading behind us we crossed the second part of the grape crop then into an orchid of oranges. Danny picked some to take back for the lads, it was then that I noticed the name on a box left for the pickers, I pull Danny's sleeve to get his attention. He looked in the direction I was pointing got ya I heard him say, for on the box was printed in English was Dominic Silva orange company. Now we needed to find his house and set up surveillance on him logging his movements trying to find the best place to take him down.

All that night we searched but still we found nothing, we will need to move closer to this area and have the others with us I told Danny. We returned to base and agreed that after dark that evening we would return and find a new base set up the night after and resume the search the second night. We ate a meal and waited till Bret and Cole returned, I explain about the writing on the box to them and they agreed a move would be in our best interest. Some of these farms are massive Cole commented what you noticed may be the first field of hundreds. Let's just hope not I replied we have been here to long already and still have not found the target. We decided to take all the equipment with us that next night and if we found a base we could move straight in, if not we would hide it. Dawn broke and we got our heads down, Danny was on first watch so the rest of us stretched out. Packing all the gear around our persons we readied to move out the others carried a box of ammo each. We will hide those when we are in the right area we can pick them up later. The decision was made that we would split up and make an individual search of the area to find a base. Once we found one we would return to where we left the ammo and wait for the others to return.

After about one hour I found a base similar to the one we had just vacated, it had the space we would need plus the cover. I headed back to the boxies where we hide the ammo only to find the guys all there waiting. Danny has found a great place Cole told me as I got close to them, running water included he said. Let's take a look at it then I answered, Cole and Bret stayed with the ammo while Danny and myself moved off. We crossed another field of orange trees then turn to our left towards some cliffs, at the base there was a mass covering of trees and undergrowth. Danny pulled away some fallen branch and we crawled though to a clearing which was just the size we needed. Water ran down the cliff into a small pool then out through the trees to a trench which ran to the other side of the field and onwards. I gave Danny the ok with the base, he went back to fetch the lads and bring the ammo. I spent the time looking around the place we could use the torch safely now due to the thickness of the trees and undergrowth. A large overhang covered most of the clearing this would give us shelter from rain. A large bolder near the base had a gap between itself and the cliff face which we could sleep hide the supplies and even cook.

I started a small fire got water from the stream in empty tin can and boiled some water, the guys arrived back. Coffee I asked as they settled down, their faces lite up by the fire you bet said Bret taking the can from my hands. After the coffee we put the equipment away, there is still time left for a patrol I told them, we left the base in the same teams as before.

Cole and Bret went west I decided to follow the stream they would need water so it seemed the right thing to do. Keeping to the right side of the stream and well away from it so has not to disturb the water we moved on into the dark. One two three orchids later some four miles from the base we found a home a graceful home. It was a manor in size ten bedrooms or more, the garage had six doors stables for twenty or thirty horses and had a small village of out buildings. This looks promising Danny whispered, yes I acknowledged this could be the one it's the sort of home I would have if I was has rich as he is. From behind a large clump of bushes we watched for a while, its twentyone thirty so there should be people about Danny commented. Yes I replied but it's to open to get up to the buildings without being seen, let's go around the other side and take a look.

Working our way around to the rear of the buildings didn't help us that much as there was still a large open space to cross before reached the house. Let's check the out buildings to see what we can find I suggested to Danny, ok he replied but let's split up and meet back here in thirty minutes. We both headed off in different directions, I checked the garage area from the rear. There was three windows covering the whole building, as I peered in I could just make out the vehicles inside it was full, each bay contained a car. That told me that nobody was out in a vehicle so everyone should be inside the building, what it didn't tell me was who was in there. From the corner of the garage building I could see the main building a bit clearer.

Eight windows covered the front, two on the ground level six on the upper floor, these six were linked by a long balcony this was held up by four thick Roman columns. Between two of the columns on the lower floor was a large double door entrance with one window each side. The whole building was white like marble with a flat roof little columns of pillers with a connecting block edged all round the roof. The building was light up with bright lights all the way around it that was what made it difficult to get close. The only chance we have was to the get on the porch which went all around the building with a wall the same style as the roof. The rear had three windows plus a large French window above was six more windows the same as the front. Both the sides had two windows on the ground floor with four above, I made my way back to Danny. What do you think I asked him? But before he could answer the back door opened and out came two men with four dogs. "Dam it" I declared in a whisper as the men chained the dogs to areas around the house.

We eased away back to a safe distance, how do we get passed them? Danny said, I don't know yet but we must find out who lives there. Back at base we sat and talked it over, we need to watch in the day time I told him he agreed and said I will find a hide where I could see the coming and going. After a drink he collected his gear he would need and returned to the house. He covered himself with soil and brush to blend in with the area and settled down to sleep till daybreak then all day he would watch the house. Cole returned with Bret just as dawn was breaking, I told them what we had found, we found nothing he told me just oranges and more oranges. This guy must own a lot of land it go's on for miles he expressed, do you think we might be in the wrong area?.

We have nothing else to go on if he is not here we will have to call the whole thing off, we would never find him by chance. Disapointment filled my heart, i hated to waste mine and the lads time but i also hated the thought of this man would escape to kill kids in the streets back home with his drugs. The name on the box told me he was here so i knew i was going to get him it was just a matter of time. Danny arrived back with us at dusk, he brought the news i wanted to hear. I saw him he told me" early this morning a member of staff left the building and left in one of the cars. Three hours later the car returned with Silva and a woman on board plus two armed bodyguards, anothercar followed with five more men. I watched them enter the house with two of the men but the otheirs went into one of the out buildings Danny continued. Thats great news I told him well done, now we must make our plans on how we can get him. These plans would have to include when where and and how we get him, as I said before I could just pop out and shoot him but we have to get away safe.

We are going to have to watch is movements, where he go's for how long and who with him. Ideally I would like to get him on his own somewhere that he would'nt be missed for a few hours giving us time to escape. It was not likely to happen that way we would just have to watch and wait and take a chance when offered to us. Danny went back with me to the house while Cole took a look with Bret at our escape route see what they could do to hold up any pursuers. That was if I targeted him at his home. At the house I used my night scope to check all the windows, first the top floor, but I was down that low I could only pick up shadows. He would have to come to the window for me to target him I told Danny, if I did that I would'nt know who was there with him. Checking the building where the bodyguards went I could see them playing pool on a table while three watched soccer on a television. Where is the power coming from I asked Danny?, The second building at the side of the house has a generator in it, also a pump that pulls the water from the steam he told me.

Those facts were log in my brain they may be needed in my plans later. I checked the downstair windows, the first window to the left of the front door was a large dinning room, I could see house staff clearing up from their meal. Danny I need to know what is in everyone of those buildings but not the house I dont think that place would be any good. You stay out tonight I will relieve you before dusk with Brett, get me as much of that information as you can I patted him on the back has I left. Danny was just carrying his pistol so he was traveling light with some food and some ammo, being light to move around would help him but I would'nt know how much till later. Arriving back at our base I was meet by Cole with a real urgent way about him, did you know that this guy you are going to pop off is the governor of this area?. That was what the celebrations was about at that village, they had just voted him in and last night he was sworn in at a big party. So thats where he came from this morning I responded, I would say so replied Cole its about a three hour return trip to the city he continued. You know if you bump him off now you will have goverment troops police as well as all his mob, Cole pressed me. We have been paid half of our money to hit this target and hit it I will I told with a touch of anger in my voice.

Cole backed off and left me thinking what should I do call the whole thing off or risk the lads to life in jail or even death. But he is a drug baron he must be stopped to many young people are dying through this mans drugs. I went into a corner by myself and spent a hour thinking it over, finally I made a decision, ok lads you go out and search for the plants. If you dont find any we give up and go home but if you find them we do the hit. We left the base and went three different ways six hours was what we had to find anything, I trusted the lads as I had known them a long time if they found they would say. After six hours I drew a blank and so did Cole then Bret arrived back I found three fields full of the stuff all covered in netting so it cannot be seen from the air he told us. You were right Cole said and pattedmy shoulder lets get Danny and plan this thing. Leaving them to get some rest I made my way to where I left Danny but when I got there he was no where to be seen. I looked towards the house from the cover of the brush and brambles, two men stood by the front door with weapons in there arms. Both carried AK47's both the dogs lay close by them, I had a bad feeling Danny was stuck out there or he had been captured. Two hours passed there was still no sign of Danny, I noticed a lot of coming and going from one of the buildings. It was not the building Danny had told me had the guards in but the one next door.

I couldn't get closer for fear of being seen and there was not a position I could get to see inside that building. The sun was now out still no sign of Danny he was in trouble I knew it but how could I get to him. Staff were arriving at the house to start work a truck pulled up with farm workers who entered a building collected tools and left for the fields. Nobody went near the building were the guards were using so I didnt see any reaction by the guards towards them. They would have kept them away if they didn't want them to see anything, I needed to get back to the boys for help. Bret was on guard when I arrived back, what is wrong he asked as I dropped to a sitting position where is Danny?. I don't know he was not at our meeting place, he could be in a hide to dangerous to move or he could be captured. Knowing Danny he would have got back if he could come what may said Cole from his lying position. Then what should we do Bret asked? wait till dark and go get him I told him thats all we can do. Lets get back to that hide and watch that house and see if we can see if he is there. If has been captured then he has not talked or this place would be crawling with the mobi told them.

Danny would never talk but everyone has a breaking point don't they, Veitnam was the place to remember that the guys that cracked. Pain has a tolerance level you can stand so much but keep upping that level and your body and brain will give. We had to go with care to get back to the hide, farm hands were wondering around the site going about there work. It was daylight the sun was burning the ground a slight breeze moved the trees dust kicked up into your eyes. Has we finally settled in our hide I look towards the house heat waves rippled from the ground but behind the house in the distance dark clouds were forming. The storm held off till the work force had gone home and dusk was starting to close over the arizon then down came the rain. Raining so hard it flooded the ground in seconds, so hard that you could'nt see through it or walk without sticking to the mud. The stream filled and burst its banks, it was a good job we raised the supplies up before we left the base they would have got full of water. We had brought our rifles with us this time and as much ammo as we could carry, the rest we raised up on the rocks covered with a ground sheet.

The stream bed had a rocky shingle bottom so we waded up the stream to get closer to the house, it prevented us form sinking in the mud. Both the guards were huddled up against the wall of the house trying to stay dry, even the dogs didnt look happy about the rain and stayed deeper to the wall. We made our way to the rear of the pump house Cole entered the building with his bag of tricks a small charge would make it look like a circuit fault. Five minutes after Cole had left the building the lights went out with night scopes we could see people running around. One circuit burnt out one of the men shouted to the house, has it been tampered with a guy on the porch asked. Dont think so just a fault, maybe damp got in, can you fix it he was asked? yes about ten minutes the man in the building replied, ok fix it. As the man turned to go into the generator Bret grabbed him one blow knocked him out Cole started to repair the generator.

I covered the door while the lads worked getting thinks working would keep the rest of the mob in doors and bringing our prisoner around for questions. Were is our buddy I heard Bret say then a dull thud which told me Bret was not waiting to long for silence from the man. Cole had the power back on in no time so everyone in the house was happy and would leave us alone. We just had to pretend we was this man we had working in the building so they dont come looking for him. Just making things safe I shouted to the guards knowing the noise from the genny would muffle my voice. ok I heard back so we now had time. Two more thuds came from Brets direction while I stayed at the door Cole came and relieved me on moving into the building I saw Bret wipe his hands. Danny is in the building that you saw all the movement earlier with one man watching over him. What about this fellow i pointed at the guy on the floor? he is dead Bret replied, Why you could have tied him up i said with anger in my voice. Save me doing it later was his reply which angered me more lets go was all i could say hide that body first.

With the body pushed well under the generator we went back out into the rain and circled around to the back of the buildings. We squeezed between two buildings, then realized the building next door to the one Danny was in was where the men bunked. We froze as there door opened and two men came out, if they had looked down the gape they would have had us. The rain was still coming down hard the ground was soggy and very sticky to walk on we needed to get Danny and get away from that place. I gestured to bret to walk out wave to the guys on the porch then enter the building where Danny was. We had looked through the side window and saw the guard had his back to the front door and was dozing. Just hoping he would not turn when the door was open two strides and Bret would knife him. If he turned Bret would have to shoot and then we fight our way out dragging Danny with us. Bret walked from the building into the open space and waved to the guards, the rain made him look like the man from the genarator building and they waved back.

One dog barked a bit but the men scalded him the dog went quiet, Bret walked in and the man turned. The blade flew through the air in a tumbling action sticking into the guards neck cutting his vocal cord and severing his artery. Terror came to the mans face but he was dead before Bret stopped him hitting the floor. Danny was tied to a chair he was out cold they had beat him bad Bret unbolted the rear door and let us in. Bret put his finger to his lips indicating the sound of laughter from the building next door. We untied Danny and Cole put him over his shoulder within a moment we was out the back door heading for cover. I think the rain saved us that night as nobody wanted to come out in it. Struggling through the mud made it hard for us but we made it back to our base the rain washed away our tracks as we went. While i checked Danny over Cole and Bret back tracked to make sure nothing would lead them to us, once they was happy the closed the entrance.

Danny came to after an hour he had badly bruised ribs but non broken, swollen jaw both eyes cut blood from his nose ran down his bare chest. Once he could talk he told us how he had been checking the buildings when a guard came around the back for a pee. I hide my gun in the hay before he got to close, i couldnt run he had his shotgun on me. Once they got me inside they went to town asking me questions, i told them i was a climber but they didnt believe me. They will know soon that you was not alone when they find the two bodies of there men for the next few days this place is going to crawl with silva's men. My words came true, search party after search party combed the area coming close to the entrance twice before they gave up. Do you think they think we have got away ? bret asked, maybe but its going to be a few nights before we find out i saw the disapointment on their faces. Look i told them with a hint of angerwe dont move till Danny is up and able to walk for himself then we get the job done and get out of here all of us. There days past before Danny felt up to walking, his rib were now blacky blue but not as tender, his left eye was still closed the swelling was going but he was still not fit.

Do the hit without me Danny told me that third morning, i will i told him but i need you fit to get out of here. Ok he said then let me make my way back to the first base near the boat then once you have done the job you can catch up with me. I put it to the lads what Danny had said and they agreed having him safe would allow us to continue with our work and get us away quicker.

We made plans for that night we would let Danny go after dark taking two days rations and some ammo with him. Testing the weight he was carrying i loaded it into a rucksack for him then i cooked a hot meal from a rabbit we cought in our traps. It was like a banquet stew with meat and ground roots which we knew we could eat and dried biscuits to mop up the gravy made from the powder in the rations. Fish tomorrow i told Danny which gave him a smile on his face, ya what time are we dinning he commented not to early i replyed with a chuckle. Soon it was time for him to leave, it was like sending your child to school for the first day i watched him go through the entrance out into the field then lost him in the dark. Will are we going out to check out the ranch house Bret asked? why not i replied we need to find out Silva's routines and were im going to hit him. Knowing i needed to give Danny time to reach the river that hit would not be tonight tomorrow maybe but not tonight. Cole filledhis bag with explosives to start setting the traps and Bret armed himself to the teeth. His shoulder straps had three small throwing knives on each side hanging down with quick release straps.

Rifle magazines filled little compartments around his torso six grenades for the M203 also slotted onto his webbing. His side arm hung in its holster at his hip with a dagger in a sheth and one in his boot. They both carried there M16 at the ready both these men were killing machines both were what you needed in a fire fight. My mind drifted back to Vietnam all those years back to a jungle patrol that we was in that got ambushed. Charlie came out of the ground everywhere, we was surrounded men were being hit every direction you looked. There was no way out but some how the four of us linked together and fought our way out. Guns blasting every face that came up in front of us, shooting clubbing stabing killing men anyway we could.

The only survivors that day was the four of us, all the others were killed twentyseven souls died that day leaving eighteen widows and fourteen fatherless children. From that day on we stuck together and all came home with our purple hearts but alive to tell the tail. The rain had left the ground sticky in places but we managed to reach the viewing point in the bushes and as i expected it had a heavy guard around the house. Two men watched the porch while two more walked the grounds with the dogs. Dobermans that was the breed of the dogs and very nasty one's watching how they pulled and snarled at their handlers. Two were tied to ground stakes about one hundred foot from the house and fifty foot apart the other two was taken around the back and tied the same distance. So now we had four dogs covering each corner of the house plus two patroling guards, another two guards patroled the porch.

It looks like we are not going to get anywere near the house Bret whispered to me, your right there i responded so i am just going to get him when he is in the open. Cole went to find some targets to help our escape, the road from the house crossed the stream so he added a explosive device. We would need to stay all night and day to watch Silva movements so any work we had to do we would need to do it now. Digging intothe soft topsoil was easy now it was wet, each of us made a coverwhich blended in with the surroundings. Once Cole returned and told us where he had set the charges we set up a watch for the night two hours on four off and i took the first watch. Sleeping wasnot easy out there, the damp ground give you a chill and the bugs bite deep into your flesh but this we was used to after Nam. I started to day dream when the dogs barking pulled me out, the guards were changing shifts which set the dogs off i noted the time it was now two in the morning. Other than the guards nobody was moving about.

Sunrise was sixthirty and we was all awake watching the guards feed the dogs and taking them in to the barn for a rest. that just left the men on the porch to watch and they just sat on the wall smoking and chat to each other. I studded the buildings, there roofs was at a hight which would allow me to see into the top rooms but there was no way up in the day time and it would be hard at night with those dogs.

Two hours later the front door opened and there stood Silva, he wore white riding trousers and white shirt, a red cravat around his neck finished off with black leather riding boots. He streched is body back and upwards as if to get the stiffness of sleep out of his bones. He had a load voice when he spoke and we heard him wish the guards good morning then told them off for sitting lazy on the wall. Both shot up to their feet and stood head bowed like noughty boys his lady came out the door at that moment, she looked like a model her riding clothes had been poured out of a bottle and hugged her body were it touched. She too wore white leggings with white blouse the buttons down low showing a ample cleavage with large swells being pushed against the cloth. Her legs slim and good shape fitted her boots like a glove she wore gloves and carried a riding crop. Her long black hair was tied up in a pony tail she was a stunner what she saw in a drug baron i dont know, yes i do "money". Five horse was lead out into the yard three guards would be going out with them, could'nt follow but we could get closer for when they come back. Soon as they rode out of sight the porch guards went inside, we backed out of our hide and followed in the direction.

We followed the horses hoof marks in the mud, Bret kept to the right of the track i took the left, this track went passed our hide with about fifty foot from the opening. About a mile on we climbed two trees and waited for their return which was two hours later and at a gallop. I watched threw my scope unattached from my rifle i could have a clear shot from the front and again after they passed this look promising. We climbed down once they had gone, you should have taken the shot i would have done the otheirs Bret said, yes and the horses would run off back to the ranch, i rasied my eyes to him. Ok its about getting out safe after we make the hit he said, correct i confirmed, its that way or not at all. Ididnt want to leave this place without hitting my target but it was getting desperate i had to get Silva somewhere alone or a blood bath. What i meant was i would have to take out the whole lot of them and that would include the women, lets do it that way said Bret when i consulted them both back at the base that night. Cole had reported nothing on all day after his ride he went indoors and never came out again, ok Cole you set as many traps as you can tonight. Bret you set up a good line of fire into the doorway of the mens hut, i will do the hit as soon as he shows his face. We risked a small fire and had some hot food and a hot drink, weapons cleaned and checked and at midnight we moved out. Deciding that after the fight we would meet the other side of the bridge before Cole distroyed it, then heading as fast as we could to the river.

It would mean traveling in the open in daylight trying not to be seen but that was the chance we had to take. I settled into the postion i had chose it had a clear line of fire from the front door to the stables Bret was about fifty meters to my left. Dogs had been put out and tied to the ground stakes, two guards patroling the grounds two on the porch the system the same as the other nights. Knowing Cole he would be out there fixing up as many traps as he could make, a few that he learned from Charlie in Nam. At first light the farming staff turned up as normal, they collected their equipment and went on their way.

I felt stiff from lying in one spot all night i riggled my toes and flexed my muscles in my legs once i took the shot i would need everything to work for my escape. The dogs were put inside the building but this time the guards patroled the grounds, this meant that Bret would need to hit these to guards first. Cole would be somewhere near so he would help with the guards on the porch. One hour past the guards changed they went to take their breakfast for some it would be their last. Another two hours past guards changed again a differant four from the early shift so that made twelve men plus there was two main men in the main house. House staff were not armed but they could get weapons, we could be up again't sixteen to twenty men. Istill wished that i could have got on one of the out buildings roofs to see into the top floor, one shot through a window may not have alerted all the staff maybe not any if he had been alone. Just then the door open, i raised the sight to my eye and forced the round into the chamber at the same time safty catch off i was ready. His two bodyguards came out first followed by his lady, then Silva was there my heart beat fast my hands started to feel sweaty.

Four horse's were brought out by two farm hands, i waited i could feel Brets eyes looking my way telling me to do it. Silva climbed aboard his horse his head was now in my sight cross section i sqeezed the trigger. His head burst open like a water melon and blood splattered in all directions especially on his lady whosewhite blouse and face was coverd in brain splatter. For a while there was a quietness, nobody moved they was just shocked then my second round took down the nearest guard and the lady screamed. Bret opened up at the two men on the porch hitting one first burst, the horses spooked and ran off with the women on board screaming. The farm hands chased after the horses while the remaining body guard tryed to make for cover firing blind as he ran. A round hit him in the chest dropping him to the ground, men were now coming out from their building firing in Brets direction.

The man on the porch was now firing at me from the doorway and he had good cover, men fired from doors windows and any cover they could find. Bret fired a grenade from his launcher it landed about ten meters from the doorway of the mobs house killing two outside and keeping the heads down of the othere's.

I waved to Bret and it did'nt take him long to be at my side, suddenly there was an explosion glancing i saw the garage go up. Lets go i shouted and we both ran heading towards the bridge, crossing the stream we heard two more explosives taking cover we waited for Cole. "Run" Cole shouted as he got near us there is a army behind me he didnt have to tell us twice, stopping to fix the wires on a fuse Cole got the bridge ready for a big bang. Bret and myself stopped about five hundred meters ahead and watched as he finished what he had to do and started towards us a large mob of people appeared behind him. Shots were fire he was hit in the shoulder but managed to keep running as the bridge went up.

The timbers went up high in the air splintering and twisting into small bits stones dirt and water mixed and landed on the crowd. Cole reached us, Lets go he said how bad are you i asked ? i will live was his answer then shots stopped me asking more. We ran through the undergrowth the mud and swamp we kept running till we could hear nothing behind us. Cole's combat shirt was covered in blood so i called a rest, lets take a look at that big fellow i said as i open his shirt. He had been lucky the bullet had entered just under his shoulder joint and gone straightthrough exiting just above his arm pit.

No bones had been hit nor arteries but he had lost a lot of blood, using two field dressings on both the front and back of the wound. After a little restwe moved off keeping to the cover of the trees to avoid being seen. We arrived at a track which by the marks told us it had been used recently and by heavy trucks, could be what they use for the dope Bret commented. Well if it is there wont be much today Cole told us i blew it up, how the hell did you do that i asked?. Well i found some fual cans that they must use for the tractors poured it into the water channels left a small incendiary device and bobs your uncle. You did get him ? Cole inquired, yes plus half his army ireplyed now i think we had better get going, just then we heard the sound of engines. Hiding behind the brush we watched two military trucks full of soldiers go passed the last one stopped about two hundred meters up the road.

The men jumped down from the tail gate and entered the undergrowth at that spot, lets go i said crossingthe track and entering the woods the other side. That was not the only time we would see troops that day, they was looking for the men that murdered the governor they were looking for us. After a good while i checked Cole's wound, it had stopped bleeding but required cleaning and some clean dressings this he would have to wait for. About four k's from our hide and Danny we saw more troops searching the area in front of us, digging slit trenchs we covered each other in branches and brush. I pull the last branch over just as the troops arrived around us, laying still i held my pistol at the ready and prayed. These men were full time soldiers and checked the area well but we was experts and knew how to hide Vietnam had taught us that. Staying were we was for a good hour after the last soldier had passed very near to our position we slowly came out from our hides. Moving with even more caution now we slowly made our way to the entrance to our first hide. As we entered Danny was there pointing his rifle at us, phew i nearly fired he stated once he saw it was us.

I knew you had got him this place as been crawling with state troops since this morning he told us. I checked my watch, god we had been seven hours making our way back here, it only seemed one hour ago i had killed a man. The rest of the day we stood guard at the opening and watched as the troops and police searched for us. Groups of people came along with sticks poking the shrub trying to flush us out it would be difficult to get to the river with all these patrols.

Lets wait till dark and see what that brings i told the lads, we had asked the captain of the boat to be off shore every night after midnight till two. He would wait fishing then move so if we was going tonight we would have to get down the river by midnight. Darkness fell, Coles wound was no worse but he was running a bit of a fever the bleeding had stopped but the wound needed medical aid. We wont be going tonight i whispered to Bret, pointing to Cole that fever has to come out, we need a doctor. Bret took a look at Cole who was now boiling up with sweat running off him, while Danny tryed to cool his forehead with water on a cloth.

That wound could have a infection he whispered back to me, i'll go and get some help later, Danny jumped in i will go too. While Danny had waited for us he had gone out hunting food and found a small town near to the river, there was a medico centre there. Maybe it would be better to take Cole there get him treated and get away after his treatment, after some thought i decided that we would all go. Moving out of the hide at ten thirty with Cole over my back we maid our way through the brush, it was heavy going but we took it in turns to carry our friend. About a hour on we reached the river and the edge of the town, it was still full of life with crews getting their boats ready for the early start. This was a small fishing town with a fish market a few stores a boat yard, it had a church and about one hundred house's. The medical centre was in the middle of the high street, next to a super market and across from a police station.

Thats just great Bret snarled how we going to get him there?, around the back to a yard were they burn the rubbish Danny answered. Cole was starting to get restless, i had to deliberate in my mind do we go in or do we chance him dying, we had been together too long to lose him. We walked slowly across the yard Bret carried Cole so Danny and myself entered the doors and carefully walked in.

The place was spotless with white tiled floors and white washed walls, a awaiting area with a reception counter was what we first came to. Danny watch that front door i told him he pressed against the wall and glanced out the glass panelled doors. The street looks quite at the moment he informed me, good lets find some help i gestured to Bret. Though a set of doors we meet a nurse who was about to scream till i grabbed her and put my gun in her ribs, there is no need to hurt her a voice came from my right. I am doctor smythe said the man standing there looking at me with his hands raised, you are the men they are looking for?. Yes i answered but i have a injured man and if you dont help him i will kill you both, the nurses eyes filled with terror. You do not need to fear us we are medical staff your friendis wounded and needs help may i look the doctor moved forward and indecated to the nurse to help.

They showed Bret a bed to put Cole down on and then went about there work with the doctor telling the nurse what he needed. You are American i told the doctor? yes was all he said and you must be hungry, there is a kitchen down the corridor second left if you would like some food. Bret left to get us all some food while i kept my eye on these two, you have many pattients here i asked as the doctor started cleaning Coles wound. Non he replied, if they are to ill we get them to hospital other than that we lick their cuts and send them home. We are the night staff incase of emergency but not very often that we get any this time of night, an odd expecting mother. Bret returned with some cooked chicken bread and coffee, have yours then give Danny a break to have some i told him. With the lads out front watching the street i talked to the Doctor how long before we can move him i asked indecating Cole. He will need some good rest, i think forty-eight hours bed rest then two weeks rest from all activities was his reply. Doc i have got to get him home tomorrow, do you mean tonight he corrected me pointing to the clock. Four-thirty the clock read my god we have got to get him out of here and kill him the doc said. What do you think i should do i cannot leave him for these people to beat on him, leave him here till tonight and see then the doc told me, he will be safe we will not give him away. My eyes had given away my thoughts, I walk the floor a little way in thought, ok we will leave him for the rest of the day but if anything happens to him we will shoot you both when we come back.

Mister i dont know you but i know why you killed president Silva! he was a eel didnt care about anything but himself. Then why are these people so happy to hunt us down?, money he replied they have been offered a lot of money from his wife for your capture. That lady will run the show the same if not harder than he did, she run the drugs side before but needed his state influence. The doc continued to tell me all about Silva's woman it looked as if the thing we came to stop will now get worse with this woman running the show. It seemed that Silva just had the power but she had the brains and know more people would get threatened to keep the drugs racket going. So you have no fear from us the doctor continued, we will look after your friend and keep him safe. I went out to the lads and told them that we was leaving Cole here, the nurse we cleaning Dannys wounds removing the dried blood and pulling cuts together with tape.

There was a twinkle in her eyei think Danny had touched the spot with her, let's go! i said we are going back to the hide to make plans, we have to talk about what we must do. Cole was asleep when we left already he looked better for his care and i had a feeling that he would be better in the doc's hands then he would be out in the wild with us. Outside we sneaked by the back doors of building but had to up our pace once a dog started to bark when we passed his home. Arriving back at the hide i set up a watch for the night giving myself a double shift at the start to give me time to think things over. Telling the lads to get their heads down i positioned myself so i could see and hear anyone moving around close to us. Bret had asked if we was going to chat now but i told him morning will do and to get some rest, i settled down to think things over. I had come here to stop a man from selling drugs to scum-bags of the world and been paid good money to do that but if his lady take's over i would'nt have achieved nothing. Would i take the guys home that night and in a few weeks bring them back to finish the job or do it now for free. Both ways was risking our live's but being here takes part of the risk out that was worth consideration. Four hours later Bret relieved me and i got my head down but my mind kept me awake for a good while. Finally i went off only to be awoke by Danny at daylight, we have company close he reported, my heart jumped as i got up grabbed Cole's rifle.

Reaching the point where Bret lay in a dozen strides i lay beside him Danny lay the other side of me, where! was all i said. Bret said nothing and just pointed, soldiers where looking under the bushes into our area but could'nt see anything for the growth of the plant life. We watched them move away before any of us spoke, when are they going to give up Danny spoke first? i dont know i replied but we need to talk. Leaving Danny watching the patrols i took Bret to our camp area, i explained what the doctor had told me and what i thought about taking out Silva's wife. But we have not been paid for a hit on her he commented once i was finished.

Thats true and we may not be but if we take her down think of the help we will be doing for the world? getting rid of one more scum bag i pushed my case. He frowned, i dont like doing this for nothing, is there not a chance we could get paid?. I will try when we get home to give a price but i will not promise you the result, ok he said just try. Bret went and took over from Danny so i could explain to him what i was planing to do and he was fine with the plan. It would mean returning to Silva's home and taking the first chance i had to do the hit, that would also depend on these patrols stopping.

The day past by with more patrol getting close to our entrance but not seeing it or finding us, night soon came and we exitied the hide to go and see Cole. This night the streets were quite not a soul could be seen a dog barked a few streets away but nothing else. We moved into the clinic via the back door this time the nurse was in the reception area and seemed pleased to see us, well Danny that is. She smile and took us into the room were we found Cole sitting up chatting to the doctor, the nurse returned to Danny who we left guarding the front door. Hi doc how is the patient tonight, He is doing fine, why not ask me Cole said with a big smile on his face, come to take me home?. We will talk about that in a moment i told him, you boys need feeding asked the Doc? you bet we do said Bret like a little boy getting a new toy. Good, the nurse brought some cooked food from her home you will find it in the staff room. Doc do you think you could give us a moment, sure i'll help your man fix some food for you all, with that he left the room. You are going to get his wife arn't you? how did you know ? the doc's a nice fella but talks a lot he said, he can read my mind too. What do you think? i asked Cole after i had put the case forward to do the hit, i think your mad was his reply. The doctor told me that the whole area is swarming with military personal and police you will not get passed them back to her home.

That we will have to try i answered, and what about me ? i am not fit to lay out in wet fields it will be a few days before i am back on my feet. I felt my head sink as i spoke we will have to do it without you, oh yes and blow yourselfs up he mimicked, Cole we will find away. I knew he was right we had been together to long for us not to know each other and with that i decided that i would take them all home. It took us another two days before Cole had the strength to walk, we spent the time ploting our way out without being seen by anyone. The doctor got us news papers so we could read the stories they had wrote about us and stories they were. One paper said we had shoot women and children and another reported that we had cut mens throats as they slept. One reported the truth that with the president six of his followers had died and five more were injured. We was FBI, CIA, Navy seals, united state's marines different papers had us down has different groups the stories just got better.

That third night we collected Cole from the hospital, I thanked the Doc has he put a food parcel under my arm. The nurse clung to Danny's arm as we made our way out the back door, i will come back for you i heard him say. Thanks Doc i shook his hand, i did my job he told me, you did a bit more than that you saved his life and kept the rest of us safe. Goodbye he said turned and he was gone back into the building the nurse followed a few feet behind him looking back over her sholder towards Danny.

Making our way to the waterside we looked for a boat, finding a fishing boat with the door open and the key still in the starter was really lucky. Danny and Bret untied the lines and i fired her up, moving out of the small harbor into the open flow of the river we got up some speed. Another stroke of luck the tide was with us and without any trouble we was out in open sea. We planned not to meet up with our fishing friends instead we would chance the open sea making for one of the west indies islands. Once there we would fly home to the States passing off as holiday makers and no problems getting passed customs or imagration. I took a compass barring and headed for Jamaca some 800 kilometers away as the crow flies.

We would not have fuel to do all the trip so we would have to use the sails for long spells. We had sailed before on the Mekong river in Vietnam so the lads knew how to work the sails. Charts currents and wind speeds and timings would play a great part of us steering into Kingston harbor. The whole thing was almost lost when we hit a storm on our second night out and had to batten down and wait it out. But we finally entered the harbor two days later passing as fishermen coming in after the storm had damaged the boat which was just a bit of sabotage by us.

After a few days resting on the beach we flew home to Florida, we each bought a ticket from the flight desk to our final destinations. We made our way to the coffee shop in the departure lounge to chat about the future then we said our goodbye's and each went for his flight.

CHAPTER TWO

SECOND HIT

I made my usual crossword puzzle message in the local magazine to let the agency who paid me know that the target was hit. Adding to the message was my information about silva's wife, and would they want me to target her now?. The payment they owed me went into my account and i paid the lads but nothing came about silva's wife. It was four weeks later on my way home from a bar where i had been having a drink and shooting some pool. That i called in my local store and picked up a six pack and some fries that i noticed the new magazine was in. Flicking the pages i noticed the crossword, paying for the goods i walked the two blocks to my apartment. I unlocked the door and entered the hall tossing the keys onto the hall stand i made my way to the kitchen.

Putting the beer into the fridge i removed a cold one out of my stock pile, knocking the top of and tearing open the fries i sat to work out the cross-word. My code was easy if you was looking for it but nobody would ever look only myself and the poeple who use it for me. First we keep the message small, then i write down the second letter from each word of the answers using the across answers first then the downs. For example one across answer is goat so i write down the O the next answer was gnat which give me a N and so on until the puzzle is finished. Looking at the letters i put together this message, ON TUES LADY AT KEN APORT MORE INF TO CUM. So they wanted me to target her. I read the message again, on tuesday the lady will be at kennedy airport more information to come. I now wait till i recive a message in my post office box giving me all the details of her movements times and the price of the hit. Tuesday was four days away so i had time to organise myself i would need weapons, but what! that would depend on where i hit her. I checked my post office box the next day there was not a thing in it so i spent the day studing a map of the area around Kennedy airport. If i was to hit her there too many poeple would get hurt, panic would set in seeing a blood covered woman they would run everywhere to get away. I would need to wait till i got that information of her movements.

That information came the following day; i open my box to find a large brown envelope, putting it away in my bag i headed home. Once inside i ripped the top open, Two photo's fell out one of silva's wife, Allana silva was her name. The other picture was of a man, Antonio Conti was the name on the back of the picture. The information on the note read, arriving at 14.00 on tuesday will then be taken by car to hotel (Hilton) were she is booked in for five days. She has a flight booked to return on sunday at 08.00am, she has a meeting arranged with the man in the picture who is a known drug operator in New york. If you can get them both we will pay you $300,000 plus expenses, our information is from a man we have planted in Conti's group so it is reliable. The meeting place is at a resturant owned by Mr conti on 5th avenue but its also a drug factory at the rear with a large work force. Distroying the note and hiding the picture's i sat and thought about what to do next, Cole i thought i would need Cole so i placed a callto him. Hi buddy i started how would you like to take a trip to New york? when, was his reply? be here for monday i will get you a room at the Hilton hotel in the name of Alan Turner, i will be there first flight in the morning he said and hung up. I rang the Hilton and made a patential ten day booking in a single room, then i checked the flights for the next morning so i could pick him up at the airport. A few drinks and some pool helped take things off my mind but i left the bar early and took a strole in the park before returning to my apartment. Next day i was at the airport early it was the day before Mrs Silva would arrive, we had a lot to plan before we would see her the next day. Cole arrived at the arrivals coffee bar where we always meet when he came to me, hi he said how are you?. Fine i replyed and what about you i hinted to the area of his wound, all healed up just a odd twing if i twist fast.

I drove to the hotel pulled up out front and the porter took the keys gave me the disk and took the car to park it. Cole picked up his key for his room and we took the elevator to his room on the forth floor. Out of his bag he pull a bottle of whisky and filled to glasses of the complimentry bar, cheers he said and we clinked glasses. Now lets hear the story of the hit he asked, Well its our lady from Colombia but there is a second target a Italian who runs a drug factory here in New york.

A few drinks later and all the details explained we went out for a meal not just any meal but italian at chinos the very resturant that Conti owned. Entering the place we encounted a member of staff have you reserved a table sir he said to me, no im afraid we have not. Just wait while i check the bookings for this everning sir, after a check ha yes sir we have a cancelation so we can offer you a table. leading the way the head waiter showed us to our table were he explained what was special for that night, he left us with a menu. Nice place Cole said twisting his head around to take in the views most was of ladies legs, but the place did have a touch of class about it. high ceilings supported long crystal light fittings mirrow tiles on the ceiling reflected the light plus your head image. Cole pointed out the amount of clevage he could see, at the end of the rows of tables was a dance area with a small stage of steps behind that.

At the sides of the stage through two doors the waiters brought out the food plus the acts for the night came out from the left door. Calling our waiter over we ordered our food, If i wanted to eat here every night could i book in advance i asked as he took our order?. Yes sir came the answer except when we have special night then you buy tickets for the show. Could you book this table for the next five nights, yes sir may i have your name? Mr Lewis i told him and slipped him a fifty tip. That will get us here for there meeting i told Cole, the waiter returned Wednesday is a big show so it is all ticket he informed me. Could i buy two tickets? yes sir they are one hundred dollers each, i gave him the money and within a few minutes he was back with my tickets.

As i was saying that puts us here for the meeting and i think it will be on that big show night a sort of treat for Mrs Silva, Cole agreed yes you could be right. We ate our meal and drank some wine and listerned to a lady singer, Cole was showen the way to the toilet which was through the left door by the stage. Once he returned we stepped outside to where a taxi was waiting and of we went back to his Hotel room. One for the road he asked me and i excepted his offer, i took a look around while i was taking a leak at the toilet he said while he poured the drinks. When you go out to the tiolet there are two doors to your left one for guys and the other for the lady's two doors directly across are for the artists. Down the small corridor you come to two double doors which leads to the kitchen he continued with his discretion.

This a very large kitchen with seven chefs and seven hands plus all the waiters entering both doors but more so the right side of the stage. I think they like that side better as they dont have to pass customers coming from the tiolets, that make's sense ireplyed. At the rear of the kitchen there is a door which opens into the delivery area at the side street, thats on the right side, then there is a big double door flush with the back wall. I saw lots of people coming and going through that door some wearing masks, thats your drugs factory he finished. We need to see behind that door if we can i said, that may be the best place to hit them. We planned the next day, i would go watch the lady arrive and follow her while Cole heads back to the resturant and watchs that back street to see when the factory stops working if it do's. Back at my apartment i sketched a map of that back area just how Cole had explained it to me, then i got my head down so i'll be fresh for the next day.

The next morning i was up and after a wash and shave i got dressed cup of coffee and toasted bread and i was on my way. First i had to call on a friend who was kitting me out with some weapons and ammo, he also had some explosives for me. We meet at a old disused drive in that nobody use's he opens his trunk i check the goods pay him and he is gone five minutes tops is all i see of him. Consealing the weapons in the trunk i started up the car and headed off to the airport to see the arrival of Mrs Silva plus any bodyguards she my bring. My mind toyed with how i was going to accomplish my hit on both parties and make it look natural, the resturant looked like the place. I drove through queens into oceanside then followed the signs to the arrivals department at the airport parking in a bay facing the front exit doors. While i watched i pictured that rear entrance at the resturant and the door at the back of the kitchen. The automatic doors opened and there she stood like a film star, she had on a head scarf which drooped around her neck on top of that she wore a wide brimmed hat.

A thin lemon dress hugged her figure hiding little of her large breasts which swelled above the neck-line. A fur stolle dangled down from each of her wrists to near the top of her short hemline, seamed stockings coveredher long legs finishing with lemon matching shoes. She was a real atractive woman it was a pity she was so evil and love's only money. Two bodyguards were in front of her and two brought up the rear but there was a young man carrying her bag and a briefcase. They made there way to a stretch limo who's driver held open the doorto let his lady in. She was followed by the young guy and two of the bodyguards, the other two jumped into a black limosine and followed as they pulled away. Bringing up the rear was yours truly but keeping far enough back not to be noticed, Mrs Silva could no be noticed as the limo windows were tinted. Judging by the way they were going it looked like they was heading straght to the Hilton hotel before they did any business.

I over took them and got there first parked the car and entered the lobby i asked at the desk if Mr james was in his room, 146 i told the desk clerk. She buzzed Cole's room but no answer sorry sir but there's no reply, fine i will wait in the bar can you let him know when he come's back. yes sir she replyed, i turned to walk away when coming towards me was Mrs Silva's group. I turned slowly and asked house phones, just there sir she pointed in the right direction and i ducked inside a hood booth. I toyed with the phone book trying hard to get her room number, Hello Mrs Silva the clerk acknowledge after she informed her who she was, your penthouse suite is already for you. You two take the bags up and check the place, me and lover will wait in the bar she told the two nearest men. Me and lover i repeated to myself she didnt waste any time mourning for her dead husband.

They moved off into the bar area taking seats near to the window i followed and sat the other side of a small partition quite close to them. Tomorrow i'm going shopping and spend a lot of money on bags dresses and shoes, i heard her say, just then the waiter arrived at the table. I think we will have a bottle of Champagne darling shetold the waiter and get my boys a beer. The bodyguards were seated near the door leaving the love birds alone but still close enough to protect her. I noticed one stearing in my direction so i picked up a paper and holding it high to cover my face i pretended to read. The waiter took my order for coffee and returned within and few moments with tray full of coffee pot water and cup saucer with complementary biscutes.

Mrs Silva's young lover was called Amos and he was in his early twenties she seemed very happy to have a play thing he was to young to understand manipulation. Finally i heard somthing i had been whating for, we will meet up with Conti at his resturant tomorrow night she said to her young friend. Once i get a order off him there will be regular money coming in from America, then we can look at europe. She poured a second glass of bubbly for each of them and sank it just as quick the glass was refilled by the waiter. The first two bodyguards returned and informed her that the rooms were fine and there is another bottle of champagne waiting. Is your rooms close by she asked them? we are right next door to your suite he informed her.

One of us will remain on your door at all times, good lets go lover she said to her young companion and off they went leaving one guard to bring up the bottle. Cole arrived at the bar door looking for me, i waved him over to were i sat coffee i asked? no thanks i need a real drink. bring us two double whiskies i told the waiter. I just saw our lady he said sounds like her young friend is in for a good time from what she was saying. Once he had is drink he started to tell me about his mornings work i got there about six he started, about twenty people arrived to start work. Were they kitchen staff i asked? no they arrived two hours later, the resturant opens at noon these people was let in and ushered through that door at the back of the kitchen. Ever hour the door was opened and a few workers came out for fresh air and a smoke, they wore white coats and masks hug around there necks.

Guards would stand with them making sure the coast was clear and no one ran off with anything, they was shoved back in once the break was over. Conti himself turn up about midday and went straight into the back so he must have a office back there as he came out later in his shirt sleeves carrying some book work. He took another belt of his whisky and then continued, once the kitchen staff came on that back door was locked and no one came out. So it appears that while the resturant is open they keep the work shop closed up? yes he agreed, i wonder when the work force finish. Depends when the work is done Cole commented if there is a lot t o do they would stay late if not they go home early. Yes but how early i dont want to kill people just because they work for a bad guy or innocent bystanders.

Most of those people will just be there to earn money they wont get the profits that Conti and his gang will get. A lot will die of drug poisoning ignorant to what they are handling, yes but somewill take drugs as a payment for the work Cole stated. They need help not death i answered we dont choose there way to live its the monsters that sell them the drugs i want.

We will get ready and go to the resturant tonight and i will try to take a look in the kitchen and look for a way to get the two of them at the same time. I went back to Cole's room and took a few hours rest as did Cole before we made ready to go out. While i follow her tomorrow i want you to try to get into her room and plant a device which we can detinate from here. Just enough to damage the room and get her and anyone in with her, that will be our back up if we dont get her at the resturant. Cole acknowledged, need some gear he said, its in my car before we go we will fetch it, guns he asked they are there too i replyed. Did she get a good look at you today? i asked Cole no not at all came his reply good try and keep it that way one of her men took a good look at me. After we got ready and collected the weaponery from the car and returned it to Cole's room we got a taxi to the resturant. Both of us were now carrying revolvers held in a shoulder holster hidden inour jackets.

These were only to be used in extreme curcumstancethe killing of Mrs Silva and Conti would have to look like a accidenta act of god. The waiter checked our resavation and the showed us to our table there was a piano on the stage a pianist was play some soft back -ground music. We could have done with something a bit livelier i whispered to Cole as we took our seat, maybe we can get him a bit livelier later with some requests. Our food came, we had ordered a three course of soup main dish of fish and a sweet of cake's italian style. The room was full now lots of couples and a few large parties so we needed to get them up encourage them to dance. Cole made his way to the pianist and whispered in his ear and before he got back to his seat the piano burst out honky tonk music. Cole jumped up in the air and went across to the nearest dancing to the music before to long there was three line on line dancers all following his steps. I took advantage and sneaked out to the toilet corridor, there was nobody about the waiters were busy clearing plates.

Looking through the small square windows at the top of the doors i could see the chef's busy at their work, only four were working the others must be having a smoke. Waiter were coming through the other door with dirty dishes and placing them on a counter ready for the dish washers to clear them. I open the door slightlyand sqeezed through bending down low so i was hidden by the work surface's of the preperation tables. Making my way to the back of the kitchen i stood behind a pot rack. I could see that every one was facing away from me so i stepped to the factory door. It was unlocked and slightly open i looked in, it was all clear so i stepped inside. There was rows of work benches each was covered in white powder and had a set of scales with a box full of plastic bags. The work force had gone home for the day but i was surprised to find they had left it in a mess, i licked my finger and touched the powder. Baking powder was the taste i got when i put my finger to my lips, it was a taste i knew from my mothers cooking days. They was leaving the powder so if they got raided they would say its a preproom for the pastry and nobody would suspect. Two offices in the corner were well furnished and had all the modern office equipment.

One was Conti's with a big leather seat and fine table, chairs for visitors were spread around the room. A picture on the table showed Conti his wife and two children i looked at it, atractive woman i thought but soon you will be a widow. There was nothing in there to help me but i would like to be in the room when he meets Mrs Silva here tomorrow night. I checked the kitchen again as i went out the door, the chef's were back from their break but they were rushing around with a new batch of orders for food.

I sneaked back the way i came exiting the door as a waiter came in, toilet i said just there he said pointing to the guys. Sitting back at our table i took a large gulp of my drink god get me another i told Cole, i took a big drink of the second before i told him what i had found. Do you think we could get them both in that office Cole inquired? maybe i replyed but we would need to cut it close with the timer. It would mean getting in before them setting a fuse waiting till they entered then firing it. I could rig a booby trap but if one should trigger it you could miss them and then we would have trouble getting a second shot. A timer would be best then we would just have to get it right with the time, yeh he said and got up to dance with a young lady who asked him.

The rest of the night was spent enjoying ourself's Cole even got up and gave them a song somthing by kenny Rodgers i think. We decided that no one would suspect two men having a good time without a care but little did they notice that we was not drinking to much, later we would be making a bomb for the place. handling explosives requires a steady hand and i knew Cole keeps a very positive side to working with the bang stuff as he calls it. The night was long we worked on our devices making two one for her room which we would only use if the resturant dont work. The second one would be planted in his office somewhere under the table. Cole would wait till the big show started, Conti would have a table for his guest so they should watch the show that will give Cole his chance to set up the device. Setting the timer for forty minutes would give them a chance to watch the show and then make to the office. To be sure we will ask on entry what time the show go's on till as we had a business callcoming back at our hotel. Once happy all was ready Cole finished off by telling me he would enter the detenators when he planted each device and set the timer for the resturant last. Sleep came but restless Veitnam battles re-fought bothers died charlies bloody traps sprung, young men never saw their home again. Some went home in boxies with only parts of the body in it, others went home to get locked away in jail or mental hospitals. The worst was the one's that lived, some with limbs missing but some scared by memory of that terrible war. I was the platoon lieutenant and i had the job of writing the lads wives, mothers, next of kins to tell them that the husband son etc died doing his duty for good old uncle Sam.

I was awaken by Cole, sorry brother i disturbed you again?, no i sleep like a log he told me, its time to get up. After i washed and dressed i went out to my carand sat waiting for Mrs Silva to come down. At nine Cole brought me a steak on rye and carton of coffee he sat with me chatting about the old days in Nam thefun time's. Times when we would pull pranks on the new guy's like harmless snake's in their bedding, tell them you heard a click when they took a stride and made them think they had stood on a mine. God they dont seem so funny now do they i asked him? no i surpose they dont but boy at the time, we both smiled. It was eleven when she finally came out of the hotel with her guards in tow, the young man held her hand and opened the car door. Iwill see you later Cole told me then left my car, i watched the her stretch limo pull away a few secounds later i followed. The reasonfor me following her today was to make sure there was no secret meeting between her and Conti. First stop was a dress shop whichshe spent over a hour picking one dress, next was a shoe shop. Two hours and three pairs of shoes later we moved on to a hat shop where she purchased six hats and two handbags.

I watched each purchase though a small pair of binoculars which i kept in the carthe one guard carried the bags to the car after each shop. Two more dresses were bought then on to a shop for underwear and finally perfume, a new suit for Amos shoes and a top coat. Five hours had passed from the time she left the Hotel to the time we returned, i parked the car up and went straight up to Coles room. How did you get on he asked me? i was bored stiff i answered but she did'nt go near Conti or his place so it must be tonight that they get together. How did you get on planting that device in her room i asked him? fine the maid went in to change the towels so i sneaked in behind her. Hid in a cupboard till she closed the door he continued, then found the ideal spot by the bed to hide the device. What damage would that do to the hotel if we have to use it? well some furniture will get damaged charring of the wall near to blast and glass shatter in the whole of the room. There was a knock on Cole's door, who is it he shouted, hotel porter sir i have your suits oh yes Cole replied and opened the door sign the book and took the garments. Looking at me with puppy eyes he just said i thought it would be nice to dress for tonight so i hired some dress suits. I smiled at him you cannot help yourself around ladies can you i said and patted him on his back.

Even in those evening suits we both knew what tonight was about there could be some lead flying about if we get caught. Cole put the plastic explosives in his heel of his left shoe the detinator was in the right heel a second watch went on his arm to use as a timer. Shoulder holsters were wore on our left shoulder being that we are both right handed one spare mag was dropped into our inside pocket. Ready we got our taxi and headed off to the resturant with nerve ends tingling but brains allert to what may happen. We entered the resturant the way we had for the last few nights with one exception this time we had to show our tickets then we was showen to our table. I ordered a round of drinks a cold beer for me and Cole had a whisky with ice and water, special tonight Italian chicken the waiter told us.

A bottle of wine was put on the table complyments of the management, the band on the stage were playing soft music some film thyme tunes plus plenty of Glen Miller not sure why they did that. The head waiter had told us that the show started at nine and would finish about ten thirty with light music continueing till they closed. There was two acts tonight some ballerinas from some school in Italy and a classical singer again Italian there acts would give plenty of time to set that explosive. Now we just hoped that they did'nt have the meeting while the show was on.

The resturant was full when Mrs Silva arrived with young Amos in tow her bodyguards escorted them to there table then retreated to the back of the room out of the way. She looked stunning in a long flowing cream dress her log blonde her cascading down each side of her ample breasts. Deep cleavage showed off more than plenty of her tits a large red stone hung around her neck likea christmas burble. Amos looked like a little mouse in his suit his bow tie made him look like the tree. Conti joined them at the table with what looked like his wife and his mother two other men sat with them bodyguards for the family. Cole had the special while i ordered a chicken salad with pasta another drink accompaned the meal. By the time the meal was finished most tables had eaten Conti's table were on there sweet, the time told me there was ten minutes to show time.

Just before the lights dimmed Cole made his way to the toilet he entered a cubical and waited till the room got quite before he made his way to the kitchen. He told me later how he entered the kitchen to find only a handful of staff who were cleaning up, the rest were in the corridor watching the show. He entered Conti's office and picked a place were he would do most damage, he was going to distory the factory too. Satisfide he had done his job he returned the way he came and joined me at the table dropping a cream cake in front of me, compliments of the managment he said. Cole ordered another round of drinks and we paid the bill, half way through act two we left the resturant tipping the head waiter on our way. We entered a bar about half a block away from the resturant and ordered some drinks, game of pool Cole asked ? why not i said rack them up. Twentyfive minutes passed and we was just into our third game when we heard the explosion everyone including ourself ran out into the street.

Its the Italian place one of the bar staff shouted we all moved down the street to see more. When we reached the the side alley we could see the back door had gone and some bodies had fell out into the unloading bay. The customers in the resturant were pouring out of the double doors at the front smoke was billowing out, the boarded windows of the factory had been blown out and flames flicked through. Lets see if we can help i shouted load so all could hear us, grabbed Coles arm and ran down the alley. Nobody followed uswe reached the door but the smoke and flames stopped us going in.

The kitchen side looked full of smoke but the factory was well ablaze, making our way back to the main street we saw the head waiter leaning on a car bonnet. What the hell happend i said to him? it was a explosion in the kitchen i think he replyed what about the staff and customers i inqiured all out except the boss and his family. My heart sunk he had not mentioned the guest that had been with the boss, The boss had a table full of people did'nt any of those people get out. Oh yes the lady and her escorts came out with me and the other customers as did the staff in the resturant and most of the kitchen staff that is except two and they would have been with the boss. He explaned that the boss had taken his wife and mother into his office to present the two chefs with a gift for their long service. Isaid no more as police were moving us back and the fire engine's were now on the scene. Missed her i said to Cole as we walked away of all the luck it sounds like Conti had to do a duty before he talked to Mrs Silva. We picked up a cab and went back to the hotel, in Cole's room we put on the television and waited for the news.

We received buletins about the explosion reporting ten dead then later it was twelve but no identifcations. Cole opened a bottle of whisky and we had a few drinks till the early hours of the morning then we got the news we were waiting for. Last night on fifth avenue therewas a explosion which killed ten people. The explosion happened at Chino's reasturant which is owned by millioner Antonio Conti who was killed in the explosion along with his wife and mother. Orfens i said allowed, what do you mean said Cole, killing them both has made there children orfens. Two friends also died with the family plus five members of Mr Conti's staff. fire experts at the scene say it is to early yet to know the caurse of the explosion but they think it was a faulty gas pipe in the kitchen. The bomb in her room i said, will go off he looked at his watch in another hour, i set the timer to go off while she was in bed. I lay back on his bed tiredness got at me and soon i was asleep cole went off in his chair.

BOOOOM the noise made me jump up from the bed, Cole told me to stay inside his room but a call on the landing called for us to use the stairs and go down to the lobby. The fire alarm was ringing out so loud you could not hear yourself think Once down stairs there was complete panic, i used this state to leave the building to avoid being questioned. Telling Cole i would see him later at my flat i removed his weapon and ammo and drove off in my car. Feeling satisfide that we had completed our mission i went to bed andfell into a deep sleep.

Again a bang awoke me but this time it was a knocking on my door, who is it i called through a locked door? its Cole came the reply. Letting him in he pushed past me put the news on, i switched the set on to the news channel and watched. The explosion at the Hilton hotel early this morning caused only damage as nobody was in the suite at the time. Police spokesmen have said they are not sure what caused the explosion but they think it could be gang warfare relating to drugs. Police are looking for the woman that had rented the room to clear her from their enqires. i shut down the set, i dont understand where did she go, it dont matter Cole replied she cannot leave without being questioned.

It is likely that she went into hiding after the resturant bomb, but where i said. Lets start with that hire limo he said picking up the phone as he flicked through the book. Hi my friend hired one of your cars and she was involved in a explosion in a resturant i just need to check she is ok. Thank you he said and put down the phone, we are in luck the car company picked up the car early this morning from a motel. Twenty minutes later we was parked outside the Motel, we sat in the car and watched for three hours then one of the bodyguards stepped out. Cole stepped out of the car to follow him twenty minutes later Cole was back with bags of goodies as well as coffee.

Where is the bodyguard? he is right behind me two seconds later the man came round the corner with his bag of goodies he had been sent out for food to. first he entered cabin 2B dropped off some of the food then went to 4B with the bulk of food and stayed there.

I would say the guards are staying in 4B Cole said i smiled at him with contempt, i saw that for myself i replyed. What would you do if you was them he asked me? well i would lay low for a few days get a car move somewhere that i can fly out from and i think thats what they will do. I decided to book a room so one of us can rest while the other keeps a eye open, i went to the reception and booked in. 1A was across the drive from 2B and we had a good view of 4B and they would have to pass us if they leave their cabin. Once inside i put a chair near the window and turned on the television.

The news channel were now saying that Mrs Silva was responsable for the bombing at the resturant. The bomb in Mrs Silva hotel room was retaliation for Mr Conti's death, this was playing right into our hands they would lay low now. Cole joined me and when i told him the news he was estatic that will keep them in doors till they work out what to do. Yes it could'nt have worked out better, the police were looking every port would be looking and Conti's contacts would think they killed him so they would be looking. This could be like the gun fight at ok corral Cole said they have only one exit and to get threw that they have to pass us. I dont want a blood bath but if i can take a shot i will, i need to get back to my apartment to collect my rifle. Just before i was about to go the door to the bodyguards room opened two guards came out and went to Mrs Silva's room.

A few moments later they came back out and walked towards the exit passing our window as they went. If you get the drink i will go and purchase a car once i fined a car lot was the conversation we heared as they passed. Once they had gone i jumped into my car and headed for my apartment, i must hurry i thought, once they have the car they could drive off anywhere. I reached my apartment entered got my rifle from its hidding place and was back on the road the full trip had took me just thirty minutes. We had been lucky for the last few days even with the way thing had turned towards Mrs Silva, but as i entered the carpark my luck ran out. Entering the drive i almost bumped into a person but stopped just short of hitting him, he looked up at me and it was the bodyguard who had been looking at me in the Hotel.

I could tell by the way he looked he had recognised me but he tryed to make out he did'nt, he waved off me nearly hitting him and rushed off towards his room. parking the car as fast as i could i made my way to our room and got inside just as the men's door open. Two men came out looking menacing holding their hands to the inside of their jackets, this told me they was armed. They starred all around as if looking for some one. Then the man that had recognised me came out and pointed towards the carpark area they both made there way towards where my car was parked. they looked my car over then walked back as they passed our window one was heard saying maybe he as had to come here afterthe hotel bomb. We will find out which room he is in and watch him the other told him, they waved the man at the door back inside the room. That was bad for me it would mean that i would'nt beable to move about so freely, the rest of the day we watched the guards move from room to room. Early into the everning my friend that had recognised me went off in the car returning with more food and drinks. Cole did the same for us not using the car knowing that they were watching but returned in a new car which he perchased from a dealer in a bar.

We dont use your car while we are here he told me mine is parked around the corner they have not seen that one. For hours we watched but no sign of Mrs Silva or her young friend, that poor kid must be worn out if she is as sexy as she looks Cole asked on a change over. lucky son of a bitch i replied and imstuck here with you he smiled and dived onto the bed and was asleep in a wink. She was not the lady i took her for i thought she would be out and about drinking and dancing taking chance's after all not everyone saw her. My thoughts came true about midnight the bodyguard got the car and pulled up outside her room, i awoke Cole. Seconds later she and her companion climbed into the back of the car A driver and one guard accompanied them while the other two watched them pull away. Cole shouted bathroom window and i was out within a second of him and sitting next to him in the car as their vehical turned out the drive.

This time we kept a real good distance from them there was not much traffic about so we stay just in sight. Cole pulled the car over about two hundred meters short after they stopped, it was a night club not the sort you would take a lady but Mrs Silva went in.

We had worked out that the two men with her had never seen me or Cole, they had left the man that know me behind to watch for me following them. So in we went, picture, s on the wall showed women topless some just had a g-string on but it looked like this could be a place were everything go's. The place was dark except for a dance area, the bar was long with two girls go-go dancing one on each end. Four topless bar tenders served you your drinks four more served the tables, we found a dark area but where we could see everything. I could see why they had chose this place police would'nt come here looking for them they would'nt expect anyone on the run to hide here. Three bra and panty clad girls danced on round stages in the middle of the dance floor and one hung from a cage from the celling. Cole call the drinks which arrived in no time, i looked around the room and found Mrs Silva sitting with Amos in a alcove alone no other guards to be seen.

Then i saw them standing by the bar in the darkest part of the club, the music got a bit loader and faster and so did the dancers. Men near the platforms pushed money into the elastic of the girls panties little squeals told us that fingers had push a little to far soon bra's were off. Men shouted orders to the girls who got sexier as they got dirtier requests. I glanced across to Mrs Silva table, she looked stuning again in a short black dress that showed her tanned legs the neckline plunged well below her breasts. From the side you could see the fulness all except her nipples. She was drinking her drink but you could see the music was having the same desire as the dancers were having. She was swaying in her seat her body moved like a snake Amos held onto her arm but he could'nt control her rythem. Soon she was dancing on her table, her hip rolls and pelvic jerks got the same calls the strippers got and soon she was slipping the straps off her shoulders.

Jumping down from her table she joined a girl on the round stage the music changed to the stripper music. The men went wild as she pulled down the top of her dress and showed off her red bra then the dress was off red panties and stockings with suspender belt covered her lower body. Her two bodyguards moved closer not to stop the action but to get a better look, she spun with her hands around her back and off came her bra. Lord she had the best tits i had ever seen, they were firm and pointed forward like cones, her nipples long and thick like bottle corks.

The shout of off off off rang around the room, she squealed with pleasure as her hands took hold of both sides of the elastic and they slipped down. First everyone stood still, but as her hands explored her sex all hell let loose and hands were grabbing at her body. Her bodyguards now stepped in slapping down some big guys while Amos grabbed her off the stage and wrapped her up in table cover. Get her out of here one guard shouted to Amos and he pushed her to the door, Mrs Silva could'nt resist one more flash and pulled open her cover. The crowed went crazy and both guards were hit and knocked to the ground, the bitch just laughed and ran out the doors. Amos was caught at the door by a big trucker and one blow put him down, bang bang two shots rang out. One of the guards had got his gun out firing into the air made the crowed forget Mrs Silva and run panicking. Lets get out of here before the police turn up Cole said, by now the club was nearly empty just a few staff picking themselves off the floor were they had dived when the shooting had started.

Outside there was a distance sound of sirens we ran to the car and drove off in the rear window i watched two police cars turn onto the club car park. There was no sign of Mrs Silva or her men, one bodyguard picked up Amos has he left the building while the other kept his gun trailed on the attackers. Cole drove around the streets like a pro race driver, making our way back to the motal in record time, parking on street we climbed back in the window. The car that they had gone out in was parked on the parking bay so they had come back. Nothing was seen or heared for the rest of that night but we was sure that after that problem they would move soon.

As i watched out of the window i was thinking to myself that soon i would need to take her down and then that body would come into my

197

mind. I had never found it hard to kill but she was a fantastic looking woman, then my mind remembered how she laughed when her two guards went down. That was the jolt i needed to bring me back on earth, picking up my rifle i wiped it over placed a round in the breech, first chance that round is yours Mrs Silva. Next morning was a hive of activity once the guards had fed her ladyship they started packing her bags in the car, I awoke Cole and he went and paid the bill. I sat in the car waiting for them to move, Cole returned just as their car pulled up to the reception. The first chance i have today i will take that shot i told Cole, so lets hope we get a good clear area with nobody in the way. They pulled away from the motel and we followed, Cole had filled our tank with fuel when he had bought the car so we was fine for a few hundred miles.

They took the southwest freeway which would take them to Mexico if they traveled the 2,086 miles. I working out a most probable route they would take with a average of four hundred miles a day at 80 mph would see them driving for five hour and take five days to get there. They could drive longer Cole said, yes but taking in fuel stops food and toilet breaks i am looking at a average. They also have five drivers who can change five times a day and do the trip in a fifth of the time. But that lady will want a bed at night not sleeping rough in a car with five men i told him, she will travel some dusty trails he continued. Thats why she will stop i pressed home, she like's her comforts plus she dont like being in the same place to long. She also as to find another buyer for her goods Cole continued and to do that she needs to get home.

We watch our distance betweenthe cars as the miles ticked away they stopped and refueled on one occasion that day and while they ate we filled our car. Cole grabbed some food from the service shop while they was in the resturant, bottles of coke and snacks would be our food this day. Cole ducked down at one of the shelving units as two of the guards came in for cigarettes, three days to get to the boarder one said thats a lot of driving. Will the car hold out the other said best get some oils and plenty of water we dont want to get stuck. Cole sneaked out as they was filling bags, Back at the car he throw me a map best check the distance to Johnson city thats were we are stopping next. He had heared them mention this in the service station, knocking the tops off two cokes i started to study the map. From New york to Johnson city is six hundred and thirty-five miles and thats a ten and a half hours drive i told him as he pulled off following their car.

Darkness was with us as we hit Johnson City they pulled in a motel and we parked up till they had gone in their cabins. Both of us were dead on our feet it was ten forty-five with the night watch and the days driving we were bushed. Cole set his alarm on his watch to go off at six he jumped the back seat and i reclined the drivers seat we were soon gone At first light i was awake, checking the motel office it said closed till nine so it was safe to get some breakfast and a wash. Across the street was a truckers stop so we drove the car over parked for a quick get away and went in. There was already three drivers in tucking into a huge breakfast and at that time my stomach was crying food. I ordered ham eggs beans with toasted bread, Cole order the same with a side of pancakes, while it was cooking we went and washed up. After a wash we returned to the eating hall and sat near a window so we could see if anyone was about at the motel. Eating that meal slowly gave my taste buds the treat of there lives, it had been a good while since we had eat a good meal. More coffee the waitress ask and poured it from a glass jug with the reply of yes from us both.

You lads are up early this morning i only get truckers at this time as a rule she said, but i had a group in a hour ago five men and a woman. My heart jumped what did they look like i asked lady was a looker with a baby boy friend and four big men. I drank my coffee paid the bill and was on the road in two minutes flat. Cole was driving we had some ground to make up and he would push the peddle they was about twenty minutes ahead of us. Why had not checked to see if their car was still there i dont no, but one good thing the food had made me feel better. Cole told me not to beat myself up over it, if we had not got that sleep we would never have made it thruogh this day anyway.

Luck was in our favour we had to stop for fuel and there they was taking a toilet break, i kept my eyes on them while Cole filled the car and rushed to pay for it. Back on the trail we was now only one hundred meters away from them far enough for them not to see us. We continued along the same route, looks like they are going for Dallas Cole said watching the road signs. I checked the map thatsnine hundred and fifty-one miles from Johnson city i told him, on this road it will take fifteen hours he replied. Lets split the driving to four hour shifts then the non driver can sleep four hours and not be so tired. In that fifteen hours we stopped twice more to take in fuel for the car and a meal for everyone, they sat in the service resturant we ate in the car. The last stop was about two hours from Dallas so we moved a little closer not to miss them pulling in for the rest of the night. Again we stopped at a motel on the south side of Dallas there was a truck stop on the same site so we ate a harty meal then. With the car filled and our guts bursting we staggered our sleep it was now midnight so we took a three hour stretch each, taking into account they left at six that morning. While i was doing that first watch i checked the maps, we would be heading for Nuevo Laredo which was four hundred and thirty -seven mile from Dallas. It would take us seven hour drive then we would be at the Mexician boarder. I had made up my mind that if i target her in mexico we would not be linked with the bombs or the death of Conti.

So many people die in Mexico under strange curcumstance and the crime never solved. I have a plan that i hope will work a plan that might get them all and look like an accident. At six oclock Cole awoke me, still full from the nights meal we sat and waited drinking bottles of water and wiping the sweat off our faces with it to. I told him that i was going to make the hit when we had cross the boarder into Mexico, along a quite stretch of road i would shoot a tyre out making the car crash. Mrs Silva's group was late this morning it was six-thirty before they amerged, they pulled the car over to the truck stop five entered while the driver filled with fuel.

Cole went into the service shop once the driver had come out and entered the resturant. He grabbed two coffees each and a bag full of snacks, the first part of the journey i would be driving so Cole could get more sleep. I had drained my second cup by the time their group came out, she still nibbling a pancake and looking a hundred Dollers in a pair of shorts and a t-shirt. The bodyguards went in front of her so they could look back at the tightness of those shorts so tight you could see her sex shape the t-shirt tide in the middle with no bra. I looked down at Cole snoring oh i wish i was in her car, shaking off the thought i watched Amos walking to the car fifty meters behind them. He looked like a little boy with a butterfly net chashing freash air, what she saw in him i dont know. Pulling off the truck stop drive i followed them again at a distance down the southbound road picking up the signs for the boarder. A thought came to my head we had stuck to the state speed limits but once in Mexico the limits are not so stricked, a lot faster with not many police patrols. If caught a few dollers will get you off such a currupt force the Mexican police, but if we get held up at the boarder they would escape us. Three hours past and we stopped for a toilet break and Cole took over, keep going i told him we need to get through the boarder before they do.

I expained to him why we needed to get there first and he agreed, so we sped off leaving them walking to the toilet as we past. Again ducked down in the back seat i saw the shape of her sex through those tight shorts and the full lenght of her nipples sticking out against her t-shirt. I was going to find it hard to bump this one off looking at that body before i pull the trigger. Both of us always carried our passport when on a local hit so if we need to we can cross the boarder ease with no troubles. Today was no exception we pulled up to the hold point walked into the hut showed our passports and answered two questions why are you visiting our country how long are you staying. Few days holiday we told the customs man, he stamped a page of our passport, have a nice stay he told us and off we went. A kilometer down the road was a large welcome board we pulled the car up and reversed behind it and waited for their group to arrive. I stood with my rifle at the ready a round in the chamber my sight fixed tight i wiped to sweat off my brow and peered down my sight. Forty minutes later their car was in my sight, taking steady aim at the front tyre i fired.

The car swerved to the left and went into a roll, five time's it rolled before it came to a stand still. Bits of the car lay everywhere a door had broke off windows smashed rear wheel buckled front wheels kept spinning. I watch through my sight and moved it to the open door the body lying there was nobody i had seen. The car was theirs but they was not in it, just then a Ford Mustang flew past the wrecked car Cole fired the engine and we was soon on their tail. They switched cars i shouted to Cole over the noise of the engine yes but how did they know he replied?. I dont think they did i told him i think they just got a faster car, Our car was fast but theirs was flying on the straights but it couldnt hold the bends thats when we closed up. The first bend they sent a hail of bullets at us but moving that fast they could'nt steady their aim. Get as close as you can i told Cole, who pushed the peddle to the metal got us a car distance away, resting my rifle on the wing mirrow i looked down the sight. Things jumped around but i made out a shape and fired, Good shot Cole shouted i saw the blood splatter that was a head hit. It was then i womans arm came out the window with a automatic hand gun and sprayed us with rounds.

Two rounds ripped into the roof tearing into the soft metal, two more hit the windshield punching two small holes. Bastard i shouted she's no lady now i will enjoy getting her, we had dropped back a good bit but my rifle had the range. Even though this was a good road a lot of dust came up off the surface due to the winds that blow the sandy desert dust across it. Wild country was all around us only a odd building but most empty for years others animals took shelter from the wind. It was one of these that Silva's car headed for turning off the road and up a dirt track. Where the hell do you think they are going Cole shouted? i dont know i replied but stay with them, their car pulled up and out they ran into the buildings. Cole pulled the car up close to a wall and we hide behind it just as a hail of bullets hit the top level of the rocks which the wall was made of some ricochets shot high into the air.

I will take the housei said you take the barn and with that Cole ran around low against the wall letting off two rounds as he went. The driver had left the engine running and the rear door behind the driver was left open this could be a trap to get us close then run off in the car. I lifted my rifle and brought the sight to rest on the fuel tank area, the first round just made a hole the second hit the spot and up went the car with a explosion. Flames shot across the gap and hit the door frame and window setting both frames ablaze.

The fuel spray also hit the wooden floor and soon the down stair area was burning, a shot came from the only upper window hitting the wall near to my arm. I felt pain a heat went through my right arm blood stained my shirt, i rolled my sleeve back to see a graze but deep into the flesh. Another shot came this time i was ready and fired my rifle, a scream of pain came and a body fell from the window. The building was now fully ablaze and smoke was starting to fill the sky, we were far enough away from the road not to be seen but that smoke. The other building was a derelict barn Mrs Silva was hold up in there with the three other men and they had Cole pinned down behind the wall. I rested my rifle in my hand with my arm on the wall to steady my shot, a shot came from the double barn doors on the second floor.

The doors were rotten and as my round hit them they splintered into the mans face forcing him back into the open, Cole sqeezed off a shot hitting the man in the chest. A burst from a automatic peppered the wall with rounds Cole rolled back behind the wall covered in dust. I made my way around the other side of the building were there was another set of doors one hung down with the top hinge broken. Moving slowly along the wall i got level with the rear door of the barn raising my head to eye level i noticed Mr Silva aiming her gun in my direction. She squeezed her trigger and a spray of rounds hit the wall low but the direction was right, i dived to my left and moved down a meter before raising again this time i fired my rifle.

Ducking down again i heard a low cry of pain, raising again i saw her stagger behind the wall of the barn clutching her shoulder. I leapt the wall and ran towards the barn wall, my heart was racing i felt sick the antipation of something happening to me was giving me chest pain. A round flew over my head a shot came from the upper floor but looking up i noticed no one, i made the wall and hugged it close. Moving along the wall i reached the door frame i bent down and crawled along the hanging door which gave me cover. Gun fire from the front told me that Cole was having a good fight but with who? in my head there was three dead guards. Silva was wounded but how bad i did'nt know that left Amos who is a whimp and had not showed us that he carried a gun so that left one guard.

I peeped from the bottom from the door, the guard was behind a old rusty seed box firing at Cole with his back to me. I lay my rifle down and pulled my revolver out of my shoulder holster. I cocked my weapon an leapt to my feet sending a round towards Mrs Silva she was knocked back by the force of the round which hit her in the chest. Blood sprayed onto the wall from the exit wound from her back her body slumped to the floor. With out time to think i turned towards the guard who had not seen me but heard the cry from Mrs Silva. Standing up he turned only for blood splater to come towards me from a exit wound in his chest caused by a round from Cole. The mans eyes glazed as he starred at me, he dropped his weapon blood ran from his mouth it was the man that had been staring at me in the hotel. He took a step forward and said i knew it was you and then fell dead, it went very quite Cole entered the front door.

A shot rang out and the round hit Cole in his left wrist "BASTARD" he shouted and fired a shot up into the barn upper floor level. I climbed the ladders to the upper floor to find Amos lying face down on the floor a hole in the corner of his eye but a great part of his head was blown open. His hand was clutching a small barreta, a weapon we call a girly gun something they would have in there purse. I retured to Cole who was sitting on the seed box wraping up his wound with a headscarf which Mrs Silva had been wearing. Mrs Silva body lay on the floor and she was still breathing but only just, who are you people she asked me? and dead. We moved the bodies to look as if they had been battling between each other and everyone had been killed.

We made our way to Mexico City were we stayed for a few days it gave us time to have a good rest and heal our wounds. The television showed the seen of our battle and called it the ok corral, but as we thought they belived it was a disagrement over drugs. Cole put stiches in his own wrist but helped me with my arm as the graze was at the back. The car we left with a poor family who was so shocked when we said its for you and gave them the keys. Checking my account to find the money had been paid after my cablegram to the agents so i trasferred Cole's to his account. It was time to split again so with a pat on the back he caught his plane while i went and boarded

CHAPTER THREE
THE THIRD HIT

After that hit on Mrs Silva i decided to have a holiday and the first two days i checked out where to go in the local travel agent. I thought about the west coast and the Pacific ocean Hawaii was in my mind, Florida also came to mind so did the west indies. My mind was made by a fine picture of Italy with its culture and sport their fine food and their women. I decided on a bit of a tour five countries in thirty days, Starting in Paris for two nights, followed by three nights in Marseille. Two nights in Barcelona then threenights in Madrid then i fly to Portugal to Lisbon for three night which ends with two nights in Porto. From there i fly to Italy where i spend three nights in Venice plus four in Roma, finally on to Munich and Berlin covering seven nights finishing in London for two night before flying home. My itinary was worked out for all the flights and connections at all the different airports, hotels were booked and all transport was booked.

My flight to Paris was in twodays time so i put out a message to all my contacts that i would'nt be around for a month. A few hours after i had posted the message the usual way in the New york papers i recieved a return message. It read while you are in Europe we may have some work, please let us know if you are interested. I replied that i was going on holiday and would be in Paris in two days time at the Savoy any results, cable me there. Two days later i was looking down from the aircraft window over at landmarks of Paris, all these place's that i had booked i had never been before.

That was with the exception of Germany which i had served there in the army. Landing was a bit on the bumpy side but we landed safe and disembarked to collect our luggage. I had decided to travel light and had only brought a holdall bag which held just what i needed for a few days. I would buy some new clothes at the stores while i am here in one of the best fashion capitals in the world. This was my answer to the French customs when i passed through and they challanged my lack of luggage, they smiled and stamped my passport have a nice trip sir. I took a taxi to the Hotel and gave the driver a heavy tip, this would insure a good service while i stay here. Making my way to receptioni picked up a New york time's off the paper rack, ibooked in and was told that i had a message.

I took the lift to the fifth floor with a bell hop he opened my door carrying my holdallputting the bag down in my bedroom he opened the window. Would sir require anything else he asked i slipped him a good tip, can you get me a bottle of scotch whisky i asked?. Of cause sir i will bring it straight up sir and closed the door behind him as he left. I took a glance out the window and in the distance i could see the Eiffel tower, it was about a kilometre away. Picking up the message i opened the tiny envelope, all it said was crossword?. I walked over to the table and picked up the newspaper i flicked the pages till i found the crossword puzzel. Working out the answers first i then broke the code, target for you in all five countries check post for info and that was all.

Taking a shower and change of clothes i decided todo some exploring of the city, down in the lobby i got the porter to get me a taxi and off i went to see the sights. I set a price with the taxi driver and he agreed to show me all the main attractions place's. Starting with the Eiffel tower which was small compared to the empire state building or any of New yorks buildings come to that. That first afternoon we covered so many place's i cannot remember them all, my driver spoke good English and told me the best places to eat and night life. He also promised to collect me early in the morning and take me to Palace of the Versailles and a river boat trip. We found the nearest cable office and i checked my account nothing had arrived yet so instructed for the cable to be sent to my hotel room.

Although i was still on holiday and aiming to enjoy this experience it would'nt hurt to improve my finances by doing the job i do best while here. Deciding to eat at the hotel that first night was what i did, taking a three course meal off the menu, i started with a soup. Frogs legs followed cooked in garlic sauce with potatoes and spinach. The final course was creme caramel all very nice but after i had finished i could have murdered a steak. Again the porter got me a taxi, my friend was off duty now so i had a new face, this man was not so good with the English language so it took a lot of sign to get him to understand me but we got there. Pulling up outside the night club that my friend had mentioned that morning i paid him and went in, the room was dark with flashing lights and load music. I took a seat in the alcove near the bar, a pretty young lady came and ask what i would like i ordered a whisky. She was back in seconds with the whisky and a table mate which she stood the glass on is there any other service i can do for you? she said with a sparkle in her eyes. Not at this moment i said reading the hint but stay around we could have some fun later once i'v had a drink.

She walked away with a smile on her face and looked back with a grin when she got to the bar. Looking around the room i noticed this was a classy place, people wore top of the range clothes wore Gucci and Armani jewelier. These were people with money not just your run of the mill young kids, Daddy was somebody within a company or a banker or even a television star. The older couples looked like royalty princes or princess with real class, i felt good mixing with these people it was so different than the pool bar i hang out at. A small hand touched my arm, hi" you lonely tonight i looked up at a real beautiful face of a woman not young but not old, hi i replied. please Dont misunderstand she continued i'm her on business from the States i'm on my own and caught your accent when you spoke she told me.

Would you like to join me i asked her, please she said and sat on the seat across the table from me, drink i enquired please i would love a Martini on the rocks dry was her answer. Calling the waitress over i ordered another whisky and a dry Martini on the rocks, again the girl took no time with the drinks and placed them down. Looks like our fun laters gone she said? you never know i replied with a cheeky grin three can have more fun, my companion also smiled at my comment. She took a sip of her drink placing the glass down to the table she asked if i danced, yes i told her but not this modern stuff. Come on she said standing up and grabing my hand it will be fun just shake your body to the music. We made it to the dance floor were she faced me and started to dance i just followed her moves. There she said over the sound of the music it's ease is it not? i nodded my head as i shook my waist and hips in time with hers. She wore a flaired skirt with a white blouse and a red scarf tied around her neck, three buttons on her blouse were undone she was showing a good sight of clevage. I was tapped on the shoulder by a young French man who cut in on the dance and started rockingand rolling with the lady.

I smiled to myself i did'nt know her name and already i had lost her, i sat back down and watched her jive. She danced good every move was like a seduction and she knew it as she spun in the dance her skirt rasied to expose her lovelly long legs. They were covered with dark seamed stockings showing her suspenders and the creamy flesh just below her panty's. she screamed has she was spun, she knew that every twirl was a show for us men. Looking towards me she gave a wave and i gavea waved back, The song finished and she came back to my table. She was wet with sweat her blouse clung to her body showing off the shape of her narrow waist, her black bra showed its self more against the wet cloth. The night moved on we drank some more we danced some more then the time came to leave the club it was now 3AM. I call a taxi for cindy, i had found out her name as the night had gone she asked me to join her so i climbed in next to her.

We did'nt say much i explained that later this day i was going on the river and would she like to come along for some fun. She asked what time as she had to go to the office first, hy maybe you could come with me then we could go boating. How could i go with you to work your boss would'nt be pleased would he? i am the boss she replyed with a big grin. Entering a drive that looked like the entrance to a palace my jaw dropped the house was a palace, you live here i said? better than that i own it. The taxi drove up to the main door which had a large square area for many cars to park, a cascade of steps went down into path that went both sides of a fountain in the centre of a pond. The doors were open by a butler, you did'nt call madam the driver was waiting to collect you. No this nice man gave me a lift in his taxi, good morning sir the butler acknowledge me and all i could do was nod my head still dum struck. You will come in for a night cap wont you she asked? yes would love to i stuttered and enter two big oak doors that was about ten feet high.

Statue's were all around the entrance hall like roman god's and godess's a marble floor had a wide runner carpet to stop you slipping. We moved through a large library into a loungewhich had two couches, one high backed with a scroled arm on one end. The other was a four seater in red leather in the style of Queen Ann, A piano covered one corner of the room and a writing bureau covered another.

A large fire place filled the main wall with book shelves attached both sides, Cindy walked to the far book shelf and pressed a book. The books opened into a well stocked bar, she poured me a whisky and she decided to have the same. I sat on the Queen Ann and glanced towards the two large windows with a double door in each that opened out onto the large patio area. This over looked the front grounds with the fountain and a maze cut garden with the drive each side. Cindy rang a bell on the table and the butler arrived, iwont be needing you anymore tonight just lock up and turn off the lights she told him. Yes my lady was all he said and departed, we had not spoke since entering but i think i was too taken aback by thesize of this home. Well what do you think of my small place she commented as she sat beside me? small! you have got to be joking this place is beautiful. I think you need to tell me more about yourself she smiled and just said not now its late and i need somthing else, taking my drink away from me she lay down.

Cindy tugged at the belt of my trousers once undone she pulled my zipper and released my manhood from its hide. Her bright red lips just kissed the end before taking the length into her mouth, my back arched as the plessure ran up my spine. With the lights now out the room was lite by the flickering of the fire, has she removed her blouse and bra the silhouette on the wall showed a fabulous pair of breasts. I removed my trousers and shirt my jockey breifs followed has did her skirt, those bare breasts and stockings and spends made me wild. I pulled her back down towards me my left hand went onto her right breast while my mouth sucked licked her left one. She moaned out and riggled with shear delight, her nipples grew as i explored them. My hand found its way onto her panty's and i followed the swell of her sex along the cloth until i reached a damp area.

She let out a squeal when i touched her clit and pull the gusset off her pussy, inserting two fingers into her sex. Please no more she cried i want you and i want you now, with out much movement my manhood dived into that love pool pushing deep. Warm and wet my manhood soon was responding to the rythem of our movement and we both cried out has the pleasure took over. We lay silent holding on to each other, my hand felt her juices flow away from her womanhood. Sleep fell on us and next i knew she was awaking me with a tray of breakfast, i kissed her on the lips.

Cindy told me how she had got married to a young businness man who dead leaving her a wealthy woman. She had kept the interior designer business going by running it by herself. After i had showered and shaved she brought me some clothes that had belonged to her husband, put these on it will save a trip back to your hotel. The butler entered and told us that the car was ready and waiting out the front, thank you Henry can you set a extra plate for tonights meal we have company. Yes madame he said and was gone, How do you know i wont to stay another nighti asked here i have only two nights left here then i move south.

Then spend them with me she cried its been so long since! i stopped her saying anymore, i too have work to do so i must go but for two nights i will stay. She hugged me tight then we moved out to the car, Peter take us to the office then later we are going to the Palace of Versailles then on to a river trip. Could you book us a beth on the boat with some lunch, yes madame. Is there anything that you would like she asked me, i looked at her full chest and smiled she leaned towards me and whispered later. Peter i called to the driver could you take me too a post office cable branch? yes sir there is one just down the road here. Jumping out as the car stopped i told Cindy i want be long, i entered and checked my cable box there was a message for me, opening it there i read the contence. We have your first meeting booked at 32b marseilla rue, Marseilla toy maker which ment bomb maker, Micheal Frombert was his name. I tore the paper into tiny bits and split the bits between three waste bins then went back to the car.

At Cindy's office i meet her team who took the calls and visited peoples home's to plan their designs for their homes. She left her team to run the show for the next two days and soon we was walking around the Palace grounds. As a designer she could talk me through the layout of each room also what she would do to the room to inprove it. Her history was very good she knew everything about the place, and who lived and died there. After a few hours we drove to the river went on the boat and was showen to a table the glass windows aloud us to see all the sights while we ate lunch. Cindy if you require me to stay with you i will need to get my things from the hotel, ok lets go up the Eiffel tower then we will stop off at the hotel she replied. The view from the top of the tower was great you could see the whole of paris but like i said the Empire state building is that high your in the clouds.

At the hotel i left Cindy in the car went to my room to get my few bits the bottle of whisky i ordered was on the table, plus a new New York times. On the paper there was a note from the desk this paper was sent in for you, i slipped it into my bag and went down to the desk. My room had been paid for so i just handed back the key, the duty manager came to ask if anything was ok and i explained that i had meet a pal. No discount was offered but he gave me the whisky free, we made our way back to Cindies home getting there with time to clean up before Henry called us for dinner. A dinner fit for a king it was, soup for starter followed by fish on salad then quail and spring vegetables ending with sorbet. Coffee was taken in the lounge, Are we going to a club tonight i asked her?better than that she said we are going to a show. She ran off to get ready while i sat there, then Henry entered if sir would follow me i will take you to your dressing room.

I followed him up the stairs to a room which was full of designer clothes, a evening suit hung from a rail all neatly pressed, i took a shower while Henry found some shoe's. Once dressed i looked in the mirrow the whole lot could have been made for me. I must be the same size as yourold master i told Henry, sir looks very much the sameas the masterthe resemblance is uncanny. He pulled out a picture from a draw and showed me, well it knocked me a back it could have been me or my twin brother if sir would be so kind not to tell my lady that i showed you that it may upset her. Mom's the word i told him and left the room as i came out onto the landing Cindy came out of her room Wow she looked like a million dollers. She wore a long white gown which fleared at the bottom and had a plunging neckline at the top thin straps held it on her, a white fur stole. You look lovely i told her and kissed her hand, you look very nice yourself she told me and the thought of the picture came back. We made our way out to the car, were are we going i asked? it's a surprise you will see when you get there she told me and got into the car.

When we stopped we was outside a fantastic theatre were swan lake was being advertised on the boards outside. This night is a total sell out Cindy told me, tickets cost a arm and a leg she continued. And did you think i could'nt afford to pay i said to her in a snarl, no no of course not i was just saying she then went quite. Climbing the steps we entered the theatre was handed our stage program and went and found our seats which was a box looking down from the side of the stage.

Two of her colleagues from work was in the box with us i let them sit up front with Cindy while i sat behind them all. I had torn the crossword page from the paper and i started doing the clues till the lights went down then for three hours i was bored. While they went for a interval drink i stayed and finished off the crossword but i waited till later to brake the code. Cindy came backfirst you are not very happy with me tonight she said, no not really i said. Why what have i done? well first when was you going to tellme i looked like your husband then you started treating me like him not letting me pay for anything. A tear filled her eye's im sorry i did not mean to do anything i just miss him so much and being with you brought him back. I promise i wont treat you like your him again, i will stay with you for the next two nights then i must go i told her. Were are you going from here she asked now wiping the tears away? Marseille i told her, we have a boat down there i could join you for a day or two.

I gave her that look which say's your doing it again, she noticed and jumped in if you want me too, Cindyyou dont know nothing about me dont you want to know. Like what she said, who i am were i'm from what do i do they are important things to know. Ok Will were are you from? just then her friends returned i'll tell you later i said and went out to the washroom. Finding a cubicle i sat and worked out my message, Target will be on a boat the night you sail for Barcelona but not sure which boat. It was signed off GANT get a new york times, which was telling me to get a paper the next day. Cindy smiled has i walked back in the box, i whispered i needed a drink i will meet you at the club later. Entering the club i loosened my bow tie and sat at the bar, my little waitress came to me what you drinking she said?. Whisky was all i said, my someone's in a bad mood, no not really just a bit tired. She did give you a good night then, it could have been better with you there i said, she laughed i'll get that drink. It was a hour later when Cindy arrived and headed for me turning down a dance offer. Will are you ok with me? sure i said forget it lets have a drink, She sat beside me on a stool, Where you from Mister she asked me. I am a New Yorker and proud of it i told her, and what do you do for a living? im a assassin i told her, now the drink is talking she replied and sipped her drink.

The rest of the night was fun we danced with each other and other people including my little waitress whom danced a sexy dance with Cindy too. By home time we was well full of drink and high spirt Cindy invited Susanna my little waitress back to the Chateau for a night cap. Henry was given the rest of the night off while we sat drinking in the lounge listerning to the music and dancing. We all raised to dance together and with the drink we all fell in a heap on the floor, laughter came from all three of us until Cindy kissed me. As the kiss ended i looked across to Susanna who just sat on the floor looking at us, pulling her towards me our lips kissed. Her body quivered with need and my hand fell onto her covered breast CIndy joined in first kissing me then kissing susanna. I eased one of Cindy's tits out from the top of her dress and held it in my hand Susanna put her mouth over her nipple and sucked it gently. Cindy moaned out loud and arched her back grabbing at Susanna she pulled open her blouse exposing her bra covered tits. I had the best of both worlds two women exposing their bodies to each other and two women including me in their games that was every mans dream.

For the next hour there was a lot of touching sucking squeezing and sexual contact ending with three heavy orgasams. We all ended in Cindies bed were i had full sex with them both before we all fell into a deep sleep till daylight broke and Cindy had to go to the office. Leaving us in bed when she went we slept on for a while then i felt the soft silky skin of a bare bottom, rubbing my manhood along theflaps of skin between her legs i soon felt moisture. My manhood slipped into that wet little cave and i heard her whipper with plesure. Soon the rythem was speeding up she pushed as hard as i did and that telling feeling went through my manhood i grabbed both her tits as i cum and she cryed out as her orgasm flowed from inside her. My manhood slipped from her pussy and then she ran a river all over the silk sheets.

We kissed and fell back into a deep sleep until Cindy came and awoke us for a bite to eat by the pool. I tryed to get her back into bed but she said i would need my strength for later. A swim was just what we needed so after a lite snack we hit the pool all naked as the day we was born. What do you want to do today Cindy asked me? well i need to get a paper i told her as i pushed my naked body against her in the water. I think a nice meal with lots of wine at a resturant followed by a night club more drink and then maybe some sex, she just smiled i'll sort the paper. She sent the driver for the news paper and while Susanna swam and Cindy showered i phoned a resturant and booked a table for three near the dance floor.

This would be my last night in Paris and i will be making the most of it at ten the next day i catch a train south. I got Susanna to ring in sick as i told her it was my night before i left and i want her tohave fun with us too. I told the girls to get ready and take as long as they like i want them both gorgeous for tonight. While they readied themselves i did the crossword finally decoded it read, weapon in a floor board in your room at hotel. Boat call The Mary Day, good luck more news tomorrow. Henry found me a very nice blue suit from the clothes cupboard and i put it on hafter a shower of coarse. Henry got the car to beat the front door, i waited on the gravel drive beside the car and waited and waited but it was well worth the wait. First out the door was Susanna wearing a long red dress which hugged her body the swell of her breasts pushed out from her plunging neckline.

Her blonde hair hung long to her shoulders with a black ribbon tied like a choker around her neck. Cindy followed in a black dress again it hugged her shape with no underwear lines showing, her large nipples pushed against the material and stuck out so inviting. Ok lets go i said jumping into the car once i had seated the young ladies, soon we was in the heart of Paris pulling up outside the cabaret resturant. Both girls giggled once they saw where i had brought them, this was a sexy resturant nice foodsexy shows.

After we entered i gave my name and we was showen to our table Champange was served i looked at Cindy, this is my treat i said and she nodded and smiled. Susanna was like a little child she was twisting and turning in her chair to look at everything, ooh i would so like to work here she told us with your figure you could i said. The watress's wore very little that served our meal just little tassels covered their nipples and a g-sting covered their lady bits. Stay up fishnet stockings black patent leather shoe's and a maids hat compleated the uniform for these girls. I dared Susanna to see if she could get dressed up like the maid that was serving us and off she went to talk to someone. I held Cindy's hand, i have had a great time in Paris and you made it even better for me so tonight is my way of saying thank you. You make it sound like its the end, that we will never see each other again after tonight, well will we i asked? tonight is not our last night we will be together again and soon.

Before she could brake into tears i kissed her. You never kiss me like that a voice hit us, Susanna stood beside the table dressed as a maid and she look great so great i could feel a stiring in my pants. With the meal finished we watched the show, the thyme tonight was women of the world and the women came out in national costumes from all over the world. We had african strippers Brazilian strippers Russian German and Greek all dancing and stripping to their music.

Then the floor was opened up to customers to try their hand Cindy sat close but Susanna was out like a shot spinning and shaking her tassels giving the single men a treat. Another hour passed before we hit the night clubs, avoiding our normal club so susanna could stay with us we traveled the full strip. Susanna meet up with a old boyfriend and kissed me goodbye next time you visit you look me up she said and was gone. Feeling the effect of the drink we got the car and went home to go straight to bed make love and crash out. I rose the next morning at nine my ticket for the train south had a reserve seat on the ten fifteen to Marseilla, I put together my bag. Henry had got the cook to cook me a harty breakfast which i had with Cindy, A New york times had been fetched for me and a food bag for the trip had been packed. The car got me to the station on time and Cindy came down to the platform with me. she had been quiet all the journey i climbed aboard the train found my seat and went back to the door while the porter put my bag on the rack.

I am going to miss you i told her, i'v had so much fun when i will be back i dont know but i will tell you i will be coming back soon. We kissed and the train started to move I am sorry Will but i have fallen in love with you she shouted, i love you too i shouted back. A emptyness filled my heart, a feeling i had never known before a feeling i hoped i would never feel again. A porter snapped me back to where i needed to be, can i get you something sir ? yes i would like a coffee please nescafe milk and suger. I picked up the paper which i read before i did the cross-word two hours later, braking the code it just said that, my target could be found at the Casino most nights. I folded the paper and glanced at my watch, working out i should arrive at Marseilla about eight tonight, resting back in my seat i dozed off awaking hours later.

The train was now in Lyon station one hundred and sixty-two miles from my target. I ordered coffee and once it arrived i open my food bag from Henry and tucked intoa nice sandwich with some cheese. The train arrived at seven forty-five, i walked across the station court to the taxi park and got into a cab. Hotel stella i told the taxi driver. The road to the hotel followed the sea front, the boats were plentyful and i had to find one in this lot. Soon we was at thefront door of the hotel, it had been modernised the year before so the paint looked clean and bright. Signing the register i requested a news paper every day i was here and took the lift to my room. Once i set down my bag i checked around the floor, i had to roll the carpet up but i finally found the loose boards by the bedside locker. prising the floorboard up with my small pen knife i found my gun wrapped in white cloth with two spare clips of ammo.

The weapon had been cleaned oiled and loaded, along with the weapon was a note. This weapon has had all the numbers removed so throw it in the sea when finished clean your prints. The man that left the note did'nt know i was a pro my skin will never touch that weapon. The note also give me all the information about my target again. His name was Micheal Frombert who was a bomb maker, he would sell his weapons to anybody who would pay his price. He had been knowen to plant his own bombs again for the right price. He was good never been caught making or using his bombs. But the FBI had got there agents to purchase them off him but never got near, knowen home a apartment in Marseilla. The address 32b marseilla rue or his boat the Mary day was were he would crash if drunk. I unpacked my bag and to my surprise ifound two light weight suits the dress suit and the other clothesthat i wore at Cindy's. So now i know why my bag was carried to the train so would'nt feel the weight of it, she had packed shirts and shoes socks and slacks. I rang down to reception to placea call to Cindys number while i put the clothes away. The call came through, Hi just ringing to let you know i got in safe and to thank you for all the clothes. I thought it was time for me to get rid of them and you looked so nice in them i hoped you didnt mind, not at all i replyed i needed to buy some new one's they are just the job. I will save the rest for when i see you again with that i heard her sob, dont cry i told her i will come back soon. I said good night and she replied i love you i told her i loved her too and put down the reciever. Pondering over what i had just said to her i realised that i really did love here, that strange emptiness is there again and wanted to see here tonight.

Staying in that night was what i choose to do, i didnt even go out for food but just finished the food pack that Henry had made up and made coffee from my room complimentry pack. It was the next morning when i first ventured out, walking along the seafront towards the harbour to start my search for the Mary day. It was just there on the first bay that i found her and across the road was the Casino which Mr Frombert liked to use frequently. Finding 32b Marseilla rue that took a lot more foot leather it was at the other end of the sea front. Seeing these areas by daylight showed me areas were i could hide in wait for him coming home but i think in this case i will be following him. If he gets drunk at the Casino he would make for the boat, if he go's night clubbing they are nearer to his apartment so that would be his destination.

The whole area was a place of beauty the boats including Mr Fromberts were of top quality they were rich mans toys. The buildings were all painted white and had a sparkle about them the streets clean but very heavy with traffic. Shopping was alittle like New York and London rolled into one, all the designer names was there strongly influenced by the Italians. Art galleries were everywhere you turned, pictures of well known artists hung in windows with security cage's around them.

The sea was a blue to hard to discribe the beach a gold sand full of young girls and boys playing volley-ball, water ski-ing and having fun. At a German beach bar i ate a brat-wurse in French bread drinking Australian beer but it was very nice.

The day went by and i enjoyed every moment of it but i needed to get back to read the paper brake the code take a shower and get ready for the night out. I was planing on watching The Mary day to see the man that go's aboard that night but waiting for me at receptionwas a envelope i took it to my room. Once the door closed i ripped it open to find a picture of Mr Frombert inside and nothing else and there was no message on the cross word that day. Tonight i would dine out in a nice resturant then try my luck on the wheel before finding a nice club to finish the evening. Bath Ithought and thats what i had, splashing all smelly stuff on my body before putting on my everning suit. Down in reception they told me the name of a very good resturant and call a taxi to get me there. After my meal which was excellent i went off to the casino to try my luck, inside was like a roman palace with water fetures and busts of romam heads. Red white and blue satin material draped the walls and large stained glass windows filled the entrance wall.

I got myself a thousand dollers worth of chips and found myself a place on a wheel, i watched for a while then i placed my first bet. Looking around the table to see who i was playing with, i notice a very tall French gent in a dress suit and bow tie his chips were high on the table. There were two young ladies who held there chips tight in there hands, A husband and wife team were across from me he was betting she was watching men in her low cut dress. Three more men filled the table all had small stacks of chips on the table, it seamed the French gent was doing the winning. losing my first bet i put some chips on the red plus some on the number sixteen.

The wheel spun and the little ball went around stopping on red sixteen my lucky number, the coupier stacked a pile of chips and pushed them to me. Lucky man the wife in the low cut dress said, i just winked at her and placed my next bet putting my chips on the black the wheel spun thirty-one black. Again chips came my way the next three bets i put my chips on the middle of four numbers and two won. I put a bet on the red and went to the bar sir could have is drinks brought to the table, yes i know i said but i just want to sit here for a moment. Red fourteen came the call the girls shouted you won let it ride i said and took a drink of my whisky. Red twenty-eight you won again the two girls shouted, once more i let it ride, red number six was the call this time i collected my winnings tipped the man and sat down to a second whisky. The chips bulged my pockets so i cashed in half of them Three thousand dollers in french frances and i still had half left. Next i tried some black jack sitting with two more women and a very pale faced man a second glance told me it was Mr Frombert and he was well drunk. The cards were dealt one face up one face down the face up was an eight i bet some chips lifting my second card it was a ace giving me nine or nineteen.

It was my turn so i tapped the table to let the girl know i was happy, throwing her cardsover showed a seven and a king she called eighteen with banker privilage of one and i had won again. losing small bets on the next two hands i moved away as Mr Frombert was getting restless and i didnt want anyone associating me with him in anyway.

The two girls were now standing by the bar so i offered them a drink they Came from Birmingham in England, Janet andJane was there name's. We went on to a club after cashing my chips i had won five thousand dollers in French frances my lucky night the girls were game too but i declined their offer of back to their place.

Explaining to the girl that i had some work on the next day so i would need to get up early in the morning which was a lie but it fell in with my plan. Promising them dinner on the everning then a night at the Casino then a club was agreeable by both of them. I slept well that night and spent the next day shopping for beach -wear, the paper had no message on it. Keeping my appointment with the girls i took them to a resturant followed by the Casino, Mr Frombert was there again this time he was sober and winning. We used another table and shot some dice winning another three grand we went onto the night club. Drinks flowed like a river and soon we was all drunk to drunk to play about so i made sure the girl got home safe and went back to my hotel. I put a note in Janets bag telling her to meet the same this evening, my plan was to find Frombert in a drunk state and kill him. I planned to drown him by sneaking out from the club making for his boat waiting for him then im going to killing him. My plan will work if i can make sure he gets drunk, he loves his drink but like tonight he was not always drunk.

Next morning the news paper code told me that he had been hired to plant a bomb in the US embassy in Germany so to get him soon. The day went slow, i spent some time on the beach trying to get a tan but my mind was working overtime on my plan and of the alternative if it did'nt work. I would have to shoot him and that would mean finding some -where quite and getting him there. I meet the girls at six and took them to dinner, from the resturant we went to the Casino like i had the last two nights drinks were ordered and we started to play the wheel. Mr Frombert was not in the place and panic started to build inside me, maybe he had left for Germany already.

Good evening Mr Frombert how are you tonight? ask the doorman, i will be better once i get a drink came the reply and my body relaxed. My luck was in again and i took money off the first four plays so i had a cheeky bet zero and to my utter delight it came up. There was screams and shouts the manager was called for it was like hitting the jackpot on a gaming machine in Vagas. I ordered Champagne for everyone and watched Frombert grab a bottle for himself, Bastard i thought but you drink as much as you like. The Manager congratulated me your cheque will be here tomorrow half a million French frances he told me. The girls were jumping with joy i was very excited myself but had to keep my head clear till later. We left the Casino later, by now Frombert was drunk.

At the night club we settled into a secluded corner, a waitress brought us drinks, i ordered a bottle of Champagne. The girls was giggling and jumping around dancing, i kept my eye on my watch, the Casino closed at two- thirty i needed to be at his boat before that. More drink went down the girls i pretended to be a little drunk, two men took the girls to the dance floor while i told them that nature was calling. Slipping out the door while they was occupied dancing but with enough Champers to keep them going for a few hours. In the open air i lengthened my stride till i could see the harbour walking down the gangway towards The Mary day. I passed a number of boats in darkness but two was still showing lights in the cabins, i just hoped they didnt walk on deck for awhile. Hiding behind a oil drum on the walkway i heard Mr Frombert, get close to the entrance gate, singing has he came. He fell once at the first boat and nearly hit the water, then bumped against one of the boats with lights on. Go to bed you drunken slob a voice camefrom the cabin but Frombert was to drunk to notice. I had removed my clothes down to my swimming shorts and waited, he stubbled again this time bumping his head. Standing up he rubbed the back of his head and must have noticed blood, shit he swore and moved forward with a shuffle. He passed my position and i grabbed him bythe throat sqeezing stoped him crying out, i lunged forward taking him into the water.

There was a big splash as we both hit the waterbut i pulled down on his shoulder to take him down. Knowing where i was going i took a deep breath he didnt know and was about to cry out which took the air out his lungs. He struggled as we went down but i had gripped him in a way that he could'nt get a grip on me to break my grip. He screamed under the water which helped his lungs fill he struggled in panick and large air bubbles bellowed out his mouth. His arms stopped waving around and his body went heavy and started sinking on its own, letting go i mademy way to the surface. I climbed the steps of the jetti and removed my wet shorts, drying my body with some nets and rags i found i redressed. Creeping out the gate i made my way back towards the club combing my hair as i went, i entered the club and sat at the table and poured myself a drink. The girls returned to the table after the last song, we thought you had left Jane told me, no i had a pee then was stopped to talk to a man who thought he knew me. He was into car racing so we just chatted away you two did'nt miss me anyway you was well into them fellows. No we came back to the table twice looking for you, how you can hardly stand i told them, drink up Janet said we will show you who can stand.

We drank the rest of the Champagne and headed of to their place with another bottle, you may feel that i am heartless bastard having fun less than one hour after killing that man. Well maybe i am but to me he was scum, He would'nt think about kids being killed by one of his devices. Cannot stand said Janet watch this then, putting on the right music they started doing the cancan throwing their dresses's in the air showing their panties and stocking tops. With the jumping up and down jane's tits came out of her dress top janet noticed and soon her's were also out. It was so funny i just flopped on the bed with laughter then the girls started stripping and my manhood stood solid in my trousers. Both noticed and before i knew it my trousers were off Jane was sucking on my manhood Janet was kissing me has i squeezed her tits. There was no feeling in this not like with Cindy it was just good sex with two women. Ileft their apartment about seven-thirty and went back to the hotel to get some sleep.

Later that afternoon i sent a cable letting them know that humpty had had a great fall, they would know what it ment. Checking the news paper there was a message for me in code it said once your target is dead leave the weapon in your room we will get rid of it for you.

The gun was still wraped up i had not open it i just slipped it under the floorboard but i would get rid of it myself i never trust anyone to clear up after me. This was my last night so i had planned with the girls to do our same routine, i had already got the hotel to ring the Casino telling them that i would be in tonight for my money. Getting ready that evening i watched the television well shaving it was not the main story but there was a mention that the body of a man was found near the mouth of the harbour. It stated that the man had drown after heavy drinking and falling into the sea near his boat, people on the boat near heared him fall twice but never heard him fall in.

Blood was found were he had fallen it matched a cut to his head. That cleared that up they was not looking for anyone and did'nt suspect fowl play. I meet the girls and they both looked worse for wear, headaces was a word of the day water was the drink with the meal. Walking into the Casino was like a surprise party everyone patted me on the back, the manager called me to a stage shook my hand and gave me a cheque for the money he owed me. Food was everywhere you turned this was a real party even the people playing on the wheel or shooting the dice were dancing around the tables. I was holding Janet and we was swaying to the music it was building up to a real frenze then it just stopped and it was back to the gaming tables. I placed a few little bets winning on two losing one, did you see the news today? jane asked me, that man that sits there was found dead in the sea he drowned. Pulling a face as if i didnt know the man Janet jumped in you know the drunk, oh him when did that happen and when did they find him. She told me the story has she had heard it from the television and he fell in she finished.

He had a bottle of my Champagne you dont think that sent him over the top, no Janet said he was a drunk, it could have happened anytime. We had a great night at the club, being the last night i let myself go I rang Cindy and lied told her i was having a boring time but i didnt lie when i said i missed her. Giving the girls a goodnight kiss and declining their offer of a good night together as a goodbye i walked back to my hotel and turned in for some sleep. My trip to Barcelona started at seven-thirty the next morning walking out to get some breakfast and pick up my paper from reception. Back at my room i pack my bag and then i rememberd the gun under the floor.

I did'nt want to take it or leave it there so out i went to the break water and throw it off the rocks into the sea. My boat is leaving from the dock at twelve-forty so i had some time to kill before my taxi picked me up to take me there. Reading my paper and doing the crossword gave me my next instructions for spain, the good news was my first part was free time. My target was in Madrid and i would get more information at the end of my Barcelona trip. Sitting having a coffee in the hotel reading room Janet and Jane turned up, we just had to say its been fun goodbye and thank you for a good few days they both kissed me and left.

Thats after i gave them a enverlope containing two five thousand franc chips to cash, play, shop or drink. Knowing them they will do all of those things and more, leaving them was not so bad they was just good friends no heart strings. The taxi arrived and i said my goodbye's there was no sign of the girls they would have hit the shops buying new dresse's. At theDock my bag was put on the boat in my cabin for me with sixteenhours of travel i had booked a cabin. We left the dock at two oclock which ment we docked in Barcalona at six to six-thirty tomorrow morning.

I stayed on deck till i could'nt see the dock anymore then went down to my cabin i washed and ordered a bottle of whisky. A porter brought the bottle to the door of my cabin, i paid him and gave him a tip. Asking what deck the duty-free shop was he told me that there was two a main supermarket on deck number two and a kiosk on the main deck. I made my way to the resturant were i had a coffee and a sandwichof chicken with salad, that would do me till i had a main course laterthat evening. Walking around the supermarket i picked up another bottle of whisky and some aftershave some soap and toothpaste. Icontinued to the main deck and watched the sea foaming and splashing like a washing machine.

The seagulls followed the boat with a hope of some tip-bit would be thrown in their direction. Remaining there for over an hour, i then returned to my room had a drink than showered, shaving made me fell fresh as i had not hadone for two days. Smelling as good as i looked i had one more drink then went for my meal, Steak the first one since i left home while eating the ships purser came to the table. There was some entertainment on in the main dance hall tonight a treat i was not expecting, a female singer plus a pop group the show started at nine.

After my meal i went out on deck again i had thirty minutes before the show so i spent it watching the sea. I wondered what the girls were up to, in the casino no doubt, Cindy i would'nt have a idea were she was but was she thinking of me. The wind started to blow and the wave's got choppy and the boat started rasie and lower in the water, water sprayed across the deck and wet my face. Moving back in doors i went back to the ballroom sat at the bar with a double whisky in my hand i watched the people dance and stagger with the sway of the boat. The pop group started the night off singing beatles songs, then came the girl singer who sung so beautifully, she mixed her songs up so you could not say she was like any one person.

The weather had cut rough and people was running out to be bad, sea sickness hit the boat like a plague. The rest of the show was cancelled due to the group being ill, i made my way back to my cabin two drinks later i was out cold sleeping like a baby. With all the course changes the boat had to make made us two hours late docking in Barcalona. I think i was the only passenger who walked off the boat without help and walking streight, a bit of a headache through the drink but other than that sound.

CHAPTER FOUR

THE FORTH TARGET

From the dock the taxi took me inland to my hotel were i was going to rest for the next two days and nights, i asked the driver to show me a few of the sights. He showed me the family church that they had been building for nearly one hundred years already. But they kept running out of money so it would be finished in another two hundred years no one alive today would see the finished thing. I got the driver to park the car as we went and had a coffee on the rambles were all the shops had tables and chairs in the centre of the street. If you sat on a seat that belonged to Sony they would bring you a catalogue out of their goods to look at and serve you with a coffee. We then went to the old cathedral which still stands on its Roman footings and a water drinking fountain which its states that if you drink from the fountain you will return again some day.

The driver told me that there was a big football match that night, Barcalona were playing A.C Milan. Never seeing football match live before i begged him to take me to the ground to see if i could get a ticket to watch the game. Not only was i lucky enough to get a ticket i was showen around the trophy room and the ground before the crowds arrived. I was take to my Hotel so i could get ready formy big night of football, being a Yankies fan i understood the rivalrybetween the two clubs. As i showered i noticed a New York timeson my bed so i turn to the cross word and completed it as fast as i could. Once the code was broke, it read, target is Manuel Damingo gun runner sells to anyone with a buck, lives in Madrid over a wine shop more news later. Pedro the taxi driver picked me up and took me back to the groundi had purchased a ticket for him too so he showed me all the place's i needed to be. We was up high in the stands but we could make out the teams, it was a great match which Barcalona won two to one.

Pedro took me to his local bar to meet his mate's and some beer lots of beer followed by lots of shots. We had a mock Bull fighti played the bull and Pedro and his mate's play matadors with tableclothes as capes. That was one fun night, one of the best on this holiday except for the time spent with Cindy. It had gone one in the morning when i arrived back at the Hotel, i decided to ring her i needed to hear her voice. It was Henry that answered the phone i am afraid madam is asleep sir he told me, she will want to talk to me. There was a long delay while he awoke her, darling she said down the phone yes its me Will i told her. I am so glad you rang i am missing you so badly she told me, i told her about the boat the trip around the city and the football match and i was the bull i told her like a excited little boy. Iam glad you are having fun she said with a tear in her voice, whats the matter i asked her? nothing i just wish i was there with you. we will be together one day i told her blew a kiss down the phone and hug up the reciever. Calling it a night i settled down to sleep thinking what Cindy had said and thinking how i felt. Next morning i went out shopping i bought a new case a pair of shoe's a couple of shirts for a dress suit and two short sleeve shirts to wear with my jeans.

The Spanish people here were so friendly i sat and chatted to a old couple that spoke good English, they had lived in Germany in the war but came home before it ended. I found a red light district where the girls would stop cars to negotiate their fee's, some looked very young about twelve or fourteen. A area that just had dirty mag shops that sold films ofa naughty nature, i was offered every thing from a big momma to a school girl. Declining the offer i went and looked for a Casino thats were i would be tonight trying my luck on that wheel. Another paper wait for me in my room when i got back, completed i broke the code of the crossword.

Domingo was at home in a flat in Madrid awating a gun deal that the agency have set up for me. Not liking the idea of meeting him face to face i cabled a message to leave it to me and that i would need a gun. That night i went to the casino taking Pedro my new found friend who came home with two months wage's as i won twenty thousend pesatos on a good run. Hitting a night club we got well drunk on lager and whisky chasers before he drove me back to my hotel and sleep. A bad head next morning stopped me getting a early train from therailway station i waited till lunch time the cought a train that took meto Madrid. I had three days here in the Capital of Spain, after a four hour train journey i walked through the station to the taxi rank and found a English speaking driver. He took me to my hotel with a promise that he would return in two hours to show me around the night life. I unpacked my case andread the paper there was no message today so i had no news of a gun or the address of my target.

At seven pablo picked me up and took me onto the streets of this lovely city, he showed me bars with people sitting outside in the warm night air guitars playing. Traffic was just as busy now as it had been coming from the station and all the shops were still open and full of customers. Pablo took me into a bar which he used with his taxi driver friends and we had a drinking contest were i came second to a man who was twice my build. Moving on to a sex bar which was exactlywhat it said it was, after you entered the door you was pestered by girls offering you sex for money. We had two drinks then moved on to a Disco bar and sang and danced the night away with a mixed crowed of girls and men. It was a real fun night i drank a little more than i should of but i was on holiday so i let myself go. Dancing with the girls who rubbed their tits in my face and arm wrestling with the boys Pablo left as he was up early in the morning. I was taken back to a house party were i found myself in bed with four girls in the morning and didnt know if i had done the dirty deed or not. I made it back to my hotel later that morning to find the paper had been delivered to my room. Opening to the cross word i cracked the puzzel to read the code, It read just paid last hit into bank make bull fight tonight letter at reception. Down at the hotel reception i checked with the clarke to see where the bull fight was that everning.

She rang around and told me there was only one that night in the main arena and booked me a seat the ticket to be collected at the reception. Spending the rest of the day shopping and looking around this fantastic city killed the time leading up to the bull fight. Not sure if i would like the show i got ready to go to the bull-ring Pablo was called and off we went to the bull-ring. Pablo was off duty once we got there and went off to find his mate who would give him free entry. Finding the reception i asked for my ticket and my letter, both items were dually given me. Opening the envelope i found a key to a locker asking the girl were the lockers were kept she pointed to a far corner of the reception. The lockers were behind a small screen wall to give you some privacy but i still open mine with caution. Inside i found a pistol which i slipped into my inside jacket pocket there was also a note.

The note told me that the wine shop was on a quiet side street in the suburbs of the city, Manuel had not left his flat for two days. As i didnt fancy the bull fight i made my way out of the stadium to a taxi rank, i showed the driver the name of the street to drop me but no house number. After a twenty minutes drive the driver told that we had turned onto the street. We passed the wine shop it was still open and there was a light above in the flat. Stopping the cab a futher two hundred meters down the road i paid the driver and waited till he left before i walked back to the shop. There was no door outside to get up to the flat i turned the corner to see if there was a back way and there i found a little alleyway. A iron staircase went up to a long balcony which serviced all the houses along that block, climbing the stairs i made my way to his front door. I had decided to go straight for him with daylight fading i knocked on the door, after a second knock a voice call something and a bolt banged as it was pulled back.

The door opened slowly but before he could see out i pushed it hard knocking him back and he fell to the floor dropping his gun. He was a small man and frail looking and no match for my build his face showed horror he knew he was in trouble and made a rush for his gun. My weapon exploded in my hand and once again two rounds hit him full in the chest blood sparyed from his back as the rounds came out. He slumped motionless his legs bent under his body and blood just spilt into a large pool on the floor. A quick look around his room told me i had hit my target as it was full of guns ammo and explosives. I made my way out as fast as i could move down the stairs down the ally and into the street, not a soul was about. No one had heard the shots so it seemed, if they had they had not responded.

Walking along the side road till i reached the corner which meet a main street i glanced back no shouts or nothing came from the area. Finding a taxi i went back to the arena mixed in with the crowd even found Pablo but dont ask me about the bull fight. After killing a man that was the only thought i had, i never saw a bull slaughterd, i just heard the crowed. After the bull fight i ate a meal and swilled it around with a few beerbefore going back to my room and sleeping the night through. There was nothing in the news the next day as a matter of fact nothing was heard for two weeks after i had left. the door must have close as i left and his body was not found till the landlord went for his rent. My third and final day in Madrid was a mixed day i sent my cable after breakfast and shopped for more clothes. I was getting a nice modern change now even some trendy stuff that i wouldnt have bought before. This holiday had been great, and cost me nothing i will have been paid for two hits this time tomorrow. Won at all the casino's that i had visited, took nothing from my account and put more back than the hoilday cost me. To top all that i have enough money to last till i go home without taking any from the bank. Clothes all paid for and more to come, i could live his life for ever just taking a target when i need to.

I got another bag to pack all my new gear in, it could cost me some excessive baggage fine at the air port tomorrow when i fly to Lisbon. No paper today so no message, that afternoon i rang Cindy to see how she was, she told me she was fine but missing me we passed some time small talking. About a hour passed before i said goodbye and hung up. The funny thing was when we hug up the pain in my chest was back that empty feeling was back that sad feeling was back. This must be love i told myself i had never felt this way before but i must finish what i was doing before i would know truly. planning the night ahead changed my packing i decided to play some roulette so left of my dress suit white shirt and bow tie. Ringing Pablo to take me in his car then arranged for a drink later in his friends bar, he dropped me at the bottom of some steps outside the casino. Taking a seat at a table i watched the first two turns of the wheel and took that time to change some money.

My night was not to bad i picked a winning number and a couple of combinations winning me ten thousand dollars. Depositing it into my account in the casino bank i meet pablo outside and off we went clubbing starting at his mates bar.

229

CHAPTER FIVE

THE FIFTH TARGET

The plane trip from Medrid to Lisbon was smooth and without any turbulance and the passage through customs and immigration was without problems. Three days and nights here are going to be a blast as this is the country i most looked forward to seeing. The sights to see are breath taking, the waters the warmest in Europe, one of the finest drinks ever tasted Port, narrow cobbled streets. This was a real treat for me, its a pity i have a target here one that i read about in todays New York news via the crossword. Franco Lebretti was my target, he was born in Italy and a mafia hit man, like myself and on equal ability to kill in a great number of ways.

This target will be hard if he gets wind of anyone getting on his trail he would have the skills to change from bear to hunter. I had heard his name before, he had killed a lot of important people over the years in lots of different countries. Another target that lived on a boat, but there would be no drownding of him, he did'nt drink or go clubing, he just liked his Italian food.

This guy you dont get too close to, i will have to take him out one of two ways, sniper shot or blow him up. Once i had booked in at the hotel and put my luggage in the room i took a walk into the city centre stopping to buy a bag of seeds and feed the birds. Then i walked the main streets checking out the shops and resturants walking through the gateways of the fortified city. Then the cobbled streets so narrow with old bars and inn's fishmongers and netmakers, you could still hear the smugglers rolling their barrels of rum. Pirates singing their sea songs while swigging their jugs of ale and porta and the girl all gigged about around them in a sexy way. In this city your mind can go so far back in time, there is evidence of all sorts of settlements Romans, Greeks, Vikings, such a fantastic place.

Taking a seat outside in a small bar i ordered a cold beer and just watched the world go by, every man was a Roman soldier and every woman was a pirates tart. Washing hug from lines which stretched across the street, old wooden signs hug from over the doors telling your trade. Menymodern shops had moved into the city but they all still had that old time look. While walking that day i noticed the place's that i was going to hang out at on the nights that i am here, some looked shady but full of characters. The rest of the day i found the marina and then sent a cable requesting a rifle to be found for me with a sight. This agency must have contacts world-wide as you get all your weapons next day latest, waiting for me in the hotel when i got back was a note under my door. The enverlope was of the A4 size and contained a picture of my target, Franco Lebretti lives on a boat called the Santa Maria. There was other places and information about his movements like he go's out fishing every evening returning late.

He likes to take long walks along the sea front, he eats at the same resturant every day. Too many routines for a man that has killed and made enemies, he leaves himself open to attacks. Washing and dressing for the night i went out to a resturant for my evening meal i then went on to a club, the place was all glass and mirrors flashing lights and dancing girls i sat and watched the dancers. A dark haired girl came to me and asked if i would like a private dance, i agreed a price and she lead me to a private room. She wore a short skirt bare midrift and a bra type top covering her tits which swelled over the cups of the garment.

I sat down while she put on the music and then started to dance to the rhythm. With her legs wide open her skirt raised over her panties showing the mound of her womanhood, her pelvis rotated and she rubbed against me. I felt the warmth of her rubbing at my manhood making it erect and ready for action i cupped her breasts and she pushed me away. Extras cost she told me in her best english, i will pay you but not here i replied to her.

Where do you want to go she asked? my hotel i answered, ok but i must finish work or the money go's to the club. I paid her for her dances and went back to the bar. She climbed up onto her platform and started to dance again and for the rest of the night she watched me, waving when the boss was not looking. I kept my drinking low so i would enjoy the plesures i had coming to me, Cindy came to mind but this was just going to be sex nothing more. With most people gone the young lady went and changed to her normal day clothes which were not much differant from her work clothes.

A short skirt which just covered her panties long boots small top which just covered her braless tities. Back at the hotel we wasted no time she stripped me off and started to explore my body, rubbing my oldman up and down she know just what a man required. licking sucking and kiss my now stiff manhood i was now ready to penatrate that very wet pussy. I dont know how long or sex went on for but when i awoke she had gone and taken the money i had left on the side cabinet.

My other money i had locked away in my suitcase under the bed. Morning was here again and it was time to start thinking about my target, i rang down stairs and ordered some breakfast, i was told i had a cable and a paper. I washed and dressed, soon my food was at my table with the paper and cable, i dipped my bread in my egg and ripped open the cable. Rifle can be picked up at the antique shop on the left side of the main square, the name of Franco's boat was a funny one, Au pied che my french was not that good, go dont get your feet wet was in there. Burning the note, i finished my breakfastleft my room heading for the big square which i got to by taxi. Stopping the taxi a block away from the shop i got out and paid the guy and walked into the square. birds flocked around my feet to eat the seeds people had thrown to them all differant types but the gulls comanded by their sheer size.

I noticed the shop and crossed the road to get to it, a bell rang on the door as i entered and a frail old man came to the counter from the rear of the shop. You have a package for me i said, im the dear hunterwhich was the code on the note to tell this guy. He said nothing just turn went back to the rear of the shop and returned moments later with a small stainless steel case and handed it to me. He turned again and without a word returned to the rear of his shop. The bell rang again as i left the shop, that had been the only sound i had heard in there except for the old mans boots on the floor. There was no weight to the case and was only twelve by eight by five in size, there would be a few rounds in a clip in with the rest of its contents. Once before i had collected one of these rifles and they were some weapon, it folded down into five parts armour lite. Taking a seat at a coffee bar i ordered a coffee the sun was very hot so i sat under the parasol to shade me from its rays. After my refreshment i walked down to the harbour and looked around, no sign of the Au Pied Che. I struck up a conversation with a old dockhand, where are all the boats i asked? fishing he replied they should be back soon.

I walked out to the mouth of the harbour to watch the boats come in, there were holiday makers with their camera's on that point so i would'nt be noticed. After one hour thefleet came in all the crews going about their work to get the fish home. Then i noticed the Au Pied Chu she was a small trawler not a yacht as i had beenexpecting with about five crew and the skipper who stood in his wheel house steering the boat in. He looked hard with his square jaw long hair and rugged face, he bellowed orders to his crew and they jumped to his comand. A boat captain he looked but a killer he was and my job was to kill him. The fishing fleet left the harbour each other day at three and arrived back about four the next day, today they was back for a celebration which was why they had come home early.

It was a Catholic celebration for the sea, the skippers had caught sardinesand crab only to use in the celebrations. Franco's crew all went home for the night only Franco remained on board the boat, i worked it out that it must be tonight that i hit my target.

If i dont hit Franco tonight he will sail the next morningand not return till the following day and to late for me to hit him. Returning to my room i opened the case to check my rifle, fitting the pieces together i assembled my rifle cleaning as i went along. Five rounds sat in a foam cut-out in the case, a small sight finished off the assembly now my weapon was ready. Dressing in dark clothing so i could blend in with the shadows i sat and waited till the darkness fell before i left to do my deed. Carrying my weapon in its case i reached the harbour by foot, the streets around were alive with the joys of celebration and very noisy. Ifound the place where Au Pied Che was mored and then found a place were i could hide but see the boat. There was a light on the small trailer but i could'nt see any movement Franco was either out on the town or below on the boat. The tied was going out so the boat was low on the jetti the gang plank was only a slight higher than the walkway. A larger boat was mored in front of Che so he could'nt jump from his to that one should things go wrong. The other side was a flat pontoon which would leave him in the open so that left the sea one side the walkway the other, to use that he would have to pass me. Waiting in a dark area i watched the boat unseen from land or sea, from land the fireworks was lighting up the sky. At sea it was lighting up the boats making it easy for me if he stepped out on deck.

Two hours passed still no movement on deck then i heard voices coming down the walk-way. Franco's face was lite up by the fireworks but he had somebody with him walking in the same direction. I could'nt fire it would give me away so i watched as the two skippers said goodnight and boarded their boats. A few more lights came on each of the boats and i waited longer till the bigger boat went dark again, still the fireworks went off but they was getting thinner. Twenty minutes passed then the door opened to the lower deck and a man stepped out, Franco lite a cigarette and leaned on the deck rail looking out to sea. A firework exploded in the sky drownding out the noise of the rifle shot, Franco head burst from the inpact of the round and fell forward.

His upper body bent over the rail and the weight pulled him over and into the sea. The darkness never aloud me to see his body float away but thats what it did. Folding away my rifle i put it into the case and went out to join the party in the street which went on to the early hours. Back at the hotel i put the rifle case under the bed then lay on the bed and went streight to sleep, sleeping sound till a knocking on my door awoke me. I had slept late and it was room service trying to get in to clean my room, i opened the door and let the young woman in. She was very nice and i took a shine to her, she wore a cotton coat type uniform and with the shape of her body just her underwear. Shetold me that she would have been finished a hour ago but had to wait for me. Begging me not to tell the boss that she had knocked my door i agreed but told her that she would have to run my bath and then scrub my back. She went and started to run the bath so stripping off i joined her, her eyes went down to my manhood and before icould say watch you cock she had her hands rubbing it. Pulling her buttons open i exposed her black underwear, touching the swells of her tits made her sigh with plesure. Soon she was naked and in the bath with me soaping my body with her tits my hand rubbed her hairy pussy it felt wet and slimy.

She raised her body up and impaled her pussy over my manhood the movement made me pulsate and climax very fast she also cryed out as she came. Later when we was dressed i asked her if she would like to go for a meal that evening, sorry but no she replied my husband will be home and with that she left. Smiling to myself i dressed and went out for my final night in Lisbon, there had been no paper that day so for the next three nights i can relax. Sending a cable saying that the baby was in the cradle and delivering the rifle back to the shop to get rid of it for me. Another good night was had and i stayed as far away from the harbour so no one could say i was seen there. There was so many visitors to the area nobody would stand out that much.

Later i heard that Franco's crew had turned up the next morning for work. They serched the boat and found the blood splatter on the deck and the police were called but with no body found they could only suspect foul play. His body was swept out to sea and had been eatten by the sea monsters that you could find out there. The next morning i was taken on a coach to Porto he second largest city in Portugal a place of real beauty and busy waterway sytem.

This city was developing that much that the population raised almost treble in five years. I had two days and nights here and i aim to see as much of this city as i can, my hotel was Av da Bouvista one of the rich area's of Porto. I had arranged for my main luggage to be sent ahead to Venice and just carried a small grip bag for the to days here.

My room was the tops a large window showed me a distance view of the river mouth with the three light house's guarding the opening. New buildings covered the whole area, white walls and red tiled roofs everywhere you looked, tennis courts were all around us sports grounds with football stadium. I left my room and and found a cab driver who would show me all the sights and thats just what he did, Museum churches and even there new hospital and university. I booked a trip along the river for the next day so i will beable to see a lot more of the city. Returning to shower and change for the night was what i did next and the driver returned to show me the food delights in their resturants. The food was a delight to my pallet and washed down with some of the finest wine i had ever tasted, after i had filled my stomach we found a bar. Drink flowed nicely till it was time for my comrade to leave me, he dropped me off at a night club with the promise he would pick me up in the morning for my boat trip. The rest of the night i watch the dancing and drank some of their home made port, i arrived back at my room in the early hours.

A paper had been posted under the door i decided to read it the next day and just lay on my bed and went to sleep. Awaking early i showered and ordered breakfast in my room, i drank my coffee as i read the paper and did the crossword.

Breaking the code the message read, Money in. new target you will find in Venice. name Roberto petrochelle Mafia hit man. More news later. A call came on my room phone it was the desk telling me my cab was waiting. I boarded the boat on time but there seemed to be some delay with us getting off, after twenty minutes i asked one of the crew what the hold up was. A body was found floating between the boats, my heart sunk do they know who it is? No just that its a man and he came in with the tied. How did they know that ? a shark had taken his head, my heart went back to normal my round had hit Franco in the head so that wound would'nt show. Soon the boat pulled away from the dock about sixty meters below our mooring a police boat was removing the body. Back in relax mode i listern to the skipper explaining that we would stop three time on this trip once go on the cable car up to the higher level of the city. After one hour we will return to the boat and continue to the old iron bridge which was the only way to cross many years ago thirty minutes then back to the boat.

Then we go to the new marina were we have lunch with a one hour break. We then travel a father hour up the river seeing the sights of the new city the return back for a close up to the three light house's before we dock. After the scare at the start of the day i had a great time the rest of it seeing all the sights i wanted to see and much more. Returning to my hotel about four i was informed that i had recieved a large envelope. Ordering a coffee i went to my room, i waited for the coffee to arrive then i opened the envelope. A picture of Roberto Petrochele looked back at me, he looked a cruel man with a weather beaten brown face. A scar covered the right side were he was slashed with a knife in a fight his attacker was found cut to bits two weeks later.

He lived in the slum area of Venice in the back street area waterways, He was a killer with no mercy. This man was not going to be my easiest target but i looked forward to the chellange after reading his murderous dossier. I made a list of my needs in Venice and sent them by cable from the reception desk, each item was coded, a hand gun was a razor, soap was explosives. Detonators and fuse was toothpaste and toothbrush, the receptionest looked a bit puzzled at me but i explained they were brands you could only get in italy. I got dressed and went out for my final night in Porto, deciding i would need company tonight i made for a resturant with a club and hopefully a companion for that night.

My flight was midday so i didnt raise till nine ordered my breakfast and sat looking out the window trying to remember the joy of the night before. I noticed a young woman at the bar of the resturant, taking a stool close by her i said hello and could i get her a drink. She told me she was waiting for her friend but would like a drink so i order her a martini on the rocks and we got to chatting. She was Swedish blond, blue eyes and a really great body, visiting a friend she meet at university who live's in this fab city, her lady friend turned up and they joined me for lunch.

They both spoke good English so the night was free from comunication problems and what a night we had. After the meal we took a cab to a casino were again my luck was in and i won fifty thousand American dollers. We drank Champagne and moved on to a night club after my money had been put into my bank account. Dancing the rest of the night away till we all returned to my hotel i ordered a bottle of bubble for my room. With the room radio on a little low as not to disturb the other guests we danced a nice waltz myself and Anna started but soon Sal the Portugise girl joined us. With the three of us clinging to each other we soon became intermet and started kissing clothing started coming off Anna removed her blouse and bra and Sal started to suck her friends nipples. Next came my shirt and trousers just leaving me in my pants and socks. Sal slipped off her dress and stood there in her underwear that light brown body sent my mind haywire and i was soon i was erect. The three of us made it to the bed, lifting Anna's skirt and pulling her panties to one side i was in her she cried out has my manhood penatrated her pussy and her wetness sent a chill down my spine.

Sal was now out of her underwear fighting to get into the action and grabbed Anna's nipples again. That feeling when my fluids gushed from me filling Sal's pussy and the looks on both of their face's as they both orgasmed. The knock on my door was the porter who had come to tell me my cab for the airport had arrived, he grabbed my bag and was gone. Reaching the room door i looked back at the two young ladies still asleep in my bed, money on each pillow to buy them somthing nice i blow a kiss and left. I arrived at the airport on time for my departure and spent some time ringing Cindy to let her know i was on my travels again. She had been out clubing with a friend and had a bit of a head on with the drink but other than that she was fine. The flight to Italy was just a few hours so i picked up a paper from the airport shop to help pass the time away. There was a message for me in the crossword so i worked it out then decoded the result to find out what the news was.

The message was in jargon but i will read it to you in plan English, The tool you need will be in a book shop near St pauls square, look under American history of water -ways and water animals. It will only be there one day so you must collect it today, i checked my watch two oclock that gave me little time to get to my Hotel then find the shop before it closes. I decided that i would make the shop first then my hotel, and thats what i did once out the airport i took a cab to the water taxie's and the waterway to St Pauls square. Asking local to the were abouts of the book shop i was pointed in the right direction.

Entering the shop i looked around there was a number of tourists getting maps or guides of the area so i just looked around. Can i help you sir? came a sweet voice from the counter, i am looking for a book American history of waterways and water animals. I will help this gentleman another voice came from behind me, turning i saw the face of a weather beaten old man. Thanks i said i would be most grateful, he lead me to a dark area of the shop and pointed to the shelves, you will find what you want up there he pointed to American history. He walked away and left me, i pulled across some steps and climbed i found my book and removed it finding a little box behind it.

Putting the box in my holdall i returned to the desk could'nt find what you wanted the girl said to me?no but i will take a map of the place i told her. I took a water taxi to my hotel it was the hotel Ateneo and was on the rio di s.luca, looking around the area as we moved i noticed the water was a dirty brown like the bottom had been stired up. The hotel had a sort of garage that the taxi turned into from the water. The water had raised as the taxi glided over a floor area covered in water which at some time been the landing stage. I got out paid the man and gave a porter my bag telling him who i was, your room is ready sir your other luggage is waiting. Once in my room I poured myself a belt of whisky from my duty free bottle and sat down to read the rest of my message. Your target is staying in a house on the street called Rio Terra it can be got to from the Grand canel then turn into the Rio dei santi, housenumber 4. Taking the box out of my bag i placed it on the table next to my glass i refilled the glass and removed the colts 45 from the box.

Laying the weapon on the table i then removed the rounds, twenty had been provided so i loaded the mag and put the rest in my coat pocket. As i stranger here i was adviced not to walk the streets at night on my own so i ordered a taxi from reception told them where i wanted to go and arranged a time i would be picked up. First i had my evening meal in the hotel resturant soup starter which was like asparigus with potatoes and noodles.

Beef olives followed as main course with icecream pancakes for desert. Two glasses of wine went down with the meal followed by a Brandy, soon i was being taken to a night club via a nice family bar calledRamarnos who's son worked at the hotel. Taking a seat at the bar i ordered my drink pulling out my street map i had bought, i looked at the index at the back and found the page and grid reference of my target. Turning to the page i found the street, following a route back with my finger i found i could get to him without going on the water. Just then a voice i had heard spoke out to me, not lost already? i turned to see the young lady from the book shop. No i was just trying to find my way around so i could see all the veiws.

The Gondolas will take you to most place's or ther sea taxi's, what about you i said will you show me around?. You are a fast mover idont know you and you ask me to be your guide, well you spoke to me first i replied with a smile. Ok you win i did talk to you first. Well i said well what she replied, will you show me the sights of Venice?. How long are you here for? just two more days and nights, i see she said its not to long then she thought for a moment then said ok. I have some time off so i will take it and show you Venice starting tonight i interupted her, what ! she said you can show me the night life two i told her. Now wait i moment she started and i interupted her again and i will pay you one thousend dollers a day.

Her face went into shock, you will pay me two thousend dollers for two full days work. correct i said a smile of happiness came to her face, is that a yes i said to her yes yes yes she replied. I ordered us both a drink and i realised that i had not asked her name, what do i call you? my name is Sofia and yours she asked its Will i replied. We made a night club were i dont know i just got onto a boat and off we went, we danced and drank but most of all we talked about Venice and New York. She saw me back to my hotel and i just kissed her hand goodnight. We arranged to meet the next day at the book shop for ten oclock first she was going to show me the palace and the bridge of sighs the around the waterways on a gondola. It was while we was on the water that she mentioned that the gondola's were run by the mafia and each of the men working t hem have to pay.

This could have been one of Roberto's jobs collecting money fromthese hard working lads and paying it to the mafia after his cut. Later we took a water taxi up the Grand canal and we passed the place were Roberto lived it was not to hard to get to from my hotel. We spent a plesent day in the sun on the water and arranged to have dinner that evening in a resturant that she loved. A enverlopeawaited me on return from the dayout, it just said be careful thisman kills without feeling men women or children dont take a chance with him. They even offered me more money to kill him than they had for the other's.

That night i have a really nice meal with Sofia but leave early so i could go and see Roberto on his home ground and hope i can take him out then. Finding my way through the walk ways crossing over small bridges in narrow streets finally i found his street and his house. There was house's on both side's of his street and a walk-way at one end with a canel at the other, i stood in the doorway across from his house it was dark. My old feeling came back, its a feeling i used to get when i was in Veitnam lying in wait for a enamy patrol or a target that i had been ordered to get. It was like a empty stomach feeling that made you feel sick, i dont know if it was the fact that i was going to kill or that i could be killed.

A light was on in the upper window but i could only see shadows and it looked more than one person. He had got company just then the door opened and i had to press to the wall of my building as the light lite up our part of the street. Roberto stood outside his door calling back inside to another person, a women came to the door with a baby in her arms, i lowered my weapon. Say bye bye to papa he said to the baby kissed the women and moved away, she stayed waving to him untill he turned the corner and she went back in. Has soon as the door closed i ran after him in the dark, peeping around the corner just in time to see him cross a bridge. I needed to keep up but not to let him see me, i was tempted to wait were i was and watch for him coming back but i decided to follow.

After a short while he entered a building which was flooded on the ground floor and you had to walk up a wooden plank to get up from the water. The building was in darkness less for some candles which had been placed in area's that was being used to walk, i walked the passage way very slow and carefully. I could hear voices through a door at the end of the walkway but as i got close to the door one of the floor boards creacked the room went quite. I found a spot to hide as the door opened slowly two men came out and looked around they both wore the Gondola boatman uniform. Roberto was making a rent collection from the men, once they was happy there was no-one about they all moved out. Following a while later i look about but they had all gone including Roberto, i raced back to the bridge there was no sign. This time i decided to wait about and watch for his return, there was no-way that he had reached is home that fast so he was out there some where. While i waited i thought about Sofia and how she had looked that night, she told me about her flat over the book shop and i wished i was there now making love to her.

The day dreaming almost cost me my life, as i looked up in front of me there was Roberto looking straight at me my shock gave me away and he came at me. His knife plunged deep into my left sholder he would have got my heart if i had not dropped down a little. I held the pain by not cryingout, he pulled the knife and went for a second lunge but the flash of my weapon lite his face for a second. He travelled back as the round hit him in the centre of his chest and blood splatter flew from his back. The street lamps picked up the look of fear in his eyes but he still lunged forward with his knife aiming for my face. Bang bang this time two rounds hit him near his throat and he fell blood gushing from his artery in his neck. I could also feel that warm sticky feeling when blood was running down your body i staggered over to where he lay and looked at him his last breath had been and gone.

A window opened and i stepped into the shade, Whats going on down there a voice shouted then another voice was that gun fire i heard. I moved slowly through the shadows keeping away from the street lights until i was a good distance away. My blood loss was making me feel sick and drained of enegy my legs was starting to feel heavy to pick up. Resting in a doorway for a moment i knew i was going to pass out and needed to get somewhere quick. Sofia was the name that came to mind and by now i was only a few streets away from the shop, falling against her door with a bang i managed to ring her bell. She shouted Will and opened my coat to take a look at my wound i will get you some help she told me, no please just get me inside and clean me up. She struggled to get me upstairs but we finally made the flat before i blacked out. Coming around it was light thesun was shining through the window, my left shoulder hurt but had been cleaned and was all bandaged up.

I tried to sit up but my head started to spin a few moments passed and the bedroom door opened. Sofia came in with a tray containing a bowl of soup bread and a cup of coffee, What time is it i asked her? its two in the afternoon she replied. You did a good job with the bandage i told her, not me she said it was Doctor i called him. What did you tell him ? i inquired from her, What could i tell him i didnt know how you got hurt that was untill a hour ago. My heart jumped what do you mean? well last night there was a fight in a back street and one man was shoot dead and the other got away wounded. You left your blood trail everywhere but imanaged to clean up most of this area before daylight. I knew you had been involved in something as i found your gun in your pocket so i got some rags and water and went back six streets cleaning up your blood drips. You had leaned over a bridge leaving a great deal of blood so i left it there the police will think you fell into the water. Thank you i said but what about your friend? he thinks you was mugged and got stabbed in the fight, he put six stitches in your shoulder by the way. Where is my gun i ask? its in that draw she pointed to a cabinet by my side, do you want me to throw it in the grand canal. No i will get rid of it, as she finished feeding me she picked up the tray and walked to the door, you made a lot of people happy last night.

She left the room before i could challange what she meant, pulling the gun from out the draw i put it away under my pillow just incase. It was a good while later when Sofia returned, What did you mean i made a lot of people happy last night?. Well the man you killed was a member of the mafia but not only was he doing their dirty work he was useing their name to line his own pockets. Roberto Petrochele was a hated man in this area but nobody was brave enough to do the job that you did she continued. The shop down stairs was paying him protection money so was other shop owners in this area, the mafia had the taxi's and Gondola's has i told you so their payments will go on. I spent the rest of that day in bed but i needed to fly to Rome the following afternoon i also needed to send a message to let them know that my target was dead. Sofia took a friend to my Hotel with a note from me explaining that i was ill and in bed so to let my friends collect my case's. Sofia sent my cable to the po.box which i used with a message that they would understand but she would not.

Two New york Times papers was in my room which they brought out with them, they had details of my next target in Berlin Germany. Sofia's friend convinced me to cancel the flight to Rome and go down the following day by train losing one day out of the four i had booked the hotel was informed that i would be a day late. That night i tried to raise from the bed but the pain was too much and i lay back down, Sofia made me some soup which made me feel a lot better. Her friend checked my wound and was pleased with its healing but he said that bed rest was what i needed not moving around to open the wound. Sofia came and sat with me later once she had finished in the shop not only the police are looking for you she told me but the Mafia too. Were have you heared that from i asked? people that live local that use the shop she replied to my question. Are you safe while im here i asked her? i dont want you involved in any of this, i became involved once i mopped up that blood.

The police nor the Mafia are looking for you directly they think you are somewhere in the canal, its who you was and who hired you to kill a mafia man. Has the only people that know your here is my friend who patched you up and myself i would say your safe. That maybe i said but the mafia would ask around the hotels and find that i didnt come back and you collected my bags due to illness. Her face changed, my god i didnt think of that, We need to move you to my friends flat then if anyone come's here i can say that you went home. In the cover of darkness i moved to Gus's flat to rest that night and the next day. The next day was Sofia's half day in the shop and that was when she was approched by a man who said he was a police officer. She told me later that she knew he was not what he said but she played along. You collected some clothing yesterday from a mans room at a hotel, why?. They belong to a friend of mine who was on holiday but he was took ill and spent two days in bed in my flat. And where is this man now?, we drove him across the boarder and we got him a flight to Munich he already as a flight booked there to Berlin. Why the questions she asked him? we had a killing the other night and we are just eliminating any loose ends.

The so called officer said his goodbyes and went on his way not even looking back as Sofia watched from the window. The local papers that day reported a gang war which ended in the killing of one man who's body was found on the street. A second man who was badly hurt is feared drowned after falling into the canal. That afternoon we spent talking about our live's and when we was children but if i would have felt better and the way that split up her skirt was making me feel i'm sure sex would have happend. When Gus came home he cooked a traditional spagetti with pasta and we washed it down with some wine from a local vineyard and it knocked me out. By the next morning i awoke full of life my wound throbbed a little but the fever gone and head clear it was time for me to move on. Sofia came to say goodbye we kissed sweetly at the station as i boarded the train to take me south to Rome, thank you for all you did for me i told her as the train pulled away. With only three days and nights here now in the beautiful city of Rome i was going to do the best i could to see as much of it as possible. At the station i got a taxi to take me to my hotel, i talked him into working for me for the next two and a half days.

He would show me all the sights by day and drink with me at night but one night iwas going to watch a show with italian ballerinas doing swan lake. A cable was waiting for me at the desk which i opened as i got to my room, well done with hit that was a hard home run. Money in more news soon. I washed off the dust of the journey before i went out for a meal with my taxi friend who took me first to his home to meet his family and friends. Wine was presented to me from all angles these were truely friendly people and they knew how to welcome you to there home's. Pepi thats what i called the taxi driver took me to the spanish steps first and we sat with a crowd of people just watching the world go by soon it got dark and hundreds of bats came out. but sitting with these people having fun together made life worth living and that was hard to think about in my trade. There was times when i was in Nam when the killing sickened me but once i had lost so many friends in so many brutal ways i stopped thinking about it. There it was kill or be killed here and now it much the same taking out killers but now i get paid well for doing it. Lets go get a drink i said to pepi, from the steps we found a bar we drank and danced with the locals most of the night till my wound ached then i drank some more to kill the pain. We got to my hotel in the early hours and i slept till noon Pepi call up to my room to see if i was going out that day.

I grabbed my paper and went down to him, he too looked a bit green but he drove around them streets like a racing driver. I read my paper in the back seat as we traveled to monumental cemetery of the Capuchin brothers. The paper just told me about my next target Alfred Bocklemann Terrorist, Kidnapper, Killer, a big man Munich born man. Folding the paper i put it away in the net rack in Pepi's cab door just as we parked up to look around this not so well known cript. The cript of the Capuchin monks everything was made of human bones from the chandiliers to the decor on walls and ceilings. As i was going to the show tonight i needed a evening suit so we stopped of a a hire shop to get one and then moved on to theTrevi fountain. Putting some coins into the fountain i made a wish stopping for a coffee and a bite to eat we finished our day at the piazza del popolo. Pepi told me that he would collect me at eight that evening to take me to the theatre he would wait to collect me and plan our next days travels.

I climbed the steps to the theatre and entered the main door. Entering a most elligant foyer two large crystal wedding cake looking chandiliers hung down from a well decorated ceiling. A red carpet filled the whole floor space and the stair went both sides of the foyer leading to the upper floor. You may ask why i am here to watch something with class, and culture, well my mother came here a few years ago when she was alive and she told me how much she loved it. She made me promise that if i ever came here i would make a show. I found the show very moving and how them little ladies could stand on the end of their toes the way they do. After the show we went for a few beer's near the Spanish steps and watched the bats flying all around the place.

Tomorrow we will see the Vatican museum and the Sistine chapel, following that with the Colosseum. We will end your tour of Rome with a trip to the Capitoline Museum, and stay till its dark so you can see the whole of Rome by night. Pepi had sat outside in his cab and planned all that for me so i got him a bottle of his favourite drink a few drinks later i was dropped off at the hotel. Once in my room i checked my shoulder in the mirror it was a bit pinky around the edges but it had closed up fine, in another week i will remove the stitches just how Guy had told me. We completed the days trips the next day and the sights were sure sights to see. The Vatican was so great with its building and the whole religion feeling of the area. the paintings on the ceiling and around the wall are master peices not to be missed if you come to Rome. The colosseum was breath taking the design the shape and the engineering that went into that place. You could picture gladiators loins and christians all fighting for their lives in there.

The crowds cheering and shouting for people to live or die, the emperor making his mind up with his thumb. Roman soldiers marching through the streets the chariots used like i would use Pepi and his cab to get around the place. We took lunch and i walked around a local market to see the traders selling the home made or home grown items.

Late in the afternoon we arrived at the Capitoline musuem which was a nice tour. But the highlight was the ruins at the back of the building and once it got dark the view across Rome was stunning. After a few drinks that night i went back to the hotel my flight being at nine-thirty the next day i would need to be up early. I gave Pepi some extra money for the service he gave me and a nice bunch of flowers for his lovely wife. There had been no news paper that day so i would now get all the information about my target when i get to Munich. My shoulder ached in the night and kept me awake but i got some sleep and awoke refreshed after my early call from the desk.

Pepi took me to the airport and waved me off as my aircraft left the beauty of Rome and started my journey to Germany. Soon we landed in Munich i collected my luggage and made my way to the forward luggage office. Filling in the paper work i paid the clark and handed over the case of clothes the would go ahead of me to Berlin a few dollers extra had it delivered to my hotel. Ifound my hotel via a cab driver who liked a drink and i hired his full services of guide as well. Retriving my room keys from the desk i went to my room there waiting for me was a New York time's.

I unpacked my holdall and put away the clothes and shoe's before i did the crossword puzzle. Alfred Bockelmann is up for hire from any terrorist organisation that will pay his fees and he will kill anyone and that include's women and children. We will send a picture via cable and any information we have, could have another target next destination. So i could have another target before i go home well at least i made some money this holiday. Cindy was so happy to hear from me, she told me that she was missing me more and more each day. I had to change hands with the phone as my injury was starting to ache, what's wrong she asked? nothing i told her i bumped my shoulder on a boat and its brusied. As i was talking i checked my arm a bit of redening was showing around the cut, i had picked up a infection. I called down to the desk after i had hung up from Cindy, to see if they had a service doctor and they had. The doctor came out within one hour and told me what i had expected that i had got a infection in my wound and i would need a course of antibiotics. He did'nt ask to many questions just that who ever had done the stitching had done a good job. Giving me fourteen tablets to clear the infection and telling me no drinking while taking them he headed for the door i will check you the day after tomorrow.

He had changed the dressing and cleaned the wound and already the pain had eased. While i sat trying to get my shirt on there was a knock on the door the porter passed me a cable-gram. Could'nt find to much about your next target except a picture which you will recieve in the post tomorrow. but every night he dines at his favorite resturant calledDallmayr in Diener strasse.

We will continue to find some more information for you, Berlin target is called Micky ODonnal. Thats all they said about my Berlin target and there was not much to go on for the first target here. Time came for my cab to pick me up, Dallmayr Diener strasse i told him, nice resturant he told me but you must book a table. You get me there i told him, ten minutes later he pulled up outside the resturant, i will wait over there he pointed to a taxi rank.

Walking into the resturant i was challanged by the head waiter, you have a reservation sir he asked. No i said but im sure you could find something and i slipped a few notes in his hand, he glanced at the cash and with satifaction he said please follow me sir. pleased with the position he found me i settled down, i could see every table in the room as i was up on a raised platform and the door was well in sight. It was filling up very fast with big parties and couples taking the tables, even though i had not seen his picture i felt i would know Alfred Bocklemann.

I watched each couple as they where showen there table, just as i was starting my soup starter a group of people arrived with a very loud man laughing even louder. You seem in a very good mood Mr Bocklemann the waiter commented, got him i thought and settle more now to enjoy my meal.

CHAPTER SIX

TARGET NUMBER SIX

So my first day passed with hopefully confident that i had seen my target, he was well dressed and well spoken. Everyone loved him he was a joker who liked to entertain his guests, spash his money but if they only knew how he earned it. Just before i settled down for the night i checked a whats on in Munich this month in a booklet and found Munich was playing Hamburg that next night. I like soccer and to see two of the this countries best teams was a bonus, i rang down to find out if they could get me a ticket.

The porter told me that the hotel had got there own box which i could shear with two more hotel customers. With that sorted i called it a night and went to sleep well i tryed that dream was back the blood the screams and the explosions. It always seemed that this dream came when i was planning to hit a target, Veitnam on a patrol we was ambushed, hit from all side's our death toll was so high just a few escaped. That memory will always be with me seeing those bodies of my buddies lying there will haunt me. I got up and made myself a drink of coffee off the guest trolly in my room, sitting in my chair i planned my day tomorrow.

A bit of shopping and sight seeing followed by the soccer match then a night club. Finding Alfreds movements and hitting him would have to happen the day after then i could take the train to Berlin the following day. The gun i had was still in my hidden compartment in my holdall but i needed a silencer and some more ammo. Writing out a cable message to the agents post office box i seal the envelope after encoding the message i will send that first thing. I ordered a breakfast at the hotel and went the full hog with two eggs over-easy pancake with honey and a pot of coffee. While i was eating i opened the big white envelope that the porter brought with my meal. In it was a picture of Alfred and to my pleasure it was the man i saw last night in the resturant. After my meal i found my cab and got him to take me to the cable office and sent my message, giving them the details of the hotel for my return message.

From there i went and looked around the shops picking up a few shirts and a pair of shoes, spending a few hours around the city. The game kicked off at four oclock so i returned to the hotel to get ready and asked the porter to book mea table at the Dallmayr for after the game. A telegram awaited me in my room it just said tool you need in box 116 at bus station, ask for key via news paper man in booth with your code word. The Hotel manager rang my room to explan thathe had arranged for the hotel minibus to take us to the ground and then take us to the place we need to go after. Use of the box is with the compliments of the hotel, i thanked him and asked about the people who were going with me. Mr and Mrs paine were from England so there would be no language problem they are only young in there twenty's. We was to meet down in reception in one hour so i made a coffee and read the paper. We meet one hour later and boy oh boy was Mrs paine a little doll, blonde with blue eye slim curvy figure with full breasts that she liked to show her cleavage. Her husband looked a bit of a lose and could not control her that was for sure, she started flirting from the time she saw me.

The box was really nice with all the makings of hot drinks a table of buffet food and a clear view of the ground. We was high up above the crowds so no one could see us i order us some bottles of drink and paid for them. The match started and Mr paine was sat glued to it while Mrs paine (carol) she told me later, was to busy mixing drinks. Five minutes into the game and Munich scored Mr Paine jumped up and down like a two year old, Carol looked at me and rasied her eyebrows to the sky. I poured myself a drink and gave Dave (MrPaine) one and he just knocked it back he did this with every drink he was given. Half time Munich still in the lead one nil, Dave was very clear that he was getting drunk and before the second half kicked off he passed out. He just cannot take his drink Carol told me, can you? i asked her i can get a bit silly when i'v had to much. How much more is that ? i asked again, another large one might do it she said with a smile i poured her a large vodka and coke. I soon had her tits out of her top rubbing her hard nipples she made a small noise with the pleasure.

Soon i had her skirt around her waist and her panties to her ankles and when Hamburg scored so did i. I removed her panties and put them in my pocket they are to remember you by i told her, she smiled you can see through this dress so has i am walking everyone will see my fanny. That will keep me wet all the time i'm out she told me, then we best keep you out. Game over Dave awoke and was told it was a draw. I invited them both for dinner but Dave said he had an head ache and would like to go back to their room, ok said Carol but i will come! later, i bet you will i whispered to her.

Dave did'nt mind so we dropped him off first then went on to the Dallmayr, each time Carol stepped into the light you could see her pussy hair. We was greeted at the door, name taken then showed to my table as Carol passed the waiter i heared him choke a little as he spotted the view. Champagne was ordered and we both took a menu off the waiter, i sat across from Carol so i could look at her cleavage. Into our soup course my target arrived again with a group of people they sat at a table two across to our left and Alfred had a clear view of Carol. She noticed him staring at her and mentioned it to me, knowing how much she liked to flirt i spun her a story. I told her he was rich and loved to spoil women, her face got really interested and made it very plain to him she was interested. She left to go to the rest room and Alfred followed her i waited to see what would happen. Fifteen minutes passed then he reapeared at his table looking very flushed, Carol rejoined me at our table looking a bit redin the face. Did you enjoy that i asked her, No! she replied he might have money but his dick is so small.

I covered my face to hide a snigger, Carol was certainly a character why she married i dont know. There was no more incidents at that meal, i dont think Alfred even looked over again. I ordered a cab back to the hotel and as we entered the lift i kissed Carol on the cheek, night cap in your room she said and pulled me out at my floor. Once in the room she pulled at my tie and opened my shirt, I have been so horny all night walking around with no knickers on then that little dick trying to do it for me she told me as she undone my belt. Now you are going to fuck me like i'v never been fucked before, pulling down my trousers as the last words came out her mouth. It was early morning when she left my room, it was also the last time i saw her but she did leave a note at reception which just said thanks for the memory.

It had been their last day on holiday and he wanted to watch the soccer match how sad was that. After i washed and shaved i went out for breakfast deciding to have it in the bus station when i pick up my tool. Making my way to the paper kiosk at the station i picked up a New York times and as i paid i gave my code, the man looked at me and passed a local paper from a box behind him. As i walked towards the luggage box's i found the key in the paper, finding 116 i opened it and took the box that was inside. Leaving the key in the box door like all the others i walked back outside and got a cab. show me some sights i told the cab driver and he responded to my request.

I opened the box in the cab and took a peep at the silencer happy that it would do the job i closed the lid and returned it to my pocket. It would have to be tonight when i hit old Alfred as at noon tomorrow i get a train to berlin and set about hitting my target there. Four days i would have in Berlin followed by two days in London then it would be back to good old New york, thinking about New york i remembered my paper from the kiosk. Checking the cross word for a message but there was nothing there was nothing much to the headlines etheir.

After driving around for two hours i got the driver to drop me off a my hotel and asked him to pick me up at six-thirty to take me to Dallmayr. The doctor has just arrived to see you sir the porter told me, please send him up i replyed. I had forgot the doc was coming but i did need him to take a look at my wound. The antibiotics are working he told me but you need the wound cleaning more often. He cleaned and redressed the wound and gave me some clean dressing to replace the one that was on. I will call in again tomorrow he told me, sorry doc but i go to Berlin tomorrow, fine just keep it clean and finish the tablets. At six-thirty the cab arrived for me, with my gun in my pocket i set out to carry out my hit on my target.

Arriving at the resturant at six-fortyfivei stated my name which is not my real name just what i use for work and the waiter showed me to my table. Ordering a drink while i read the menu would slow things down as i did'nt want to be finished eating before Alfred came in. Just recieving my starter as Alfred came into the door with some friends, they took their seats at a table four down from mine. Making no sign that i was watching him so people would notice i noted his every movement. He was dressed to kill tonight if youwill pardon the comment but he had a few young ladies in tow so he had dressed to impress them. white shoes and white trousers pink jacket with a white shirt and pink cravat.

His company was in fits of laughter at the way he was entertaining them and drink was flowing by the bottle full two to three on the table at a time. My second course arrived and the empty plate was cleared, i ate slowly bringing no attention at all to myself. I had just finished my main course when Alfred stood up to go to the toilet he bumped the table which knocked down a wine bottle red wine ran all over the ladies dress. While the room was in eruptions i took my chance to move to the toilet, I entered a cubical closed the door and waited.

It was a few moments when a pair of voices came into the room full of excitment about the spilt wine incident. Has i was wiping the wine off her lap i was rubbing her pussy and she loved it Alfred said to his mate. One went into a cubical the other i heard washing his hands, the hand washer finished and shouted to Alfred i will see you back at the table. From the rustle of clothes it told me Alfred was passing motion, i screwed the silencer to the gun and waited till i heard his trousers get pulled up before i stepped outside my cubical. Ten seconds later Alfred opened his door and the shocked look on his face has he saw my gun was that of a scared man.

He grabbed for the inside of his coat but three bumps from my weapon hit him in the chest and his body flew back into the cubical. I followed him in and locked the door behind me, his last breath left him as he died. Sitting him down on the toilet i adjusted his clothes to look like he was still on the toilet. Opening the door i slipped out turning the engaged sign with a key locked the door closed. I glanced under the door and it just looked like he was still using the toilet. His blood was running down his chest between his legs and down the pan, nothing hit the floor. Making my way back to the table again trying not to raise anyone's eyes to me, after sitting down i ordered my sweet and a coffee and brandy. Ten minuetes later one of Alfreds friends checked the toilet and came back telling the table he is still on the loo.

I downed my brandy and got my check paid and left the resturant, found a cab casino i instructed and in due time we arrived outside. With another good win in the bank i made my way back to my hotel stopping on a bridge to drop my gun and silencer. My hands shaked most of the night they always did after a hit but sleep came and went and i was awoke next morning by the porter giving me my early call. Would you like me to help you pack sir? he asked me, no i can manage it i replied just make up my bill for me. Ok sir here is your paper, put it on the bedside table i told him and i will see you down stairs in a few minutes. I opened my paper and found there was a message within it but decided to work it out on the train.

There was a hour and a half before my train left for Berlin so once i got to the station i had breakfast picked up a local paper and some magazines. The headlines of the local paper read Local man found dead in famous resturant toilet. The train pulled out on time, i settled down in my berth to read my papers especially the crossword as the message seemed a large one. Micky O'Donnal is a member of the IRA plus black panther he has a lot of backing so we have got you some help should be at the station waiting for you. Help waiting i said to myself i wonder who, i finished reading the Times and turned to the local paper. The story of Alfred was on the front page, man found shot dead in famous resturant toilets.

A friend who was with him at the resturant said i was talking to him then i left him for a moment or so and when i went back he was dead. A police spokes man stated that they where making inquires to who was in the resturant at the time. Naming the dead man as Alfred Bockelmann they are not ruling out gang war as mr bockelmann was involved in under world activities. Reading the papers and magazines made my journey go very fastand before i knew it the train porter was announcing that we would be arriving in Berlin in five minutes. Making my way to the carriage door we soon pulled into Berlin and stopped at platform five. I called a porter to take my two extra case's that i had bought for the extra clothes i had got in Munich and my holdall.

Walking off the platform i handed my ticket to the collecter and look out for anyone holding up my name. Not a sign of anyone so i went outside and hailed a cab, with all my luggage in we made our way to my hotel. Booking in i asked if there was any messages? no sir we have nothing for you. I went up to my room and unpacked leaving the case's that i had sent early. A knock came to my door and i went and opened it, stood there to my surprise was Cole and Danny they pushed passed me with a bit of a rush. What are you two doing here? i stated, Coletold me that a message had been sent to him to get a friend and get out to Berlin. Telling me the target and the dangers i could see why they needed us to come and help you. Well now you will need to tell me the dangers you are talking about i said to them but first i gave them both a hug. I ordered a bottle of whisky up from reception, Cole said it would be safer if we was not seen together.

Once i poured them a drink using the one glass and the glass in the bathroom for my teeth i swigged the bottle. Ok whats this about? i asked impatienly, well you have been traveling around europe bumping off bad guys. The law dont care who you are and have not tied up that these killings are linked. But the under world have noticed some of there contacts around Europe have been killed and have put out a contract on you.

How will they know who i am? they dont but they would only need to get a itinery of all people that have traveled around the countries where there has been a hit then they could find you. my heart sunk why had i not thought about they could be linked with the underground. Ok what do we do i asked? well it seems the person who has been given the job to find out who you are is Micky O'Donnal.

The agency what him hit as well so they have sent us to help you. Should i change hotels, no just play things as normal Danny spoke for the first time, with us hanging loose we will be able to get all we need to get him. Already we no where he hangs out but he always has a gang with him, there is a garage were they all work handling drugs and stolen goods are stored there. What about weapons, if you grab your holdall we will show you our room and it will answer your question, we moved down the corridor to their room. We can watch your front door from here Cole told me as we entered the room i could see nothing but a mess, empty boxies lay over the floor.

Each bed had a armoury of weapons on it including plastic explosives, we was about to clean up Danny told me we've been unpacking the goods. Angency have notifide the local secret service that we are here and who we are watching but will not get involved unless we ask. There is one of their men out the front who is tuned into our radio which he pointed to me, he will tell us if any strange face's arrive. We will never be seen together and will always leave alone and the others will follow five minutes apart. Cole showed me the different weapons we had, hand guns three Walter pp 7.65 cal two 10round mags to each. Three Smith & Wesson39-2 9mm with two 8 round mags to each wo Mac-10 machine guns effective from 50meter.45Acp 1,145 rounds/min two 30round mags each. One Ithaca model 37 shot gun 13in barrel 16 gauge.

Finally three KA Bar knifes. There was three smoke and six H.E Grenades plus a large amount of plastic explosives with detinaters. You have enough tostart a war i told them both, thats what we may need to do. Well im on holiday i told them so im going to do what other holiday -makers do and explore the city, see you later and i was off. Jumping into a cab brandenburg gate i told the driver and off we went, looking back i saw Danny jump into a cab a good way behind me. What i did'nt know was that Cole was going to take a look at the mobs garage. We drove around for about one hour, danny in the cab behind me still watching my back, i asked the driver where he went for a drink when off duty. The little bar that the driver took me too was a nice small local bar that you would'nt expect to find holiday makers.

Taking a seat i told the driver to get the man out of the cab behind me and bring him in. Danny entered the bar and pretended not to know me, do you want a drink i called to him? he walked across to me and said i'll have a beer. If these people are looking for me they will find me what ever we do so lets not jerk about lets look for them and not give them a chance to look for me. Thats why Cole is out there now confirming that we can find them at the garage HE'S DOING WHAT! i shouted.

Do you know where this place is? no i have only been out here today myself, Cole came out two days ago.

I downed my beer and we both jumped into my cab and went back to the hotel. Entering my room i open one of the case's that i had forwarded to the hotel. From a sealed compartment in the case i pulled out six passports all with my picture on all in different name's. Do you all think i am stupid!, every boarder i crossed i had a different name i didnt have the same name ever. Police or mob have not got a clue who they are looking for at the moment. But how did you book everything to get here Danny asked me? differant travel agencys and cable bookings using the name i was going to travel in on that flight or ship. They would have to check every flight made to them countres from the hit to the next hit and they would'nt find the same name on any other flight.

Now we have lost Cole i started to say just has he came through the door, i gave him a rocket for what he did and you of all people would know me well enough not to full for that. Now we have got all that shit out the way take it from me they only know that their men have been hit by who they dont know. Get me a pen and paper and while its fresh in your head write down everything you noticed on that garage, doors in, windows, fire escapes, rooms on the front rooms on the back. The amountof men basicily what we are up against, i did'nt see that many Cole told me, then we keep watching until we know. For an hour he drew a map of the garage has he remembered it, and for that hour i fired questions at him. Still not happy i decided to go look for myself after dark taking you two as back up like we always do. Cole looked at me hurt i'm sorry Will but i just thought it not safe for you, ok i said but from now on its our old routine it works. Just then there was a call on the radio, Cole answered it there is a strange man walking around outside the hotel, roger that. As myroom was at the front we went to take a look, peering through the window from behined the curtain we saw the man.

He did'nt look much like a gangster or a killer but they never do but this one was nothing a young lady came out of the hotel and they went off arm in arm. Darkness fell over Berlin and the night entertainment started, come on we can find a bar close to that gargage and heve a few beers. Cole had hired a car so we jumped in that to go out a cab driver may remember things once the target has been hit. We choose a bar about two blocks from the garage there was plenty of bars in between us so not much chance of seeing Mr O'Donnal. We left the bar about midnight and walked the two blocks to were the garage was, the front was on the main street but to get to the rear you had to take a alley. Danny watched the front while myself and Cole went down the alley one ether side with our weapon at the ready. It was really dark the only light was a single bulb hanging above the garage rear door.

The rear of the garage had a fenced compound with a double gate to let the cars in or out, this was chained with a big padlock. The fence was held up with steel poles the whole thing would rattle if you tryed to climb it. There was a small window to the right of the two wooden doors on the building, the doors were high enough to let a removals lorry in. In the yard there was all the usual things you would find in a garage, used tyres oil drums empty crates which spare parts had arrived in. A air machine was attached to the wall with its hose wrapped around the hanging point.

There was a larger window to the left which was a office and through this window we could see a light and shadows moving around. Cole climbed the fence which i held steady to cut down the noise, over he ran across the yard to the small windows. He spent some time looking in then moved to the big window looking through just as the light came on and he dropped down. I moved into the shadows across the street but could see the two figures in the office both wore sholder holsters with a hand gun holstered in it. After a few moments of pottering around they left the office Cole glanced through the window and took note of what he could see. Regrouping back at the car we exchanged notes of things we noticed, Cole had noticed seven men in the back room. Weapons and ammo in boxies also in with the seven i had noticed my target but he never stayed still for one moment for me to judge his size. A table made with a large piece of hardboard lay across four oil drums to make a table on which there looked like packs of money. This looked like O'Donnal's hide, i would have liked to have done him there and then but there was to many things stacked against us and the last thing was to risk the boys. We decided to have another drink but closer to our hotel so we could get home easier and not roam the streets looking for the way home.

Two large steine later we was finishing off our chat in our own little corner, Danny was saying that there was a great point across the road which you could see most of the inside of the garage. In the jungle i would find a spot where my target would use and i would wait for him to get a good shot and escape. But when you are in a built up area you have to look at the dangers around. passers- by that may get caught in the cross fire. Explosions or fire that could cause damage to innocent peoples property.

The safety of your men and yourself and a way to escape the area if things go wronge. In this case drums of oil which could explode or contaminate water if it leakes into rivers streams or wells we may kill for money but we are not heartless. Back at the hotel we got our heads down in our own rooms as i entered mine a newspaper was lying on the floor by the door. Going to the crossword page i broke the code all it told me was that O'Donnel lived in a small apartment near to the wall and that the area was derelict.

I planned my next day to check the area then on the night attack the garage and try to get my target, if he is not there i will look for him at home. The next morning we went out for coffee, ham and eggs, i then explained my plan. Today each of us has a job to do, Cole i need a truck somthing that will smash them gates and doors. I dont care where or how you get it just get one. Danny i will need you to follow me and watch my back i'm going into the devils back yard and i dont want any surprises.

CHAPTER SEVEN

TARGET NUMBER SEVEN

We explained to the cab drivers were we wanted to go and just before we reached the wall we got out to walk the rest. Danny stayed a good one hundred meters behind me but looking at this area we must of stood out. It looked like a place that the rest of the world had left behind, the building were old some well before the first world war some lived in most not. Some being pulled down some falling down there was not a lot of goverment funds going into this area. A empty veiwing point stood close to the wall, it had not been used for a long time. Some used to have dummies put in them just to give the Russians the idea that they was being watched.

The Russians always had men in their towers two to be correct, one Russian and one east German as the Russians did'nt trust the Germans. We walked a block or two but did'nt see nothing of O'Donnal or his men but then we cut some luck, a holiday maker approched me. Are you the Irish guy who is selling sweets he asked me, sweets was a code name for drugs. I told him no but i was looking for some sweets too, well i was given this corner he told me i will take a look down there i said and moved away from him.

Once around the corner i found a place were i could watch him as he paced the cobbled road. Where he stood was a house that covered the corner with a large site of rubble next door and all around the other side of the street till you hit the paint splashed Wall. I hid in the rubble and saw Danny do the same feather up the street and we watched the man. Five minutes later i saw two men come from out of the rubble but where from god only knows. They checked the area then approched the man who asked them the same question that he had asked me. Has the man answered him he turned to see if anyone was about and it was O'Donnal and one of his mob. With a rifle i could have took him down from there but by the time i got in range with my pistol he would be gone.

The manopened his wallet to get his money out and O'Donnal snatched it from his hand and thumbed him in the face. O'Donnal and his man took of like a pair of rabbits back into the rubble and i dashed from my hide towards them but lost them in the rubble. Danny found me on the derelect site, the fella is fine he said just a small cut on his forehead and four thousand dollers lighter. Four thousand Dollers i repeated who carry's that much money? well he wont do it again replied Danny. Spread out and look i told him they just disapeared in this rubble, we moved apart and after five minuetes Danny called Will over here. My route to Danny was slow has the bricks made me stumble a few times and nearly fall but i got to him in the end.

He pointed down by his feet and there was a man hole cover the lid replaced but signs showing that it had been moved. I lifted the lid slowly andlooked inside, it was dark but there was light about two hundred meters up the pipe. I climbed down it was dry but very smelly Danny followed behind, lets make to the light i told him see whats up there. Has we walked we passed two more man holes both had been opened and used but resealed. Rats run about freely and did'nt seem bothered by us we reached the light which was a larger works running across the pipe we was in. Light bulbs hung down from a gas pipe on the ceiling one side of the pipe had a water flow channel.

Our pipe had a step which went down to a pathway that run along side the water channel. Which way Danny said east or west? the question shook me it could only go so far east or it would go into east Berlin yet the water was moving from that direction. Lets take a look how far we can go east then take a look the other way i told Danny, why not split and meet back here in twenty minuetes. Ok but you be careful and dont take any risks, with that we parted he went west i took east. I walked along that damp pipe for ten minuetes before i came to a gate which was not locked just pulled too i could here voices talking a bit fether along the pipe line. One had a Irish accent but they were both talking Russian, i looked up at the roof above the gate.

The shock hit me there in red writing was welcome to east Berlin with a crossed hammer and thistle. I turned and headed back the way i came i would have liked to have been able to understand what they was saying but Russian was not my lingo. Cole was the man i needed he spoke it like a native he spent some time in Berlin with the Army. Danny arrived back at the pipe step a short while after me, find anything? i asked just a pumping station but there are lots of ways out up ladders. What about you? once i explained what i had seen and heared strange he said once i had finished. What do you think he is up to?selling ivan drugs he asked?, could be i replied you could be onto the truth there. Once we hit the street we found a cab and headed back to the hotel tonight we would attack the garage. I told Cole what had happend in the pipe and he just said this O'Donnal has his fingers in lots of pie's. Cole told us about his day, he had found a spot to hide the van and parked the hire car there.

Then he walked a couple of kilometers and found a truck stop and waited till a van of suitable weight camealong. As soon as the driver entered the cafe he stole the van, Driving it to his hide and emptied its cargo of kids toys. He told us that he did'nt want the cargo to get damaged so thats why he hide it in the bush's. Sitting in the lads room we discussed the plan for that night, we cleaned the weapons and loaded them with ammo. Filling the spare magazines with rounds we layed them on the table in readiness as we did our weapon. We locked our room and went down stairs for our evening meal, we needed to make thing look normal.

A paper had arrived but there was no coded mesage on it, as we sat at the table i read the news from home as we waited for our Bratwerst mit pomfritts un kartoffel saladt. Returning to our room with a few beer we watched the television and i noticed as i always do how quite the lads were. Danny was wiping the oil from his revolver, while Cole pumps rounds into his shot gun only to reject them again. We all got a few hours sleep awaking in the dark of night, ok lets go, they both got to there feet and stowed their weapons. Cole wore cross chest holsters with two revolvers one under each armpit.

The 16 gauge went under his large coat knife in his left boot and two grenades in his pockets with explosives and detinaters. Danny had one shoulder holster with revolver and another revolver in his waist band knife in right boot and his Mac-10 under his jacket. There was not any difference between myself and Danny i also carried a Mac-10. Has we had done at the evening meal we all went down at different time's as not to appear together. Once out of sight of the hotel i jumped into the car with the lads and off we went to the van hideout to collect the van. Cole puts some explosive into the van to explode on inpacked with the heavy building door and not the gate. Our plan was to ram the gate then head for the doors were Cole would jump before inpacked, Danny will give us covering fire. As the door go's down Cole and myself will rush in, and in the confusion hit our target.

It was ten-thirty when we got to the block before the garage and let Danny out, we would give him ten minutes to get in position. The area was quite but being a industrial area that was to be expected, one factory in the area was working a night shift we could hear the press shop banging out the car body's. This noise would block out some of our gun fire, it could also cut out some of the explosions. Cole and i checked our weapons again we did'nt want any jams or misfires, its time Cole told me. I got out at the corner of the alley and ran down to the side of the gate, a light was on in the office and i counted at least four shadows Cole came around the corner at a fair speed he turned and hit the gate full on.

One side flow into the air the other came off its hing and clattered to the floor a face appeared at the window just as Cole jumped and the van hit the doors. One burst from my Mac-10 shattered the glass and sent the man flying backwards into the room. It all went silent for a few seconds but as the door crashed to the floor there was a might of excitment coming from the men inside. Danny open up at the office window and gun fire was returned, Myself and Colerushed into the garage rear firing as we went. Cole got the first two with his shotgun as they came out a small room in the corner or thethe inspection area. The first one took the blast in his stomach and his body went into the inspection pit. The second got off one shot which flew way over our heads but he did'nt get off a second as his body was sent back into the room he had come from. Two guys had set up behind some crates two more were behind a work bench if we did'nt do somthing fast we would be cought in a cross fire.

A smoke grenade gave us the cover we needed to move and both myself and cole did just that. How many men we were up against we did not know but they were coming out of the floor boards, a burst from my Mac-10 put paid to the two men behind the bench. Cole had the two behind the crates pinned down with his pump action shotgun, every shot he made sent debris flying everywhere cans bottles tools wood glass anything that was not screwed down.

A round hit the upright beam that i was hiding behind a quick glance told me that a man stood on the stairs to the upper offices and another was on the landing. With a weapon in each hand i dived forward, there was whistles as rounds passed my body telling me they was close. A burst from the Mac burst open the stomach of the man on the stairs. Two more rounds left my hand gun, one hitting the man on the landing in the throat sending him over the hand rail and onto the floor. I dont know how but parts of the building were now on fire, shots from Danny told us that things were happening outside. Running out the front door we noticed two cars race away, we let off a few shots after them putting some holes in the cars. Your man got away Danny told me as he arrived by our side he was carrying a bag i think it was money Danny continued. I think you are right Cole confirmed from beside me, we just ran passed a table of drugs and another full of weapons but no money.

He may have grabbed as much of the drugs and money as he could carry and i know where he was going to sell it. Danny also confirmed that one of the men was wounded and had to be helped into the car, thats good i replid now lets get out of here those sirens are getting louder. We made it back to where Cole had hid his car and drove back to the Hotel, again we parked up down the street and went in ten minutes apart. I went to my own room switched on the tv set and ran the bath, peeling off my shirt i noticed blood on the sleeve. At first i thought i had been hit again but it was my old wound it had opened up a little but nothing i could not repair myself. I held a towel on my arm to stop the blood flow and it did the trick in seconds i then took out the spare dressing that the doctor had left me. I stepped into the bath sat down to relax away the ache's and pains of the last few dayshas i did the news came on the television and the garage fight was top lines.

They found a great deal of weapons and drugs so think it was a deal gone wrong. Nine bodies where found at the scene some had been burn't but others had been on he criminal wanted list. A list of weapon were posted they was all Russian with enough ammo to start a war. The bath was just what i needed and after a slug of whisky i retiered to my bed and slept the night through.

The next morning i got the hotel to change my flight to England for the next day and said i would require the room for one extra night. I sent a coded message to the agency explaining the sittuation and i was staying one more night to finish the job, i then awoke the lads. Cole dressed my wound for me then we planed the day, once fed i left the hotel with the lads following later, meeting at the car we set off back to the area that we found the tunnel. Parking the car away from the area where O'Donnal mugged the drug user we set off on foot looking for their cars, street after street we looked.

Finally we found them parked in a derelect street with only a dozen house's being lived in. The one car had bullet holes all over its trunk and the light glass covers had been smashed. The second had a large stain of blood on the back seat, parked slightly away from the buildings so if found we would'nt know which door to kick in. Cole kept his eye on the cars while Danny and myself went to check the tunnel to see if anyone was down there. Finding the cover that we entered before i climbed down.

Thats when i noticed with the bit of light the daylight gave us the blood stain at the bottom of the ladder. We both cocked our weapons, were would they take a injured man? not across to the east surely Danny whispered to me. I would'nt think so, the Russians dont get involved with small time gangsters, but what if this is something bigger. What have you got in mind i asked him? im not sure yet but i think we will need to tread a bit softly. The light was still showing at the other end of the tunnel and we took great care to step down on to the pathway once we got there.

A blood trail went left towards the Russian sector. We moved slower now as the tunnel twisted and turned and the last thing we wanted would be to walk into someone coming the other way. We reached the point where i was forced to turn back the last time but this time there was no voices to be heard. Has i peeped around the corner i could see a opening to the left with light coming from a room, must be the workmans rest room Danny whispered to me. I sneaked a glance through the door and there was a man laying on a bed, he had a very pasty pale face and his eyes had a hint of blue around them. There was not another soul in the room, i walk across to the man and pulled back his covers a make shift bandage had been put on his wound but blood was pouring through.

He has not got long i told Danny recovering the guy, take a look around while i take a look down the tunnel. I followed the path a short way when i heard voices and stuck myself like glue to the wall of the tunnel, i schuffled a bit closer to the voices. O'Donnel was standing at a ironbar fence with two of his men he was talking to a Russian officer and four guards who were on the other side of the bars. The water flow now went underground more so there was a flat floor on both sides for them to stand on and the bars were fixed to the floor. The bars also went into the water stopping anyone coming out from the east to the west. Were O'Donnel stood there was a gate with chains and padlocks all over it, so if i get you the rest of the money you will have the guns and ammo here tomorrow night he said to the officer who just nodded.

It is important that you dont let me down, your gun's will be here the officer groaned plus your explosives. I moved back slowly as the conversation seamed over, getting Danny out of that room just before they arrived back. At first i planned to jump them there but with those Russians involved i needed to hear more of this plan. It was not long before i had the full story, Where you going to get the money for the guns? boss one of his me asked. Those drugs i managed to escape with will get the cash we need. What about the men that run in with the police last night has left us short handed. Dont worry the Russian will provide us with a hundred on the day we hit the Americans Embassy, two of there drivers willram the gates.

The only information i didn't get was when this man would carry out this attack, i would need to get my information to the Embassy. The last thing we heard was the wounded man had died and they throw his body into the water and was carried away with the flow. Danny and myself made it back too Cole without getting noticed, he set both cars with a tracking device after he heard our story. It was obvious that O'Donnel and his men were living down the drain works as they never came out.

I cabled the agency all the information we had and asked to pass it on to the Embassy and American military so they will be on alert. Cole set the reciver to our car and we took in turns to watch the device while the other two got some sleep. It was two hour into my watch about ten that evening when i started the engine of our car and started following the indecator on the reciver screen. I picked up their car in a distance and was able to follow by sight pulling up a good sixty meters behind when they stopped. We was in a bar and club area and we watched as a group from their car went into a crowded bar.

This time it was Cole and myself that followed, grabing two bar stools we sat down and made a casual glance around. O'Donnel sat at a table with four other men, his gang were spread around the room watching thepeople around them and that included us. Cole whispered i will beback and set off towards the toilet passing close to O'Donnels table.

Two men stood up as Cole got near but he just walked passed and through the toilet door, O'Donnel indecated to sit down to them. On his way back from the toilet Cole stopped to talk to two ladies very close to O'Donnels table, just as the money changed hands. A briefcase was passed to one of the men who took it to the toilet area to check, he returned and nodded to his boss, who nodded at O'Donnel with the transaction done they all got up and left. I invitedthe two ladies to join us while Cole went out and got Danny, there is no rush to get back i told them nothing was happening till the next night. We was able to let loose that night drinking and dancing one lady called a friend to join us so we all paired off. I think these were working girls up in the corner on the dark side of the room i could see Cole pushing his hand between his ladies legs.

Her legs opened to accomadate his hand and she exposed stocking topsred panties and a very hairy pussy. Coles fingers soon had that pussy purring, in the mean time Danny was up dancing one hand on her back the othere squeezing a mellon sized tit which was almost out of her top. My lady was slim but her breasts were as large as i had seen, i just touched her knee and her legs fell open. Stocking suspenders and tight black panties was soon in view, But i mean to the bar not just me. I bought some bottles of drink and we all made our way to the car and squeezed in, i entered the hotel first and distracted the night porter while the lads and girls sneaked up stairs. The night porter handed me a cable message from the agency i read it on the way up in the lift, INFORMATION PASSED TO THE AMERICAN EMBASSY AND OUR TROOPS. IF RUSSAINS INVOLVED BE CAREFULL DONT RISK YOUR LIFE'S. I join everyone in the lads room a few drinks and i whisk my young lady back to my room telling the lads to enjoy themselves.

Trying to enjoy the delights the lady was offering but the thought of what tomorrow may bring took the cream of the cake. We did get it together towards the end but it was not good sex. Sometime in the night the girls had left but not before they had looked around for our money finding nothing as i told the lads to hide it somewhere safe under their matteress and lay on it. next morning i recieved another message from the agency to let the rebels do their transaction with the Russians so we can get some evidance. Cole went out and bought a camera and some 400 filmspeed film so the light in the tunnel should be enough to use without a flash unit. While Cole was out Danny and myself cleaned all the weapons and loaded the magazines with rounds.

We got through the day with a little sight seeing we made our way to the embassy and the barracks to see how the security looked. We didn't get to close but noticed there was a sharpness about the guards, ram barriers were posted behind the gates and no cars were aloud in to the grounds. Machine guns had been mounted on the guardhouse and out buildings, the guards trebled. The day passed and we readed ourselves for our nights work we carried two weapons each as we had the night of the garage. We carried more explosives this time we was going to do some damageto that drain. The moniter told us that the cars were stationery parked the same place as the day before, we watched till dark then Cole attached a explosive device to both of them.

This time Danny set himself some cover watching the lid on the tunnel but when he got there the lid was already off. All three of us went down this time, what we didn't know was that O'Donnel had sent his second incommand to pay the Russians. He had gone to recruit some men from outside the city and to steal some vans for the raid.

The information was got when just as we reached the opening in the tunnel two men walked into us, Cole was fast with his knife cutting his throat before he could scream. Panic showed on the mans face as he tried to breath but with his windpipe cut he couldn't, Danny hit theother man with his weapon knocking him cold. Blood sprayed from the gaping wound covering Cole who lay the man down in the water as he died. Damn i'm covered in this shit now and it will stink before i get back to the hotel, pulling the second man up by his coller he dragged him up the pipe to the ladders. Cole swap clothes with the guy while he is out cold, i told him and thats what he did, both me and Danny went in bits when we saw how shortthe trousers were. When are you going to attack theEmbassy i asked the man when he came too, go fuck yourself he told me, Cole pulled his knife let me have him we can wait for the attack. I have not cut any ears off since Nam, Cole said throwing me a winkas he brought his knife up towards the guys right ear, no no no wait!. You have something to say i told the man, has i watched the sweat run down his brow, the attack is at noon tomorrow.

He told me everything from where O'Donnel was to how the attack would take place the next day. Take him to the back of our car tie him up and put him in the trunk we will hand him over to the police i told the guys. He got out the car very quite but pushing Danny into Cole they both fell and the guy ran to his car. No Cole shouted but is call went on silent ears, Booooom the explosion sent the second car flying through the air and our car shook. The lads were strugling with their hearing for a few hours after that, i was fine has i was in the car but the jolt opened my wound again. i managed to get a message off to the agency to let them know when the attack wasgoing tobe. They would warned the troops also the German police so everyone would be waiting for the raiders tomorrow inculding us.

Another night we had a few drinks and a pork schnizzle meal with mushrooms and fries once the attack was over tomorrow i would be flying to London and some good English food. That night i even gave Cindy a call i was missing her so much, she said she was really missing me to and could she join me in England. i told her i would be working and wouldn't have no time with her whenshe hung up she sounded upset. Before i turned in i checked on the boy, Cole took a look at my shoulder your wound is getting infected he told me mybe you should sit tomorrow out there is more than enough to sort that little lot out. I cannot miss it i told him that Irish fuckers mine and i mean to get him.

We said our goodnights after he dressed my wound and back to my room i went. I didn't sleep well with the pain of my wound and the thoughts of the next day i poured myself a large whisky and sat in the chair. My thoughts went to Cindy, i think i love that girl two good belts of whisky and i was asleep awoken five hours later with the lads at the door.

Its time to go Will Cole told me, how is your shoulder? its fine i lied it ached like hell my arm pit was on fire but i had to see this through. I booked out of the hotel and had my bags forwarded to the airportmy flight to England was ten that everning the lads had a flight at four the next morning. Cole drove the car and parked it so we could see the gate's of the Embassy and also watch the traffick coming down the road towards it. The guy we had captured had told us the raid was going to be first light thirty minutes after the gaurds had changed. But unknown to them they would have only seen a small amount change not the sixty or more in hiding awaiting them to call.

The Police were hid in doorways well out of sight we looked around and could'nt see a soul around that area. I rubbed my shoulder and Cole noticed, that hurting you he enqired? no its just a bit stiff i replied, you never was a good lier Will after this im taking you to a doctor. He knew it would have been no good trying to stop me now. A few early morning workers left their homes making there way to work, most on bicycle's which all play its part in making things look natural. It was too early for children so they would be safe in doors, just this odd few men and women which the rebels will see as normal. Thirty minutes later a heavy van came to the top of the road and parked, two minutes another one joined it.

A group of people got out of the vehicles and split both side's of the road. The two vans opened up there throttles and speed forward towards us showing no sign of stopping. When they was about fifty meters from the embassy opening the guards slammed a large crash gate shut which locked to the walls and floor with large bolts.

Then the men inside the wall opened up with their small arms, the vans where peppered with rounds. The first swerved into the gate and was halted on inpact, the second just ploughed into the rear of the first. It bounced off the rear of the first and just rolled to the wall, for a few seconds there was quiet but soon their was men leaping out the back doors. Not knowing of the extra men laying in wait they scrambled up the wall only tobe cut down by rifle fire, both van were now ablaze. Screams came from the men stuck inside as the flames licked at their flesh some gunfire came from inside but not a round left the van.

The men inside were shooting themselves before suffering the pain they would get from the flames, the area was soon full of the smell of burning flesh. While the action was going on with the vans the group that had left the vans were now charging down both side's of the road they had been joined by a large group of about one hundred men. They wore civilian clothes but fought like soldiers, these were the Russian troop provided by the theRussian officer. The first to come in contacted with them was the German police but they was out skilled and out gunned losing around ten men with the first volley. The Russians had brought some fearful weapons and grenades from RPG's were now hitting the wall cutting a hole into the embassy grounds.

Russian troops stormed through the hole only to meet up with the troops of the Marine corps and abloody battle was fought. Myself, Danny and Cole went looking for the Irishman and his gang, up till now they had not been seen. Do you think he was in one of the vans Cole asked me?i dont think he would put his self in that much danger. Just then four of the gang came around a corner firing a mixture of weapons, two police officers was in their line of fire and took almost every round. The officers bodies jerked and jumpped as each round hit its target, limbs came away from there torso's leaving them laying on the floor like sloughtered cattle. Myself and the lads waisted no time and opened up with our own weapon has we rushed forward towards the group. One flew into the air backwards as a round from Cole's shotgun hit him tearing out his guts. Anothers head burst open like a melon has both me and Danny put rounds in it, blood spray splattered both our face's as it was caught in the breeze. The battle on the Embassy wall was at its full heat, bodies were falling like flies in and outside the grounds. The other two men that we confronted turned and ran towards a carO'Donnels face appered at the open window, stand and fight you cowards he shouted.

His men just continued towards him and a burst from his machine gun cut them down a secound burst sent us diving to the ground. His driver released the clutch on the carand with a wheel spin it raced away with O'Donnel firing at anything that moved. Get the car i shouted to Cole i know were he is going, as i looked down Cole was holding Danny he had been hit in the chest. We forced a field dressing to his wound to stop the flow of blood his eyes had glazed and his flesh had started to go gray with the blood loss. Talk to me Danny i shouted at him and i tapped his arm every time he closed his eye's, two ambalance men joined us and took over his care. Go and get him for me Danny whispered to us as he was put into the ambalance the doors closed and away he went. Looking around men were still fighting on the wall but soon around twenty men layed down their arms and surrendered to the police and Marines.

His words rang out in my ears Go get him for me, get the car i told Cole again. We was on the road within ten minutes behind their car O'Donnel would be looking for a hideout before he could get outthe country. But i knew the only place he had left was that pipeline but this time he would be waiting with what was left of his men. Cole slowed the car as we turned into the old derelict area each shadow turned our weapons towards it in anticipation of a ambush. Each fallen wall looked like a rampart of a fort and great cover for your enemy, the loose rubble on the floor was camouflage for any sniper, ground i would use myself. Cole stopped the car along side a wall were the house was still standing but had lost its doors and windows, lets both play sniper this time Cole said in a whisper. We entered a opening that used to be the door and climbed the stairs to where once we would have found the bedrooms.

Crawling low we looked through the door which was once a opening to the balcony, Nothing! so we moved out behind some rubble to take a better look. looking across the land we could see a variety of rubbish, old boilers prams pipes wire bricks and lots of rust. The wall stood at the end of this bit of land and at the height we was we could see a bit into the east but only a bit. Cole said there and pointed to the drain cover we was looking for, can you see anything of O'Donnel or his men i asked not a soul came the reply. I am going down and make for that manhole cover i whispered to Cole cover me then follow once i get there?, he acknowleged with a nod.

I backed out of the balcony on my hands and knees and only got up once i had the full cover of walls on all side's of me. I eased down the stairs slowly trying to keep my feet off the debris. My left foot just touched the step and a bottle rolled away from my foot, it bouncied down four steps before it smashed on the concrete and i froze.

A shower of bullets hit all around the the front door and i heard Cole return fire i clamberred back up stairs and stood at a distance that i could talk to Cole. Where are they? two to the left in that pile of junk, the other one was directly in front of you as you leave the front door. Ok give me two minutes then lob a smoke grenade towards the guy in front and a blast to keep the other two's heads down. I followed my last routine down the stairs just a little faster and i reached the bottom just as the grenade blow and Cole fired. I was out the door and running to my right away from the gunmen the purple smoke to thick for the guys to see what had happend.

Diving for cover before they realised what had happendi hit the rubble shoulder first and i felt my wound open up again. Icould feel the blood trickle under my armpit and down my side but i had no time to worry about it and found myself some cover. Cole was now heading towards me but the smoke was thining so i gave a burst from my machine gun which forced the gangs heads down. You ok Cole asked me, just a old wound i told him but he understood and just smiled, when this is over was all he said. now you keep them busy here and i will get around the back of them hetold me and off he went under a burst of my fire. This time i was glad to let him do the running around as i felt weak and sick i just lay there watching their postion for movement. Cole moved from one load of rubble to the next until he had clear views of the two gang members positions.

A burst from a automatic weapon hit the ground all around me missing my leg by centimetres i rolled to a new position just as Cole open fire behind them. The guy in the front position on his own took both barrels of Cole's shotgun sending him up and backwards into the air his stomach all ripped open.

The other two tryed to run but found it hard on the rubble to keep their footings and stumbled about, one managed to get some distance but Cole was after him. The other ran into my sight and was stopped dead by the impact of my round it hit him dead centre of his forehead. I had seen this before when a man is dead before he hits the floor but he seemed to stand there for sometime before he fell. I considered another round but then he dropped like a doll who's strings had been cut with a blood mass as a face. The final man took both of Coles barrels in the back, his chest just blow out snapping his ribs as the impact forced its way through his body. A hail of bullets hit all around the two of us i rolled behind a old water tank and this time Cole landed hard on his ankle.

I look across to were the shots came from just in time to see O'Donneland two of his men go down the hole. You ok i asked Cole? four minute mile is out he told me and went to stand "woo" the hundred metres is not in either. You sit there and i will take a look at what is happening i told Cole, dont risk your life he said the police are bound to be here soon just wait for them. I will be fine i told him and moved off slowly keeping myself under cover of the rubbish and rubble untill i was near to the man hole. Not a sound could be heard other than the flow of traffic a few streets over in the new part of the city. A siren was going off but that was on the other side of the wall i crawled up on my hands and knee's and looked down the man hole. There was no light at the end of the tunnel i climbed down slowly till my feet touched the floor of the pipe.

My shoulder was giving me some pain now and i could still feel the blood running down my side. I moved along the pipe to my left but every step told them i was coming there was that much debris laying about the floor. Every step no matter how light i placed my foot would wake up an army of sleeping men glass, stone's, and tin rattled down that pipe. Then there was a flash of light and a round whistled past my head, i had kept low if i had not i would have been dead. I sqeezed the trigger of my weapon and a burst of rounds hit the walls and top of the pipe ricocheting along the pipe. I heard a groan i had hit my enemy there was no return fire, i crawled along the pipe until i came to a body. My hand touched it first it was warm and sticky with blood my hand was covered in it. I searched for life but i found no sign there was no breath no heart beat no nothing god take his soul. Has i got closer to the opening were the two pipes connected there was light coming from the left. I took a peep up at the ceiling and saw that the light bulbs had been smashed all along that part of the pipe. Shots flicked the wall all around me chipping bits of the pipes covering me in dust and concrete chips that filling my hair and nostrils.

The shots were coming from the right side of the main tunnel away from the russian sector, i slide to the pipe floor. Keeping low i moved slowly towards my attacker the glass from the light bulbs cut into my hands but it didnt stop me the thought of killing O, Donnel kept me moving. The noise of rushing water got louder as i neared the pumping station, a big sluece door was lit by a red light over the top of it warning that it was closed. A small resevouir spread out in front of the door which caught the water leaking from the sluece door then ran along the channel to the russian sector. Above the door was a small walkway which stopped at a wheel that opened the sluece. More shots rang out hitting the walls forcing my head as low as it would go covering my face in the shit and slime that lay there. Anger made me open fire from were i lay spraying the whole of the sluece room with a burst that would have killed an advancing army. Two bodies ran up the ladder onto the walkway one fired in my direction the other went for the wheel, he was going to flood the pipe.

Speed of movement was against me to save myself i needed to move now or die. I gave a final burst from my weapon and dived for the opening that i had came through to escape, my hands grabbed the opening just as the water hit me. The water rolled my body over once forcing me to loose grip my mind told me this is it the water will drag me along hitting everything in its way. Cutting into my flesh i would get drawn down to a watery grave, then i felt hands grab my jacket and pulling me clear.

Trying to get my breath i looked up at the unshaven face of Cole, i knew if i left you alone you would get into trouble he told me. I just smiled at him and patted his arm then went back in search of the enemy. The water was still rushing passed our point but was not as deep now most ran down the wellwhich is where i would have ended if not for Cole. The two men on the walkway were still holding tha position but had lay low so has to make a smaller target. Cole fired his shot gun spraying the hole walkway area with pellets. One man jumped up and got off one round before a burst from my weapon tore into his chest leaving three large holes, his partner soon followed with a single shot to his head. one body remained on the walkway his arm dangled over the bottom rail the first man fell over the top rail and went down the well.

The final man had climbed up to another cover and escaped to the surface only for the police to pick him up. O'Donnel was still down here somewhere, we moved slowly trying not to splash the water to hard to give us away. We headed east towards the Russian sector, taking each step as slow and as calm as we could. Just around the turn in the tunnel we heared the voice of the Irish rebel telling his men to fight on till the death. They was at the room were we found the dying man and watching the area that we would arrive from. The water had flooded the room and they was knee deep, Cole still limping pushed around me and throws a grenade.

They was ready for it and ducked back into the room O'Donnel ran out before the exposion and ran towards the Russians. The grenade blew sending water splashing everywhere and making a small creater near the room enterance. Dont shoot a voice call we are giving up, Cole moved level with me so we could both see who was coming out.

Throw out your weapons i shouted and two machine guns plunged into the water. be careful i told Cole as one man came out with his hands above his head. The other man followed but was very close to the first we could'nt see his hands, its a trap i shouted just as the front man ducked. His partner stood with a AK47pointing towards us but two barrels and a long burst from my weapon got the jump on the guy and before he got a round off he and his partner were dead.

Their bodies floatred in the water then flopped down the small step and into the deeper water of the channel to be sweeped away into the grill that stopped you going into the Russain sector. Cole sat rubbing his ankle, you stay here i told him i'v got work to do and i moved off down the tunnel. I kept close to the wall but the lighting at this part of the tunnel was a lot brighter and there was little places to find cover. Reaching another bend i moved forward with caution rat ta tat tat the distingushed sound an AK47 makes but this time there was more than one.

I ducked down but no rounds came my way, i took a glance around the bend and to my astonishment on the floor in front of me was the body of O'Donnel. Russian troops stood the other side of the gate with smoke coming from their weapons. The officer in charge spoke has he noticed me with my hands held up, this man was killed trying to cut open the gate and enter the Russian sector and add the escape of east Germany prisoners. Cut open i said looking at the blood soaked body of the Irishman, the officer spoke to one of his men. A set of wire cutters was pushed though a gape in the grill they dropped close to the body. This incedent is closed, what about all the dead bodies and wounded men you have here in the west? i asked him.

I have no knowlodge of this, goverments will discuss what action will be taken if our soldiers were involved, good day comrade he said and left. I made my way back to Cole, you ok he asked? yes just dandy now my job is complete and i can enjoy my last bit of the holiday. He smiled what about that young lady you have fallen for, i did'nt reply i just helped him up with my good shoulder and made our way out.

Out in the fresh air the police was waiting and after we explain what had happend we was put in a car and taken to hospital. Cole had broken a bone in his foot and got it plastered i finally got the treatment i needed for my wound and Danny had two weeks bed rest with the wound he got. Visiting them both in there rooms i thanked them for their work and told them what they had been paid which pleased them very much.

What are you going to do now Cole asked me? well im going to get my flight to England and see the sights. I will rest this wound before i go back home and see what come's once i am back there i told them. What about you two? this wound will heal quick so i will be ready for any jobs the agency offer me Danny replied. What about you Cole? Im going to have a two month holiday and enjoy some of this money, Canada fishing he continued, i'v always fancied catching salmon up there.

I left the lads in Germany they were in safe hands and took a flight back to England after four days and a dozen phone calls to Cindy i took a flight to France and married that girl of mine.

THE END

Printed in the United States
By Bookmasters